ACHIEVE

®

EXAM SUCCESS ▪ 2nd EDITION

A Concise Study Guide and Desk Reference

DIANE ALTWIES, PMP
JANICE PRESTON, PMP
FRANK REYNOLDS, CAPM

J.ROSS
PUBLISHING

Copyright ©2014 by Core Performance Concepts, Inc.

ISBN 978-1-60427-087-7

Printed and bound in the United States. Printed on acid-free paper.
10 9 8 7 6 5 4 3 2 1

Library of Congress Cataloging-in-Publication Data

Altwies, Diane, 1962-
Achieve CAPM exam success : a concise study guide and desk reference / by
Diane Altwies, PMP, Janice Preston, PMP, & Frank Reynolds, CAPM. -- 2nd
edition.
pages cm
Includes bibliographical references and index.
ISBN 978-1-60427-087-7 (pbk. : alk. paper) 1. Project
management--Examinations--Study guides. 2. Project
management--Examinations, questions, etc. 3. Project
management--Certification--Study guides. I. Reynolds, Frank, 1943 February
26- II. Preston, Janice. III. Reynolds, Frank. IV. Title.
HD69.P75A457 2013
658.4'04076--dc23
2013040238

This publication contains information obtained from authentic and highly
regarded sources. Reprinted material is used with permission, and sources
are indicated. Reasonable effort has been made to publish reliable data and
information, but the authors and the publisher cannot assume responsibility
for the validity of all materials or for the consequences of their use.

All rights reserved. Neither this publication nor any part thereof may be
reproduced, stored in a retrieval system, or transmitted in any form or by any
means, electronic, mechanical, photocopying, recordings, or otherwise, without
the prior written permission of the publisher.

The copyright owner's consent does not extend to copying for general distribution
for promotion, for creating new works, or for resale. Specific permission must be
obtained from J. Ross Publishing for such purposes. Direct all inquiries to
J. Ross Publishing, 300 S. Pine Island Road, Suite #305, Plantation, 33324.
Office 954-727-9333; Fax 561-892-0700; Web www.jrosspub.com.

Core Performance Concepts, Inc., is a Registered Education Provider of PMI.
Project Management Institute (PMI), Project Management Professional (PMP),
Certified Associate in Project Management (CAPM), Organizational Project
Management Maturity Model (OPM3®), and the Project Management Book
of Knowledge (*PMBOK® Guide*) are registered marks of the Project Management
Institute, Inc. PMI does not endorse or otherwise sponsor this publication.

Attention: Corporations, Professional Organizations, Universities, and Colleges:
quantity discounts are available on bulk purchases of this book. For
information, contact salesandmarketing@jrosspub.com.

TABLE OF CONTENTS

CHAPTER 11 **RISK**

CHAPTER 12 **PROCUREMENT**

W hen I teach a project management class, I always ask my students why they are taking the class and what they are hoping to achieve. One of the most common responses is that they want to know how a project should be run. Or put another way, they want to know—what are the best practices, tools, and techniques for planning and executing projects? You may have asked similar questions when you were acting as a project manager, participating on a project as a team member, or being responsible for overseeing projects.

With more work being accomplished through projects, you might find yourself on a team that has little or no experience with how projects should be done, and your organization may not have a proven methodology for you to follow. Why is a proven methodology important? Current research shows us that only about 62% of projects are meeting their original business goals, and projects run by organizations following standard practices are more successful than those without such practices. One of the goals of this book is to present a methodology using best practices, tools, and techniques to successfully achieve project goals.

The Certified Associate in Project Management (CAPM) credential was created for anyone involved in projects to get project work done more effectively by improving project management processes. Whether you are a student, new to project management, changing or advancing your career, or already serving on a project team, the CAPM can launch a career path or take it to the next level. Through studying for the CAPM, you will be developing and demonstrating skills—and more importantly, learning key concepts that you can apply to work, career advancement, and personal goals.

What is so powerful about the methodology in this book? The methodology is based on the recognized project management best practices found in the Project Management's Institutes, *A Guide to the Project Management Body of Knowledge (PMBOK® Guide)* Fifth Edition. What sets the PMI standard apart is that it is recognized and applied as the best practice for all industries across all countries around the world. Think about the power of having all team members aligning their work to the project manager around globally accepted standards. There is power when team members, stakeholders, and sponsors understand common concepts for getting project work done. What makes this possible? When teams form, they can be productive more quickly because everyone knows his or her role and responsibilities. Each member of the team has a common understanding of processes and methodology, and each speaks the same "project language." Much of project work today is done with global teams, and that trend is increasing. Having a global standard leverages the power of using dispersed resources and improves start-up time for culturally diverse project teams.

How will you use this book? This book will guide your preparation for the CAPM exam. It presents the material in logical sequence, covering all the key concepts in an easy-to-understand format. In addition, you will also find exam tips, practice questions, and sample exams to help you be successful.

Equally important, you will use this book as a reference guide after the exam. I recommend that you keep this book handy and refer to it throughout the life cycle of your projects—no matter what your role is or whether you are using project management skills to achieve goals at work and in your personal life. You will find that this book is an excellent resource for tools and techniques based on a proven methodology that will lead to overall project success.

Diane L. White, PMP

Diane L. White is a Project Management Professional (PMP) and has earned a Masters Certificate in Information Technology from George Washington University. She has a Masters of Arts and a Bachelors of Arts in Education from the University of South Florida, Tampa, FL, U.S.A. Diane has been managing projects for over 20 years in the information technology and telecommunications industry.

Diane served on the Project Management Institute's global Board of Directors from 2011 to 2013. Prior to that, from 2000 to 2009, she was on the board of the PMI Tampa Bay chapter where she served for two years as the chapter President. She has spoken at many PMI conferences and events. In addition to her active involvement with PMI, Diane teaches for the University of South Florida's Certificate in Project Management program and volunteers in the community as a project leader.

The *PMBOK® Guide,* published by PMI every four years, is the basis for the Certified Associate in Project Management (CAPM) credential. The most recent update, released in January 2013, is officially called the *PMBOK® Guide* Fifth Edition, but is popularly known as the *PMBOK® Guide* 2013. Within one year, the changes in the *PMBOK® Guide* will be reflected in the CAPM exam. For the 2013 *PMBOK® Guide,* the exam changes took effect in July of 2013. The CAPM Exam consists of 150 questions. Fifteen of those questions are field-testing questions to see if they are appropriate. The 15 trial questions will *not* count towards the pass/fail determination. So only 135 of the 150 questions will actually count towards your score.

For those who have been using the *PMBOK® Guide* 2008, the following paragraphs describe the major changes for *PMBOK® Guide* 2013. If you have not used the 2008 Guide, you can skip the remainder of this preface.

The *PMBOK® Guide* Fifth Edition has been significantly improved from its prior editions. For those who are familiar with the *PMBOK® Guide* Fourth Edition, you will find that the new *PMBOK® Guide* addresses and speaks to the business community in general, with major improvements in consistency as well. We highlight below a few of the key changes as they relate to helping students prepare for the CAPM exam. To see a full list of changes from the *PMBOK® Guide* Fourth Edition, reference Appendix X1 of the *PMBOK® Guide* Fifth Edition.

One of the major changes made in this version of the *PMBOK® Guide* is the addition of a 10th knowledge area: Stakeholder Management. The table below and on the following page highlights the changes by each knowledge area.

Knowledge Area	*PMBOK® Guide* Fourth Edition Processes	*PMBOK® Guide* Fifth Edition Processes
Integration	• Develop Project Charter • Develop Project Management Plan • Direct and Manage Project Execution • Monitor and Control Project Work • Perform Integrated Change Control • Close Project or Phase	• Develop Project Charter • Develop Project Management Plan • Direct and Manage Project Work • Monitor and Control Project Work • Perform Integrated Change Control • Close Project or Phase

Knowledge Area	*PMBOK® Guide* Fourth Edition Processes	*PMBOK® Guide* Fifth Edition Processes
Scope	• Collect Requirements • Define Scope • Create WBS • Verify Scope • Control Scope	• **Plan Scope Management (Added)** • Collect Requirements • Define Scope • Create WBS • Validate Scope • Control Scope
Time	• Define Activities • Sequence Activities • Estimate Activity Resources • Estimate Activity Durations • Develop Schedule • Control Schedule	• **Plan Schedule Management (Added)** • Define Activities • Sequence Activities • Estimate Activity Resources • Estimate Activity Durations • Develop Schedule • Control Schedule
Cost	• Estimate Costs • Determine Budget • Control Costs	• **Plan Cost Management (Added)** • Estimate Costs • Determine Budget • Control Costs
Quality	• Plan Quality • Perform Quality Assurance • Perform Quality Control	• Plan Quality Management • Perform Quality Assurance • Control Quality
Human Resources	• Develop Human Resource Plan • Acquire Project Team • Develop Project Team • Manage Project Team	• Plan Human Resource Management • Acquire Project Team • Develop Project Team • Manage Project Team
Communications	• **Identify Stakeholders (Moved)** • Plan Communications • Distribute Information • **Manage Stakeholder Expectations (Moved)** • Report Performance	• Plan Communications Management • Manage Communications • Control Communications
Risk	• Plan Risk Management • Identify Risks • Perform Qualitative Risk Analysis • Perform Quantitative Risk Analysis • Plan Risk Responses • Monitor and Control Risks	• Plan Risk Management • Identify Risks • Perform Qualitative Risk Analysis • Perform Quantitative Risk Analysis • Plan Risk Responses • Control Risks
Procurement	• Plan Procurements • Conduct Procurements • Administer Procurements • Close Procurements	• Plan Procurement Management • Conduct Procurements • Control Procurements • Close Procurements
Stakeholder Management	Was not defined	• **Identify Stakeholders (Moved)** • **Plan Stakeholder Management (Added)** • **Manage Stakeholder Engagement (Moved)** • **Control Stakeholder Engagement (Added)**

In comparing the *PMBOK® Guide* Fourth Edition to the *PMBOK® Guide* Fifth Edition, you will also note that a few processes have been removed, added, or combined, but for the most part the major structure of the *PMBOK® Guide* processes has stayed in tact. A total of 47 processes exist in the *PMBOK® Guide* Fifth Edition, increased from the previous 42 processes in the prior edition. The five process groups have not changed. However, a new knowledge area—Stakeholder Management—has been added.

As stated, the biggest change in this edition is a new knowledge area—Project Stakeholder management, which is Chapter 13 in the *PMBOK® Guide*. Much of the content was previously included in the Project Communications Management knowledge area. PMI's goal with this new knowledge area is to highlight the importance of effectively engaging all stakeholders, especially those external to the project, in project decisions and project execution.

You will also see some general changes throughout the new edition. PMI has developed some basic rules for defining and using inputs, tools and techniques, outputs (ITTOs), project documents, and the project management plan. You will see more consistency in titles of the various processes. Processes in the monitoring and controlling process group typically all start with the word 'control,' and each knowledge area has a planning process that requires the project manager to plan the management of that process group. Take a look and you will see the consistency PMI has adopted.

Finally, this edition has been harmonized with other PMI standards, such as the glossary of terms with the *PMI Lexicon of Project Management Terms*. The *PMI Lexicon of Project Management Terms* is the central body of terms that all of PMI standards will reference.

Now lets look at each chapter individually for some specific changes.

Chapter 2, Project Management Overview, has been reorganized significantly, and several new descriptions have been added for predictive, iterative, incremental, and adaptive (agile) life cycles.

In Chapter 3, Processes, PMI clarified and made the use of three terms more consistent. Read the definitions of work performance data, work performance information, and work performance reports. Look at how they are being more consistently used throughout the *PMBOK® Guide*.

In Chapter 4, Integration, PMI now differentiates between the project management plan and the project documents. Project documents are not intended to be part of the project management plan. The project management plan should stay focused on defining the project management processes for the project.

Chapter 5, Scope Management, added a new process called Plan Scope Management. A key highlight in this chapter is that an emphasis has been changed in the Validate Scope process; the expectation is not just that deliverables will be accepted, but that they must add value and fulfill project objectives.

Chapter 6, Time Management, like the chapter on scope, has added a new process called Plan Schedule Management. Additional clarification has been provided on the differences between management reserves and contingency reserves, as well as between resource leveling and resource smoothing, and agile concepts have been introduced.

Chapter 7, Cost Management, also has a new process called Plan Cost Management. In addition, this knowledge area has been updated to reflect the changes made in the *Practice Standard for Estimating* and *Practice Standard for Earned Value Management*, 2nd Edition, and further clarifies the differences between management reserves and contingency reserves.

Chapter 8, Quality Management, has had limited changes; however, several other widely used quality models and quality tools have been referenced showing their relationship with the five process groups.

In Chapter 9, Human Resources Management, PMI has expanded on the benefits and disadvantages of virtual teams.

For Chapter 10, much content has been moved to the Stakeholder Management knowledge area, and only a few minor changes have been made to specific process names.

Chapter 11, Risk Management, introduces the risk profile and the terms risk attitude, risk appetite, risk tolerance, and risk thresholds. This chapter has also changed the term positive risk to opportunity risk.

For Procurement Management, Chapter 12, the only significant change has been changing a process name to Control Procurements.

Diane, Frank, and Janice would like to recognize the hard work and contributions of the many individuals who have helped us make this book a success. Both of us believe in the CAPM credential as a tremendous way to provide future project managers, project management team members, and project participants an opportunity to excel in their respective project roles and demonstrate their knowledge and willingness to improve their skills. All project managers want CAPMs on their team!

We would like to thank Steve Buda, Drew Gierman, and the team at J. Ross Publishing for their guidance, patience, and support in developing this study guide and desk reference; we would also like to thank Jessica Haile and Jessica Padilla for their diligent work as our editors.

Illustrations in this book have been provided to us by Rita Lee who can be contacted at ritaasialee@gmail.com.

Thanks also to Metafuse, Inc., who permitted us to use screen shots from their flagship product, Project Insight™, web-based project management software, for many practical examples in the book. Special thanks to Janelle Abaoag for helping us with the graphical images.

There are certainly others, whose names are not here but who contributed as participants in our workshops, challenging us to defend our statements and the answers to the questions we have written. Without all of these individuals' support and involvement, this book would not have become a reality.

INTRODUCTION

Congratulations! Your curiosity about the project management profession and what is involved in attaining the proficiency status of a Certified Associate in Project Management (CAPM) will lead you to many achievements. As you may know, the guide to the Project Management Body of Knowledge (*PMBOK® Guide*), which is published by PMI, is revised every four years. The revision of the *PMBOK® Guide* is followed by corresponding changes to the CAPM certification exam questions. The current edition of the *PMBOK® Guide* is the 2013 edition (Fifth Edition), and it is often referenced as the *PMBOK® Guide* 2013. This study guide is closely related to the *PMBOK® Guide* and has been revised to match the *PMBOK® Guide* 2013. Before you begin, make sure you know what version of the *PMBOK® Guide* you need to study, and determine your target time for taking the CAPM exam. However, if your purpose is simply to find out more about the project management disciplines and the exam process, then any version will provide you with valuable information.

Our purpose in creating this study guide is to provide you with a consolidated source of material that, used together with the material contained in the *PMBOK® Guide* and your experiences as a project manager, project management team member, or project participant, should be all you need to pass the CAPM exam.

Janice, Frank, and I have been teaching project management concepts for many years, and we believe that project success comes not just from the knowledge the project manager has, but from each person participating in the project, regardless of his or her roles. The success of any project is directly related to the competency of the whole team. This book is meant to enhance that understanding and improve the overall effectiveness of any team.

To help you succeed and to make effective use of your study time, the chapter topics in this study guide match the chapters in the *PMBOK® Guide*, and each includes material covering concepts described in the 2013 *PMI CAPM Exam Content Outline* and PMI's *Code of Ethics and Professional Conduct*.

To facilitate learning, we've incorporated into this study guide a series of examples, class exercises, and case studies to increase your understanding of the key tools and techniques of project management.

Answers to the class exercises can be found at the end of each chapter. Proposed answers to the case studies can be downloaded from the WAV™ section of the publisher's website at www.jrosspub.com/wav.

In addition to examples, class exercises, and case studies, each chapter contains a series of sample exam questions that reflect what a candidate may experience when sitting for the CAPM exam.

We have *not* included in this study guide all the inputs, outputs, tools, and techniques described in the *PMBOK® Guide*. You *must* go through the *PMBOK® Guide* in detail to become familiar with the deliverables, tools, and techniques of the many processes.

Our objective in creating this work has been not only to create a study guide, but also to provide anyone involved in projects a desk reference for becoming a more effective project manager. This study guide provides you additional value to what is described in the *PMBOK® Guide* by offering explanations and examples, as well as going beyond the *PMBOK® Guide* to topics that reinforce these concepts and improve project manager competency.

At the end of Chapters 4 through 13, you'll find additional guidance on becoming a better project manager. These exercises and activities have been used in many project settings and can provide the new project manager assistance in getting started.

The *PMBOK® Guide*, by design, is not meant to provide detailed step-by-step instructions to the project manager in a project setting. We hope you will find that this study guide provides you the information needed to understand the concepts of the *PMBOK® Guide* more thoroughly and enable you to use its tools, techniques, and methods in real-world environments.

Remember also that the exam tests your knowledge of generally accepted project management processes. Your particular industry and/or area of specialization will have different ways of doing the same thing, but PMI is administering the test, so you need to know "the PMI way." Throughout the book you will find highlighted exam tips that aid in your studies.

We have included an assessment test in Chapter 1 that you should take before you continue on to further chapters. It will help you focus on those areas of your knowledge and experience that are the weakest and save you time by allowing you to skim over the areas in which you are already knowledgeable. These assessment questions may also help you decide if you need to take a course on project management principles or a CAPM exam preparation course before attempting the actual exam. Chapter 14 is a final exam to help you confirm your understanding of the material.

Alongside the concepts and methodologies introduced here, we showcase screen shots from a popular enterprise project management software system, Project Insight™. As there are many tools for project managers, such as collaborative and web-based software solutions, where appropriate we will show you views of Project Insight™ as examples of certain concepts.

After you achieve your CAPM credential and gain more experience, you may consider taking the Project Management Professional (PMP®) exam, also administered by PMI. This is a more extensive exam requiring additional experience for you to be approved as a certified project manager. Use our *Achieve PMP® Exam Success: A Concise Study Guide for the Busy Project Manager*, 5th Edition, book to help you pass the PMP exam. The PMP exam is focused more on evaluating and responding to project situations and requires a knowledge beyond just the *PMBOK® Guide*.

All purchasers of this book will have access to online practice exams. A key to success in passing the CAPM exam is taking several practice exams, in particular, automated exams such as what we provide. Directions regarding how to access the online CAPM practice exams can be found after registering for this book's WAV™ material at the publisher's website (www.jrosspub.com/wav). You will have access to this testing site for 45 days following your registration and can run an unlimited number of 150-question CAPM exams with random combinations of over 1000 questions.

Finally, we would like to emphasize that you should by no means assume that studying this study guide replaces reading the *PMBOK® Guide*; both books should be used together. We suggest the following study method:
- Start by doing an overview of a chapter in the *PMBOK® Guide* (paging through the chapter to get a big picture of what the chapter is about and how it is organized). This should take about two or three minutes.
- Read the *Certified Associate in Project Management Credential Handbook*, available online at www.pmi.org, to understand the latest in applying for and obtaining your CAPM credential.

- Do the same with the equivalent chapter in this study guide. Note that Chapters 1 and 2 of the *PMBOK® Guide* are combined into Chapter 2 of this study guide.
- Next, read the *PMBOK® Guide* chapter carefully, asking yourself, "What do I need to learn from what I am reading?"
- Next, read the corresponding study guide chapter carefully to find the tips and important points to learn.
- Perform all the class exercises in the study guide and review your answers with your instructor, classmates, or a friend also studying for the exam, and take a look at the answer key within each chapter.
- Then reread the *PMBOK® Guide* chapter in chunks, referring back to the study guide.
- Download the WAV™ files case study materials from www.jrosspub.com/wav website.
- Perform the case studies throughout the book and compare your answers to what has been provided.
- Download the WAV™ files process charts and review the interdependencies of each of the *PMBOK® Guide* processes.
- Make notes or flash cards to help you remember essential information. Use these notes later to test yourself so you can narrow your focus on the information you may need to revisit.
- Next, do the sample exam questions at the end of each chapter in the study guide. If you find there are any concepts where you are weak, you may want to read up on them by accessing the related reference material and practicing with additional exam questions.
- Use the online test bank to perform practice tests by simulating actual 150 question exams or arranging questions by knowledge area.
- Finally, reread the *PMBOK® Guide* chapters, this time very quickly, so you end with the overall picture rather than being buried in details.

Good studying and good luck with building your project management skills and knowledge. We look forward to hearing from you and celebrating your achievements. News of your success as well as any suggestions or comments on our study guide can be sent to us by email to info@cpconcepts.net.

Diane Altwies, Janice Preston, and Frank Reynolds

Core Performance Concepts, Inc.

Core Performance Concepts, Inc., a training, curriculum, and services provider, was established in 2005 by Diane C. Buckley-Altwies and Janice Y. Preston. Answering the need for high-quality courses, curriculum, and organizational transformation services for adult learners, Core Performance Concepts provides turnkey solutions for:

- Leadership
- Project Management (including agile methodologies)
- Process Improvement (such as Six Sigma and lean concepts)
- Business Analysis

Core Performance Concepts believes that organizations can *only* succeed through the people they hire. Having a knowledgeable and effective workforce that understands organizational strategy and demonstrates critical skills will enable success for any business.

Our hands-on, interactive curriculum—whether on ground or online—provides the student the necessary knowledge to prove competency in the workplace.

With over 50 years combined professional and corporate experience delivering strategy for organizations, we understand the importance of good fundamental knowledge and efficient processes, and we strive to help organizations succeed.

Diane Altwies, MBA, PMP, has been managing software development projects for nearly 30 years as a program manager or project manager in the insurance, financial services, and healthcare industries. She is the CEO of Core Performance Concepts, Inc. She continues to teach and consult for organizations on various program management, project management, and business analysis topics and develops advanced courseware topics for project managers. Diane is a frequent speaker at professional meetings and symposia across the country. She is a Fellow of PMI Orange County and has an MBA in Finance and Marketing and a BA in Production Management, both from the University of South Florida. In addition to this book, she has co-authored two others: *Program Management Professional: A Certification Study Guide with Best Practices for Maximizing Business Results* and *Achieve PMP® Exam Success: A Concise Study Guide for the Busy Project Manager*.

Janice Preston, MBA, CPA, PMP, has been managing projects for more than 25 years in industries as diverse as real estate, finance, healthcare, and technology. For more than 15 years, she has developed course curricula in project management and has been responsible for creating several project management certificate programs at leading universities. She writes and speaks on many project management topics, including team leadership, communication skills, earned value, cost control, and procurement. She is considered an expert in the field of risk management and has consulted on updates to the *PMBOK® Guide*'s risk management knowledge area. She is a Fellow of PMI Orange County and has an MBA in Finance and Accounting from the University of Missouri and a BA in Education from the University of Central Florida. Her other publications include *Achieve PMP® Exam Success: A Concise Study Guide for the Busy Project Manager*.

Frank Reynolds, CAPM since 2008, was a PMI-Orange County Chapter 2006 Project Management Fellow and a PMP from 1992 to 2005. Frank has over 35 years of experience in project management in a variety of industries, professions, and cultures. He has been acknowledged for supporting clients whose projects demand the integration of a variety of disciplines. Throughout his career, Frank has often consulted with and trained project managers and project participants in manufacturing, information technology, transportation, urban design, telecommunications, engineering, and construction in multidisciplinary project settings. He has taught and consulted extensively in the United States and China as well as Dubai, Brazil, Spain, France, Poland, Singapore, and Malaysia. Frank is a frequent speaker at professional meetings and symposia across the country. He is a pioneer in training members of project teams and promotes PMI's Certified Associate in Project Management certification.

Downloadable Resources at
www.jrosspub.com.

Value-added material is available from the WAV™ Web Added Value™ Download Resource Center at www.jrosspub.com.

At J. Ross Publishing we are committed to providing today's professional with practical, hands-on tools that enhance the learning experience and give readers an opportunity to apply what they have learned. That is why we offer free ancillary materials for download on this book and all participating Web Added Value™ publications. These online resources may include interactive versions of material that appears in the book or supplemental templates, worksheets, models, plans, case studies, proposals, spreadsheets, and assessment tools, among other things. Whenever you see the WAV™ symbol in any of our publications, it means bonus materials accompany the book and are available from the WAV™ Web Added Value Download Resource Center at www.jrosspub.com.

Downloads available for *Achieve CAPM® Exam Success: A Concise Study Guide and Desk Reference*, 2nd Edition, include:

- Directions for how to use the online test bank with your unique serial number found on the inside front cover of this book
- A flashcard study aid of key terms and concepts
- A self-study exercise on understanding the interdependencies of all 47 processes defined in the *PMBOK® Guide*
- A case study answer key
- A training aide for better understanding process interdependencies

STUDY TIPS

CHAPTER 1 | **STUDY TIPS &**
ASSESSMENT EXAM

1

WHAT IS A CERTIFIED ASSOCIATE IN PROJECT MANAGEMENT (CAPM)?

A CAPM is a project manager or project participant who:
- Has been responsible for individual project tasks in his or her area of expertise
- Has a demonstrated understanding of the fundamental knowledge, processes, and terminology as defined within Project Management Institute (PMI) standards
- Has a high school diploma, or equivalent, with at least 1,500 hours of experience as part of a project management team *or* 23 hours of project management training
- Has passed a CAPM exam administered by PMI

CAPM EXAM SPECIFICS

The exam has the following characteristics:
- It assesses the knowledge and application of globally accepted project management concepts, techniques and procedures
- It covers the ten **knowledge areas** and the five **process groups** as detailed in *A Guide to the Project Management Body of Knowledge*, Fifth Edition (*PMBOK® Guide*)
- It contains 150 multiple choice questions
- It includes 15 questions that are pre-exam questions being field-tested by PMI that do not affect your exam score
- It takes up to three hours

The table on the following page summarizes the distribution of exam questions across each of the 13 chapters of the *PMBOK® Guide*.

Note that the information in this chart may change from time to time. Consult the PMI website (www.pmi.org) for the most current information.

PMBOK® Guide Chapters	% of exam	Approximate # of questions
Chapters 1 to 3: PM Overview and Processes	15%	23
Chapter 4: Integration	12%	18
Chapter 5: Scope	11%	17
Chapter 6: Time	12%	18
Chapter 7: Cost	7%	10
Chapter 8: Quality	6%	9
Chapter 9: Human Resources	8%	12
Chapter 10: Communications	6%	9
Chapter 11: Risk	9%	14
Chapter 12: Procurement	7%	10
Chapter 13: Stakeholder Management	7%	10
Total	100%	150

STUDY TIPS

Below is a list of recommended study tips from project managers who have successfully passed the CAPM exam. Think about each one and determine which suggestions are the best for your learning style.

- Develop a plan for studying; see page 1-17 for a sample study plan utilizing the *PMBOK® Guide* and this study guide
- Follow the plan on a daily or weekly basis; it is important for you to commit to studying
- Make a checklist of things you need to study
- Plan your study sessions with time limitations
- Vary tasks and topics during lengthy study periods
- Find one special place for studying and use it only for that
- Eliminate distractions
  · If daydreaming, walk away

1

- · Take brief breaks (5 to 10 minutes) after about 50 minutes of study
- Continue to test yourself
  - · Use lots of practice exams
  - · Create your own exams
  - · Your goal should be to consistently achieve 80% correctness
- Understand the big concepts first
  - · Restate, repeat, and put in your own words
- Memorize
  - · Important people mentioned in this textbook and their contributions to project management
  - · Formulas
  - · Processes and their order
  - · Inputs, tools and techniques, and outputs of each process
  - · Key terms from the *PMBOK® Guide*
- Use memorizing methods such as:
  - · Flip-charts
  - · Diagrams
  - · Mnemonics
  - · Memory searches (relate to past experiences)
- Prepare for the exam day
  - · Get a good night's rest
  - · Avoid last-minute cramming
  - · Have a good breakfast
  - · Leave books at home
  - · Use the calculator on the electronic testing system
  - · Go with a positive attitude
  - · Get to the exam site *early*

EXAM TIPS

The exam tests your knowledge of the *PMBOK® Guide* by asking you many questions on definitions and inputs, tools and techniques, and outputs, and it has many situational questions that determine how well you apply *PMBOK® Guide* concepts to real-life situations. Most people can succeed if they follow these simple steps on test day.

- · Use the 15 minute tutorial time to do a brain dump on the items you have memorized

- Relax before and during the exam
  - Take deep breaths
  - Stretch about every 40 minutes
  - If you get nervous, try to relax
  - Give yourself a goal and reward yourself
  - Resist the urge to panic
- Read each question carefully
- Be especially alert when double negatives are used
- Reread ALL questions containing negative words such as "not," "least," or "except"
- If a question is long and complex, read the final sentence, look at the answer choices and then look for the subject and verb
- Check for qualifying words such as "all," "most," "some," "none," "highest-to-lowest," and "smallest-to-largest"
- Check for key words such as "input," "output," "tool," "technique," "initiating," "planning," "executing," "monitoring and controlling," and "closure"
- Decide in your mind what the answer should be, then look for the answer in the options
- Reread the questions and eliminate answer choices that are *not* correct
- The correct answer, if it's not simply a number, will include a PMI term
- Make sure you look at *all* the answer choices
- Mark questions to come back to

TIME MANAGEMENT DURING THE EXAM

- Keep track of time (you have approximately 1 minute and 15 seconds for each question)
- Set up a time schedule for each question
- Allow time for review of the exam
- To stay relaxed, keep on schedule
- Answer all questions in order without skipping or jumping around
- If you are unsure, take a guess and mark the question to return to later; do not linger

- For questions involving problem solving:
  - Write down the formulas before solving
  - If possible, recheck your work in a different way (for example, rationalize)
- Subsequent questions may stimulate your memory and you may want to reevaluate a previous answer
- A lapse in memory is normal
- You will not know all the answers
- Take your time
- Do not be in a rush to leave the exam
- Before turning in the exam, verify that you have answered all questions

FAQS ABOUT THE EXAM

- Can you bring materials with you?
  NO
- What is the physical setting like?
  It is a small room or cubicle with a computer, chair, desk, and trash can
- Can you take food or drink into the exam area?
  NO food or drink is allowed
- Can you take breaks during the exam?
  YES, you can go to the rest room or take a break to clear your mind, but know that your clock is ticking all the time, so you need to determine if you have time for a break
- What are the time constraints?
  You have 3 hours (with an additional 15-minute tutorial and 15-minute survey)
- Are the exam questions grouped by knowledge area such as scope, time, and cost?
  NO, the 150 questions are randomly scattered across the process groups and knowledge areas
- Can you take paper and pen into the exam area?
  NO, pencils and paper are supplied
- Can you see both the question and the answers on the same screen?
  YES

1

- Is there a way to cross out or eliminate options that you immediately know are not correct? NO, you can work only on a piece of scratch paper
- Is there a way to mark questions when you are in doubt of the answer? YES
- When you are done, can you review the exam? YES
- Can you review just the questions you marked as doubtful? YES
- Do you get immediate exam results? YES, if you are taking an online exam, after you are done, hit the SEND button and then the computer will ask if you are sure; after you hit SEND, you will fill out an online evaluation of the exam process consisting of about ten questions; a testing center staff person will give you a detailed report of your results

---

TIP
Come up with your own creative phrases to remember the processes in each of the ten knowledge areas.

MEMORIZATION TIPS FOR PERFORMANCE DOMAINS, PROCESS GROUPS, KNOWLEDGE AREAS, AND PROCESSES

PMI defines the field of project management as consisting of five **performance domains**:
- Initiating
- Planning
- Executing
- Monitoring and Controlling
- Closing

Each domain contains tasks and the knowledge and skills which are required to competently perform these tasks. There are also cross-cutting knowledge and skills, which are used in multiple domains and tasks.

In alignment with the five performance domains are the five **process groups**. Each process group contains two or more processes. The process groups with their corresponding process counts are:
- Initiating (2)
- Planning (24)
- Executing (8)
- Monitoring and Controlling (11)
- Closing (2)

This yields a total of 47 processes. The process groups are discussed in detail in Chapter 3 of this study guide.

There are ten **knowledge areas**. Each of the processes, in addition to belonging to a process group, also belongs to a knowledge area. The knowledge areas with their corresponding process counts are:
- Integration (6)
- Scope (6)
- Time (7)
- Cost (4)
- Quality (3)
- Human Resources (4)
- Communications (3)
- Risk (6)
- Procurement (4)
- Stakeholder Management (4)

The individual processes are discussed in the knowledge areas (Chapters 4 through 13).

Table 3-1 of the *PMBOK® Guide* has a comprehensive chart that cross-references the individual processes, knowledge areas, and process groups.

Many people like to use creative phrases that jog the memory to remember lists and sequences. Examples of memorable phrases follow for the five process groups and the ten knowledge areas.

1

Memorization Tip for the Five Process Groups:

Henry **I**nitiated a committee named **PEMC**o to **C**lose down the railway line.
1. Initiating
2. Planning
3. Executing
4. Monitoring and Controlling
5. Closing

Memorization Tip for the Ten Knowledge Areas:

I've **S**een **T**hat the **C**ost of **Q**uality **H**as **CR**itical importance to my **P**roject's **S**uccess.
1. Integration
2. Scope
3. Time
4. Cost
5. Quality
6. Human Resources
7. Communications
8. Risk
9. Procurement
10. Stakeholder Management

You may want to devise your own memorization tips for processes in each of the knowledge areas. Here is an example of a **memorization tip for the Project Scope Management processes**:

Planning **S**cope **M**eans you **C**reate **R**eal **D**irection, a **S**ense of a **C**an-**W**in attitude and a **ViS**ion for **C**ontinued **S**uccess.
1. Plan Scope Management
2. Collect Requirements
3. Define Scope
4. Create WBS
5. Validate Scope
6. Control Scope

1

FORMULAS, EQUATIONS, AND RULES

Some formulas, equations, and rules must be memorized to answer exam questions effectively. The most important items to remember are listed here. Most of these are discussed in more detail in the following chapters.

1. Project Network Schedules

Network schedules are created after duration estimates and the relationships between the work packages have been determined. Following a path(s) from left to right makes a forward pass.

- **Forward pass**
  - Yields early start (ES) and early finish (EF) dates
  - Early finish = early start + duration
  - *Rule*: If there are multiple predecessors, use *latest* EF to determine successor ES

After all paths have been given their forward path, they are traversed from right to left to make a backward pass.

- **Backward pass**
  - Yields late start (LS) and late finish (LF) dates
  - Late start = late finish – duration
  - *Rule*: If there are multiple successors, use *earliest* LS to determine predecessor LF

Once the forward and backward passes have been completed, the total float for the node can be calculated by:

- Total float = late finish – early finish

2. Normal Distribution

Normal distribution, commonly known as a bell curve, is a symmetrical distribution, as shown in Figure 1-1. Each normal curve can be distinctly described using the mean and sum of the values.

The possibility of achieving the project objective in the mean time or cost is 0%, with a 50% chance of falling below the mean and a 50% chance of exceeding the mean. Adding one or more standard deviations (σ) to the mean increases the chances of falling within the range. The probability of falling within 1σ, 2σ, or 3σ from the mean is:

- $1\sigma = 68.27\%$
- $2\sigma = 95.45\%$
- $3\sigma = 99.73\%$

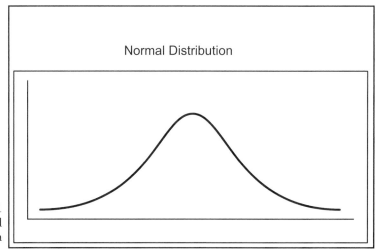

Figure 1-1
Normal
Distribution

Normal Distribution

3. Triangular Distribution

When there are three possible values, each of which is equally likely, the distribution takes on the shape of a triangle, as shown in Figure 1-2.

- With A = lowest value, B = highest value, and M = most likely value, variance for a task (V) (variance is not on the exam) is
  - $V = [(A - B)^2 + (M - A)(M - B)] \div 18$
- Mean (μ)
  - $\mu = (A + M + B) \div 3$
- Standard deviation (σ)
  - $\sigma = \sqrt{V}_p$

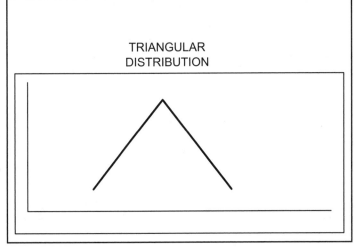

TRIANGULAR
DISTRIBUTION

Figure 1-2
Triangular
Distribution

4. Weighted-Average or Beta/PERT Distribution

The beta distribution is like the triangular distribution except more weight is given to the most likely estimate. This may result in either a symmetrical or an asymmetrical (skewed right or skewed left) graph. An asymmetrical graph is shown in Figure 1-3.

- Where O = optimistic estimate, ML = most likely estimate, and P = pessimistic estimate, variance for a task (V) is:
  - $V = \sigma^2$
- Mean (μ)
  - $(\mu) = (O + 4ML + P) \div 6$
- Standard deviation (σ)
  - $\sigma = (P - O) \div 6$

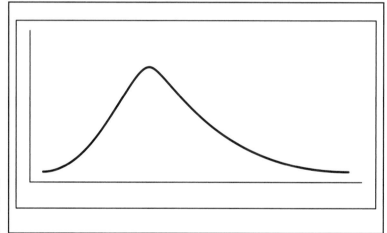

Figure 1-3
Weighted-Average
or Beta/PERT
Distribution

5. Statistical Sums

- The project mean is the sum of the means of the individual tasks: $\mu_p = \mu_1 + \mu_2 + \ldots + \mu_n$
- The project variance is the sum of the variances of the individual tasks: $V_p = V_1 + V_2 + \ldots + V_n$
- The project standard deviation is the square root of the project variance: $\sigma_p = \sqrt{V_p}$

6. Earned Value Management

Earned value management is used to monitor the progress of a project and is an analytical technique. It uses three independent variables:

- **Planned value (PV)**: the budget or the portion of the approved cost estimate planned to be spent during a given period
- **Actual cost (AC)**: the total of direct and indirect costs incurred in accomplishing work during a given period
- **Earned value (EV)**: the budget for the work accomplished in a given period

These three values are used in combination to provide measures of whether or not work is proceeding as planned. They combine to yield the following important formulas:

- **Cost variance (CV)** = $EV - AC$
- **Schedule variance (SV)** = $EV - PV$
- **Cost performance index (CPI)** = $EV \div AC$
- **Schedule performance index (SPI)** = $EV \div PV$

Positive CV indicates costs are below budget. Positive SV indicates a project is ahead of schedule.

Negative CV indicates cost overrun. Negative SV indicates a project is behind schedule.

A CPI greater than 1.0 indicates costs are below budget. An SPI greater than 1.0 indicates a project is ahead of schedule.

A CPI less than 1.0 indicates costs are over budget. An SPI less than 1.0 indicates a project is behind schedule.

1

7. Estimate at Completion

An **estimate at completion (EAC)** is the amount
we expect the total project to cost on completion and
as of the "data date" (time now). There are four
methods listed in the *PMBOK® Guide* for computing
EAC. Three of these methods use a formula to
calculate EAC. Each of these starts with AC, or
actual costs to date, and uses a different technique
to estimate the work remaining to be completed, or
ETC. The question of which to use depends on the
individual situation and the credibility of the actual
work performed compared to the budget up to that
point.

- A **new estimate** is most applicable when the
  actual performance to date shows that the
  original estimates were fundamentally flawed
  or when they are no longer accurate because of
  changes in conditions relating to the project:
  - EAC = AC + New Estimate for
    Remaining Work

- The **original estimate** formula is most
  applicable when actual variances to date
  are seen as being the exception, and the
  expectations for the future are that the
  original estimates are more reliable than
  the actual work effort efficiency to date:
  - EAC = AC + (BAC – EV)

- The **performance estimate low** formula is
  most applicable when future variances are
  projected to approximate the same level as
  current variances:
  - EAC = AC + (BAC – EV) ÷ CPI

  A shortcut version of this formula is:
  - EAC = BAC ÷ CPI

- The **performance estimate high** formula is used when the project is over budget and the schedule impacts the work remaining to be completed:
    - $EAC = AC + (BAC - EV) \div (CPI)(SPI)$

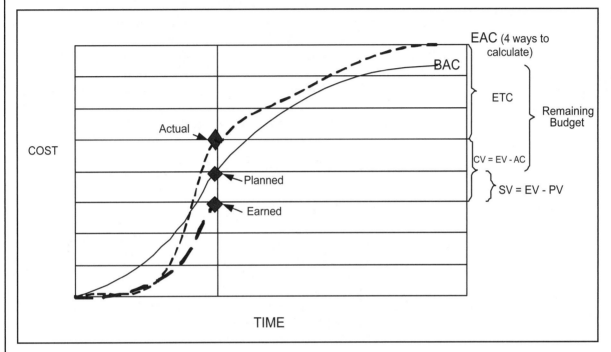

Figure 1-4
Earned Value
S-Curve

Figure 1-4 above indicates how many of these EAC formulas can be used to graph information. Formulas to be used with the figure above include:
- $CPI = EV \div AC$
- $SPI = EV \div PV$

8. Remaining Budget

- $RB = $ Remaining PV
    or
- $RB = BAC - EV$

9. Budget at Completion

- $BAC = $ the total budgeted cost of all approved activities

10. Estimate to Complete

The estimate to complete (ETC) is the estimate for completing the remaining work for a scheduled activity. Like the EAC formulas above, there are three variations:
- ETC = an entirely new estimate
- ETC = (BAC – EV) when past variances are considered to be atypical
- ETC = (BAC – EV) ÷ CPI when prior variances are considered to be typical of future variances

11. Communications Channels

- Channels = $[n(n - 1)] \div 2$
  where "n" = the number of people

12. Rule of Seven

In a control chart, the "rule of seven" is a heuristic stating that if seven or more observations occur in one direction either upward or downward, or a run of seven observations occurs either above or below the mean, even though they may be within the control lines, they should be investigated to determine if they have an assignable cause. The reason for this rule is that, if the process is operating normally, the observations will follow a random pattern; it is extremely unlikely that seven observations in a row would occur in the same direction above or below the mean.

The probability of any given point going up or down or being above or below the mean is 50-50 (i.e., 50%). The probability of seven observations being consecutively in one direction or above or below the mean would be calculated as 0.50^7, which equals 0.0078 (i.e., much less than 1%).

SAMPLE STUDY SCHEDULE

Week/Day	Knowledge Area/ Domain	PMBOK® Guide Chapter	Study Guide Chapter	Goals
1	PM Overview	1 and 2	2	25 questions
2	Processes	3 & Annex A1	3	25 questions
3	Integration	4	4	25 questions
4	Scope	5	5	25 questions
5	Time	6	6	25 questions
6	Cost	7	7	25 questions
7	Quality	8	8	25 questions
8	Human Resources	9	9	25 questions
9	Communications	10	10	25 questions
10	Risk	11	11	25 questions
11	Procurement	12	12	25 questions
12	Stakeholder Management	13	13	25 questions
13	Review	1 to 13	2 to 13	75 questions
14	Review	1 to 13	2 to 13	75 questions
15	Practice	1 to 13	2 to 13	150 questions

SAMPLE ASSESSMENT EXAM

Readers should give themselves 61 minutes to answer these 50 sample exam questions. This timing is similar to the average time per question recommended by PMI in the actual CAPM exam.

1. What is the benefit of following the communication plan to collect and distribute information?

   a) It allows an efficient flow of communications
   b) It identifies and documents the approaches used to communicate
   c) It enables the project manager to use interpersonal skills effectively
   d) It ensures that information is flowing to all project stakeholders

2. Which of the following organizational process assets might influence the Control Communications process?

   a) Meeting management and facilitation techniques
   b) Organizational culture and government standards
   c) Report templates and record retention policies
   d) Information management systems and listening techniques

3. Communication technology is a tool and technique of which processes?

   a) Manage Communications and Manage Stakeholder Engagement
   b) Plan Communications Management and Manage Communications
   c) Control Communications and Control Stakeholder Engagement
   d) Plan Communications Management and Plan Stakeholder Management

Notes:

4. Your project data shows that, at some point in the time during execution, the earned value (EV) is $10,000 and the actual cost (AC) is $7,500. The cost variance (CV) is:

   a) There is insufficient data to make a determination
   b) <$2,500>
   c) 1.333
   d) $2,500

5. On November 1, $1,200 worth of work on activity A was planned to have been completed. The work accomplished was worth $1,300. What is the schedule variance?

   a) <$100>
   b) $100
   c) <$150>
   d) $150

6. Cost Management is primarily concerned with:

   a) The cost of resources needed to complete schedule activities
   b) The cost of resources for acquiring the project team
   c) The cost of resources needed to complete the schedule activities excluding subcontracted items
   d) The cost of resources and materials for on-going operations

7. The estimate that relies on the actual cost of a previous similar project as a basis for estimating the current project is a/an:

   a) Parametric estimate
   b) Bottom-up estimate
   c) Three-point estimate
   d) Analogous estimate

Notes:

8. What is the key benefit of the Determine Budget process?

   a) It determines how much the project will cost
   b) It provides guidance on how funds will be spent
   c) It creates a cost baseline used to measure performance against
   d) It allows you to determine whether or not variances require corrective action

9. Outlining and guiding the team selection to obtain an effective team is a key benefit of which process?

   a) Acquire Project Team
   b) Plan Human Resource Management
   c) Develop Project Team
   d) Manage Project Team

10. The human resource process which improves the competencies of team members to enhance project performance is the _____ process.

   a) Manage Project Team
   b) Develop Project Team
   c) Plan Human Resource Management
   d) Acquire Project Team

11. Managing the team most requires an emphasis on _____, conflict management, and leadership.

   a) Communication
   b) Organizational structure
   c) Performance monitoring
   d) Time tracking

12. What impact does a matrix organization have on project team management and development?

   a) Team development is simplified
   b) Team development becomes more complex
   c) No impact
   d) Team development does not take place in matrix organizations

Notes:
_____
_____
_____
_____
_____
_____
_____
_____
_____
_____
_____
_____
_____
_____
_____
_____
_____
_____
_____
_____
_____
_____
_____
_____
_____

13. Formally ending a project and providing lessons learned is a key benefit of which process?

   a) Validate Scope
   b) Control Quality
   c) Close Project or Phase
   d) Close Procurements

14. The _____ process finalizes all activities across all process groups to formally close the project or phase.

   a) Closing processes
   b) Close Procurements
   c) Controlling processes
   d) Executing processes

15. What is an action to make sure that work performed in the future aligns with the project management plan?

   a) Risk responses
   b) Corrective actions
   c) Preventive actions
   d) Defect repairs

16. Performance data that is analyzed and integrated is called:

   a) Work performance completed
   b) Work performance data
   c) Work performance information
   d) Work performance reports

17. Integration is primarily concerned with:

   a) Effectively integrating the processes that are required to accomplish project objectives
   b) The appropriate level of rigor to achieve the desired project performance
   c) Dividing projects into phases to provide better management control
   d) Facilitating the formal authorization to start a new project or project phase

Notes:

18. A narrative description of products to be supplied by a project is the:

   a) Project scope statement
   b) Charter
   c) Project statement of work
   d) Contract

19. PMI members must adhere to:

   a) Customer quality assurance policies
   b) Professional responsibility guidelines
   c) A code of ethics
   d) Best business practices

20. The CCB is responsible for reviewing and approving or rejecting change requests. These actions are accomplished during what type of meeting?

   a) Decision making
   b) Option evaluation
   c) Information exchange
   d) Change control

21. The project management plan and its subsidiary plans are:

   a) Mandatory on every project to ensure success
   b) Progressively elaborated in subsequent processes
   c) Developed by the project sponsor
   d) Specified the same way for projects in all application areas for all sizes of projects

22. The life cycle that includes high level vision but not a detailed plan is preferred when an organization needs to reduce the complexity of a project or manage changing scope is:

   a) Agile
   b) Adaptive
   c) Predictive
   d) Iterative

Notes:

23. As you hold meetings with your project sponsor, the needs of the sponsor will become more clear, which will enable your team to develop the requirements of the project. The process group which enables this increased specificity is:

a) Monitoring and controlling
b) Planning
c) Initiating
d) Executing

24. Completing and settling the work of the contract is a process called the _____ process.

a) Close Project or Phase
b) Close Procurements
c) Administer Closure
d) Contract Administrator

25. During which step of the procurement process are the proposals received?

a) Plan Procurements
b) Control Procurements
c) Close Procurements
d) Conduct Procurements

26. The process that includes reviewing and documenting how well a seller is performing is:

a) Plan Procurements
b) Control Procurements
c) Close Procurements
d) Close Project of Phase

27. The contract type in which the seller is reimbursed for all costs and receives a negotiated fee is:

a) Firm fixed price
b) Fixed price incentive fee
c) Time and materials
d) Cost reimbursable

Notes:

28. The technique that examines quality practices implemented, nonconformity with quality policies, and compliance with an organization's quality process is:

    a) Quality audits
    b) Cause and effect analysis
    c) Flowcharting
    d) Process analysis

29. A key input into the Control Quality process is:

    a) An activity list
    b) Evaluation criteria
    c) Work performance data
    d) A project scope statement

30. One main benefit of the _____ process is that it guides the project manager on how quality will be managed throughout the project.

    a) Project Quality Management
    b) Plan Quality Management
    c) Perform Quality Assurance
    d) Control Quality

29. A key input into the Control Quality process is...

    a) An activity list
    b) Evaluation criteria
    c) Work performance data
    d) A project scope statement

30. One main benefit of the _____ process is that it guides the project manager on how quality will be managed throughout the project.

    a) Project Quality Management
    b) Plan Quality Management
    c) Perform Quality Assurance
    d) Control Quality

Notes:

_____

_____

_____

_____

_____

_____

_____

_____

_____

_____

_____

_____

_____

_____

_____

_____

_____

_____

_____

_____

_____

_____

_____

_____

31. Reserve analysis compares:

    a) The effectiveness of the risk management process to the project objectives
    b) Current project cost estimates with similar past project costs
    c) Project performance to the planned schedule
    d) The amount of contingency reserves remaining to the amount of risk remaining

32. Which of the following are tools and techniques of the Plan Risk Management process?

    a) Checklist analysis and assumptions analysis
    b) Monte Carlo simulation and decision tree
    c) Meetings and expert judgment
    d) Probability and impact matrix and risk categories

33. The purpose of _____ is to determine potential positive or negative affects on schedule, cost, quality, or performance.

    a) Assessing consequences
    b) Defining probability
    c) Identifying risks
    d) Developing responses

34. A major benefit of performing the Perform Quantitative Risk Analysis process is that it:

    a) Documents identified risk events and potential responses
    b) Provides a quick and low cost method of identifying high-priority risks
    c) Changes the Project Management Plan to eliminate a threat
    d) Supports the project manager's ability to make decisions to reduce uncertainty

Notes:

1

35. In monitoring and controlling a project, which of the following tasks would you perform?

    a) Maximizing team performance through mentoring and communicating status to get feedback from stakeholders
    b) Measuring performance to identify variances and managing changes to scope, cost, and schedule
    c) Using control charts to ensure deliverables meet quality standards and implementing the quality plan
    d) Assessing corrective actions to be taken and implementing approved changes to meet project requirements

36. Which of the following organizational process assets are likely to influence the Plan Scope Management process?

    a) Issue and defect identification procedures
    b) Infrastructure and personnel administration
    c) Organization culture and market conditions
    d) Policies and lessons learned

37. The process of defining and documenting stakeholders' needs to meet project objectives is called:

    a) Plan Scope Management
    b) Plan Stakeholder Management
    c) Collect Requirements
    d) Define Scope

38. Providing a description of requirements that are included in the project scope is a key benefit of which process?

    a) Plan Scope Management
    b) Collect Requirements
    c) Define Scope
    d) Create WBS

Notes:

1

39. The scope baseline for a project includes:

    a) Project scope statement, WBS, and WBS dictionary
    b) Project scope statement, procurement statement of work, and project statement of work
    c) Requirements, project scope statement, and procurement statement of work
    d) Project statement of work, project scope statement, and product analysis

40. The goal of capturing customer feedback and measuring customer satisfaction at the end of a project is to:

    a) Satisfy customer requirements
    b) Communicate to stakeholders
    c) Enhance customer relationships
    d) Update your knowledge base

41. Which process will assist the project manager in increasing support for a project?

    a) Identify Stakeholders
    b) Plan Stakeholder Management
    c) Manage Stakeholder Engagement
    d) Control Stakeholder Engagement

42. Which of the following are tools and techniques of Manage Stakeholder Engagement?

    a) Expert judgment and analytical techniques
    b) Communication methods and interpersonal skills
    c) Meetings and information management systems
    d) Stakeholder analysis and classification

Notes:

43. Outputs from the Manage Stakeholder Engagement process include:

    a) Issues log and communications management plan
    b) Project management plan updates
    c) Project document updates and change log
    d) Organizational process assets

44. Determining how to deal with each stakeholder is a key benefit of which process?

    a) Identify Stakeholders
    b) Plan Stakeholder Management
    c) Manage Stakeholder Engagement
    d) Control Stakeholder Engagement

45. Which of the following are inputs to the Control Stakeholder Engagement process?

    a) Project documents and expert judgment
    b) Organizational process assets updates and meetings
    c) Work performance information and change requests
    d) Issues log and project management plan

46. The technique for reviewing performance over time to determine if it is improving or getting worse is called:

    a) Trend analysis
    b) Critical path method
    c) Critical chain method
    d) Earned value management

Notes:

47. Which of the following are enterprise environmental factors that affect planning to manage the schedule?

a) Organizational culture, resource availability, and project management software
b) Monitoring and reporting tools and historical information
c) Templates, schedule control tools, and policies
d) Change control, risk, and schedule control procedures

48. How will estimated resource requirements effect duration estimates?

a) Resources who are lower skilled will increase cost
b) Resources who are only available 20% of the time will reduce the duration
c) Resources with high skills may reduce the duration
d) Resources can be leveled over the project duration

49. The approved schedule model that can be changed only through formal change control is called a:

a) Schedule management plan
b) Progress report
c) Schedule baseline
d) Variance analysis

50. The process that determines what resources and what quantities of each resource will be used is called:

a) Sequence Activities
b) Define Activities
c) Estimate Activity Durations
d) Estimate Activity Resources

SAMPLE ASSESSMENT EXAM ANSWERS

with explanations and references are in Chapter 15, Appendix A.

Notes:

This book has free material available for download from the Web Added Value™ resource center at *www.jrosspub.com*.

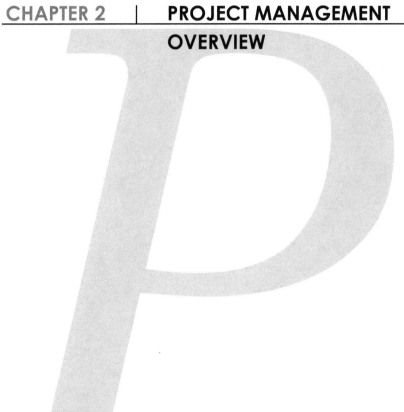

CHAPTER 2 | **PROJECT MANAGEMENT**
OVERVIEW

2

2

2

PROJECT MANAGEMENT OVERVIEW

Chapters 1 and 2 of the *PMBOK® Guide* provide a basic structure to the field of project management. These chapters provide an introduction to project management, the context and environment in which projects operate. Together, these two chapters give an overview of the project management discipline. These chapters in the *PMBOK® Guide* themselves are not about knowledge areas, but they contain many important definitions and concepts that must be understood before attempting the remaining chapters of the *PMBOK® Guide*.

Overview questions on the CAPM exam mainly cover definitions, concepts, and approaches. You must be familiar with PMI terminology. Projects, programs, project management, stakeholders, project and product life cycles, organizational structures, and influences are among the topics covered.

Knowledge Area Processes

The *PMBOK® Guide* is defined in terms of ten knowledge areas and five process groups. Within each knowledge area, processes are defined. It is important to know each of the processes within the matrix of the knowledge areas and process groups. The *PMBOK® Guide* defines a total of 47 processes. The table below outlines the distribution of processes across the five process groups.

Process Groups	Initiating	Planning	Executing	Monitoring and Controlling	Closing
Numbers of Processes	2	24	8	11	2

2

Key Definitions

Business value: the entire value of a business; the total sum of all tangible and intangible elements.

Colocation: project team members are physically located close to one another in order to improve communication, working relations, and productivity.

Constraint: a restriction or limitation that may force a certain course of action or inaction.

Enterprise environmental factors: external or internal factors that can influence a project's success. These factors include controllable factors such as the tools used in managing projects within the organization or uncontrollable factors that have to be considered by the project manager such as market conditions or corporate culture.

Good practice: a specific activity or application of a skill, tool, or technique that has been proven to contribute positively to the execution of a process.

Operations: ongoing work performed by people, constrained by resources, planned, executed, monitored, and controlled. Unlike a project, operations are repetitive; e.g., the work performed to carry out the day-to-day business of an organization is operational work.

Organizational process assets: any formal or informal processes, plans, policies, procedures, guidelines, and on-going or historical project information such as lessons learned, measurement data, project files, and estimates versus actuals.

Portfolio: a collection of programs, projects, and additional work managed together to facilitate the attainment of strategic business goals.

> **TIP**
> Read the *PMI Lexicon of Project Management Terms*. It provides the foundational professional vocabulary.

Product life cycle: the collection of stages that make up the life of a product. These stages are typically introduction, growth, maturity, and retirement.

Program: a group of related projects managed in a coordinated way; e.g., the design and creation of the prototype for a new airplane is a project, while manufacturing 99 more airplanes of the same model is a program.

Progressive elaboration: the iterative process of increasing the level of detail in a project management plan as greater amounts of information and more accurate estimates become available.

Project: work performed by people, constrained by resources, planned, executed, monitored, and controlled. It has definite beginning and end points and creates a unique outcome that may be a product, service, or result.

Project life cycle: the name given to the collection of various phases that make up a project. These phases make the project easier to control and integrate. The result of each phase is one or more deliverables that are utilized in the next few phases. The work of each phase is accomplished through the iterative application of the initiating, planning, executing, monitoring and controlling, and closing process groups.

Project management: the ability to meet project requirements by using various knowledge, skills, tools, and techniques to accomplish project work. Project work is completed through the iterative application of initiating, planning, executing, monitoring and controlling, and closing process groups. Project management is challenged by competing and changing demands for scope (customer needs, expectations, and requirements), resources (people, time, and cost), risks (known and unknown), and quality (of the project and product).

TIP

Reference the glossary of the *PMBOK® Guide* frequently to learn PMI terminology.

2

2

Project management information system: the collection of tools, methodologies, techniques, standards, and resources used to manage a project. These may be formal systems and strategies determined by the organization or informal methods utilized by project managers.

Stakeholder: an individual, group, or organization who may affect, be affected by, or perceive itself to be affected by a decision, activity, or outcome of a project.

Standard: a document that describes rules, guidelines, methods, processes, and practices that can be used repeatedly to enhance the chances of success.

Subproject: a component of a project. Subprojects can be contracted out to an external enterprise or to another functional unit.

THE PURPOSE OF PROJECT MANAGEMENT STANDARDS

The *PMBOK® Guide* provides an organized description of the generally recognized good practices, or standards, of project management. It defines and explains the application of useful knowledge, processes, skills, tools, and techniques that are applicable across industries, technologies, organizations, cultures, and systems. These generally recognized standards are applicable to most projects most of the time and are based on a consensus about their value and utility.

It is important to note that a standard is not always and everywhere applicable. This is important to all project participants because the *PMBOK® Guide* states that "the organization and/or project management team is responsible for determining what is appropriate for any given project." A standard is not a law or an enforced or enforceable regulation.

2

WHAT IS A PROJECT?

Projects are collections of uniquely combined processes that spend capital resources in the present for possible benefit in the future. This kind of work is quite distinct from operational work, which is the day-to-day work to produce goods, services, improvements, and information.

Ongoing work, called operational work, usually involves an iterative process and is the basis of producing revenue for a given organization. Most enterprises exist primarily to continuously, or in batches, produce those things that intermediate and final consumers want or need.

All organizations have components of project and components of operational work. Web-hosting systems, hospitals, and food-processing firms are primarily operational. There are some enterprises that exist not to produce many copies of a product or continuous services but to construct or otherwise produce a singular end result; such enterprises are centered around that one project. Some of these are construction firms, custom software developers, or product design specialists.

Figure 2-1 below graphically depicts the difference between project work and ongoing operations.

PROJECTS

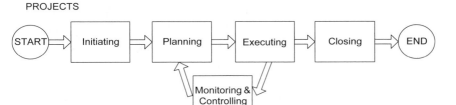

On-Going OPERATIONS

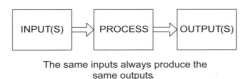

The same inputs always produce the
same outputs.

Figure 2-1
Project Work and
Ongoing Operations

2

WHAT IS PROJECT MANAGEMENT?

Project management is the application of knowledge, skills, tools, and techniques for unique activities to meet the requirements in a project, system, or service not previously fulfilled. Projects are conducted using five process groups: initiating, planning, executing, monitoring and controlling, and closing.

In this study guide we discuss how project management affects or is affected by three distinct groups of team members: the **project manager**, the **project management team**, and the **project team members**. The knowledge, skills, tools, and techniques required of one of these groups may be different from, but no more or less important than, what is required in other groups.

Project managers through project management team members and project team members produce an expected outcome by balancing the requirements of the scope, schedule, quality, budget, and other project constraints.

Another distinctive characteristic of project management is **progressive elaboration**, which is the idea of starting with an end result in mind, without knowing all the intermediate steps required to achieve it, and working to build that end result. Unlike operational work, the technical processes and interactions of a project are incompletely specified. It is for this reason that planning, executing, monitoring, and controlling are typically performed repetitively through a sequence of phases.

The act of elaborating progressively means that the project team can begin on a project without knowing everything that will need to be accomplished in order to achieve the final result. Work that is well defined needs to be delivered early in the project so that it can proceed, while work that is required at a later date is decomposed after the project has started.

This approach also means that members of the project management team and the project team performing the work may be assigned different kinds of activities in

> **TIP**
> Figure 1-1 on page 5 of the *PMBOK® Guide* demonstrates the interactions possible between programs and projects.

2

each phase. It is also likely that project participants will come and go as needed, as the project gains the benefit of appropriate expertise and loses the experience of those associated with the project from the beginning.

RELATIONSHIP BETWEEN PROJECT MANAGEMENT, PROGRAM MANAGEMENT, AND PORTFOLIO MANAGEMENT

Project management, as formalized in the *PMBOK® Guide*, represents the foundation of professionalism in providing the world's unique products, services, information, and systems. In addition to project management, there are two other aspects of the *PMBOK® Guide* that need to be considered: programs and portfolios.

Program Management

Program management is the act of managing a group of related projects in a coordinated way to obtain benefits and control not available by managing projects individually. There are basically three types of relationships among projects in a program.

One kind of program can be a set of projects and subprojects that are related to producing a single outcome for operations. Such a program might involve an internal project to achieve the benefits of the results delivered by three external projects and associated subprojects. Consider a utility company who will be building a new power plant. The utility company may be responsible for the construction of the power plant itselve, however, the clearing of the land for the new construction and the laying of the power lines from the power plant will be performed by highly qualified subcontractors.

A second kind of program might be a phased or chronological set of projects like the implementation of two nuclear power plants over a period of fifteen years.

2

A third kind of program might be associated with a project management office in which a number of projects might be clustered because they are all based on a common technology such as solar power generation, clients in the same industry, or enhancements for the same product.

Portfolio Management

TIP
Review and understand Table 1-1 on page 8 of the *PMBOK® Guide*. It shows the differences between projects, programs, and portfolios as each relates to scope, change, planning, management, success, and monitoring.

The concept of portfolio management for projects was built on what was originated by financial investment managers. The idea built on the diversity of objectives that individuals and firms had for the outcome of their investment of capital. From an individual's point of view, younger people could afford to take greater risks with their retirement funds and seek greater returns on their investments. On the other hand, retired individuals might be more concerned with conservation of their capital, assuring a more modest return for their lifetimes.

Strategic business planners adopted this concept of capital investment philosophies for start-up firms, growing firms, and mature firms.

Portfolio management in recent years has shifted from being exclusively the domain of a chief financial officer to being shared with all levels of the organization. This is because a firm that wishes to maximize the return on invested capital may have to choose investments by balancing return maximization with potential risk. This could take the form of the development of a new product line, spending on marketing and promotion, buying a complementary business line, or purchasing a desirable financial instrument.

Class Exercise 2-1

Review the scenarios in the table below. Determine if the situation would be considered a project, program, or portfolio.

Scenario	Project, Program, or Portfolio?
XYZ canning company supports all of the canning for ABC Growers. For each vegetable product line, XYZ canning company provides 10 different packaging options. When one packaging option changes, the project manager will typically be responsible for upgrading all vegetable product lines.	
An organization has authorized funding to create a new manufacturing process that can be leveraged in 3 of the 6 product lines it offers.	
Smith Company is a retail enterprise with a wide variety of products that it offers its clients. Typically the company likes to maintain an inventory of products that provide the retail enterprise a minimum of a 10% profit margin. Any project selected must be evaluated to ensure that this profit margin is not impacted.	

PROJECTS AND STRATEGIC PLANNING

Projects are initiated in organizations for a variety of reasons. In most cases, projects are intended to improve or enhance the organization's ability to reach its strategic goals. Strategic planning places and prioritizes projects in one or more portfolios in order to:
- Meet market demands
- Maintain and upgrade plans and processes
- Educate or train to avoid problems and increase productivity
- Meet customer requests
- Take advantage of technological advances consistent with an organization's stance towards innovation adoption
- Meet legal requirements
- Meet a social need
- Take into account environmental considerations

2

Projects are critical to an organization's ability to meet its strategic objectives. Organizations that realize this need strongly emphasize the importance of good project management practices.

PROJECT MANAGEMENT OFFICE

TIP
It is important for CAPM exam candidates to understand the differences between project management and PMO management.

Project management office (PMO) is a fairly vague term. PMOs can take on many different structures and purposes for an organization, such as:

- Managing shared resources across projects
- Identifying and communicating project methodologies, best practices, and standards
- Developing and managing project policies, procedures, templates, common tools, and documentation
- Coordinating communication across projects and among individuals with shared or complementary responsibilities
- Coaching
- Monitoring compliance

The PMO is an additional layer of organization dedicated to helping project managers. Although most often found in matrixed or projectized organizations, it may exist in any type of organizational structure.

There are definite impacts to organizations that wish to create and maintain a PMO. Figure 2-2 below outlines the pros and cons of a PMO.

Figure 2-2
PMO Pros and Cons

PROS	CONS
• Emphasis on project management career paths • Less anxiety among project managers about the next assignment at project completion • Centering of project management competencies • Standardization of the project management system • Centralized management	• Additional layer of hierarchy • Some of the adverse aspects of a matrix organization • All of the adverse aspects of a projectized organization • Lack of application knowledge by the project managers

2

Recognize that the project manager's role in a project is different from that of an individual who manages a PMO. Figure 2-3 below outlines these differences.

Figure 2-3
Roles of the Project Manager
and PMO Manager

Project Manager	PMO Manager
• Project managers focus on the immediate needs of the project • Project managers control the project management team and project team participants to meet project objectives • Project managers at the work package level control scope, schedule, cost, and quality trade-offs	• PMO managers review program scope changes for opportunities and risks • PMO managers attempt to maximize, optimize, or satisfy shared resources • PMO managers manage overall risk, opportunities, and interdependencies of all projects at their level of the enterprise

The *PMBOK® Guide* outlines three types of PMOs that may be seen in organizations today.
- Supportive or consultative PMOs focus on best practices
- Controlling PMOs focus on compliance
- Directive PMOs directly manage projects

PROJECT MANAGEMENT IN OPERATIONS MANAGEMENT

It is important to know that project and operations management are different. As previously mentioned, operations are ongoing and continue to exist until their results are no longer necessary. For the most part, project management exists to make sure the revenue- and service-producing operations are effective, efficient, and value producing. For example, projects may be initiated to improve an operational process or the quality of an existing product. In these instances, the projects are initiated and concluded by integrating the new processes into the existing operational environment.

> **TIP**
>
> In practice, project management organizations may be placed at various levels of the larger organizational hierarchy, and may even be hybrids of the types discussed in this study guide.

2

Projects intersect with operations during the course of a project in many ways, including:

- At each initiation or closeout phase
- When developing a new product or making expansions, changes, or improvements to an existing product
- While improving operations or product development processes
- At divestment of the operations at the end of a product life cycle

At each juncture, deliverables and knowledge are transferred from the project to operations to begin to harvest the benefits of any improvement, expansion, or reorganization.

Within a given operational organization, projects done for the benefit of only that unit are typically managed by functional managers as secondary, informal activities.

Operations managers may also be stakeholders in projects, especially when projects cross organizational boundaries but directly impact the operational manager's span of control. Their roles, in addition to being functional project managers (perhaps of a subproject to implement an expected outcome), might be as sponsors, champions, or owners of the project itself.

Business Value

Business value is the entire value of the business. It includes all the tangible and intangible elements like brand, public benefit, and stockholder equity, to name a few.

Effective portfolio, program and project management, organization is what organizations need to have in place to meet strategic objectives and create business value.

2

PROJECT MANAGEMENT ROLES AND SKILLS

Projects are not delivered by project managers alone. It takes the coordination and cooperation of various individuals and organizations to successfully deliver projects. Those working on a project fall into two broad categories:
- The project manager
- The project participant

Role of the Project Manager

Operational management and project management are different because their core processes are different. Operational management is about continuous or cyclically recurrent work that produces a stream of revenue or other benefits to an enterprise. Project management harnesses the temporary involvement of diverse individuals who produce a desired outcome in which one step or phase drives the next one until the outcome is achieved.

A project manager initiates, plans, executes, monitors and controls, and closes out sequentially dependent phases of work until the benefits of a project can be harvested by the sponsoring operational enterprise. A project manager may report to a functional manager and/or program manager with respect to the work of the individuals and the value of the intermediate and final work products they create. Project managers plan and deliver, during the course of the project, the metrics for individual components and work products, as well as costs, schedules, scope, and quality. A project manager may also report these and similar metrics to a program manager and/or portfolio manager.

2

Project Management Skills

Individual project managers and members of a project management team require a variety of competencies to fulfill their assignments.

- **Project management knowledge competency** is what project managers know
- **Project management performance competency** is what project managers can do
- **Personal competency** is how project managers behave based on their attitudes and personal characteristics

Throughout this study guide we discuss the various kinds of knowledge, skills, and competencies that are necessary to succeed as a project manager and as a project team member.

TIP

It is important for CAPM and PMP exam candidates to understand the various types of processes, inputs, tools and techniques, and outputs outlined in the *PMBOK® Guide* and be able to recognize them as such on the exam.

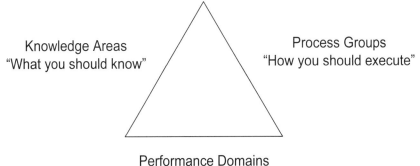

Figure 2-4
Knowledge, Skills,
and Competencies

Knowledge Areas
"What you should know"

Process Groups
"How you should execute"

Performance Domains
"What you should do"

Role of the Project Participant

Project participants often work as subject matter experts (SMEs) in the realm of their expertise. As SMEs, they give cultural, social, international, political, and physical contexts to the project environment. Even the most seasoned project manager is dependent on contributing participants, especially those on the project management team who bridge the potential gap between SMEs and the project manager.

ORGANIZATION CULTURES AND STYLES

Projects can be conducted in a wide variety of organizations. Which organizational context and specific organizational structure is adopted varies with the needs of the project. How a project is organized must reflect the **enterprise environmental factors** and the mixture of linguistic, ethnic, enterprise, and professional cultures, as well as the history of projects conducted in that setting.

Those sponsoring and conducting a project need to recognize and build on the resources available in the specific project environment, including the:
- Degree to which visions, values, norms, beliefs, and expectations are shared
- Availability, understanding, and experience of participants of policies, methods, standards, processes and procedures
- Authority and responsibility consistent with the aggregate work culture
- Work ethic, work hours, location, and relationships
- Risk tolerances
- Ways in which team members are motivated and rewarded
- Overall operational environment

ORGANIZATIONAL COMMUNICATION

Organizations today, more often than not, are affected by the globalization of our workforce. Most project teams work in some form of virtual team. Organizational communications have a great impact on how well projects are performed. The project team needs to determine the best method for communicating on each project.

2

ORGANIZATIONAL STRUCTURES

PMI stresses the importance of organizational structures because the organizational structure will often constrain the availability of resources for a project.

Functional Organizations

Figure 2-5
Pros and Cons of a Functional
Organization

In a functional organization, each employee is in a hierarchical structure with one superior. Staff is often grouped by specialty, such as accounting, marketing, or engineering. The pros and cons of a functional organization are shown in Figure 2-5 below.

PROS	CONS
• Flexibility in staff use • Availability of experts for multiple projects • Grouping of specialists • Technological continuity • Normal advancement path	• Client is not the focus of activity • Function rather than problem oriented • No one fully responsible for a project • Slow response to the client • Tendency to suboptimize • Fragmented approach to a project

Included in a functional organization is the use of what is frequently called a **project expeditor** (PE) or a **project coordinator** (PC).

The PE is a facilitator who acts as the staff assistant to the executive who has ultimate responsibility for the project. This person has little formal authority. The PE's primary responsibility is to communicate information between the executive and the workers. This type of structure is useful in functional organizations in which project costs are relatively low.

TIP
Become familiar with Table 2-1, Organizational Structures on Projects, on page 22 in the *PMBOK® Guide*.

The PC reports to a higher level in the hierarchy and usually holds a staff position. A PC has more formal authority and responsibility than a PE. A PC can assign work to functional workers. This type of structure is useful in a functional organization in which project costs are relatively low compared to those in the rest of the organization.

Matrix Organizations

It is important to understand the differences between weak, balanced, and strong matrix organizations. The pros and cons of a matrix organization are listed in Figure 2-6 below.

Figure 2-6
Pros and Cons of a
Matrix Organization

PROS	CONS
• Project is the point of emphasis • Access to a reservoir of technical talent • Less anxiety about team future at project completion • Quick client response • Better firm-wide balance of resources • Minimizes overall staff fluctuations	• Two-boss syndrome • More time and effort needed to acquire team members • Functional managers may be reluctant to share top performers • Conflicts of authority between project manager and functional manager • Careful project monitoring required • Political infighting among project managers

Matrix organizations have:
- A high potential for conflict
- Team members who are borrowed from their functional groups and who are therefore caught between their functional manager and their project manager (but as projects draw to a close, these team members know they have a "home" with their functional groups)
- Team members who only see pieces of the project and may not see the project to completion
- An advantage in relatively complex projects in which cross-organizational knowledge and expertise are needed
- Project managers whose authority and time on a project increase from weak (lowest level of authority) to balanced matrix to strong matrix

2

Projectized Organizations

In a projectized organization, team members are often colocated and the project manager has a great deal of independence and authority. However, team members worry about their jobs as a project draws to a close. Figure 2-7 below shows the pros and cons of a projectized organization.

Figure 2-7
Pros and Cons of a
Projectized Organization

PROS	CONS
• One boss • Project manager has a great deal of independence and authority • Team members are often colocated • Team members are treated as insiders • Most resources are involved in project work	• If not tracked closely, hourly costs may become inflated while specialists are waiting between assignments or are on call • Bureaucracy, standards, procedures, and documentation may result in an abundance of red tape

COMMON THEMES ACROSS THE *PMBOK® GUIDE*

As you read through the *PMBOK® Guide*, you will find some commonality among all processes. Figure 2-8 on the following page highlights some of these commonalities within each of the process groups.

This figure is a subset of the full identification of inputs, tools and techniques, and outputs. Note that the inputs **enterprise environmental factors** and **organizational process assets** are identified in all of the process groups except closing. In addition, **expert judgment** is a tool and technique for *every* process group. It is actually a tool and technique in 17 processes.

	Initiating	Planning	Executing	Monitoring and Controlling	Closing
Inputs	• Enterprise Environmental Factors • Organizational Process Assets	• Enterprise Environmental Factors • Organizational Process Assets	• Enterprise Environmental Factors • Organizational Process Assets	• Enterprise Environmental Factors • Organizational Process Assets	• Organizational Process Assets
Tools and Techniques	• Expert Judgment • Facilitation Techniques	• Expert Judgment • Facilitation Techniques	• Expert Judgment • Meetings	• Expert Judgment • Meetings	• Expert Judgment • Meetings
Outputs	• Charter	• Project Management Plan	• Deliverables • Work Performance Data • Change Requests • Project Management Plan Updates	• Approved Change Requests • Change Log • Project Management Plan Updates • Work Performance Reports	• Final Product • Organizational Process Asset Updates

Figure 2-8
Commonalities among
Process Groups

KEY *PMBOK® GUIDE* CONCEPTS

Organizational Process Assets

One of the concepts that has captured the attention of business leaders and practitioners in the last decade has been the idea of knowledge management. This became apparent during the radical changes in computer systems running up to the Y2K response planning in the late 1990s. Knowledge management was originally pursued by service organizations such as accountancy and management consultant firms whose stock-in-trade was the conduct of short-lived engagements, other than projects. Technical, organizational, and relationship knowledge resided solely in individuals and in working groups. The departure of an individual or a group from an enterprise often meant that significant information and capital goods also left the organization as well.

Other organizations realized how much of their innovative processes and tools were carried in the brains of their managers and specialists. This recognition is reflected in the importance of formally-communicated and documented processes and procedures as well as other repositories of enterprise know-how in the corporate knowledge base.

Because projects are temporary, if care is not taken, any lessons learned may be forgotten. In addition, projects can take advantage of existing knowledge to increase the effectiveness of a project team. PMI categorizes this knowledge as "assets" to the organization. These organizational assets come in two categories:
- Processes and procedures
- Corporate knowledge base

Processes and Procedures

Processes and procedures were the first of these organizational process assets to be formalized and documented. This occurred because of quality improvement initiatives based on communicating among individual performers and teams, improved methods, and other formats of best practices.

Class Exercise 2-2

In the table on the following page, describe four to six organizational process assets of your organization that are typically leveraged. Identify the benefit of each asset.

2

Organizational Process Asset	Benefit of that Asset

Corporate Knowledge Base

The heart of knowledge management is the ability to avoid enterprise amnesia. It is not enough to document. It is vital to know what is available and how to access it. Indexing is a necessary but not sufficient characteristic of any knowledge base. Two characteristics make a corporate knowledge base sufficient to assure that the knowledge and understanding of prior performance remain in the organization and be applicable to future performance.

The first characteristic is to identify the gatekeepers of a knowledge base. A gatekeeper is an individual or team that has experience with a variety of the projects, problems, and processes that an enterprise has previously utilized. Utilization is a matter both of the successful application of knowledge and the unsuccessful or inappropriate application of knowledge.

The second characteristic is to have capabilities similar to popular web search engines in which unstructured pathways for access simplify the relationship of a current need or problem to prior attempts and successes.

Class Exercise 2-3

In the table below, identify two or three lessons you've learned in prior projects that you would like participants in other projects to understand and take advantage of.

Identify the consequences, if any, of the lessons not being addressed and identify any benefits that could be recognized if implemented on future projects.

Lesson Learned	Consequences	Benefits to Future Projects

Enterprise Environmental Factors

In order to make sense of the *PMBOK® Guide*, the context of managing projects needs to be understood. Many of the project management competencies depend on knowledge of the environmental factors of the enterprises involved in a project. The *PMBOK® Guide* addresses, to a greater or lesser degree, adaptations or extensions of general business knowledge.

The environment in which the project management team and the project team work is critical to the success of any project. Ignoring environmental factors can be hazardous. Enterprise environmental factors are the inclusive factors facing an organization. All participants in a project need a common understanding of environmental factors, which can include:
* Organizational culture and structure
* Government or industry standards
* Infrastructure, such as existing facilities and capital equipment
* Existing human resources
* Personnel administration
* Company work authorization systems
* Marketplace conditions
* Stakeholder risk tolerances
* Commercial database
* Project management information systems

2

Class Exercise 2-4

Consider your own organization. In the table below, list three enterprise environmental factors that affect the projects you work on. Identify how each impacts your projects.

Consequences	Benefits to Future Projects

These concepts of **organizational process assets**, **processes** and **procedures**, **corporate knowledge base**, and **enterprise environmental factors** will be addressed numerous times throughout all of the *PMBOK® Guide* knowledge areas. The CAPM candidate must understand these thoroughly and be able to identify them in a project setting.

2

PMBOK® GUIDE IMPACT ON ALL PROJECT PARTICIPANTS

The *PMBOK® Guide* appropriately offers the perspective of the project manager when discussing each process. In reality, a project manager may have a greater or lesser involvement in the initiating, planning, executing, monitoring and controlling, and closing processes. For the purposes of preparing for the CAPM exam, it is fruitful to look at processes not just from the project manager's point of view but also from the perspective of groups in which CAPM participants can be found. For each process group, it is worthwhile to understand the project from the standpoint of all stakeholders who contribute to the project, as well as from the standpoint of other project participants with roles such as project owners and sponsors, project management team members, and team members on the larger, more fluid project team.

Stakeholders

As previously mentioned, everyone who has some personal or financial interest or stake in the conduct and/or outcome of a project should be identified as a stakeholder. In essence, everyone who directly or indirectly encounters the project, its primary or secondary outcomes, or other unintended consequences has some "skin in the game."

Stakeholders may have a positive opinion or even a negative opinion of a project. Regardless, they are stakeholders.

Stakeholders who are informed of and trained in the processes and knowledge areas (and their respective roles in participating in a project-managed endeavor) improve the likelihood of a project delivering stakeholder benefits. It is for this reason that having a CAPM on a project increases the likelihood of successful projects and improves the livelihood of project stakeholders.

There are many different types of stakeholders. It is up to the project manager and the project management team to identify stakeholders and their relationship to the project. The *PMBOK® Guide* recognizes the importance of identifying stakeholders, which is why the latest edition has singled out the importance by creating an entirely separate knowledge area dedicated to stakeholders.

Beyond the actual project participants and the project sponsor, project stakeholders can come from other areas within the organization or external to the performing organization. Consider the following when identifying the stakeholders on your project:

- Sponsor
- Customers
- Users
- Sellers
- Business partners
- Organizational groups
- Functional managers
- Consultants
- Government entities
- Project team
- Other countries

Class Exercise 2-5

Using the list above as a guide, can you think of any other stakeholder groups within the projects you are working on that can be either positively or negatively impacted by your project? Indicate these stakeholders and their impact in the table on the following page.

Stakeholders	Stakeholders' Impact

Project Owners and Sponsors

The primary linkage between the owners and sponsors and the project is clearly the project manager. Owners and sponsors frequently have the largest and most obvious financial stake in a successful project outcome.

Project Management Team

A project management team is the leadership subset of a larger project team. The head of this team is the project manager. However, depending on the scope and duration of a project, a project manager may have individuals to whom he or she has delegated authority for significant processes. Members of a project management team may have leadership, managerial, or supervisory involvement and may be identified by titles such as project leader, technical leader, project administrator, team leader, or supervisor. Organizations with collective bargaining units may also have members of trade unions or professional guilds for whom a foreman might be identified.

2

Project Team

A project team is the superset of which the project management team is the primary source of management and supervision. A project team is usually characterized by a fluid membership, variability in size, and changes in its members' roles when assignments span project phases.

The project management team focuses on the supervision of individuals during execution and monitoring and control processes.

Project team members often have important formal and informal leadership roles, the most obvious being technical leadership, which is often based on technical knowledge and experience. Such leadership is not just in project team members' specialty, but in their capacity to work with complementary specialties that may provide input or support or may receive output from a given project activity. Equally important are participants in projects who have the ability to propose ideas to, persuade, and collaborate with peers, subordinates, and formal leaders.

The composition of project teams can and will vary greatly based on many factors. Certain factors such as reporting relationships, culture, location, and dedicated or part-time resources need to be evaluated and planned for accordingly.

GOVERNANCE ACROSS THE PROJECT LIFE CYCLE

TIP
The approach to project phases, when different from what is normally followed in an organization, should be documented in the project charter.

Project governance should be described in the **project charter** and subsequently refined in the **project management plan** as the public approach to the conduct of the project. The project must address the applicable scope, budget, schedule, and quality within the constraints and context of the sponsoring organization or within a program consisting of one or more projects.

Governance is an oversight function that is aligned with the organization's governance model. The program management office may play a part in project governance depending upon the type of PMO being used.

CHARACTERISTICS OF THE PROJECT LIFE CYCLE

Project life cycles define the phases that a project goes through from initiation to closure, the technical work to be done in each phase, the skills involved in each phase, the deliverables and acceptance criteria for each phase, and how each phase will be monitored, controlled, and approved before moving to the next phase. As indicated in Figure 2-9 below, the resources necessary to execute a project phase increase as the project progresses. They are at their highest during the implementation/execution phase and rapidly taper off during the termination/close phase.

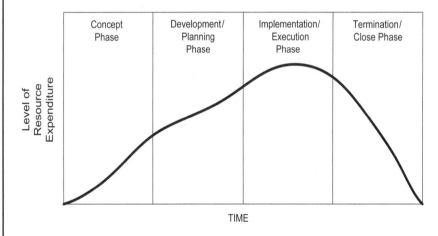

Figure 2-9
Resource Expenditure
Across Phases

A typical project life cycle contains the following four phases and likely deliverables:

The **concept phase** typically has the following deliverables:
- Feasibility studies that clarify the problems to be solved
- Order of magnitude forecasts of cost
- A project charter to grant permission for the project to proceed

2

The **development and planning phase** typically has the following deliverables:

- The scope statement
- A work breakdown structure (WBS)
- A schedule baseline
- A determination of budgetary costs and a developed budget
- Identification of resources and team members with levels of responsibility
- A risk assessment
- A communications management plan
- A project plan
- Control systems and methods for handling change control

The **implementation and execution phase** typically has the following deliverables:

- Execution results for work packages
- Status reports and performance reporting
- Procurement of goods and services
- Managing, controlling, and redirecting (if needed) of scope, quality, schedule and cost
- Resolution of problems
- Integration of the product into operations and the transfer of responsibility

The **termination and close phase** typically has the following deliverables:

- Formal acceptance
- Documented results and lessons learned
- Reassignment or release of resources

The phase structure provides a formal basis for control. The conclusion of each phase presents a scheduled opportunity to continue, redirect, or terminate a project. A management review will determine the continuance or termination of a project consistent with the informed consent of the sponsor.

Each phase end provides an opportunity to refine and revise the project management plan for the succeeding phase and the project as a whole. The initiation of the succeeding phase provides an opportunity to release staff

2

and other resources, repurpose staff or resources, and add staff and resources consistent with the different needs of the succeeding phase.

There are two basic types of phase-to-phase relationships: sequential and overlapping.

Distinct **sequential phases** are often called for because of the absence or uncertainty of the information needed to proceed with the dependent phase. This may occur due to a project's dependence on the discovery of some knowledge or the acceptance of a design. This may also occur due to financial gating by a funding authority, which releases subsequent funding only with the full acceptance of the outcome of the preceding phase.

Overlapping phases is another common practice when a project has low uncertainty and/or commitment of funding for the duration of the project. Overlapping phases may, however, increase risk because any assumptions of circumstances or performance may not be justified until the preceding phase is completed.

A project conceivably may have both kinds of **phase-to-phase relationships** during its planned conduct or may be forced to adopt a revised relationship because of unforeseen circumstances.

The *PMBOK® Guide* additionally looks at the different types of life cycles:
- Predictive life cycles
- Iterative or incremental life cycles
- Adaptive, agile, or change-driven life cycles

In project planning and replanning, the project manager and sponsor must be in agreement that the approach adopted or revised fulfills the needs of the sponsor and is consistent with the currently agreed-to budget, schedule, scope, and quality expectations.

> **TIP**
> Predictive life cycles are typically preferred when the product to be delivered is well understood.

> **TIP**
> Iterative or incremental life cycles are generally used when scope details become clear as each phase is completed. This works well in highly complex projects.

> **TIP**
> Adaptive, agile, or change-driven life cycles work well in a rapidly changing environment.

The life cycle of a project is only one aspect of the overall **product life cycle**. A project can be initiated to determine the feasibility of a product in the introductory stage of a product life cycle. There may be a second project to address the design and development of the product once the feasibility study has determined the viability of the product.

The number of projects initiated to support the product life cycle will vary from organization to organization and from product to product.

Project life cycle phases and **product life cycle phases** are often defined similarly. For example, a project life cycle may start with a feasibility phase to determine if the project can achieve its objectives, while the first phase in a product life cycle might consist of a market study to determine if the product will meet sales goals.

THE INFLUENCE CURVE

The ability to influence the outcome of a project with minimal impact to cost is high at the beginning of a project and decreases as the project progresses. The impact or cost of such project changes is low at the beginning of a project and increases as a project progresses, as seen in Figure 2-10 below.

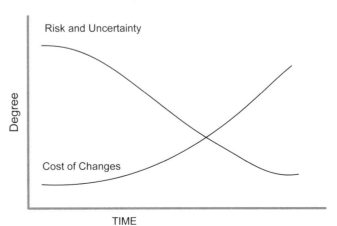

Figure 2-10
The Influence Curve

2

To put it in context, any change that is identified early in the project life cycle would be less costly to implement, if approved, than a change that is identified in later phases.

PRODUCT VERSUS PROJECT LIFE CYCLE RELATIONSHIPS

A project has a limited duration, has a specific beginning and end, and produces a unique outcome. Its life cycle begins with little staff, ramps up through planning and acquisition of staff and resources, then through successive phases, creates and delivers the defined outcome. A project is then closed and resources released to other purposes.

A product's life cycle may begin with a project, which produces an outcome that is the product, its support processes, and systems for operations. The product is typically the heart of the operational function of an enterprise. The life of a product is indeterminate. A product's life typically follows a cycle of slow initial adoption, and then, if successful, rapidly increases in market penetration and ultimately tapers off as the market for it is saturated. Ultimately, the product becomes obsolete and as it tapers off in revenue, is terminated with withdrawal from the market or cessation of production.

Organizations may initiate projects in order to extend the life of a product through product enhancements, quality improvements, or a variety of options that increase the marketability of the product.

Consider the examples of a smart phone and a CD player. Smart phones, in the current market, are reaching their maturity stage. Smart phone manufacturers are continuing to enhance products to extend their marketability by adding features and capacity. CD players, on the other hand, are most likely in the obsolescence stage. The popularity of MP3 players has overshadowed the CD player market, causing many CD player manufacturers to leave the market.

The discipline of product management often includes the sponsorship of additional projects to introduce new models of a product, penetrate new markets, improve internal operational processes, integrate outside suppliers, or outsource work to suppliers or partners.

PROJECT PHASES

Project phases work on the principle of **progressive elaboration**, in which one phase produces work products, refined plans, additional knowledge, and expertise for use by a succeeding project. In some cases, one phase must absolutely complete before the succeeding phase can begin. This sequential approach works in some circumstances, often because a dependent phase cannot begin with insufficient information, unavailable components, or external uncertainties.

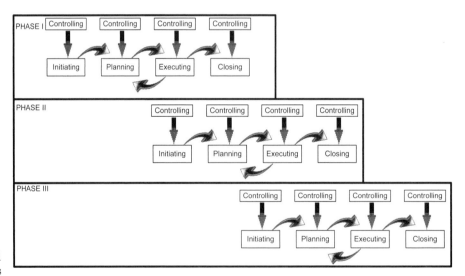

Figure 2-11
Overlapping Phases

In other cases, as depicted in Figure 2-11 above, phases may be overlapping with a greater or lesser degree of concurrency. For example, Phase II could start during the executing phase of Phase I, or after the end of the closing phase of Phase I. Overlaps will be driven by the needs of the project.

2

The design of the project process is one of the critical decisions that a project manager must obtain from the project sponsor. There are risks in any approach, which must be made clear to the project sponsor and participants.

THE CODE OF ETHICS AND PROFESSIONAL CONDUCT

The PMI *Code of Ethics and Professional Conduct* describes the expectations that we, as project managers, have of ourselves and of our fellow practitioners. It articulates the ideals to which we aspire as well as the behaviors that are mandatory in our professional and volunteer roles. The PMI *Code of Ethics and Professional Conduct* is broken into four sections: responsibility, respect, fairness and honesty. Below is a summary of each of the four sections.

Responsibility

As practitioners in the global project management community, we aspire to:
- Make decisions and take actions based on the best interests of society, public safety, and the environment
- Accept only those assignments that are consistent with our background, experience, skills, and qualifications
- Fulfill the commitments that we undertake
- Take ownership and make corrections promptly when we make errors or omissions
- When we discover errors or omissions caused by others, communicate them to the appropriate body as soon as they are discovered
- Protect proprietary or confidential information that has been entrusted to us
- Uphold this code and hold each other accountable to it

> **TIP**
> Read PMI's *Code of Ethics and Professional Conduct*. You can find a downloadable version of the code at www.pmi.org.

And we require the following of ourselves and our fellow practitioners:
- Uphold the policies, rules, regulations, and laws that govern our work and professional and volunteer activities
- Report unethical or illegal conduct to appropriate management
- Bring violations of this code to the attention of the appropriate body for resolution
- Only file ethics complaints when they are substantiated by facts
- Pursue disciplinary action against an individual who retaliates against a person raising ethical concerns

Respect

As practitioners in the global project management community, we aspire to:
- Inform ourselves about the norms and customs of others and avoid engaging in behaviors they might consider disrespectful
- Listen to others' points of view
- Directly approach those people with whom we have a conflict or disagreement
- Conduct ourselves in a professional manner

And we require the following of ourselves and our fellow practitioners:
- Negotiate in good faith
- Do not exercise the power of our expertise or position to influence the decisions or actions of others in order to personally benefit at their expense
- Do not act in an abusive manner toward others
- Respect the property rights of others

2

Fairness

As practitioners in the global project management community, we aspire to:
- Demonstrate transparency in our decision-making process
- Constantly reexamine our impartiality and objectivity, taking corrective action when appropriate
- Provide equal access to information to those who are authorized to have that information
- Make opportunities equally available to qualified candidates

And we require the following of ourselves and our fellow practitioners:
- Proactively and fully disclose any real or potential conflicts of interest to the appropriate stakeholders
- Refrain from engaging in the decision-making process or otherwise attempting to influence outcomes when a conflict of interest may be present
- Do not hire or fire, reward or punish, or award or deny contracts based on personal considerations
- Do not discriminate against others based on, but not limited to, gender, race or age
- Apply the rules of the organization without favoritism or prejudice

Honesty

As practitioners in the global project management community, we aspire to:
- Earnestly seek to understand the truth
- Be truthful in our communications and in our conduct
- Provide accurate information in a timely manner
- Make commitments and promises in good faith
- Strive to create an environment in which others feel safe to tell the truth

And we require the following of ourselves and our fellow practitioners:

- Do not engage in or condone behavior that is designed to deceive others
- Do not engage in dishonest behavior with the intention of personal gain or at the expense of another

Class Exercise 2-6

Describe a time when you encountered conduct or the consequences of conduct that appeared to be contrary to the best interests of society, public safety, or the environment. What action, if any, did you take? In retrospect, do you understand why you might have chosen a different course? Write down your thoughts below.

_____

_____

_____

_____

_____

_____

2

Class Exercise 2-7

Recall a situation in which you that you were in an informal setting with people from different linguistic, ethnic, or professional world views. Recount a story that you told or heard in such a setting in which a misunderstanding had a humorous result or illuminated how people can see the "same thing" differently.

_____

_____

_____

_____

_____

_____

Class Exercise 2-8

PMI defines "abusive manner" as "conduct that results in physical harm or creates intense feelings of fear, humiliation, manipulation or exploitation in another person." Recount a time in which you felt you were treated in an abusive manner or inadvertently caused someone in a project to feel that he or she was treated in an abusive manner.

_____

_____

_____

_____

_____

SAMPLE CAPM EXAM QUESTIONS ON PROJECT MANAGEMENT OVERVIEW

1. The *PMBOK® Guide* is a standard which:

   a) Indicates how project managers can maximize profits from new projects
   b) Shows how to combine several smaller projects into one large project
   c) Describes good practices for the project management profession
   d) Is seldom followed by project managers in real life applications

2. A project is an endeavor with a well-defined purpose that is:

   a) Ongoing and repetitive
   b) Unique and temporary
   c) A combination of interrelated activities
   d) Started and ended on certain days during each month

3. What needs is the project manager responsible for satisfying?

   a) Sponsor, client, and operational needs
   b) Project, operations, and customer needs
   c) Task, team, and individual needs
   d) Task, sponsor, and client needs

4. A management structure that standardizes project-related governance processes and facilitates sharing resources is:

   a) Program management
   b) Portfolio management
   c) Project management office
   d) Project management

Notes:

2

5. One difference between the role of a project manager and a PMO is that:

   a) Project managers focus on specific project objectives, while PMOs manage program changes
   b) Project managers optimize the use of shared resources, while PMOs manage assigned resources
   c) Project managers manage the overall risks and opportunities, while PMOs control a project's scope, cost, and time
   d) Project managers manage the methodology and metrics used, while PMOs manage individual reporting requirements

6. Projects and operational work are both:

   a) On-going
   b) Constrained by limited resources
   c) Temporary
   d) Unique

7. Projects can intersect with operations at various points during the product life cycle, including:

   a) During improvement of operations or at each closeout
   b) Before the project charter is approved by the PMO
   c) When the team is deciding what type of life cycle to use
   d) After the project has been finished and has been fully transitioned to operations

8. In a projectized organization, team members often:

   a) Have two bosses during the project
   b) Strengthen their technical skills
   c) Return to a home department at the end of the project
   d) Are totally focused on one project

Notes:

9. Conditions that influence project planning and execution but are not under the project team's control are:

   a) Scheduling software
   b) Issue and defect management databases
   c) Enterprise environmental factors
   d) Performance measurement criteria

10. The person or organization who approves the project's product, service, or result, and who may be internal or external to the project, is the:

   a) Sponsor
   b) Customer
   c) Regulator
   d) Functional manager

11. One value of breaking large or complex projects into phases is that it:

   a) Encourages cost containment throughout the life of the project
   b) Allows a review at the start of each phase to ensure the continued business value
   c) Gives the project team the power to reject changes and avoid scope creep
   d) Provides the ability to assign multiple project managers

12. When one phase starts prior to the completion of the previous phase, it is called a(n) _____ relationship.

   a) Overlapping
   b) Dependency
   c) Phase-to-phase
   d) Sequential

Notes:

2

13. An oversight function used throughout the project life cycle that provides the team with a structure, processes, and decision-making model is called:

a) Portfolio management
b) Organizational governance
c) Program management
d) Project governance

14. Major project problems, such as extended timelines, can be caused by:

a) Overlooking negative stakeholders
b) Allowing too many stakeholders on the project
c) Acknowledging negative stakeholders
d) Determining stakeholder requirements

15. In which type of organization is project team building generally most difficult?

a) Functional
b) Matrix
c) Projectized
d) Project expediter

Notes:

ANSWERS AND REFERENCES FOR SAMPLE CAPM EXAM QUESTIONS ON PROJECT MANAGEMENT OVERVIEW

Section numbers refer to the *PMBOK® Guide*.

1. **C** **Section 1.1 – Initiating**
   Although D) may be an accurate answer in your organization, the correct answer is C).

2. **B** **Section 1.2 – Initiating**
   A project has a definite beginning and a definite end to create a unique product, service, or result.

3. **C** **Section 1.7 – Initiating**
   The task refers to the project work.

4. **C** **Section 1.4.4 – Initiating**
   PMOs centralize and coordinate the management of projects under their domain.

5. **A** **Section 1.4.4 – Initiating**
   B), C) and D) have the roles of project managers and PMOs reversed.

6. **B** **Section 1.5.1 – Monitoring and Controlling**
   A) operational work is ongoing; C) projects are temporary; D) projects are unique.

7. **A** **Section 1.5.1 – Closing**
   Generally, projects and operations intersect when a portion of the project work needs to involve operations.

8. **D** **Section 2.1.3 – Initiating**
   Know the pros and cons of the various organizational structures. A) by definition, team members report to only one entity in a projectized organization; B) team members tend to lose some technical skills when they are not part of their technical specialty group; C) is an advantage of the matrix organization; with projectized organizations, team members will be let go if there is not another project to work on.

2

9. **C** **Section 2.1.5 – Initiating**
A), B), and D) are all organizational process assets.

10. **B** **Section 2.2.1 – Initiating**
The customer is the one who ultimately approves a project and therefore must be satisfied.

11. **B** **Section 2.4.1 – Monitoring and Controlling**
A) cost may actually increase by separating a project into more phases; C) phases do not help manage changes on a project; D) although a project may have multiple project managers, it is not a primary benefit of breaking up a project into phases.

12. **A** **Section 2.4.2 – Executing**
An overlapping relationship is one form of phase-to-phase relationship.

13. **D** **Section 2.2.2 – Initiating**
Project governance is a comprehensive, consistent method of controlling the project.

14. **A** **Section 2.2.1 – Monitoring and Controlling**
Although any of these could cause extended timelines, the biggest problem is overlooking stakeholders.

15. **B** **Section 2.1.3 – Executing**
Team building is easiest in A) and is next easiest in C); the organizational structure of the performing organization is a constraint in organizational planning and will affect team building.

2

ANSWERS TO CLASS EXERCISES

Class Exercise 2-1: Project, Program, and Portfolios

Scenario	Project, Program, or Portfolio
XYZ canning company supports all of the canning for ABC Growers. For each vegetable product line, XYZ canning company provides 10 different packaging options. When one packaging option changes, the project manager will typically be responsible for upgrading all vegetable product lines.	Program
The organization has authorized funding to create a new manufacturing process that can be leveraged in 3 of the 6 product lines it offers.	Project
Smith Company is a retail enterprise with a wide variety of products that it offers its clients. Typically the company likes to maintain an inventory of products that provide the retail enterprise a minimum of a 10% profit margin. Any project selected must be evaluated to ensure that this profit margin is not impacted.	Portfolio

Class Exercises 2-2, 2-3, and 2-4: *PMBOK® Guide* Concepts

****For Class Discussion Only****

Class Exercise 2-5: Project Stakeholders

****For Class Discussion Only****

Class Exercises 2-6, 2-7, and 2-8: Professional Responsibility

****For Class Discussion Only****

WAV — Web Added Value™

This book has free material available for download from the Web Added Value™ resource center at *www.jrosspub.com*.

PROCESSES

3

3

PROJECT MANAGEMENT PROCESSES, PROCESS GROUPS, AND THE INTERACTION OF PROCESSES

PMI has created a standard which documents the processes needed to manage a project. The processes are based on best practices for most projects most of the time. However, PMI recognizes that not all of the processes need be, or even should be, applied to all projects all of the time. Project managers and their teams need to consider each process and determine if it is appropriate to their specific situation. PMI calls this process **tailoring**. PMI feels that the processes and interactions among processes described in the *PMBOK® Guide* should serve as a baseline for a project management methodology. Like any baseline, there will be variances, and those variances must be documented.

Knowledge Area Processes

Knowing the 47 project management processes and the process groups in which they belong is important for any CAPM candidate. The chart below defines the five process groups and the various knowledge areas that have processes from that group included.

Initiating	Planning	Executing	Monitoring and Controlling	Closing
Integration	Integration	Integration	Integration	Integration
Stakeholder Management	Scope	Quality	Scope	Procurement
	Time	Human Resources	Time	
	Cost	Communications	Cost	
	Quality	Procurement	Quality	
	Human Resources	Stakeholder Management	Communications	
	Communications		Risk	
	Risk		Procurement	
	Procurement		Stakeholder Management	
	Stakeholder Management			

3

Key Definitions

Input: a tangible item internal or external to the project that is required by a process for the process to produce its output.

Output: a deliverable, result or service generated by the application of various tools or techniques within a process.

Tailor: the act of carefully selecting processes and related inputs and outputs contained within the *PMBOK® Guide* to determine a subset of specific processes that will be included within a project's overall management approach.

Technique: a defined systematic series of steps applied by one or more individuals using one or more tools to achieve a product or result or to deliver a service.

Tool: a tangible item such as a checklist or template used in performing an activity to produce a product or result.

PROJECT MANAGEMENT PROCESSES AND PROCESS GROUPS

The *PMBOK® Guide* defines five process groups required for any project. They are:
- **Initiating**: defining and authorizing the project (or phase of the project)
- **Planning**: defining objectives, refining them, and planning the actions required to attain them
- **Executing**: integrating all resources to carry out the project plan
- **Monitoring and Controlling**: measuring progress to identify variances and taking corrective action when necessary
- **Closing**: bringing the project or phase to an orderly end, including gaining formal acceptance of the result

The process groups are *not* project phases. In fact, it is not unusual to see all of the process groups represented within a single phase of a larger project, as depicted in Figure 3-1 below.

Figure 3-1 Interaction of Process Groups (*PMBOK® Guide* Figure 3-2)

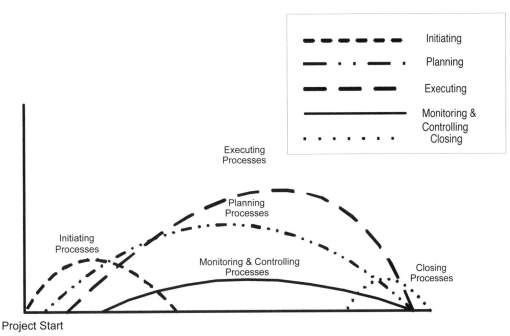

3

> **TIP**
>
> In preparing for the CAPM exam, take the time to read carefully Annex A1 of the *PMBOK® Guide*. PMI has put a lot of thought into the descriptions of the process groups, the interactions of the processes within them, and the relationships of each process group to the other process groups.

Each process group contains a number of processes, as listed below, but PMI has also identified ten topic-related knowledge areas. The processes associated with a particular knowledge area all address a single topic. For example, the processes within the time knowledge area address defining and planning the project schedule. The *PMBOK® Guide* is organized around these knowledge areas.

Chapters 4 through 13 of the *PMBOK® Guide* define each of the knowledge areas and their related processes in detail, covering integration, scope, time, cost, quality, human resources, communications, risk, procurement and stakeholder management. This study guide is organized the same way to facilitate the CAPM candidate's study.

Initiating Process Group

Keep in mind that the initiating process group, like all process groups, is scalable from initiating a project to initiating a project phase, to initiating a subproject, and to initiating a major project activity. In most cases the initiating processes are not fully staffed because they tend to occur in anticipation of starting a level of effort and represent the first work to be conducted in that unit of work.

The initiating processes may be repeated as participants and stakeholders are identified and added as the project moves from phase to phase.

There are only two processes defined within the initiating process group:

1. Develop Project Charter
2. Identify Stakeholders

3

Planning Process Group

The nature of discovery and the uniqueness of necessary project activities demand that project management team members take advantage of the specialized knowledge and skills of other project team members. It is often recognized, in retrospect, that many plans are made by those who will not actually perform the work. This is realistic in that high-level planning must be undertaken even prior to the initiation of a project as well as during the initial project formation, which results in the **project charter**.

The planning process group is the largest, with 24 processes, emphasizing PMI's commitment to and the importance of planning as a key indicator of success.

1. Develop Project Management Plan
2. Plan Scope Management
3. Collect Requirements
4. Define Scope
5. Create WBS
6. Plan Schedule Management
7. Define Activities
8. Sequence Activities
9. Estimate Activity Resources
10. Estimate Activity Durations
11. Develop Schedule
12. Plan Cost Management
13. Estimate Costs
14. Determine Budget
15. Plan Quality Management
16. Plan Human Resource Management
17. Plan Communications Management
18. Plan Risk Management
19. Identify Risks
20. Perform Qualitative Risk Analysis
21. Perform Quantitative Risk Analysis
22. Plan Risk Responses
23. Plan Procurement Management
24. Plan Stakeholder Management

3

The key concept in the planning process group is that initial plans have value even though more detailed plans will be developed later by individuals who will lead activity groups.

Executing Process Group

From the standpoint of this process group, formal preparation for working as a project team member makes the work of the project management team more effective.

This process group implicitly recognizes the continual nature of project team formation. The management theorist Dr. Bruce Tuckman is famous for his work with the stages of team formation, which will be discussed in the human resources knowledge area. His original work shows that a team, when formed, goes through four stages: **forming**, **storming**, **norming**, and **performing**. Later he added a last stage in recognition that some teams are in fact temporary, a stage called **adjourning**.

The executing process group is where the majority of work and team interaction take place. There are eight processes defined in the executing process group.

1. Direct and Manage Project Work
2. Perform Quality Assurance
3. Acquire Project Team
4. Develop Project Team
5. Manage Project Team
6. Manage Communications
7. Conduct Procurements
8. Manage Stakeholder Engagement

Monitoring and Controlling Process Group

It is in this process group that project team members who are well-informed and enabled by the project management team provide the greatest contribution to a project.

In many cases this work resembles operations work and it is project team members, the participants in the tasks within project activities, who must perform this critical work. Monitoring and controlling begins with the performing individuals ratifying their understanding of their assignments. It continues as the team members responsible for various activities validate the initiation of each discrete work assignment.

It is also in this group of processes that being a CAPM becomes critical. A CAPM, like all other PMI certification holders, PMI members, and PMI volunteers, is bound by the PMI *Code of Ethics and Professional Conduct*. Day-to-day work in the fine details of a project often presents project participants with the kind of ethical and professional challenges that at first seem merely technical or "business as usual." It is in individual work and working relationships that symptoms of dilemmas or actual violations not only of ethics but also of regulations and laws are encountered.

The *PMBOK® Guide* has defined eleven processes within the monitoring and controlling process group:

1. Monitor and Control Project Work
2. Perform Integrated Change Control
3. Validate Scope
4. Control Scope
5. Control Schedule
6. Control Costs
7. Control Quality
8. Control Communications
9. Control Risks
10. Control Procurements
11. Control Stakeholder Engagement

Closing Process Group

One of the values of the fact that processes can be scaled from major deliverable to phase or project is the opportunity to review the conduct of the work as completed. This review is most effective when it involves as many participants in the project as possible, including sponsors, champions, project management team members, the project team participants, and other stakeholders. The closing processes can be used to assure that the lessons learned are actually applied. Project managers do not want to wait to apply lessons learned in the next major work product. Many important lessons can apply to the next major activity or the next phase of a project. Project team members might not remain with a project until project closing; however, many may transition into or out of activities or phases.

Two processes are defined for the closing process group.

1. Close Project or Phase
2. Close Procurements

Work Performance Data, Work Performance Information,andWork Performance Reports

In the *PMBOK® Guide*, a very specific distinction is made between work performance data, information, and reports.

- **Data** are raw observations and measurements that are identified as activities are performed
- **Information** is data that has been analyzed in context
- **Reports** are the physical or electronic representation of work performance information compiled in project documents

An easy way to remember these differences is that work performance data are typically outputs of a process. Information is typically an input, while reports can be either an input or an output.

Class Exercise 3-1

In the **WAV™ files** there are charts of the 47 processes with the inputs, tools, techniques, and outputs for each process. Print out each chart, and then cut out and rearrange the processes for each one of the process groups.

The charts of each process will also make a very portable quick reference that can be used as a study aid.

TIP
Review Figure 3.3 in the *PMBOK® Guide*. It demonstrates graphically the interactions between the processes.

3

3

SAMPLE CAPM EXAM QUESTIONS ON MANAGEMENT PROCESSES

1. The Closing Process Group consists of which two processes?

   a) Close Project or Phase and Close Procurements
   b) Close Project and Conduct Lessons Learned
   c) Close Project or Phase and Accept Deliverables
   d) Close Project or Phase and Close Contracts

2. In which process group does a project manager assess the performance of the team?

   a) Executing
   b) Initiating
   c) Monitoring and controlling
   d) Planning

3. Good sources of information or techniques to determine detailed project requirements include:

   a) Project charter, budget plan, and the quality management plan
   b) Project charter, lessons learned, and team brainstorming techniques
   c) Feasibility studies, work breakdown structure, and the Gantt chart
   d) Project charter, focus groups, and the statement of work

4. Which process group consists of the processes used to complete the work defined in the project management plan?

   a) Closing
   b) Executing
   c) Initiating
   d) Planning

Notes:

5. The raw observations and measurements identified during project activities are called work performance:

   a) Completed
   b) Data
   c) Reports
   d) Information

6. The four sections of PMI's *Code of Ethics and Professional Conduct* are:

   a) Ethics, responsibility, respect, and truth
   b) Responsibility, respect, fairness, and honesty
   c) Honesty, truth, fairness, and professional responsibility
   d) Responsibility, respect, fairness, and ethics

7. An application area is defined as:

   a) The alignment of project objectives with the strategy of the larger organization by the project sponsor and project team
   b) A category of projects that have common components significant in such projects, but are not needed or present in all projects
   c) Projects, programs, subportfolios, and operations managed as a group to achieve strategic objectives
   d) A group of related projects, subprograms, and program activities managed in a coordinated way to obtain benefits not available from managing them individually

8. Performance domains include:

   a) Plan-do-check-act cycles, control charts, and histograms
   b) Communications, schedule development, risk management, and performance improvements
   c) Initiating, planning, scheduling, tracking, implementing, closing, and professional responsibility
   d) Initiating, planning, executing, controlling, and closing

Notes:

9. Which is the process primarily concerned with authorizing a project or project phase?

   a) Collect Requirements
   b) Develop Project Charter
   c) Project Planning Process
   d) Develop Project Scope

10. A limiting factor that affects the execution of a project, program, portfolio, or process is a/an:

    a) Constraint
    b) Estimate
    c) Assumption
    d) Exclusion

11. _____ processes coordinate people and other resources to carry out a project plan.

    a) Initiating
    b) Planning
    c) Controlling
    d) Executing

12. The two processes within the initiating process group are:

    a) Develop Project Management Plan and Develop Scope Statement
    b) Develop Project Management Plan and Develop Preliminary Project Scope Plan
    c) Develop Project Charter and Identify Stakeholders
    d) Develop Project Charter and Develop Scope Statement

13. Which of the following is the process group that includes those processes required to track and review project performance?

    a) Planning
    b) Closing
    c) Executing
    d) Monitoring and controlling

Notes:

14. One of the tasks that may be necessary for a project manager to perform during project closing is:

   a) Developing a human resource plan to release project team members
   b) Defining detailed project requirements to meet project scope and deliverables
   c) Implementing a transition plan to transfer the project to operations
   d) Administering contracts for procured materials, supplies, and outsourced labor

15. The team members on a tornado disaster recovery team will monitor their project by:

   a) Updating the risk register and response plans based on new information
   b) Documenting final acceptance of the cleanup phase of the project
   c) Ensuring that volunteers implement quality standards for dealing with hazardous waste
   d) Developing a plan to transfer the project operations to local agencies

Notes:

3

ANSWERS AND REFERENCES FOR SAMPLE CAPM EXAM QUESTIONS ON MANAGEMENT PROCESSES

Section numbers refer to the *PMBOK® Guide*.

1. **A   Section 3.7 – Closing**
   There are only 2!

2. **A   Section 9.4 – Executing**
   Team performance assessment is an output of the Develop Project Team process.

3. **B   Domain II – Task 1 – Planning**
   The budget plan, quality management plan, WBS, Gantt chart, and statement of work would be completed after detailed project requirements are defined.

4. **B   Section 3.5 – Executing**
   A) includes finishing and wrapping up the project; C) includes defining and authorizing the project; D) includes all the planning activities that take place.

5. **B   Section 3.8 – Executing**
   Know the difference between data and information; data are typically inputs to many processes and information is the output.

6. **B   Section 1.3 – Initiating**
   See PMI's *Code of Ethics and Professional Conduct*.

7. **B   Section 3.2 – Initiating**
   A) is the definition of project governance; C) is the definition of a portfolio; D) is the definition of a program.

8. **A   Overview – Initiating**
   The performance domains give an overview of what skills project managers must have to be successful in managing projects.

9. **B   Section 3.3 – Initiating**
   A), C), and D) are planning processes.

10. C Sections 4.0 and 5.3.3.1 – Initiating
A) is a limitation and may be real or perceived;
B) is an uncertain but hopefully educated guesses;
C) is a factor that is considered to be true; D) may or
may not be a constraint, but it is more likely to be
an assumption and should be specified.

11. D Section 3.5 – Initiating
This is a description of the executing process group.

12. C Section 3.3 – Initiating
The Develop Project Charter process is in the
Integration knowledge area, and the Identify
Stakeholders process is in the Stakeholder
Management knowledge area.

13. D Section 3.6 – Monitoring and Controlling
These processes are used to identify and initiate
required changes to the project management plan.

14. C Domain V – Task 5 – Closing
A) and B) take place in the Planning Performance
Domain 2; D) is part of the Executing Performance
Domain 3.

**15. A Domain IV – Task 4 – Monitoring and
Controlling**
B) belongs to the Closing Performance Domain 5;
C) belongs to the Executing Performance Domain 3;
D) belongs to the Planning Performance Domain 2.

Web
Added
Value™

This book has free material available for download from the
Web Added Value™ resource center at *www.jrosspub.com.*

CHAPTER 4 | **INTEGRATION**

4

I

4

INTEGRATION MANAGEMENT

The CAPM exam addresses critical project management functions that ensure the coordination of project practitioners who produce various elements of the project. The *PMBOK® Guide* explains that the processes in project management are integrative in nature. They involve making trade-offs among competing objectives to meet stakeholders' needs and expectations. Integration processes drive the associated knowledge area processes within each of the process groups; all process groups are addressed by one or more integration management processes. These processes interact with each other as well as with processes in the other nine knowledge areas.

It is important to note that integration occurs within as well as outside the project. For example, project scope and product scope must be integrated, and project work must be integrated with the ongoing work of the organization (such as operations and deliverables from various technical specialties). One of the key tools or techniques used to integrate the processes and measure project performance is **earned value management**. Earned value reporting is introduced in this chapter and is utilized for performance measurement in time management (Chapter 6), cost management (Chapter 7), and communications management (Chapter 10).

Project management team members work with a variety of project stakeholders to act, unify, consolidate, articulate, and integrate contributions to complete the project in order to fulfill stakeholder requirements and expectations. Project team members contribute to choices about **resource allocation**, **trade-offs**, and **interactions** within and among project and product demands.

Integration produces interactions that are not always foreseen. It is the interaction among human beings involved in building the project outcome that creates a higher level of complexity.

> **TIP**
> Earned value techniques are interwoven throughout the *PMBOK® Guide*. This vital management tool is supported by PMI's College of Performance Management. You can find this material summarized in the Exam Overview and Assessment Section immediately preceding the first chapter of the *PMBOK® Guide*.

4

The continuing integration of people and activities results from a fundamental characteristic of all projects: **progressive elaboration**. The needs of a project are understood with increasing clarity as the project progresses; therefore, each stakeholder's understanding of the project differs throughout the project's life cycle.

Progressive elaboration accompanies project integration management beginning with the project's initiation and continuing throughout the **project life cycle**.

Project participants face many challenges that differ from those faced by workers and managers in operational settings. Members of project teams (and especially project management teams) participate in coordinating the integration of:
- Project work with ongoing operations
- Product and project scope
- Schedule, budget, metrics, and reporting
- Skills, knowledge, and deliverables from vendors, stakeholders, and performing organizations
- Risks and risk response plans
- Performance and quality objectives

All six of the project integration management processes contain the tools and techniques of **expert judgment**.

Knowledge Area Processes

Within the integration management knowledge area there are six processes within five process groups.

Initiating	Planning	Executing	Monitoring and Controlling	Closing
Develop Project Charter	Develop Project Management Plan	Direct and Manage Project Work	Monitor and Control Project Work Perform Integrated Change Control	Close Project or Phase

4

Key Definitions

The definitions given here and in subsequent chapters of this study guide are terms used throughout the *PMBOK® Guide*.

Application area: a category of projects that share components that may not be present in other categories of projects. For example, approaches to information technology projects are different from those for residential development projects, so each is a different application area.

Change control: the procedures used to identify, document, approve (or reject), and control changes to the project baselines.

Change management: the process for managing change in a project. A change management plan should be incorporated into the project management plan.

Expert judgment: judgment based on expertise appropriate to the activity. It may be provided by any group or person, either within the organization or external to it.

Objective: something toward which work is to be directed, a strategic position to be attained, a purpose to be achieved, a result to be obtained, a product to be produced, or a service to be performed.

Project management information system (PMIS): the collection of tools, methodologies, techniques, standards, and resources used to manage a project. These may be formal systems and strategies determined by the organization or informal methods utilized by project managers.

Project management methodology: any structured approach used to guide the project team through the project life cycle. This methodology may utilize forms, templates, and procedures standard to the organization.

DEVELOP PROJECT CHARTER PROCESS

The Develop Project Charter process is used to formally authorize a new project or validate an existing project for continuation into the next phase. Knowing the contents of a charter is vital for members of the project team as well as for those with project management team responsibilities. Everyone should know the circumstances resulting in the project sponsor's authorization of the project, especially how and why the project has been initiated or has been continued or redirected. Knowing the priority of the project relative to other projects and the sources of funding helps all participants know how to allocate their effort and attention to the project with respect to concurrent assignments.

Sources of Project Work

Projects are initiated as a result of a problem to be solved, an opportunity to be exploited, a business requirement to be met, or a law or regulation with which to comply. Many organizations have more projects than resources, so commitment regarding which projects to undertake is based on urgency and importance.

The initiation of a project can begin with the convergence of project(s) carried in the project portfolio, new product or service proposals, legal rulings, and a coming together of a variety of stakeholders' demands, needs, and desires.

Three primary categories from which a project can be initiated are: the **project statement of work**, the **business case**, and an **agreement**.

Project Statement of Work

The statement of work (SOW) is an input in the form of a narrative description of the products or services to be delivered by the project. Project participants need to review the SOW to understand that, as the work proceeds, they can use their individual knowledge and expertise to refine this statement.

Business Case

The business case provides the business perspective for which the project is being initiated. This high-level document, refined in the course of progressive elaboration, deals with the business need(s) being addressed by the project. It includes the cost/benefit analysis as a basic justification for the project. Some examples of the business reasons addressed by a project include:

- Market demand
- Business need(s)
- Customer request
- Technological advancement
- Legal requirement
- Social need

Members of project management or project teams may be selected for their expertise or experience in specialties associated with business reasons for undertaking a project.

The business case should include specific and measurable expectations of the project called **objectives**.

Objectives give the project a purpose, defining what the expectations from a business perspective are. For example, stating that the business wants to improve efficiency is not an objective. Stating that the business wants to increase the throughput an automobile line worker can produce by 10% is an objective.

4

One way to validate a "good" objective is to define every objective in terms of whether it is "SMART" or not, as depicted in Figure 4-1 below.

S	Specific
M	Measurable
A	Achievable
R	Realistic
T	Timely

Figure 4-1
SMART
Objectives

Class Exercise 4-1

Look at the list of potential objectives below. Rewrite them to be SMART.

Potential Objective	Rewritten Objective
Deliver two new products to market this year.	
Increase market share of a compact automobile product line.	
Increase a shipping department's efficiency for new order placements.	
Reduce the cost of handling customer service calls.	

Agreements

An agreement is similar to a project SOW in that the request is initiated by an external entity. More formality is typically needed when a project is initiated based on a formal request from an outside entity. An agreement to initiate a project will usually include a defined SOW as well as the business case and a rationale for the request.

There are several types of agreements that may be used in project work. A contract is a more formal version of an agreement. The **project procurement knowledge area** discusses the formation of and components included in agreements and contracts.

Project Charter

The charter represents an agreement between the sponsor and the assigned project manager. There are occasions when a project manager is named without the existence of a project charter or even a formal initiation of the project to which a project manager is assigned. In the charter's absence, an assigned project manager should choose to create a charter in collaboration with the project sponsor.

> **TIP**
>
> See Figure 4-3 on page 67 of the *PMBOK® Guide* to understand how the charter feeds many of the planning processes.

The project sponsor is the one who signs the project charter ratifying his or her selection of the project manager. The naming of the project manager is the critical characteristic of the charter. It establishes that the project has been approved to be undertaken and managed by a formally assigned project manager.

Many project management team members are often identified in the original charter while others are identified in subsequent amendments. The charter is the medium to document informed consent of all the stakeholders who are providing financial, human, and equipment resources to a project or a project phase. Publication of this document makes explicit all roles and responsibilities and represents participants' informed consent regarding their explicit obligations.

4

Each recipient of the charter needs to read the charter from the point of view of his or her assignment. Upon reading the charter, each individual should clarify anything he or she doesn't understand with the project manager or the member of the project management team to whom he or she reports.

Individuals working on project activities should pay special attention to the implications of approaches to the project in terms of the project's maximization and optimization, as well as in terms of how project requirements are satisfied.

Other considerations when developing the project charter are the boundaries or existing artifacts that the project participants will be working within or have access to. PMI categorizes these as **enterprise environmental factors** and **organizational process assets**.

Enterprise Environmental Factors

Selecting and assigning project participants is key to obtaining knowledge and experience in using governmental or industry standards, reacting to or influencing marketplace conditions, and benefiting from components of the organization's infrastructure. Such required inputs help avoid non-conformance with a project's quality dimensions, non-compliance with regulations, and overlooking best practices for delivering the project or producing its outcomes.

Successful project teams understand the environment of an organization and plan and respond accordingly.

Organizational Process Assets

Individuals selected to participate in a project bring different kinds of experience to the project. As valuable as experience within an organization is, the acquisition of participants with complementary histories of accomplishment but who have worked in different organizations enriches a project's requisite variety of performance skills.

In addition, organization artifacts from prior similar projects can be leveraged in the planning phases of a project, as well as throughout the project. The intent here is to not always create things from scratch. Use the existing resources where applicable, both people and processes.

Class Exercise 4-2

On the following page is a sample project charter for BEST CONSULTING. You will note that not all information is known at this time. Identify three to five questions that you may have as a project participant if handed this project charter.

1. _____

_____

2. _____

_____

3. _____

_____

4. _____

_____

5. _____

_____

Project: Children's Charity Fundraiser Project Manager: Henry Optimo Project Sponsor: Mark Smith	Date: 1/1/14

Project Definition	As the CEO of a local consulting business, BEST CONSULTING, you have a passion to give back to the community. The local Children's Charity is your company's charitable organization of choice. This year you would like to plan and execute a "first" fundraising event for the local Children's Charity.
Business Justification	This project is being initiated based on your organization's corporate initiative to become more involved in the community and increase the brand image of BEST CONSULTING.
Major Project Deliverables	Hold an annual fundraising event.
Major Stakeholders	• Mark Smith, CEO • Tom Wang, VP of Business Development and Sales (Sponsor) • Mary Johnson, Marketing VP • Tom Filips, Children's Charity Public Relations Manager • The project team • The community
Project Support and Authority	Henry Optimo, Project Manager • He has full authority to select and manage the volunteer team.
Project Objectives: describe quantifiable criteria used to measure the completion of project scope; define quality criteria for product or service acceptance	• Raise $300,000 for the local Children's Charity in this first event. • Raise awareness within the state about the Children's Charity • Develop a core staff of volunteers that will participate in this fundraising event and become the leaders of any future charitable events that the consulting organization wishes to support • Develop a repeatable process for planning and executing charitable events
Constraints and Assumptions	• Constraints: minimal if any direct costs should be incurred on this project; wherever possible, volunteer resources will be used and donations will be made by organizations to support the fundraising efforts • Assumptions: most participants in this project will be volunteers and be employees of BEST CONSULTING
Known Risks	If BEST CONSULTING doesn't put a good process together for delivering successful charitable events, the objectives of BEST CONSULTING raising the expected funds or increasing awareness of the charity will not be realized. In addition, the success of this single event will drive whether or not the organization will continue to support events like this in the future.
Procurement Items	None at this time

Acceptance
Project Sponsor: _____ Date:_____

Project Manager: _____ Date:_____

Case Study 4-1

You have been hired by a team of investors to manage a new website project. Your task is to create a website for a new business venture, LUV Music, that focuses on selling music-related products for all music genres.

Based on initial discussions with the investors, you've outlined and have received approval on the following objectives:

1. Create a 10-page website that introduces LUV Music to the domestic and international markets.
2. Generate at least $50,000 in revenue from the LUV Music website in its first year with at least a 5% increase annually.
3. Create a website that attracts clientele globally. Domestic activity should not exceed 60% of web activity and 80% of total revenue.
4. Create a website that targets clientele that are in the upper middle class. More than 50% of the customer base should have income levels greater than $150,000.

Using the template provided in the downloadable WAV™ files, create a project charter for this project.

The project stakeholders and initial project team for the LUV Music project are defined as follows:
- John Smith: primary investor and sponsor
- Susan Newby: investor, marketing
- Holly Berri: web developer
- Mark Spinner: music aficionado

Identify any initial constraints or assumptions that may be present for this kind of project as well as known potential risks.

4

Expert Judgment

The tools and techniques cited in the *PMBOK® Guide* for the Develop Project Charter process are expert judgment and facilitation techniques. Such judgment is largely provided by the project sponsor, the project manager, and those who may ultimately be named to the management team of the project being initiated.

Expert judgment is not just what an individual knows or is able to do. Such judgment can be accessed when a team member knows who can do the required work or provide needed information. Such individuals may be known by project participants as members of their professional networks or of their communities of practice or communities of knowledge.

Expert judgment is frequently provided by project management team members. Project managers also provide important expert judgment to their assignments. The project manager's contribution is often in his or her breadth of knowledge and ability to discern the quality of judgment provided by project management team members, project team members, and critical stakeholders (who have in-depth expertise in specialties demanded by a project).

The challenge for each project team member, regardless of assignment, is to provide judgment based on his or her expertise, which is consistent with his or her abilities.

In the context of the project charter, the balancing of four factors—scope, quality, time, and budget—requires an articulation of the relative importance of each of the four factors and a shared understanding at the individual contributor level.

There are times when one of these factors is the primary driver in decisions made on a project. For instance, if something of value must be delivered by a certain date, time constrains the project and is therefore the most important, or driving, factor in the development of the project. A scope-constrained project would be one in which a project cannot be completed until all of the "must haves" in the SOW for the product are present and acceptable to the project sponsor.

Facilitation Techniques

Facilitation techniques are mentioned several times within the *PMBOK® Guide*. Project managers are regularly called upon to facilitate conversations and to solve problems to ensure that a project progresses successfully. Effective facilitation techniques include:
- Brainstorming
- Conflict resolution
- Problem solving
- Meeting management

We will address many of these techniques throughout this study guide.

DEVELOP PROJECT MANAGEMENT PLAN PROCESS

The Develop Project Management Plan process integrates all the **subsidiary plans** from the various knowledge areas into one cohesive whole. This complete, consistent, and coherent document is the **project management plan**. It is crucial that the project manager and the project team spend sufficient time in creating the project management plan because this document serves to:
- Reduce project uncertainty
- Improve the efficiency of work
- Provide a better understanding of the project objectives
- Provide a basis for monitoring and controlling the project

> **TIP**
> Review Figure 4-5 on page 73 in the *PMBOK® Guide* to understand how the project management plan is integrated within the *PMBOK® Guide* knowledge areas.

The contents of the project management plan vary with the size, complexity, formality, and uniqueness of a project. Business, technology, and culture also shape the nature of the plan. Most importantly, the diversity, transience, and ability of project participants involved must be harnessed in the plan's creation and continued refinement. Throughout the project, this dynamic document must serve as a communication and educational tool for all stakeholders.

PMI emphasizes four concepts of planning:
- Planning begins during the initiating phase of a project
- Planning does not end until the project ends
- Planning is an intellectual process that runs through all the other processes of the project
- Planning is iterative; as the project proceeds, the project manager must involve all stakeholders as needed to plan, replan, and plan again

The concept of planning pulls together four of the major deliverables of the various knowledge areas, as depicted in Figure 4-2 below.

Figure 4-2
Planning
Deliverables

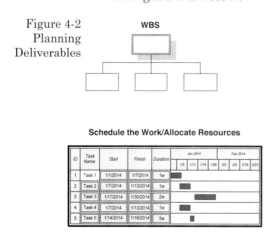

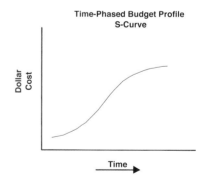

The **work breakdown structure** (WBS) represents the ruling scope document; it reinforces progressive elaboration, which results in specific work packages, activities, and deliverables, as depicted in Figure 4-2 on the previous page, which are the basis of all planning.

The **schedule**, like the one shown in Figure 4-2, reflects the work to be performed and defined by the WBS over time and is used to measure project performance. The work applied over time is quantified in terms of dollars and produces a **time-phased budget** like the one in Figure 4-2, which summarizes the effort expressed in resource costs that are expended to produce each deliverable. This is the source of data used to display cumulative costs, total planned cost, and actual cost in an **S-curve**.

Throughout the remainder of this study guide, we use these four graphic elements of the WBS, Gantt chart, time-phased budget, and S-Curve to orient the discussion to the most frequently updated and used **deliverables**.

Project Management Plan

A project management plan is more than just a set of instructions. It is not just a WBS or an output of Microsoft Project™. Planning is collaborative, analytic work, the objective of which is to integrate the plans of various individuals with their own specialties into intermediate and final work products that will fulfill the expected outcomes of a project. Its purpose is to guide project execution. It is a collection of formal documents appropriate to communicate the information needs of the audience.

The project management plan provides a standard communication tool throughout the lifetime of the project and a verification of and agreement on objectives and requirements among all stakeholders. The plan is documented and approved by both the customer and the sponsor. All **baselines** for tracking, control, analysis, communications, and integration elements are incorporated into the project management plan.

The project management plan can be updated from time to time as the project warrants. You will note that project management plan updates are identified as outputs in many of the *PMBOK® Guide* processes.

TIP
Know the key elements of the project management plan.

The *PMBOK® Guide* outlines typical elements that are included in a project management plan. Included in the downloadable WAV™ files is a sample project management plan template that has been created to help you complete the many exercises included in this study guide.

The project management plan is normally organized so that it may be created, updated, and most importantly used for coordination, monitoring, and controlling at a summary level or at selectable levels of detail. This means that the plan is usually made up of subsidiary plans. Each **subsidiary plan** is also expected to offer access as needed on a summary or detail level. Plans are usually substantially updated as a result of progressive elaboration. The completion of preceding work provides the basis for decisions on approaches to planning subsequent work.

TIP
See Table 4-1 on page 78 of the *PMBOK® Guide* for the differences between the project management plan and project documents.

The primary input to the development of the project management plan is the project charter. It is important to bear in mind that the ten knowledge areas outlined in the project management plan lack sequential or precedence relationships. The charter is the conceptual center of the project management plan, which is made up of subsidiary plans with roots in all knowledge areas.

Baseline Plans

TIP
The assigned individual must be given the time and means to validate the effort, duration, and commitment assumptions upon which the baseline plan for the assignment is based.

A baseline plan is a snapshot in time for which the project team has gained agreement on and against which performance will be measured. A baseline plan is not modified unless material changes have occurred warranting a change to what actual performance should be measured.

There are three specific baseline plans defined within the *PMBOK® Guide*:
- **Scope baseline plan**
- **Schedule baseline plan**
- **Cost baseline plan**

If a project is materially changed, it means that the aggregate of added, changed, or deleted activities, of actual results, or of forecasts for activities have exceeded current agreements. In other words, if the latest acceptable delivery date, expected scope in terms of features and performance, maximum acceptable cost, and specific quality dimensions are acceptable, the project remains within its baseline plans and therefore has not materially changed.

Baseline plans may be combined in order to establish a performance measurement baseline which can be a valuable part of earned value measurement.

However, if one or more of the dimensions—scope, schedule, or cost—materially changes during project performance, then monitoring produces large exceptions. If there are too many exceptions across the project's dimensions, sponsors and other stakeholders lose confidence that the project will produce the intended benefits within specific cost, time, scope, and quality dimensions.

Enterprise Environmental Factors

The development of the project management plan is dependent on the enterprise environmental factors impacting the organization. Factors that put somehow constrain or otherwise place boundaries on a project could include:
- Governmental or industry standards
- Project management information systems
- Infrastructure
- Personnel administration

Organizational Process Assets

Organizational process assets that may be available for use by the project management team could include:
- Standardized guidelines, work instructions, proposal evaluation criteria, and performance measurement criteria
- Project management plan templates
- Change control procedures including the steps by which official company standards, policies, plans and procedures, or any project documents are to be modified and how any changes will be approved and validated
- Project files from past projects
- Historical information and a lessons learned knowledge base
- A configuration management knowledge base containing the versions and baselines of all official company standards, policies, procedures, and any project documents

Expert Judgment

Depending on the uniqueness of the knowledge, skill, or technical leadership required, significant project results can be obtained through a team member's personal knowledge of who can achieve such results. This may result in the identification of a technical consultant or specialist who may be temporarily retained in a formal capacity to accomplish something unavailable within the project team. However, it is often the case that information, help, or access to needed experts may be obtained informally.

Developing a project management plan is a highly collaborative activity. It requires all participants to provide insight based on their project assignment roles, activities, or task responsibilities. It also requires the ability to articulate and document their specialty contributions so that others with different backgrounds (cultural, linguistic, and technical) can contribute, critique, and cooperate on common work efforts. As with

4

> **TIP**
> The project management plan is started in the Develop Project Management Plan process, but it gets updated by other planning, executing and monitoring and controlling processes.

most work products, people providing expertise need to negotiate a common understanding and check with each other for the degree of acceptance required on a project.

Facilitation Techniques

Putting a project management plan together that the team will follow throughout the life of the project requires the collaboration of many individuals. The project manager must leverage several facilitation techniques such as brainstorming, conflict resolution, problem solving, and meeting management in order to bring consensus to the group.

Outputs from Planning in All Other Processes

All planning outputs of the planning processes in the other nine knowledge areas, including subsequent updates to the project management plan, are inputs to and integrated in the Develop Project Management Plan process. All subsidiary plans are subject to the same progressive elaboration that is pulled together in the Develop Project Management Plan process.

Plans from each knowledge area are periodically updated as planned or as required by circumstances throughout the life of a project. Regardless of the frequency or means by which plans are changed, each practitioner has a responsibility to contribute to the change initiation process. And project practitioners need to respond to changes initiated by others.

4

DIRECT AND MANAGE PROJECT WORK PROCESS

The Direct and Manage Project Work process is the primary process whereby the project management plan is put into action. Most project resources and costs are expended in this process. Important tools and techniques used in this process are **expert judgment**, the **project management information system** (PMIS), and **meetings**.

In order for the project management plan to be executed, work is assigned to individuals by the project manager and then monitored for the completion of deliverables and work results. Therefore, the key outputs of this process are **deliverables**, **change requests**, and **work performance data**. Since project activities are performed by people, the project manager must understand the organizational structure and individual motivations of the people working on a project. These skills are addressed within the Develop Project Team process of the human resources management knowledge area.

Managing project work is based on the premise that actions are taken in concert with both members of the project management team and members of the project team. There are many actions that project participants may perform to execute the work, both explicitly and implicitly. These activities are identified in the project management plan and are designed to achieve the project's objectives.

Some key aspects of the Direct and Manage Project Work process include:
- Work performance
- Project deliverables
- Work assignments

Performing the work identified in assigned activities is necessary to accomplish project requirements. Project requirements are not the same as project deliverables. Project requirements are defined by the stakeholders receiving the project outputs. Project requirements define what is expected of the project output. For example, a project deliverable may be a software application. The project requirement may be a software application to support the course registration process of a university.

TIP
Review Figure 4-7 in the *PMBOK® Guide* to see how the Direct and Manage Project Work process interacts with all the other knowledge areas.

4

Creating project deliverables is often the result of intermediate work to accomplish project requirements. This is the work most often measured by the PMIS.

Each member of the team must be validated as having acquired, having oriented, and having been given an opportunity to successfully achieve the work assigned. Often such work has been identified, specified, and estimated prior to the arrival of the individual expected to perform the received time, cost, scope, and quality constraints. If necessary, participants must be trained to be able to successfully complete the work they are assigned, and the schedule must be adjusted to account for that training.

Managing and directing individuals who are part of the project management team along with the rest of the project team members requires a clear understanding of a project's outcome, the relationship, and timing of efforts planned to achieve it.

In order for the project manager and project management team to successfully execute a project, all participants must have a complete knowledge and understanding of the **project management plan**, **approved change requests**, **enterprise environmental factors**, and **organizational process assets**.

Expert Judgment

In order to successfully execute a project, the project manager and project management team must use expert judgment, as they do in other areas of project management.

Expert judgment ultimately boils down to project managers, supervisors, and other team members needing to be conscious of delegation upwards and downwards. Downward delegation is frequently covered in conventional managerial texts and processes. Upward delegation is critical to project success because the collaboration challenges posed by doing so-called "normal" things differently or performing activities that are new or unknown to project participants are even greater than they would be otherwise.

Project Management Information System (PMIS)

The PMIS is part of the **organizational process assets** that can help collaboration among members of the project management team and others contributing to a project. If the project management team and project team members are properly trained, they will be better equipped to understand the differences in the timing of reports, billable versus non-billable hours, and the significance of interim status reports associated with each activity assigned.

It is important to understand that there is a large variety of users of the PMIS resources available as organizational process assets. The input and use of information in the PMIS are important factors in the project's communications management plan. Knowledge and skills in use of the PMIS cannot be taken for granted, so the human resources management plan may also be impacted by having to account for training in the use of the PMIS.

Class Exercise 4-3

Review the potential activities that are included in the *PMBOK® Guide* Section 4.3, pages 80-81. Identify which activities appear to be the biggest challenges for your organization. Discuss how your organization leverages expert judgment and the PMIS to support the activities of the Direct and Manage Project Work process.

1. _____

_____

2. _____

_____

3. _____

_____

4. _____

_____

Meetings

The *PMBOK® Guide* recognizes that much of what a project manager does to facilitate the execution of a project is to hold meetings. Effective meeting management should be at the top of the list of management skills a project manager possesses. The project manager must understand the purpose of each meeting and ensure that the agenda and the participants invited bring resolution to that purpose. Meetings tend to be one of three types:
- Information exchange
- Brainstorming, option evaluation, or design
- Decision making

Outputs of the Manage Project Work Process

No matter how the project team arrives at the end of a project or phase, the outputs of the Direct and Manage Project Work process result in physical **deliverables**, **work performance data**, and **change requests**. As a result of the activities performed in this process, the **project management plan** and the **project documents** may need to be updated.

Deliverables of the Manage Project Work Process

More than 80% of effort of a project is expended in producing the project's infrastructure and its intermediate, component, and final deliverables. This effort, however, is the basis for the bulk of the work packages, activities, and individual tasks that are explicitly defined in the **WBS** and sequenced using the **critical path method**.

Individuals assigned to a project provide unique, verifiable products, results, or capabilities to perform a service as specified in the project management planning documentation. Their individual and collaborative expertise in accomplishing these assignments is the objective of project management. As in marketing, where "nothing happens until something is sold," in projects, "no useful result is delivered until skilled individuals are organized to produce it."

Work Performance Data

Work performance data are gathered through work execution and passed to the controlling processes for analysis. Types of work performance data include:
- Work completed
- Key performance indicators
- Technical performance measures
- Start and finish dates of schedule activities
- Number of change requests
- Number of defects
- Actual costs

Change Requests

There are three principal ways change requests can be generated:

1. Sponsors and the stakeholders they represent may generate requests directly through the Integrated Change Control process.
2. Members of the project team may be contacted directly by the sponsor or stakeholders to make a change that team members must route through the formal change control process.
3. Project participants may originate a change request through the same change control process based on their own observations or as a result of performing assigned quality management responsibilities.

It is critical to keep all change requests under formal control. Requests for a change can be direct or indirect and externally or internally initiated, and they can be optional or legally or contractually mandated. The reasons for changes may include:

- Corrective action
- Preventive action
- Defect repair
- Updates

Project Management Plan Updates

Project management team members or project team members as directed may update subsidiary project management plans as a result of approved material additions, subtractions, or changes. Significant changes in budget, schedule, scope, or quality must be brought to the attention of the project manager so a determination can be made as to the need for changes in one or more baseline plans.

4

Project Document Updates

Many project documents require periodic updates, often performed by members of the project management team assigned to project administration duties. Such documents include **risk registers** and **stakeholder registers**, as well as data and **WBS dictionaries**.

MONITOR AND CONTROL PROJECT WORK PROCESS

As the work of a project is carried out, deliverables or work results are created. Issues arise or changes come about in the form of **change requests**. The project manager and team continuously monitor performance by comparing actual performance against the project management plan and determining if corrective or preventive actions are necessary.

> **TIP**
> Review Figure 4-9 in the *PMBOK® Guide* to see how the various knowledge areas provide inputs to the Monitor and Control Project Work process.

The *PMBOK® Guide* may give the impression that monitoring and controlling are strictly sequential activities, with monitoring coming first and then controlling. It also may give the impression that this process is performed only by the project manager or the project management team.

Depending on the activities performed and the individuals or organizations performing them, monitoring and controlling may in fact be performed concurrently, and by many different types of people. Individuals participating in a project are the first line of defense in monitoring and controlling project work. The second level of monitoring is the ongoing collaboration of other team members providing continuous feedback among themselves. This is especially true when individuals are performing work that they have not performed before or seen performed by any other member of the project management team.

The primary outputs of the Monitor and Control Project Work process are change requests. Change requests can be one means by which project participants influence the completion of a project or provide alternatives to deal with any unanticipated variance performance.

In order to successfully monitor and control projects, the project manager and project team need information. Information comes in the form of the **project management plan**, **work performance information**, **validated changes**, **schedule forecasts**, **cost forecasts**, **enterprise environmental factors**, and **organizational process assets**.

Enterprise Environmental Factors

Remember that as projects progress, enterprise environmental factors may change or additional factors may become relevant to the completion of projects.

Consider an organization that has been recently purchased by a prior competitor. The environment of the project has significantly changed and must be considered by any project team for the project to be successful.

Organizational Process Assets

Just as the project environment may change during the course of a project, so may the assets necessary to manage a project also change or additional assets may become available or unavailable.

Expert Judgment

The project management team uses **work performance information** to compare actual to planned performance in order to identify the interactions among scope, schedule, budget, and quality metrics.

4

Project participants working with colleagues on assigned activities determine when to escalate problems and issues and when to resolve them among themselves. Informal assistance and formal activities such as peer reviews can be used to recommend revisions or revise a course of action.

Expert judgment is an important tool and technique for identifying the urgency and importance of work performance information.

Analytical Techniques

The Monitor and Control Project Work process involves tracking, reviewing, and reporting progress in order to meet performance objectives defined in the project management plan. The goal of analyzing project data in monitoring and controlling processes is to be able to forecast potential outcomes. There are many kinds of analytical techniques that can be employed. Look to your own organizational process assets for appropriate ways to analyze your organization's data.

Project Management Information System

The PMIS for each organization can be an excellent resource for the project manager in managing and evaluating project performance. Automated tools, databases, and other data storage features can facilitate the project manager's effectiveness.

Meetings

Data to monitor and control projects is not always available from within the reports provided from a PMIS. Meeting regularly with team members and stakeholders to assess the status of a project can highlight areas needing attention that might not otherwise have been noticed.

TIP

Know the types of analytical techniques that may be available to the project manager. They include:
- Root cause analysis
- Forecasting methods
- Failure mode and effect analysis
- Fault tree analysis
- Reserve analysis
- Trend analysis
- Earned value management
- Variance analysis
- Regression analysis
- Grouping methods
- Causal analysis

Outputs of the Monitor and Control Project Work Process

The outputs of the Monitor and Control Project Work process include **change requests**, **work performance reports**, **project plan updates**, and **project document updates**.

- Change requests result from monitoring work and determining if changes are warranted; some changes are required to deliver on the original project scope while others are reviewed for future applicability and prioritization
- Work performance reports can come in many forms; current status, exceptions, recommendations, justifications, and informational notes are all types of performance reports
- Project management plan updates and project document updates are natural by-products of the Monitor and Control Project Work process; responding to changes or information triggers may warrant redirection in how a project is managed or documented

> **TIP**
> It is important to know the types of schedule and cost reports associated with work performance information.

PERFORM INTEGRATED CHANGE CONTROL PROCESS

Changes are inevitable in projects. The Perform Integrated Change Control process coordinates changes across the entire project by determining that a change has occurred, managing a change when it does occur, and ensuring that a change is controlled and agreed upon. Through the use of the Perform Integrated Change Control process, the project manager is able to be in control and make necessary adjustments to ensure the project's success.

> **TIP**
> Review Figure 4-11 on page 95 of the *PMBOK® Guide* to understand how each knowledge area provides inputs to the Perform Integrated Change Control process.

The Perform Integrated Change Control process goes hand-in-hand with the Control Communication process in communications management to integrate the subsidiary change control processes found in the scope, time, cost, quality, risk, and procurement knowledge areas.

The typical steps of this process are:
- Project participants provide documented change requests to the project manager and the change control functions
- Change requests are screened, assessed, and either returned to the originator of the request or prioritized and sent on to be processed by the individuals responsible for the area in which the change is to be made
- Individuals are assigned to work on changes according to the assigned priority of changes as additional or supplemental tasks; the individuals accountable for implementing change requests may be either members of the project management team or members of the project team at large
- Change management administrators then generate updates to the appropriate subsidiary plans and assure that the PMIS reflects these revised or new activities
- Change management administrators maintain a **change management log** showing the status of each change request; this log allows the project management team to see clearly the additional work commitment.

Configuration Control

Configuration control is a systematic procedure that refers to change management. It is focused on the specification of the deliverables and the processes. Configuration control protects both the customer from unauthorized changes by project team members and the project team members from new or undocumented requirements changes from the customer.

A configuration management system is:
- A collection of formal documented procedures used to apply direction to and control the compliance of products and components with project requirements
- A subsystem of the PMIS

- A set of procedures for submitting proposed changes, validating change requests, tracking approval or rejection of these proposed changes, and defining the various levels of authorized changes
- In some areas, inclusive of the change control system

The purpose of configuration management is to ensure compliance with stated requirements by:
- Defining the control process which identifies and documents the characteristics of the configurable items (project products or components)
- Controlling and managing change requests to suit the characteristics of configurable items
- Ensuring the integrity and consistency of the configurable items and approved modifications through the use of internal and external audits

In order to perform integrated change control, project managers and the project management team require knowledge of the **project management plan**, **change requests**, **work performance reports**, **enterprise environmental factors**, and **organizational process assets**.

Change Requests

Directing and managing project work generates change requests that can include corrective actions, preventive actions, defects, and updates. Monitoring and controlling project work is likely to produce updates, while generating additional or revised preventive and corrective actions and defect repairs.

All of these change requests are inputs to the Perform Integrated Change Control process and are reviewed and processed.

Enterprise Environmental Factors

An organizational or project environment could experience changes that warrant handling within the Perform Integrated Change Control process. Consider a new market entrant who begins to take market share away from your organization or a new regulatory requirement that warrants modifications to an existing project. Either situation would indicate that you should make some changes yourself, and these changes would result from the environment in which your organization exists.

Organizational Process Assets

Process assets specific to change control include, but are not limited to:
- Change control procedures, which include how project documents as well as official enterprise standards, policies, and procedures will be modified
- Other change control procedures, which include how any changes will be approved, validated, issued, and tracked to their final resolution
- A process measurement database
- Procedures for authorizing changes
- A configuration management database
- Updates to subsidiary plan files

Expert Judgment

While a proposed change may seem isolated, each change (like each risk item) should have an "owner" whose responsibility is to find the interrelationships and potential impacts of the change on the project's outcome and the project plan. This individual may seek out expertise from a wide variety of sources, including:
- Customer, sponsors, and subject matter experts who may or may not be members of the project team

- The project management office, which
  may provide administrative or technical support
  or access to unique talent
- Representatives of industry groups or professional
  or technical associations
- Members of the communities of practice or
  knowledge with which project team members may
  be affiliated

Meetings

Change control meetings are common within the Perform
Integrated Change Control process. There may be a
number of **change control boards** whose roles and
responsibilities are delineated and who provide actual resources to screen and prioritize change requests.
All decisions are documented and communicated to all
involved stakeholders as actions are planned and tracked
in the PMIS. This is another example of responsibilities
assigned to project participants who may not be members
of the project management team.

Change Control Tools

Managing change requests and their associated resulting decisions is an important function of the Perform
Integrated Change Control process. Understanding why
certain changes have been approved and others have not
can assist the project manager in successfully closing the
project.

Class Exercise 4-4

The construction industry, having historically faced rampant uncontrolled changes, has pioneered change control. There is a class of project documents called "as builts." These documents highlight how the project outcome has diverged from the blueprints, schematics and other forms of documentation. Identify three to five other situations in which industries have built unique processes to reflect the reality of change in projects?

1. _____

2. _____

3. _____

4. _____

5. _____

Outputs of the Perform Integrated Change Control Process

The Perform Integrated Change Control process outputs are similar to many of the other process outputs within the project integration management knowledge area. They are **approved changes**, a **change log**, **project plan updates**, and **project document updates**.
- Approved change requests should be acted upon by the project team
- A change log records activities of the change control process
- Project management plan subsidiary plan updates need to maintained, and the baselines for scope, schedule, cost, and quality need to be adhered to (but these updates often go unreported); a lack of tracking at this level may result in scope creep
- Project document updates must also be addressed; undocumented changes often result in substantially weakened end-results for a project

The "scope creep"

CLOSE PROJECT OR PHASE PROCESS

The Close Project or Phase process is one of the two processes in the closing process group. The other process is the Close Procurements process described in the project procurement management knowledge area.

The Close Project or Phase process occurs not just at the end of the project, but also at the end of each phase.

In comparison, the Close Procurements process occurs for each specific procurement. All project procurements must be closed by the end of the project.

Expert Judgment

Specialists from the project management office, such as internal or external auditors, may be involved in assuring that fiduciary responsibility has been exercised and generally-accepted principles have been adhered to. Closing a project may also involve governmental inspections and audits from municipal, state, provincial, national, or even international entities.

Members of the project team may be involved in inspections and walk-throughs based on their technical or organizational expertise and authority.

Analytical Techniques

Many of the same analytical techniques previously discussed can apply during the Close Project or Phase process to provide the necessary confidence that the project has successfully delivered on its objectives.

Meetings

Lessons learned, closeout, user groups, and other review meetings are helpful in ensuring final sign-off and acceptance of a project.

TIP
There are many exam questions about the similarities and differences between the two processes within the closing process group.

TIP
Review Figure 4-13 of the *PMBOK® Guide* to see the interactions of the Close Project or Phase process with other processes.

4

Outputs of the Close Project or Phase Process

The two outputs of the Close Project or Phase process can occur throughout the project, either at a phase's end or at the overall conclusion of the project. These two outputs are the **final product, service**, or **result** and any **updates to the organizational process assets**.

Acceptance or transition of the final product, service, or result that a project was authorized to produce is the goal of every project. Much in the same way that a project charter is the formal authorization for the start of a project, a formal statement that the terms of the performance agreement, service-level agreement, or contract have been met ends a project or a phase.

At the end of each phase or project, the **organizational process assets updates** are accepted and archived as a critical part of the organization's "memory." These assets provide the means for identifying best practices, the basis for training and analysis, and vital records in the event of post-implementation audits or litigation. These assets include:
- Formal acceptance or project closure documentation
- Project files
- Historical information

PROFESSIONAL RESPONSIBILITY

Integration management is about initiating, planning, executing, monitoring and controlling, and closing projects successfully. Success can be measured in terms of managing the project within the constraints presented, such as time, cost, scope, or quality. When considering the four aspects of professional responsibility—responsibility, respect, fairness, and honesty—the project manager must keep certain things in mind at all times:

- Always include key stakeholders in the definition and sign-off of project objectives and acceptance criteria
- Report actual project performance accurately
- Be fair in your assessment of changes that are within scope or out-of-scope
- Strive to ensure that the recipient of the project is satisfied with the product, service, or result delivered

It is the project manager's responsibility to ensure the success of a project. It is also the project manager's responsibility to accurately reflect the performance of the project to its customers and stakeholders.

4

KEY INTERPERSONAL SKILLS FOR SUCCESS

The interpersonal skill highlighted in this chapter is:

Leadership

Leadership involves getting project work completed by helping others focus on achieving the objectives of a project. Key elements of leadership include respect and trust. Respect is addressed as part of the PMI *Code of Ethics and Professional Conduct*.

At the beginning of a project, it's critical that project managers create a vision that is compelling, motivating, and inspiring. Throughout a project, the project manager will need to help team members grow into a high performing team by building and maintaining trust, mentoring, coaching, and providing feedback.

As a project closes, leadership skills are necessary to gain acceptance of the project deliverables and ensure that the project objectives are met and that stakeholders are satisfied.

BE A BETTER PROJECT MANAGER

Exercise: successful change control management.

Purpose: many project managers separate the process of creating the project charter from the management of project changes. In reality, they are tightly linked. The ability to manage the project charter from within the Integrated Change Control process will aid in keeping scope creep at bay and ensure that the client stays happy.

Steps:

1. As soon as a project charter document is generated, store that document in a centralized location that *all* project participants can access (without giving all participants the authority to update it, of course).

2. Review the project charter at the kickoff meeting with the entire project team, including sponsors, and allow for some time for questions and answers. This will provide further clarity to the entire team about the purpose of the project and the high-level scope.

3. During the course of planning the project, continuously review the project charter with the team and notify the sponsor if you feel the team is increasing the scope.

4. During the execution of the project, ensure that any requested change goes through a change control process and that the change control process includes a reference to the project charter. Every change that is to be approved must point back directly to an existing project objective or, if the change is approved to add scope, the project charter should be updated to reflect that change by someone with the requisite authority.

In short, make the project charter a living document in your project.

SAMPLE CAPM EXAM QUESTIONS ON INTEGRATION MANAGEMENT

4

1. A key objective of integration management is:

   a) Integrating actions that are crucial to project completion
   b) Defining and controlling what is included or not included in a project
   c) Planning and controlling costs
   d) Ensuring that the project satisfies the needs for which it was undertaken

2. A project sponsor should be:

   a) At a level high enough to fund the project
   b) External to the performing organization
   c) A person who addresses the collection, distribution, access, and updates of project information
   d) The project risk owner

3. The project charter should be issued by:

   a) The project manager
   b) The individual in charge of strategic planning
   c) The functional manager supplying the most resources to the project
   d) A manager at a level appropriate to provide funding and resources

4. The project management plan defines:

   a) How a project is executed, monitored, and controlled
   b) The project and what needs to be accomplished
   c) The schedule baseline
   d) The statement of work

5. Organizational process assets that influence the development of the project management plan include:

   a) Existing facilities, equipment, and web interfaces
   b) Employee hiring, development, and termination guidelines
   c) Standardized guidelines and performance measurement criteria
   d) Organizational culture and management practices

6. The integration process that is part of the planning process group is:

   a) Define Scope
   b) Develop Project Management Plan
   c) Develop Project Charter
   d) Develop Project Schedule

7. Information from project activities that is routinely collected as the project progresses is called:

   a) Verified deliverables
   b) Work performance data
   c) Change requests
   d) Acceptance criteria

8. Approved change requests that document actions to bring a project back in line with the project plan are called:

   a) Risk response plans
   b) Corrective actions
   c) Preventive actions
   d) Defect repairs

Notes:

4

9. The Monitor and Control Project Work process is concerned with:

a) Implementing the project management plan and managing risk
b) Comparing projected project performance with the budget baseline
c) Completing the work defined in the project management plan
d) Having a comprehensive list of all schedule activities

10. You are managing your website redesign project and want to take into account the organization's environment. Which factors should you consider?

a) Communication requirements of the organization
b) The organization's work authorization system
c) Processes to review time and expense reports
d) Procedures to define issues

11. A project is complete when:

a) All work has been completed
b) The customer has formally accepted the project results and deliverables
c) Financial records for the project have been added to the project archives
d) The project manager has arranged the project closure celebration

12. Determining the actions necessary to transfer the project products to the next phase is part of what process?

a) Develop Project Management Plan
b) Develop Project Charter
c) Close Procurements
d) Close Project or Phase

Notes:

13. Which of the following is an enterprise environmental factor?

   a) Template for the risk register
   b) Human resources health and safety policies
   c) Existing design team resources
   d) Cost estimating policies

14. What kinds of actions take place during the Direct and Manage Project Work process?

   a) Collect stakeholder requirements and develop a WBS
   b) Identify quality criteria and risks related to them
   c) Obtain materials and equipment and manage team members
   d) Decide on information to be shared and how it will be distributed

15. When you have completed the Perform Integrated Change Control process, what will you do next?

   a) Recommend defect repair
   b) Implement approved change requests
   c) Recommend preventative actions
   d) Rebaseline the schedule

Notes:

ANSWERS AND REFERENCES FOR SAMPLE CAPM EXAM QUESTIONS ON INTEGRATION MANAGEMENT

Section numbers refer to the *PMBOK® Guide.*

1. **A   Section 4.0 – Initiating**
   B) is an objective of scope management; C) is an objective of cost management; D) is an objective of quality management.

2. **A   Section 2.2.1 – Initiating**
   The project sponsor should also be the initiator or issuer of the project charter.

3. **D   Section 4.0 – Initiating**
   The charter is a document that formally authorizes a project. It is such an important document that it has its own process, the Develop Project Charter process.

4. **A   Section 4.2.3 – Planning**
   B) is the definition of the project scope statement; C) is defined by the schedule network analysis; D) is a narrative description of products or services to be supplied by a project.

5. **C   Section 4.2.1.4 – Planning**
   A), B), and D) are all enterprise environmental factors.

6. **B   Section 4.2.3 – Planning**
   The Develop Project Management Plan process documents the actions necessary to define, prepare, integrate, and coordinate all subsidiary plans.

7. **B   Section 4.3.3.2 – Executing**
   Although verified deliverables could result as a project progresses, it is work performance data that is routinely collected.

8. **B   Section 4.3.3.3 – Executing**
   Know the differences between corrective action, preventive action, and defect repair.

9. **B** **Section 4.4 – Monitoring and Controlling**
A) and C) are part of the Direct and Manage Project Work process; D) is part of the Create WBS process.

10. **B** **Section 4.4.1.6 – Monitoring and Controlling**
A), C), and D) are all organizational process assets.

11. **B** **Section 4.6.1.2 – Closing**
An important output of the Close Project or Phase process is the confirmation that the project's product has met customer requirements and there is formal acceptance by the customer. C) and D) are important but not the best indication that a project is complete.

12. **D** **Section 4.6 – Closing**
The Close Project or Phase process is performed at the end of each project or phase, when decisions are made to continue with or terminate a project.

13. **C** **Section 2.1.5 – Initiating**
A), B) and D) are all organizational process assets.

14. **C** **Section 4.3 – Executing**
A), B), and D) are all planning, not executing, activities.

15. **B** **Section 4.5.3 – Monitoring and Controlling**
A) and C) are inputs to the Perform Integrated Change Control process; D) there is no requirement to rebaseline the schedule.

ANSWERS TO CLASS EXERCISES

Class Exercise 4-1: Objectives

Potential Objective	Rewritten Objective
Deliver two new products to market this year.	Offer two new products to the mid-market client base by end of fiscal year 2015.
Increase market share of a compact automobile product line.	Increase the compact automobile product line market share by 10% by end of fiscal year 2016.
Increase a shipping department's efficiency for new order placements.	Improve shipping department efficiency for new order placements by reducing time from order to shipment by three days within three months of new process implementation.
Reduce the cost of handling customer service calls.	Reduce the per call cost of handling customer service calls from $9 per call to less than $5 per call within six months of project delivery.

Class Exercise 4-2: Project Charter

This is not an all-inclusive list. You may come up with others items.

1. Is there a particular preference as to when the event is held?

2. Does the organization have any resources that have experience working on these kinds of projects or events?

3. Are there any expectations regarding the quality of the fund raiser? Are there fund raisers the sponsors have attended that they consider a success and that they would like to emulate?

4. What do the sponsors mean by raising awareness?

5. What, if any, incentive is there for the employees to participate?

Class Exercise 4-3: Expert Judgment and PMIS

**** For Class Discussion Only ****

Class Exercise 4-4: Change Control

**** For Class Discussion Only ****

ANSWERS TO THE CASE STUDY CAN BE FOUND IN THE WAV™ FILES

This book has free material available for download from the
Web Added Value™ resource center at *www.jrosspub.com.*

SCOPE

CHAPTER 5 | **SCOPE**

5

SCOPE MANAGEMENT

Scope management is fundamental to the success of any project. This knowledge area focuses on articulating the intent of the project and defining the work necessary to complete the project successfully. To develop the project scope, there must be an understanding of how **project deliverables** are broken down into smaller, more manageable components and how the delivery of these components is managed and controlled.

The role of the project manager includes defining the work, ensuring that only the work of the project is being completed, and preventing additional work (**scope creep**) not defined in the project from being initiated.

Knowledge Area Processes

Within the scope management knowledge area there are six processes within two process groups.

Planning	Monitoring and Controlling
Plan Scope Management Collect Requirements Define Scope Create WBS	Validate Scope Control Scope

Key Definitions

Chart of accounts: the financial numbering system used to monitor project costs by category. It is usually related to an organization's general ledger.

Code of accounts: the numbering system for providing unique identifiers for all items in the work breakdown structure (WBS). It is hierarchical and can go to multiple levels, each lower level containing a more detailed description of a project deliverable. The WBS contains clusters of elements that are child items related to a single parent element; for example, parent item 1.1 contains child items 1.1.1, 1.1.2, and 1.1.3.

5

Control account: the management control point at which integration of scope, budget, and schedule takes place and at which performance is measured.

Decomposition: the process of breaking down a project deliverable into smaller, more manageable components. In the Create WBS process, the results of decomposition are deliverables, whereas in the Define Activities process, project deliverables are further broken down into schedule activities.

Parking lot: a technique for capturing ideas and recording them for future use.

Planning package: a component of the WBS that is a subset of the control account to support known uncertainty in project deliverables. Planning packages will include information on a deliverable but without any details associated with schedule activities.

Project charter: a document issued by the project initiator or sponsor that formally authorizes the existence of the project and provides the project manager with the authority to apply organizational resources to project activities.

Project deliverable: a unique and verifiable product, result, or capability that is an output of the project itself.

Project objective: the purpose toward which the project is initiated.

Requirements traceability matrix: a matrix for recording each requirement and tracking its attributes and changes throughout the project life cycle to provide a structure for changes to product scope. Projects are undertaken to produce a product, service, or result that meets the requirements of the sponsor, customer, and other stakeholders. These requirements are collected and refined through interviews, focus groups, surveys, and other techniques. Requirements may also be changed through the project's configuration management activities.

Rolling wave planning: a progressive elaboration technique that addresses uncertainty in detailing all future work for a project. Near-term work is planned to an appropriate level of detail; however, longer-term deliverables are identified at a high level and are decomposed as the project progresses.

Scope baseline: the approved detailed project scope statement along with the WBS and WBS dictionary.

Scope creep: the uncontrolled expansion of a product or project scope without adjustments to time, cost, and resources.

WBS dictionary: houses the details associated with the work packages and control accounts. It is the level of detail needed as defined by the project team.

Work breakdown structure (WBS): a framework for defining project work by breaking it down into smaller, more manageable pieces; it defines the total scope of the project using descending levels of detail.

Work package: the lowest level of a WBS; cost estimates are made at this level.

PLAN SCOPE MANAGEMENT PROCESS

Plan Scope Management is the process that documents how scope will be defined, validated, and controlled. Planning for scope management is important as an input to the overall **project management plan**.

In this process, the project manager defines the processes that guide the project team for preparing the detailed project scope statement, for creating the WBS, for maintaining and approving the WBS, for defining how formal acceptance will be obtained, and for controlling how requests for changes will be processed.

5

Expert Judgment and Meetings

The primary tools and techniques needed for the Plan Scope Management process are **expert judgment** and **meetings**. Often, projects are so similar in nature that experience from previous projects can be leveraged to define and/or modify how scope will be managed in the current project. Meetings are one of the best means of utilizing expert judgment and are often required to review and finalize a project plan.

An output of the Plan Scope Management process is, of course, the **scope management plan**. Additionally, the **requirements management plan**, which describes how requirements will be analyzed, documented, and managed is defined. This plan is a subsidiary plan within the project management plan. Similar to other subsidiary plans, the approach to the requirements management plan can start with an organizational standard and be adjusted to the unique needs of the project. See the downloadable WAV™ files for a complete sample project management plan for the Fundraiser Road Race.

Figure 5-1
Scope
Management
Plan

Scope Management Plan

Project Name: Fundraiser Road Race
Date: 2/2/14

The project manager will have full authority to assign work to project resources and work directly with stakeholders to manage the overall project scope.

Scope will be defined out of the work breakdown sessions. Each task will be defined utilizing a work-package document similar to the work-package document provided.

The deliverables, objectives and time associated with each work-package will be developed based on the agreed upon schedule and priorities. Where possible, those responsible for doing the work will be involved in the work-package definition process.

Any work that is identified as out-of-scope will be directed to the project manager for initial review and decision. If a cost is estimated beyond the need for additional volunteers, the project manager will meet with the project sponsor to make a final determination.

COLLECT REQUIREMENTS PROCESS

The Collect Requirements process defines and documents what is needed to meet **project objectives**. Additionally, this process addresses the project manager's responsibility for managing stakeholder needs and requirements to meet the project objectives.

In collecting requirements, the project manager is guided by the **scope management plan**, **requirements management plan**, and **stakeholder management plan**.

The **project charter** is a document that outlines the project objectives. Although the project charter is an official document authorizing a project, it does not provide the level of detail needed to clearly define the work that needs to be completed in order to satisfy the project objectives.

To successfully collect requirements, the project manager must have a project charter and an understanding of the project stakeholders, which would be available in a **stakeholder register**.

In our fundraiser project, one objective outlined in the project charter is to generate at least $300,000 for the charity.

This objective does not provide enough detail to plan the activities that will result in meeting the objective. In order to determine how to meet this objective, the project manager should coordinate an exercise to determine the detailed needs of the stakeholder(s).

This process is typically performed by an analyst. The outcome of this analysis is a detailed listing of requirements. Requirements can be grouped and categorized in different ways. Many organizations identify requirements as project, product, technical, or non-technical requirements.

There are many options for gathering requirements. The *PMBOK® Guide* outlines eight different tools and techniques. We will discuss two of the most commonly used tools: interviews and group decision-making techniques.

Interviews

Interviews can be formal or informal with the various stakeholders. It is extremely important that the focus of an interview stay on topic with the **project objectives**. Whenever requirements are gathered, the analyst and the project manager must approach the interview in a very structured manner and with specific outcomes in mind. There is room for more spontaneous questioning as the interview progresses, but the ultimate goal is to determine the needs of the stakeholders, which will aid in achieving project objectives.

Depending on the stakeholder being interviewed, the questions will vary. Therefore, for each stakeholder a separate **interview plan** must be developed.

For BEST CONSULTING, the matrix in Figure 5-2 on the following page resulted from the business analyst interviewing the CEO of BEST CONSULTING.

TIP

When interviewing, always plan what questions you want answered to eliminate confusion and increase the chance of receiving applicable information.

Objective	Question	Response from CEO
Raise $300,000 for the local Children's Charity in this first event.	What kind of venues do you feel will allow your organization to raise the $300,000 for the Children's Charity?	"I think we should look at a couple of venues and determine which may optimize our objectives. I'd look at a road race, a golf outing, a black-tie affair, or a music festival."
Raise $300,000 for the local Children's Charity in this first event.	Which of these venues do you think has the best opportunity for BEST CONSULTING to raise the $300,000 based on the cost of the event?	"Based on my experience with being involved in various events, the golf outing and the black-tie event will probably cost around $100,000 to hold due to the fact that we may not be able to have the venue costs donated. The music festival and road race will not be as expensive since the venues are easier and less costly to rent. We should probably reach out to an organization that specializes in these types of events to find out what the typical costs are."
Raise awareness within the state about the Children's Charity.	Of these venues you've identified, which one(s) do you believe will allow us to reach the most people?	"Similar to the last question, the golf outing and black-tie event will only allow us to have a limited number of participants, but in general the folks that would be invited to these events will be more affluent and will tend to donate more. With our current client base, we should be able to invite many of our customers and vendors who would be willing to write a big check for us. The music festival and road race will absolutely reach more people because of the lower cost of entry. So if we really want to reach the most just from an awareness standpoint, I would lean toward a festival or race."
Develop a core staff of volunteers that will participate in this fundraising event and become the leaders of any future charitable events that the consulting organization wishes to support.	How many people would you like to be in our core staff of volunteers?	"I think a team of six people would be best, not too large and not too small."
Develop a core staff of volunteers that will participate in this fundraising event and become the leaders of any future charitable events that the consulting organization wishes to support.	Do you want to include *only* current employees of BEST CONSULTING?	"I want a team that is dedicated to helping our organization continue to give back to the community. I think we should have at least 1/3 from our organization, but other volunteers can come from elsewhere."
Develop a repeatable process for planning and executing charitable events.	How many events do you think we should deliver each year?	"I think we should hold a minimum of one per year."
Develop a repeatable process for planning and executing charitable events.	What do you think would be a good measurement of continually improving our charitable event process?	"I believe that we should always be striving to increase our contribution to charity annually. So if we start with $300,000 this year, then I would expect that this number could grow annually. Whether we do one event or five, the total contribution each year should grow."

Figure 5-2
Interview Matrix

Case Study 5-1

In our LUV Music case study, we have the following scope description: create a website for the new business venture LUV Music that focuses on selling music-related products for all music genres.

For this project, there are four objectives. In conducting an interview, each question must be focused on the objective(s) you are trying to achieve. Below is a start to our interview plan. In this example, you are interviewing a focus group of musicians. Take a few minutes to create additional questions in the question column for each of the project objectives.

Objective	Question	Response (Musician Focus Group)
Create a ten-page website that introduces LUV Music to the domestic and international markets.	What attracts music lovers to new music websites?	
Generate at least $50,000 in revenue from the LUV Music website in its first year with at least a 5% increase annually.	What kinds of products do music lovers purchase online?	
Create a website that attracts clientele globally. Domestic activity should not exceed 60% of web activity and 80% of total revenue.	What is the difference between domestic and global clients? What features do they look for?	
Create a website that targets clientele that are in the upper middle class. More than 50% of the customer base should have income levels greater than $150,000.	Is there a correlation between affluence and what products are available for purchase on the website?	
Create a website that targets clientele that are in the upper middle class. More than 50% of the customer base should have income levels greater than $150,000.	What markets should LUV Music be targeting if it wants more than 50% of its clientele to have income levels greater than $150,000?	

Group Decision Making

In many projects, as **requirements** are being identified, the stakeholders will have differing opinions about how the project should meet its objectives. It will be up to the project team to gather and assess these **alternatives** to determine which path or paths should be followed in order to best meet the project objectives.

Applying a method of group decision making is often necessary to choose between the many options. These methods are:
- **Unanimity**: gaining a consensus in which everyone agrees with a single course of action
- **Majority**: applying a greater than 50% criteria for voting on a recommended action
- **Plurality**: when no majority is available, the option with the greatest number of votes will be selected
- **Dictatorship**: a single person is identified as the sole person responsible for making a decision

In our Fundraiser Road Race, the team has identified several possible fundraising options, as depicted in Figure 5-3 below.

Options	Possible Revenue Opportunity	Anticipated Costs	Potential Attendance
Golfing Outing	$500,000	$100,000	150
5 or 10k Road Race	$450,000	$50,000	2,000
Black-Tie Affair	$625,000	$100,000	200
Music Festival	$350,000	$95,000	1,200

Figure 5-3
Fundraising
Options

Utilizing a table such as the one above, a high-level assessment of several **key performance indicators** are listed (i.e. revenue, costs, attendance). A key performance indicator should be defined based on the objectives spelled out in the project charter. For this event, the project has the objectives of raising money for the charity and raising awareness in the community regarding the charity.

In order to facilitate good group decision making, only factors relevant to these objectives should be defined. For example, it would make no sense to evaluate whether or not the customers of BEST CONSULTING would be attending the event since there is no objective addressing whether those customers will attend.

Case Study 5-2

For the LUV Music website project, a primary objective is to produce revenue for the organization. Brainstorm various ways to produce revenue on the website by filling out the following table:

Option	Objective Gain	Probability of Achieving Objective	Cost of Achieving Objective	How to Prove?

The primary outputs of the Collect Requirements process are the **requirements documentation** and **requirements traceability matrix**. The results of the tools and techniques that are employed in this process are critical to maintaining and controlling the scope of the project.

A requirements traceability matrix is critical to controlling **scope creep** in that it looks at each requirement of the project and links those requirements directly back to a specific project objective. Managing requirements tightly ensures that the project will stay focused on the delivery of the project objectives. Those that do not will most likely experience excessive change requests and a high potential for scope creep.

Throughout the project life cycle, a requirements traceability matrix may be updated to reflect additional details and/or changes. A simple example of a requirements traceability matrix is shown in Figure 5-4 below.

Figure 5-4
Requirements
Traceability Matrix

Objective	Requirement
Raise $300,000 for the local Children's Charity in this first event.	• A total of $300,000 is expected to be raised • A minimum of $200,000 needs to be raised from corporations
Raise awareness within the state about the Children's Charity.	• A pre- and post-survey will be conducted to measure awareness • A marketing plan must include reaching out to more than 10,000 individuals and/or corporations in the local market
Develop a core staff of volunteers that will participate in this fundraising event and become the leaders of any future charitable events that the consulting organization wishes to support.	• Identify four BEST CONSULTING employees who will commit three years to supporting charitable events for the organization • Develop a role and responsibility matrix for the four core volunteers
Develop a repeatable process for planning and executing charitable events.	• The process must be formally documented • The process developed must describe the actual results and lessons learned for each process step

DEFINE SCOPE PROCESS

Defining the scope, which requires a detailed description of the project and product, is critical to project success. Project managers must use the purpose or business need of the project as a means to manage scope and avoid scope creep. This may seem odd, but so often, even when the scope is well defined early in the project, there is a natural tendency for people to lose sight of the purpose of the project and begin to add scope unknowingly.

The project manager is responsible for making sure the project team members fully understand the scope of a project and manage their activities to the delivery of that scope and *nothing more*. Any **assumptions**, **risks**, and **constraints** defined early in the project are embedded in the scope statement.

The primary deliverable of the Define Scope process is the **project scope statement**.

Facilitated Workshops

Facilitated workshops are a key tool available to the project manager. In order to move a project forward, activities need to be completed and decisions need to be made. Workshops, as a tool, are most effective if managed efficiently. Involving knowledgeable people in these workshops allows the project manager to leverage the **expert judgment** of these individuals.

In the phase of a project in which the project manager is trying to define the scope of a project, a facilitated workshop may be needed to bring a group of stakeholders together on the specific deliverables to be produced.

For the fundraiser for Children's Charity, a decision is made to proceed with the road race, since on the surface it appears to provide the greatest opportunity to attain the dollar goal as well as reach the greatest number of patrons.

The "scope creep"

Once this initial decision is made, additional decisions may need to be made. For any meeting, the project manager should create an agenda. In Figure 5-5 below is an example of an **agenda** for a meeting to expand on the understanding of scope and to identify any additional deliverables.

Meeting Topic: Road Race Planning session
Date or Meeting: 1/15/14
Place of Meeting: Corporate Board Room
Time of Meeting: 9:00am – Noon

Attendees Required:
Mark Smith, CEO
Mary Johnson, Marketing VP
Henry Optimo, Project Manager
Scott Trivolo, Community Outreach Director
Gail Hotchkins, Event Planner
Tom Filips, Children's Charity Public Relations Manager

Optional Attendees:
Mitch Bellows, Marketing Support

AGENDA

Time	Topic	Presenter	Time
9:00am	Introduction	Henry	10 min.
9:10am	Review Project Charter and Scope	Henry	20 min.
9:30am	Work Brainstorming Session	Gail	90 min
11:00am	Lunch Break & Review	Gail	30 min
11:30am	Recap and Next Steps	Henry	30 min

DECISIONS REACHED
1.
2.
3.

NEXT STEPS
1.
2.
3.

ACTION ITEM	ASSIGNED TO	DATE ASSIGNED	DUE DATE
1.			
2.			
3.			
4			

Figure 5-5
Agenda

Facilitating workshops is not an easy task. Challenges will inevitably be presented that a project manager will need to address and overcome. Let's explore some of these situations and discuss them.

Class Exercise 5-1

For the situations defined below, what should the project manager do?

Situation	Response
During the work brainstorming meeting, Mary Johnson started identifying the work to be done, but whenever other people wanted to identify tasks to be completed, Mary interrupted them and did not allow them to complete their thoughts.	
Tom Filips, the Children's Charity public relations manager, identified several other opportunities for BEST CONSULTING to add value to the community which could be used for the charity. Some of his ideas were: 1. Use BEST CONSULTING resources for internal Children's Charity projects. 2. Joint market our companies together by linking to each other's websites from within our respective websites. 3. Plan a golf event, since a major golf pro has a child who was recently diagnosed with cancer.	
Scott Trivolo, who is a key internal sponsor for this event, sat at the end of the conference room table and didn't contribute any thoughts in the first 90 minutes of the meeting.	

Parking Lots

Often, topics or ideas come up in meetings that are good, but not truly part of the project scope. As the project manager, you can put these ideas in parking lots so they aren't lost or forgotten, but they aren't contained within the scope of the current project either. Parking lot items are simply appropriately recorded for later referral.

Case Study 5-3

For the LUV Music website project, create an agenda to evaluate the alternatives previously listed for increasing revenue. Determine which would serve the project objectives best and which should be moved to a parking lot.

Product Analysis

When managing a project that affects or creates a product, the project manager has additional considerations in defining the scope and deliverables necessary for successful completion of the project. For example, if a company produces computers in mass quantities, there may be additional considerations regarding the type of components needed for the product, such as **quality**, **grade**, or **vendor sourcing**.

> **TIP**
> When new services are delivered as a result of the project, additional considerations include process standardization, staff development, and training.

When managing projects that produce a service or result, these kinds of considerations are not as prevalent.

Alternatives Generation

In the context of scope management, alternatives generation is a tool and technique that can be leveraged to determine different ways to execute a project to deliver the product, service, or result.

For our Fundraiser Road Race, there could be several alternatives that could be employed to deliver the scope of the project. Some alternatives include:
- Hire an organization that specializes in organizing and delivering road race fundraisers
- Build a team internally to plan and deliver the road race
- Hire a consultant to advise the team on critical aspects of planning and delivering the road race

For the project manager, these alternatives need to be discussed and determined as part of defining the scope of the project.

5

> **TIP**
>
> The project scope statement should define what is *not* included in the project as well as what *is* included within the project.

Once the appropriate level of analysis is completed in the Define Scope process, the output of the process is a **project scope statement**. The project scope statement should succinctly define the work included in the project as well as the work that will not be included. The scope statement should be reviewed and approved by the sponsor and key stakeholders.

For the Fundraiser Road Race, the following scope statement was developed and approved by the CEO of BEST CONSULTING.

> *BEST CONSULTING is initiating this project in the hopes of developing a team of volunteers and a process that will allow BEST CONSULTING to regularly give back to the community. Included in this year's plan is an effort to plan and deliver a Fundraiser Road Race for the Children's Charity. The goal will be to donate $300,000 as a result of the fundraiser.*
>
> *This newly developed team of volunteers will be supported by a hired consultant to help the team establish a successful process for planning and executing fundraising events at least once annually. All efforts for this event will be performed by volunteers either from within BEST CONSULTING or from outside sources. Wherever possible, all expenses for the effort should be donated by sponsors to maximize the amount that will be donated to the Children's Charity.*

As you can see from the CEO's statement above, the scope statement gives the project manager, stakeholders, and project team a high-level understanding of the following:

- Why the project is being initiated: a corporate commitment to give back to the community
- What the deliverable(s) of the project are: a successful road race that will provide over $300,000 to the Children's Charity and raise awareness about the charity (note that deliverables and objectives are not the same)
- Clarification on key things that are *not* included in the project: hiring more employees is not planned

The purpose of the scope statement is to provide a baseline of expectations that the project team can go back to if ever there is a question regarding what is included or *not* included in the project. Of course, this scope statement still doesn't provide the level of detail for the project team to act on. That level of detail will be developed within the Create WBS process.

The project scope statement is the first component of the **project management plan**.

Case Study 5-4

For the LUV Music website, create a scope statement as a result of employing various tools and techniques of scope management, either defined in this book or as part of the *PMBOK® Guide*.

CREATE WBS PROCESS

The process of creating a WBS helps the project manager and the project team further articulate all the work that is included in a project. The WBS defines the work necessary for the project team to deliver in order to fulfill the **scope** and **project objectives**.

Work Breakdown Structure

A WBS is a depiction of the project in terms of deliverables. It may look like an organization chart or an outline list. Its purpose is to define *all* of the work necessary to deliver on the project scope.

Deliverables are different from objectives, although at times an objective can be a deliverable.

Objectives are defined early in the project initiation phase. A project is initiated to affect the organization in some way. These effects are defined as objectives. Whether objectives are improving revenue and/or efficiency or increasing competitiveness (a few common objectives), they are rarely measured at the conclusion of a project.

> **TIP**
> In addition to measuring the success of projects in term of meeting schedule or cost, it is important to measure the attainment of the project objectives.

Deliverables are tangible results of work being performed within the project. The collection of deliverables for the project can result in another deliverable and, ultimately, deliverables are used to provide value to the organization through the attainment of the project objectives.

Class Exercise 5-2

In the table below identify whether the item is a deliverable or an objective.

Example	Deliverable or Objective?
Provide technical documentation for the maintenance of green technology engines.	
Improve profitability by 20% through the development of three new green technology products in 2015.	
Create an energy-efficient engine as a new product for an automotive parts organization to increase revenue by 10% in 2016.	
Deliver tents to the Fundraiser Road Race venue in case of rain.	
Design marketing materials for the Fundraiser Road Race.	
Research marketing websites to determine the most cost-effective way to reach more than 10,000 people in the community.	
Increase awareness of the Children's Charity through the successful execution of the Fundraiser Road Race.	
Achieve an attendance of greater than 1,000 at the Fundraiser Road Race.	

Control Accounts and Work Packages

The **WBS** consists of basically two types of components: control accounts and work packages. **Control accounts** are a summary-level component. A control account is used to summarize both subsidiary control accounts and work packages that make up the control account.

In Figure 5-6 on the next page, marketing, marketing production, and surveys would be considered control accounts. The marketing control account consists of four deliverables: research for outreach opportunities, marketing plan, marketing production, and surveys.

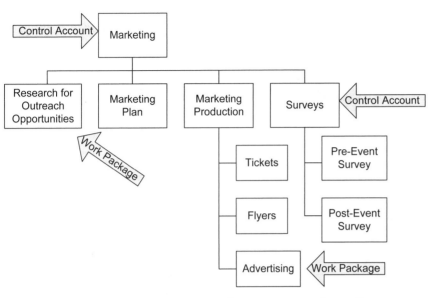

Figure 5-6
WBS Control Accounts
and Work Packages

The marketing production control account consists of three deliverables: tickets, flyers, and advertising. The surveys control account consists of the deliverables pre-event and post-event surveys.

A **work package** is the lowest level of the WBS and defines a specific deliverable to be produced. Typically, resources are assigned to work packages and *not* to control accounts.

In our example, resources would be assigned to all of the boxes with the exception of marketing, marketing production, and surveys. In theory, all deliverables defined below a control account should encompass *all* the work necessary to deliver the control account deliverable.

Our WBS shows that the delivery of tickets, flyers, and advertising constitutes *all* the work required to deliver marketing production. If, in this analysis, you realize something is not included, additional work packages should be created. For example, if as a result of the research for the outreach opportunities control account, you realize that marketing production should also include the mailing of marketing packages to a targeted list of individuals, you could enhance your WBS (similar to the one in Figure 5-7 on the following page).

> **TIP**
> Work should *only* be assigned at the work package level, leaving the control accounts to be summarizations of work packages.

Figure 5-7
Enhanced
WBS

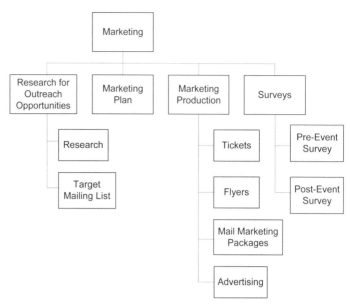

Planning Packages and Subprojects

In addition to control accounts and work packages, WBS planning packages and subprojects may be identified. A planning package is a component of the WBS that is used as a placeholder for work to be done that has not yet been detailed to the level of work to be performed. Very often, early on in the project, the project team may not be able to provide enough details to define the work to be done; however, team members know that work will need to be performed. Using a planning package would be appropriate in such cases.

Subprojects can also be part of the WBS. In many cases, a group totally separate from the project team is responsible for delivering a major component either internally or externally with a vendor. The WBS should be decomposed to the level of work that will be the responsibility of the internal group or external vendor. It is not necessary for the project team to detail any work within subprojects to be completed by another team as it will be managed by a different entity.

Each component of the WBS is typically identified by a WBS ID, a numbering system that relates work packages to control accounts and determines how work and costs are summarized and reported.

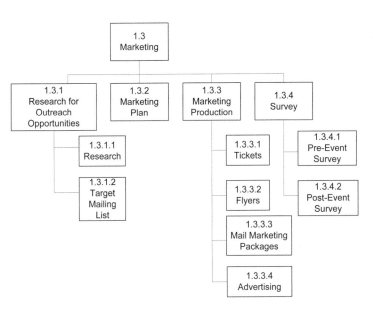

Figure 5-8
WBS ID

For our marketing component of the Fundraiser Road Race WBS, the WBS ID would look something like Figure 5-8 above.

The primary output of the Create WBS process is the WBS itself. Secondary outputs of the Create WBS process are the **WBS dictionary** and the **scope baseline**. The scope baseline is a more comprehensive document that includes the **project scope statement** as well as both the **WBS** and the WBS dictionary.

Decomposition

Decomposition is the tool and technique used to determine all the deliverables necessary to deliver on the project scope. Decomposition is performed by continuously breaking down the details of a deliverable to smaller, more manageable components.

Decomposition can continue to the detail level that is required to best manage the work. For example, with our Fundraiser Road Race, one deliverable may be advertising. Advertising could certainly be broken down into smaller components such as newspaper, magazine, and local websites; however, if a volunteer is found who has extensive knowledge about advertising, the project manager may not need to detail out the work any further than advertising. Not detailing the work assumes that the volunteer associated with the advertising deliverable will manage the entire component of work and will not require added oversight by the project manager.

If, for instance, there were two volunteers, one with expertise working with websites and the other one knowledgeable about newspaper advertising, there would be no one with extensive knowledge of magazine advertising. The project manager might in this case choose to break down advertising to the next level and manage each of these components separately on the WBS, as depicted in Figure 5-9 below.

Figure 5-9
WBS Decomposed

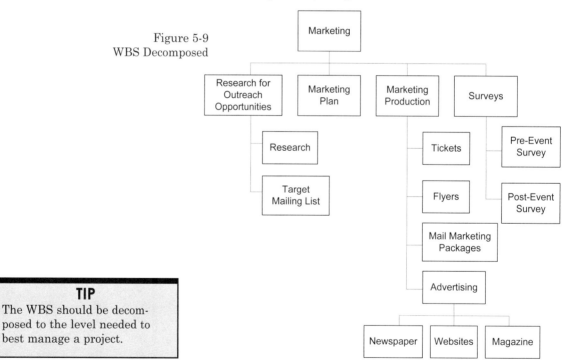

TIP
The WBS should be decomposed to the level needed to best manage a project.

As decomposition progresses, the project team should document the details of each work package in a form called the **WBS dictionary**. A WBS dictionary includes information on each work package that is important for managing the work to be performed. Details include the WBS ID, code of accounts, description of work, responsible organization, schedule milestones, schedule activities, resources required, cost estimates, quality requirements, and acceptance criteria, to name a few. An example WBS dictionary for the newspaper advertising work package might be similar to one in Figure 5-10 below.

WBS ID: 1.3.3.4.1 – Newspaper Advertising

Description: Advertise the Road Race in the local newspaper, both the daily newspaper as well as the weekly entertainment publication. Advertisements in the daily newspaper should begin two months prior to the event and the weekly entertainment publication four months prior to the event.

Responsibility: Marketing – Henry Optimo – Consultant 1

Schedule:
 Milestone: Daily newspaper submission deadlines
  Weekly entertainment newspaper submission deadlines
 Predecessor: Advertising Designs from Marketing Plan
 Successor: Event Date

Schedule Activities:
1. Request submission packages from local newspaper for both daily and weekly publication
2. Create advertisement layout
3. Review layout with sponsor and gain approval
4. Submit advertisement per submission deadlines
5. Review publisher proof and approve
6. Confirm ad published per schedule

Resources Required:
Consultant 1 – Marketing coordinator
Admin 1 – Layout team
Sponsor 1 – Layout review and sign-off

Cost Estimates:
Coordinator: 20 hours estimate
Layout team: 5 hours estimate
Review & sign-off: 4 hours estimate

Quality Requirements:
Date, time, location and cost of event must be clearly communicated, including sign-up instructions.

Acceptance Criteria:
Advertisements are published per the agreed-upon schedule.

Figure 5-10
WBS Dictionary

After discussions with the BEST CONSULTING team, the WBS in Figure 5-11 below was created for the Fundraiser Road Race:

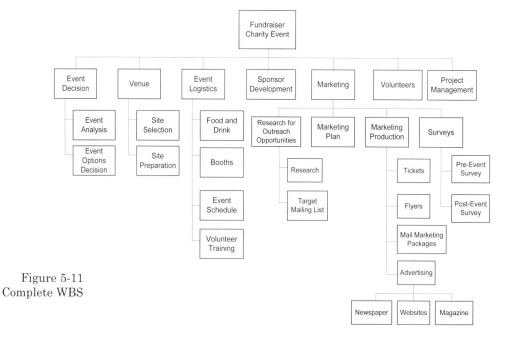

Figure 5-11
Complete WBS

Case Study 5-5

Below is the start of a WBS for the LUV Music website. Perform a decomposition and detail the WBS further based on what you know of the project that has been defined in the project scope statement.

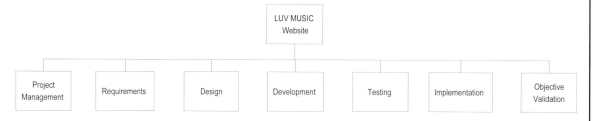

Categorization of the WBS

How you organize your WBS is up to you and your organization. In the example on the previous page, the WBS is organized "functionally" by department. There are other options to categorize your WBS. Your decision should depend on how you want to report performance.

If you want to report progress based on each functional group, then organize your WBS functionally. On the other hand, if you want to report progress based on a sequential process, you may organize your WBS in that way. Note that the case study WBS has been organized sequentially.

VALIDATE SCOPE PROCESS

When projects conclude, it is important to formally determine that all of the deliverables planned for are delivered. The Validate Scope process within the monitoring and controlling process group enables the project team members to confirm that they have successfully delivered the project. The Validate Scope process occurs throughout the project as deliverables (which have been defined in the WBS) are completed.

Note that confirming that deliverables have been accepted usually occurs *after* the Control Quality process, which is concerned with the correctness of these deliverables.

Accepted deliverables and **change requests** are the key outputs of the Validate Scope process.

Inspection

Inspections are called many different things, such as **reviews**, **audits**, **walk-throughs**, **checkpoints**, and **prototypes**. An inspection includes any process of determining if the deliverables have indeed been delivered. Project managers use the WBS to help them determine if all deliverables have been completed successfully.

5

Inspection does not occur at only one point in time. It should be planned for throughout the project life cycle as deliverables are completed. In many cases, inspection is naturally performed as handoffs occur.

For example, if a business analyst is expected to create the **requirements documentation**, and that requirements documentation is an input to the creation of a test plan, then the quality assurance analyst receiving the requirements document will review the document for completeness and its usefulness in the creation of the test plan. If there is a problem, the quality assurance analyst should work with the business analyst to rectify any discrepancy.

Case Study 5-6

For the LUV Music website, identify ten places at which inspection should be used to verify scope and what that process will be to verify completeness of the deliverable.

Accepted Deliverables

As the result of performing inspections throughout the project life cycle, a confirmation of deliverables being accepted should be recorded. It may be recorded within the **project schedule**.

Change Requests

In many cases, an inspection may determine that a deliverable is complete; however there may be something identified that could improve the deliverable. If the issue being identified is considered out-of-scope, a change request may need to be created.

A change request is a formal request to modify the project scope in order to meet a *new* requirement. A sample change request form is shown in Figure 5-12 on the next page.

> **TIP**
> Requests to modify the project for in-scope items do not warrant a change request. These should be addressed as defects and fixed accordingly.

```
┌──────────────────────────────────────────────────┐
│                 CHANGE REQUEST                     │
│                                                    │
│ Project Name:                   Date:              │
│ Project Manager:                Requestor Name:    │
│ Request Decision:  Approve [__] Reject [__]        │
│                                 Date Reviewed:     │
│ Priority:                                          │
│ [__] High – Mission Critical, Urgent   Reason for Priority: _____ │
│ [__] Medium                     _____   │
│ [__] Low                        _____   │
│                                                    │
│ Business Problem:  [to be filled out by Requestor] │
│                                                    │
│                                                    │
│ Business Implications:  [to be filled out by Requestor] │
│                                                    │
│                                                    │
│ Requirements and Options:  [to be filled out by Business Analyst] │
│                                                    │
│                                                    │
│ Current Process Impacts:  [to be filled out by Business Analyst] │
│                                                    │
│                                                    │
│ System Implications:  [to be filled out by Business Analyst & Technical Architect, if applicable] │
│                                                    │
│                                                    │
│ Proposed Changes:  [to be filled out by Business Analyst & Technical Architect, if applicable] │
│                                                    │
│                                                    │
│ Risks:                                             │
│                                                    │
│ Recommendation:                                    │
│                                                    │
│ Approved By:                                       │
│ Business Representative    _____       │
│ Project Manager            _____       │
│ Project Sponsor            _____       │
└──────────────────────────────────────────────────┘
```

Figure 5-12
Change
Request Form

5

CONTROL SCOPE PROCESS

Controlling scope is one of the more difficult aspects of managing projects. Most project managers will agree that a scope statement that has not been thoughtfully written and does not clearly articulate what is included in (as well as excluded from) the project leaves the scope subject to interpretation. This interpretation is one of the primary causes of scope creep.

The outputs of the Control Scope process include **work performance information** and **change requests**.

The "scope creep"

Variance Analysis

The purpose of variance analysis is to determine if variances exist that require corrective or preventive action. As many project managers know, project scope can easily begin to creep if even small variances in scope are overlooked.

If created well, the **charter** (or contract statement of work), the **requirements documentation**, the **scope statement**, the **WBS**, and the **WBS dictionary** are all that are needed to eliminate scope creep.

Once the analysis of a situation is completed, the project manager will be involved in determining whether a formal change request should be created.

In managing scope, **work performance information** is needed to confirm that deliverables have indeed been delivered and validated. The project manager is responsible for ensuring that this information is captured and must assess the magnitude of variation from the original scope baseline. Scope is one aspect of work performance measures and is easily identified as deliverables are completed and are accepted or rejected.

Figure 5-13 below shows a sample work performance information for the Fundraiser Road Race.

Figure 5-13
Work Performance
Information

Class Exercise 5-3

Review the following situations for the Fundraiser Road Race. Determine if each situation is in-scope or out-of-scope and whether any additional work should be performed.

Situation	In-Scope or Out-of-Scope
The project sponsor wishes to add 200 additional mailing addresses to the targeted mailing list. Accommodating this request would be considered . . .	
The market researcher has identified six different marketing opportunities: television, newspaper, magazine, email/websites, billboard, and radio. Newspaper, magazine, and websites are chosen due to BEST CONSULTING's business relationship and the fact that it is willing to support the charity at no cost. Mary Scott has been approached by the local television studio wanting to run a story on the charity event in exchange for 20 tickets to the road race. Accommodating this request would be considered...	
The market researcher has identified six different marketing opportunities: television, newspaper, magazine, email/websites, billboard, and radio. Newspaper, magazine, and websites are chosen due to BEST CONSULTING's business relationship and the fact that it is willing to support the charity at no cost. John Smith's father owns a billboard maintenance company and can help obtain the use of ten billboards the week before the road race for 50% off the cost of a weekly lease. These billboards are on a major highway and could increase visibility by 200%. The use of billboards would be considered . . .	
The marketing plan spells out the requirements for a post-event survey. The current plan is to send out an email survey to all the participants in the event. As development of event tickets commences, a project team member realizes that the team has not planned for collecting the attendee email addresses during sign-up for the event. Adding the email request to all the materials—tickets, flyers, and all aspects of advertising—would be considered . . .	

Change Management

A key responsibility of the project manager is to ensure that an appropriate **change management process** is in place for the project. A change management process is implemented for the sole purpose of reviewing and determining whether or not requested changes are considered within the scope (in-scope) or outside the scope (out-of-scope) of the project. Typically, a change management process includes an entity called a **change control board** (CCB) whose responsibility is to review and either approve or deny change requests.

A CCB should include members of the project team and other key stakeholders, including the customer. The CCB's purpose is to objectively evaluate the requests being submitted and determine any actions to be taken.

A strong **change control process** reduces the risk of scope creep.

PROFESSIONAL RESPONSIBILITY

The scope management knowledge area is about defining what work will be performed and what will not, as well as managing the work to that definition. When considering the four aspects of professional responsibility—responsibility, respect, fairness, and honesty—the project manager must keep certain things in mind at all times:

- Define requirements as thoroughly as possible
- Set correct expectations
- Don't hide the results of the Verify Scope process
- Don't tell a client *no* just because a request has not been detailed out early enough

It is the project manager's responsibility to provide accurate, unbiased information regarding the scope of a project. Even if the news appears bad, in the long run, the client will appreciate honesty over deception.

5

KEY INTERPERSONAL SKILLS FOR SUCCESS

The interpersonal skill highlighted in this chapter is:

Decision Making

Many decisions must be made to finalize requirements and scope. Decision styles that may be used by a project manager include:
- Command
- Consultation
- Consensus
- Coin flip

These styles may be affected by the relationships among stakeholders, including trust and acceptance, or external constraints such as time and quality. There are a number of decision-making models, all of which include some form of these steps:
1. Define the problem
2. Generate ideas about solutions
3. Evaluate solutions
4. Communicate and gain support for the solution selected
5. Conduct a post-implementation evaluation of the result

BE A BETTER PROJECT MANAGER

Exercise: Create a WBS.

Purpose: Involve the entire team in creating the WBS.

Steps:

1. Bring Post-it™ notes and markers to the meeting.
2. Have a general idea of the WBS categories that will be used to measure performance.
3. Let everyone on the team brainstorm all the deliverables on the project. Have them write each deliverable on a Post-it™ and stick it on the wall. There should be no attempt to order any of the stickies at this time.
4. Continue brainstorming until ideas are exhausted.
5. The next day, come back and ask if anyone has thought of any additional deliverables during the break. Add those to the wall.
6. Now show the team the categories against which the project is being measured. Have them group each sticky under the appropriate category. In some cases a category may have been missed, so feel free to add it.
7. Next, within each category, look at the deliverables and determine if there are any additional control accounts needed to group deliverables under the category. If so, add them.
8. Verify that for every control account or subcategory the team feels confident that *all* work necessary for the project has been captured in the WBS.

SAMPLE CAPM EXAM QUESTIONS ON SCOPE MANAGEMENT

1. A key input to the Define Scope process is:

   a) Requirements documents
   b) WBS dictionary
   c) A project scope statement
   d) A risk register

2. The formal and informal policies, procedures, and guidelines that can impact how a project is managed are called:

   a) Communication requirements analysis
   b) Organizational systems
   c) Organizational process assets
   d) Enterprise environmental factors

3. Which of these statements is a good description of a work breakdown structure?

   a) It is a hierarchical decomposition of the total scope
   b) It describes work that has been assigned to organizational units
   c) It defines the chart of accounts
   d) It is created after budgets and schedules have been developed

4. The Validate Scope process outputs include:

   a) Influencing the factors that create project scope changes
   b) Documenting the completed deliverables that have been accepted
   c) Obtaining the stakeholders' formal acceptance of the completed project scope
   d) Monitoring specific project results to determine whether they comply with relevant quality standards

Notes:

5. A WBS _____ will include detailed descriptions of work packages and control accounts.

   a) Planning package
   b) Chart
   c) Dictionary
   d) Decomposition

6. The primary concern of validating scope is to ensure:

   a) The project will be completed on time
   b) The acceptance of the work results
   c) The correctness of the work results
   d) A scope change has occurred

7. The scope management plan should include:

   a) A description of project deliverables, justifications, and objectives
   b) A description of how formal verification will be obtained and how scope changes will be handled
   c) A description of the project's product and all supporting details
   d) A description of how scope changes will be integrated along with corrective actions and lessons learned

8. Uncontrolled changes are often referred to as project _____.

   a) Scope creep
   b) Change requests
   c) Requirements
   d) Defect repair

Notes:

9. What needs to happen once change requests have been approved and those change requests have had an impact on project scope?

   a) The scope baselines should be updated
   b) The change request should be delivered after the initial project
   c) The change request should be reviewed by the change control board
   d) The charter should be reviewed by the change control board

10. The scope statement should include:

   a) The business need that the project has been undertaken to address
   b) Product scope description and project deliverables
   c) Clear responsibility assignments
   d) A summary budget and milestone schedule

11. Which of the following are inputs to the Create WBS process?

   a) Scope management plan and project scope statement
   b) Requirements documentation and decomposition
   c) Enterprise environmental factors and expert judgment
   d) Project scope statement and procurement statement of work

12. Prototypes, benchmarking, and context diagrams are tools and techniques used in the _____ process:

   a) Plan Scope Management
   b) Collect Requirements
   c) Define Scope
   d) Create WBS

Notes:

13. Providing a basis for defining and managing project and product scope is a key benefit of which process?

a) Plan Scope Management
b) Collect Requirements
c) Define Scope
d) Create WBS

14. A major tool and technique used in the Validate Scope process is:

a) Inspection
b) A Pareto chart
c) A histogram
d) Statistical sampling

15. As a project participant on a business process improvement project for a strategic business process, you take over a project that is about 25% complete. There are a lot of questions about what work is included in each of the work packages. The best place you should look is:

a) The scope statement
b) The project charter
c) The activity list
d) The WBS dictionary

Notes:

ANSWERS AND REFERENCES FOR SAMPLE CAPM EXAM QUESTIONS ON SCOPE MANAGEMENT
Section numbers refer to the *PMBOK® Guide*.

1. **A** **Section 5.3.1 - Planning**
   B) is an output of the Create WBS process; C) is an output of the Define Scope process; D) is an output of the Identify Risks process.

2. **C** **Section 2.1.4 - Planning**
   A) summarizes the informational needs of the project stakeholders; B) define whether or not an organization is project-based or non-project based; D) may include items such as organization's culture, human resources, and marketplace conditions.

3. **A** **Section 5.4 - Planning**
   B) is a use of the WBS; C) the chart of accounts is an accounting term; D) the WBS is used to create budgets and schedules.

4. **B** **Section 5.5 - Monitoring and Controlling**
   A) is the purpose of the Control Scope process; C) is the purpose of the Validate Scope process; D) is the purpose of the Control Quality process.

5. **C** **Section 5.4 - Planning**
   A) is less detailed; B) does not show details; D) is a technique of the Create WBS process.

6. **B** **Section 5.5 - Monitoring and Controlling**
   The main output of the Validate Scope process is accepted deliverables. The Validate Scope process differs from the Quality Control process, which is concerned with the correctness of work results.

7. **B** **Section 5.1 - Planning**
   It is easy to remember that the scope management plan is from the planning process group. Choice D is incorrect because it contains outputs from a controlling process. Choices A and C list some of the contents of the scope statement.

8. **A Section 5.6 - Monitoring and Controlling**
   Change is inevitable on projects. It is the responsibility of the project manager to have a process for managing changes and still deliver on the objectives of the project.

9. **A Section 5.6 - Monitoring and Controlling**
   Only approved change requests should be updated in the scope baseline.

10. **B Section 5.3.3.1 - Planning**
    A and D are part of the charter and not the scope statement; C is included in a Responsibility Assignment Matrix (RAM).

11. **A Section 5.4.1 - Planning**
    Decomposition and expert judgment are tools and techniques of the Create WBS process.

12. **B Section 5.2.2 - Planning**
    The Collect Requirements process uses many different techniques to define what is needed.

13. **B Section 5.2 - Planning**
    A) the main benefit of this process is that it defines how scope will be managed; C) the main benefit of this process is that it defines what is included in scope; D) the main benefit of this process is to break the work down into manageable pieces that can be planned and controlled.

14. **A Section 5.5.2 - Monitoring and Controlling**
    B, C, and D are all tools and techniques of the Control Quality process.

15. **D Section 5.4 - Planning**
    The scope statement and project charter do not have information at the work package level. Activities are smaller breakdowns of work packages.

ANSWERS TO CLASS EXERCISES

Class Exercise 5-1: Meeting Facilitation

Situation	Response
During the work brainstorming meeting, Mary Johnson started identifying the work to be done, but whenever other people wanted to identify tasks to be completed, Mary interrupted them and did not allow them to complete their thoughts.	The objective is to allow others to talk and share their ideas. The project manager should address Mary directly, but at a break or after the meeting. Something that could be said to Mary is, "You have great ideas; however, let's make sure we hear from everyone." What you want to avoid is discouraging Mary from participating in future exercises. You are only trying to modify her behavior.
Tom Filips, the Children's Charity public relations manager, identified several other opportunities for BEST CONSULTING to add value to the community which could be used for the charity. Some of his ideas were: 1. Use BEST CONSULTING resources for internal Children's Charity projects. 2. Joint market our companies together by linking to each other's websites from within our respective websites. 3. Plan a golf event, since a major golf pro has a child who was recently diagnosed with cancer.	These ideas should be placed in a parking lot. They appear to all be out-of-scope. Any parking lot items should be validated to confirm that they are truly out-of-scope and then recorded for future reference.
Scott Trivolo, who is a key internal sponsor for this event, sat at the end of the conference room table and didn't contribute any thoughts in the first 90 minutes of the meeting.	At a break, or after the meeting, take Scott aside and try to assess why he is not participating.

Class Exercise 5-2: Deliverables versus Objectives

Example	Deliverable or Objective?
Provide technical documentation for the maintenance of green technology engines.	Deliverable
Improve profitability by 20% through the development of three new green technology products in 2015.	Objective
Create an energy-efficient engine as a new product for an automotive parts organization to increase revenue by 10% in 2016.	Objective
Deliver tents to the Fundraiser Road Race venue in case of rain.	Deliverable
Design marketing materials for the Fundraiser Road Race.	Deliverable
Research marketing websites to determine the most cost-effective way to reach more than 10,000 people in the community.	Objective
Increase awareness of the Children's Charity through the successful execution of the Fundraiser Road Race.	Objective
Achieve an attendance of greater than 1,000 at the Fundraiser Road Race.	Objective

5

Class Exercise 5-3: Variance Analysis

Situation	In-Scope or Out-of-Scope
The project sponsor wishes to add 200 additional mailing addresses to the targeted mailing list. Accommodating this request would be considered . . .	In-scope. On the surface, this request appears to be in-scope and should be accommodated.
The market researcher has identified six different marketing opportunities: television, newspaper, magazine, email/websites, billboard, and radio. Newspaper, magazine, and websites are chosen due to BEST CONSULTING's business relationship and the fact that it is willing to support the charity at no cost. Mary Scott has been approached by the local television studio wanting to run a story on the charity event in exchange for 20 tickets to the road race. Accommodating this request would be considered . . .	Out-of-scope at first glance. However, since the television studio is interested in helping for seemingly no cost, the team may want to consider it. Since all resources, except for the consultant, are volunteers, taking advantage of this opportunity may be considered wise if someone has the time available.
The market researcher has identified six different marketing opportunities: television, newspaper, magazine, email/websites, billboard, and radio. Newspaper, magazine, and websites are chosen due to BEST CONSULTING's business relationship and the fact that it is willing to support the charity at no cost. John Smith's father owns a billboard maintenance company and can help obtain the use of ten billboards the week before the road race for 50% off the cost of a weekly lease. These billboards are on a major highway and could increase visibility by 200%. Use of billboards would be considered . . .	Out-of-scope.
The marketing plan spells out the requirements for a post-event survey. The current plan is to send out an email survey to all the participants in the event. As development of the event tickets commences, a project team member realizes that the team has not planned for collecting the attendee email addresses during sign-up for the event. Adding the email request to all the materials—tickets, flyers, and all aspects of advertising—would be considered . . .	In-scope. It appears to be a critical activity that is needed in order to successfully deliver on the project objectives.

ANSWERS TO THE CASE STUDIES CAN BE FOUND IN THE WAV™ FILES

Web Added Value™

This book has free material available for download from the Web Added Value™ resource center at *www.jrosspub.com.*

TIME

CHAPTER 6 | **TIME**

6

6

TIME MANAGEMENT

The time management knowledge area is focused on the definition and control of the **project schedule**. Time management is linked with **scope management** in that the work to be delivered in scope management must be defined in terms of activities to be performed along a specified timeline. Time management is also concerned with the ability of a project to meet any **schedule objectives** that may have been defined as part of the **project charter** and making any adjustments to the schedule to maintain the project's ability to meet these schedule objectives.

The identification of the appropriate sequence of activities, the estimated effort and duration of activities, and the monitoring and controlling of the completion of the activities are the responsibility of the project manager.

Knowledge Area Processes

Within the time management knowledge area there are seven processes within two process groups.

Planning	Monitoring and Controlling
Plan Schedule Management Define Activities Sequence Activities Estimate Activity Resources Estimate Activity Durations Develop Schedule	Control Schedule

Key Definitions

Activity attributes: similar to a WBS dictionary because they describe the detailed characteristics of each activity. Examples of these attributes are description, predecessor and successor activities, and the person responsible for the activity.

Contingency reserve: budget within the cost baseline or performance measurement baseline that is allocated for identified risks that are accepted and for which contingent or mitigating responses are developed.

Crashing: using alternative strategies for completing project activities (such as using outside resources) for the least additional cost. Crashing should be performed on tasks that are on the critical path. Crashing may result in additional or new critical paths.

Critical path: the path with the longest duration within a project. It is sometimes defined as the path with the least float (usually zero float). A delay of a task on the critical path will delay the completion of the project.

Fast tracking: overlapping or performing in parallel project activities that would normally be done sequentially. Fast tracking may increase rework and project risk.

Float: the amount of time that a schedule activity can be delayed without delaying the end of a project. It is also called slack or total float. Float is calculated using a forward pass (to determine the early-start and early-finish dates of activities) and a backward pass (to determine the late-start and late-finish dates of the activities). Float is calculated as the difference between the late-finish date and early-finish date. The difference between the late-start date and the early-start date always produces the same value for float as the preceding computation.

Free float: the amount of time that a schedule activity can be delayed without delaying the early start date of any successor or violating a schedule constraint.

Grade: a category to differentiate items with the same functional use but not the same characteristics.

Hammock: summary activities used in a high-level project network diagram.

Lag: the amount of time a successor's start or finish is delayed from the predecessor's start or finish. In a finish-to-start example, activity A (the predecessor) must finish before activity B (the successor) can start. If a lag of three days is defined, it means that activity B will be scheduled to start three days after activity A is scheduled to finish.

Lead (negative lag): the amount of time a successor's start or finish can occur before the predecessor's start or finish. In a finish-to-start example, activity A (the predecessor) must finish before activity B (the successor) can start. A lead of three days means that activity B can be scheduled to start three days before activity A is scheduled to finish.

Level of effort: an activity that does not produce definitive end products and is measured by the passage of time.

Logical relationships: there are four logical relationships between a predecessor and a successor: finish-to-start, finish-to-finish, start-to-start, and start-to-finish.

Milestone: a significant point or event in a project, program, or portfolio.

Predecessor: the activity that must happen first when defining dependencies between activities in a network.

Project network schedule calculations: there are three types of project network schedule calculations: a forward pass, a backward pass, and float. A forward pass yields early-start and early-finish dates, a backward pass yields late-start and late-finish dates, and these values are used to calculate total float.

Quality: the degree to which a set of inherent characteristics satisfies the stated or implied needs of the customer. To measure quality successfully, it is necessary to turn implied needs into stated needs via project scope management.

Resource calendar: a calendar that documents the time periods in which project team members can work on a project.

Resource optimization techniques: techniques that are used to adjust the start and finish dates of activities that adjust planned resource use to be equal to or less than resource availability.

Resource leveling: a technique in which start and finish dates are adjusted based on resource constraints with the goal of balancing demand for resources with the available supply.

Schedule activity: an element of work performed during the course of a project. It is a smaller unit of work than a work package and is the result of decomposition in the Define Activities process of project time management. Schedule activities can be further subdivided into tasks.

Scheduling charts: there are four types of scheduling charts: the Gantt chart, the milestone chart, the network diagram, and the time-scaled network diagram.

Standard deviation: the measurement of the variability of the quantity measured, such as time or cost, from the average.

Statistical terms: the primary statistical terms are the project mean, variance, and standard deviation.

Successor: the activity that happens second or subsequently to a previous activity when defining dependencies between activities in a network.

Triangular distribution or **three-point estimating**: takes the average of three estimated durations: the optimistic value, the most likely value, and the pessimistic value. By using the average of three values rather than a single estimate, a more accurate duration estimate for the activity is obtained.

Weighted three-point estimates, or **beta/PERT**:
the program evaluation and review technique (PERT)
uses the three estimated durations of three-point
estimating but weighs the most likely estimate by a factor
of four. This weighted average places more emphasis on
the most likely outcome in calculating the duration of an
activity. Therefore, it produces a curve that is skewed to
one side when possible durations are plotted against their
probability of occurrence.

What-if scenario analysis: the process of evaluating
scenarios in order to predict their effect on project
objectives.

PLAN SCHEDULE MANAGEMENT PROCESS

Plan Schedule Management is the process of establishing
the policies, procedures, and documentation for planning,
developing, managing, executing, and controlling the
project schedule. Planning for schedule management is
important as an input to the overall **project
management plan**.

In this process, the project manager provides guidance and direction about how the project schedule will
be managed for a project. By leveraging information
defined in the **project charter** and the **scope
management plan**, such as the method for defining
formal acceptance, the project manager uses expert judgment, meetings, and analytical techniques to develop the
schedule management plan.

Expert Judgment and Meetings

Expert judgment and meetings are needed to develop the
schedule management plan. Often, projects are similar
in nature, and that experience can be leveraged to define
and/or modify how the schedule will be managed in the
current project. Meetings are often required to review
and finalize the project management plan.

Analytical Techniques

There are many different methodologies, tools, and approaches that project teams can employ in establishing and maintaining schedules. The project team must evaluate these options and determine the best approach for the project and the organization.

The only output of the Plan Schedule Management process is the **schedule management plan**, which is a subsidiary plan to the project management plan. A sample schedule management plan is given in Figure 6-1 below.

Figure 6-1
Schedule
Management Plan

Schedule and Cost Management Plan
Project Name: Fundraiser Road Race
Date: 2/2/14
Any issues identified through normal communication channels must be presented to the Project Manager for review and determination of priority. Once prioritized, they will be incorporated into the overall schedule.
Project Insight will be the tool of choice for maintenance of the project schedule and work-package assignments.
Some items will not be considered a priority, however they will be recorded as such for consideration at a later time. These un-prioritized items will be retained in an excel spreadsheet table and will be reviewed periodically for prioritization.
As progress is reported based on work-package completion, there may be either co-dependencies affected—positively or negatively—and/or availability of resources will become a critical path item. The Project Manager's role will be to continuously monitor those dependencies and either address them directly or work with Sr. management to ensure any risks are minimized.

DEFINE ACTIVITIES PROCESS

Once the project team has defined the scope and a comprehensive list of deliverables is ready, as defined by the **scope baseline**'s WBS, the project team can begin to detail out the activities that need to be performed in order to actually deliver those deliverables.

Defining activities bridges the Create WBS and Develop Schedule processes, which include the identification of major milestones. Each **WBS work package** requires activities to be performed in a specified order to successfully deliver the work package. Defining Activities provides the basis for estimating, scheduling, executing, monitoring, and controlling project work.

The primary outputs of the Define Activities process are an **activity list** and a **milestone list**.

Decomposition

Just as decomposition is used to develop the initial WBS, decomposition is also used to break down the deliverables of the WBS into even smaller components, called **activities**. Activities are defined as the tasks that need to be completed to deliver a deliverable. Activities are the components of the WBS that will be sequenced and scheduled to produce the deliverables.

A test for knowing whether or not the WBS has been detailed to an appropriate level of activities would be to ask yourself the question: "If I perform each of the activities for the work package, will the deliverable be complete?" If the answer to the question is no, then additional activities need to be defined.

For the Fundraiser Road Race project, Figure 6-2 on the following pages provides a list of activities that have been defined.

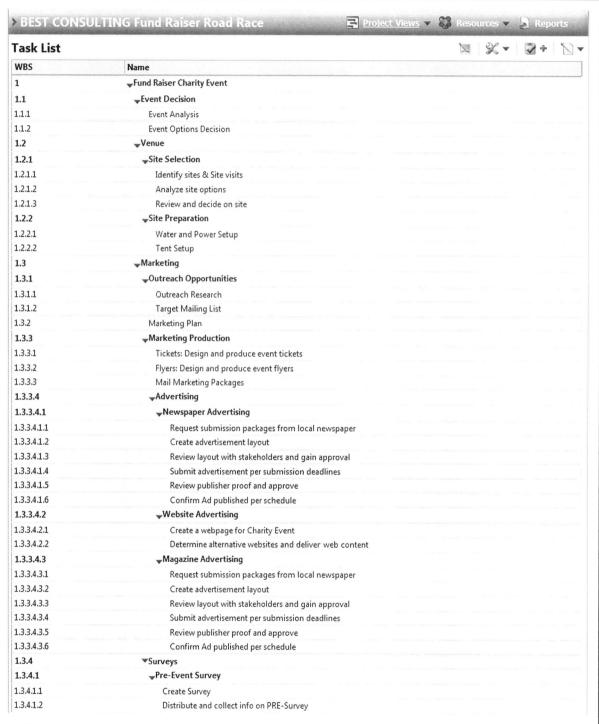

Figure 6-2
List of Activities

1.3.4.2	▼Post-Event Survey
1.3.4.2.1	Create Survey
1.3.4.2.2	Distribute and Analyze POST-survey results
1.4	▼Event Logistics
1.4.1	Food and Drink
1.4.2	▼Booths & Entertainment
1.4.2.1	Booth & entertainment site map
1.4.2.2	Assign sponsors to booths
1.4.2.3	Determine schedule of booth events and entertainment
1.4.2.4	Setup and takedown of booths and stage
1.4.3	▼Event Schedule
1.4.3.1	Develop event schedule
1.4.3.2	Assign volunteers to support each event
1.4.4	Volunteer Training: Develop and deliver training for all event day volunteers
1.5	Sponsor Development
1.6	Volunteers
1.7	Project Management

Milestone List

Milestones are significant points or events in a project. They are typical dates that do not have any duration. They can be mandatory, such as those required by contract, or optional, based on the desires of the client. In Figure 6-3 below is the Fundraiser Road Race milestone list. These milestones are subsets of the WBS or activity list. These activities have more significance to the project and should be highlighted.

Milestone	Milestone Date	Mandatory
Finalize Event Decision	Within 1 month of project start	Yes
Site Selection	Within 2 months of Event Decision	No
Newspaper Advertising Deadline	TBD	Yes
Magazine Advertising Deadline	TBD	Yes
Hold Event	Within 1 year of project start and no later than 12/31/14	Yes

Figure 6-3
Milestones

Case Study 6-1

Using your WBS for the LUV Music website, create an activity list and milestone list. Use decomposition to define activities and the templates below and on the next page for your results.

WBS ID	Deliverable	Activity	Milestone (Y/N)

Milestone	Milestone Date	Mandatory

Rolling Wave Planning

As stated in the *PMBOK® Guide*, rolling wave planning is a form of **progressive elaboration** that is used when the work in the near term is planned in detail and any future work is planned only at a high level and is detailed out at a future time.

This tool and technique is often used when a larger project is broken up into various phases of delivery. For example, when a company is looking to create a brand new product, the first phase of the project may be only to perform a market analysis on what kind of product may be worth pursuing. The project may consist of several phases, such as market analysis, product design, product development, production development, and product support. As each phase of the project comes to a close, enough information should be available for the project team to start detailing out the deliverables and activities of the subsequent phase.

Expert Judgment

Project team members with experience and skill in project scope statements, WBS, and project schedules provide expertise in defining activities. Expertise with cost, quality, scope, and software tools can also add value to continuous scheduling reviews and revisions.

SEQUENCE ACTIVITIES PROCESS

Knowing what deliverables are necessary to deliver the scope of the project and the activities that need to be performed to produce the deliverables does not ensure that the project will be a success. Knowing the sequence of the delivery of those activities and performing them in a logical order does ensure that efforts are efficiently applied to the activities.

Sequencing activities logically based on defined predecessors and successors is called the **precedence diagramming method**, and doing so delivers a **project schedule network diagram** to the project team. The schedule network diagram differs from the WBS and the activity list because it allows the project team to see the interdependencies of each activity and it gives the team a sense of the general flow of the project.

Precedence Diagramming Method (PDM)

The precedence diagramming method utilizes the list of activities produced in the Define Activities process. The purpose here is to identify which activities need to be performed and in what order. Although four types of **logical relationships**, which are also called dependencies, are defined within the *PMBOK® Guide*, planning a project based purely on the most common type of relationship, the **finish-to-start** relationship, will result in a schedule that is conservative or the longest in duration. Once the initial schedule is defined, the project manager and project team can utilize the other types of dependencies (**finish-to-finish**, **start-to-start**, or **start-to-finish**) to adjust the schedule if the conservative schedule is not acceptable.

TIP

Ideally, a project has one start and one finish.

TIP

The precedence diagram does not have any relationship to the control accounts defined as part of the Create WBS process.

Class Exercise 6-1

In scenarios below, which kind of logical relationship, or dependency, is being described?

Scenario	Logical Relationship/ Dependency
The training manual can be started about one week after testing of the new system has begun.	
All of the testing cycles need to be completed before the training documentation can be finalized and signed off on.	
The volunteers need to be trained before the team can start setting up all the booths for the event.	
The street sweepers cannot start cleaning the streets until all the cars parked on the street have been moved.	
The golf course superintendent turns on the sprinklers after each hole is fertilized.	

To demonstrate, the chart in Figure 6-4 below is an example of a sample project using finish-to-start relationships based on knowing only the predecessors. An activity with no predecessor is the first activity in the project.

Figure 6-4
Finish-to-Start
Relationships

WBS ID	Activity Description	Predecessor
1.1	Activity A	---
1.2	Activity B	1.1
1.3	Activity C	1.2
2.1	Activity D	1.2
2.2	Activity E	1.1
3.1	Activity F	2.2, 1.3
4.1	Activity G	2.1
4.2	Activity H	4.1
4.3	Activity I	1.1
4.4	Activity J	4.1, 4.3
5.0	Activity K	4.4, 3.1

The activities are then laid out in a left-to-right sequence based on the predecessors defined. A **precedence diagram** for our sample would look like the one in Figure 6-5 below. The benefit of this view is a better understanding of the order in which activities need to be performed.

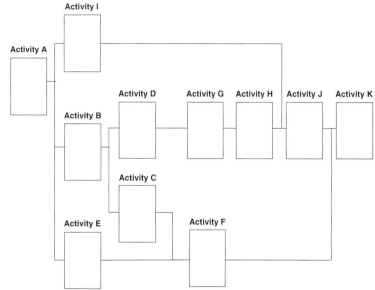

Figure 6-5
Precedence
Diagram

Class Exercise 6-2

For the Fundraiser Road Race, create a precedence diagram for the project using the predecessors defined for each activity on the following pages.

BEST CONSULTING Fund Raiser Road Race

Project Views ▾   Resources ▾   Reports

Task List

WBS	Name	Predecessors
1	▾Fund Raiser Charity Event	
1.1	▾Event Decision	
1.1.1	Event Analysis	
1.1.2	Event Options Decision	Event Analysis
1.2	▾Venue	
1.2.1	▾Site Selection	
1.2.1.1	Identify sites & Site visits	Event Options Decision
1.2.1.2	Analyze site options	Identify sites & Site visits
1.2.1.3	Review and decide on site	Analyze site options
1.2.2	▾Site Preparation	
1.2.2.1	Water and Power Setup	Review and decide on site
1.2.2.2	Tent Setup	Review and decide on site , Identify sites & Site visits
1.3	▾Marketing	
1.3.1	▾Outreach Opportunities	
1.3.1.1	Outreach Research	Event Options Decision
1.3.1.2	Target Mailing List	Sponsor Development , Event Analysis
1.3.2	Marketing Plan	Event Options Decision
1.3.3	▾Marketing Production	
1.3.3.1	Tickets: Design and produce event tickets	Marketing Plan
1.3.3.2	Flyers: Design and produce event flyers	Marketing Plan
1.3.3.3	Mail Marketing Packages	Target Mailing List , Tickets: Design and produce event tickets , Flyers: Design and produce event flyers
1.3.3.4	▾Advertising	
1.3.3.4.1	▾Newspaper Advertising	
1.3.3.4.1.1	Request submission packages from local newspaper	Marketing Plan
1.3.3.4.1.2	Create advertisement layout	Request submission packages from local newspaper
1.3.3.4.1.3	Review layout with stakeholders and gain approval	Create advertisement layout
1.3.3.4.1.4	Submit advertisement per submission deadlines	Review layout with stakeholders and gain approval
1.3.3.4.1.5	Review publisher proof and approve	Submit advertisement per submission deadlines
1.3.3.4.1.6	Confirm Ad published per schedule	Review publisher proof and approve +10d
1.3.3.4.2	▾Website Advertising	
1.3.3.4.2.1	Create a webpage for Charity Event	Marketing Plan
1.3.3.4.2.2	Determine alternative websites and deliver web content	Create a webpage for Charity Event , Outreach Research
1.3.3.4.3	▾Magazine Advertising	
1.3.3.4.3.1	Request submission packages from local newspaper	Marketing Plan
1.3.3.4.3.2	Create advertisement layout	Request submission packages from local newspaper
1.3.3.4.3.3	Review layout with stakeholders and gain approval	Create advertisement layout
1.3.3.4.3.4	Submit advertisement per submission deadlines	Review layout with stakeholders and gain approval
1.3.3.4.3.5	Review publisher proof and approve	Submit advertisement per submission deadlines
1.3.3.4.3.6	Confirm Ad published per schedule	Review publisher proof and approve

6

1.3.4	Surveys	
1.3.4.1	Pre-Event Survey	
1.3.4.1.1	Create Survey	Marketing Plan
1.3.4.1.2	Distribute and collect info on PRE-Survey	Create Survey
1.3.4.2	Post-Event Survey	
1.3.4.2.1	Create Survey	Develop event schedule
1.3.4.2.2	Distribute and Analyze POST-survey results	Create Survey , Project Management [FF], Setup and takedown of booths and stage
1.4	Event Logistics	
1.4.1	Food and Drink	Review and decide on site
1.4.2	Booths & Entertainment	
1.4.2.1	Booth & entertainment site map	Review and decide on site
1.4.2.2	Assign sponsors to booths	Booth & entertainment site map , Sponsor Development
1.4.2.3	Determine schedule of booth events and entertainment	Water and Power Setup , Assign sponsors to booths
1.4.2.4	Setup and takedown of booths and stage	Food and Drink , Volunteer Training: Develop and deliver training for all event day volunteers , Tent Setup
1.4.3	Event Schedule	
1.4.3.1	Develop event schedule	Determine schedule of booth events and entertainment , Determine alternative websites and deliver web content Confirm Ad published per schedule , Mail Marketing Packages , Confirm Ad published per schedule
1.4.3.2	Assign volunteers to support each event	Volunteers , Develop event schedule
1.4.4	Volunteer Training: Develop and deliver training for all event day volunteers	Assign volunteers to support each event
1.5	Sponsor Development	Event Options Decision
1.6	Volunteers	Event Analysis
1.7	Project Management	Event Analysis
		Add Predecessors

Case Study 6-2

For the LUV Music website, use the template on the following page to identify the predecessors for each activity. Create a precedence diagram for the project.

Note: at this time, do not fill in the dependency, duration, or cost columns.

WBS ID/ Deliverable	Activity Name	Predecessor	Dependency	Duration	Cost

6

6

Dependency Determination

The logical relationships between activities are also called dependencies because they indicate how each activity may or may not be dependent upon each other. In addition, there are four other dependencies that need to be understood before any project can be scheduled:
- Mandatory
- Discretionary
- Internal
- External

For each activity, the project team must determine the type of dependency to be used. Knowing the type of dependency will help determine for the team how team members can affect the overall **project schedule**.

Knowing which dependencies are **mandatory dependencies** is important in that these dependencies cannot be changed. The project manager may be able to affect the duration of the activities that are dependent, but will not be able to affect the relationship itself. An example of a mandatory dependency would be that the foundation of a home must be complete before framing can begin.

Discretionary dependencies are those the project team has the most control over. Activities with discretionary dependencies, by definition, mean that there are other options for accomplishing these activities in a variety of orders with a variety of different resources. Most activities within a project tend to be discretionary. For example, installing electrical wiring on the house could be started at various points in time. Wiring is not dependent upon the completion of the framing.

The dependencies typically within the project team's control are called **internal dependencies**. They are relationships between defined project activities. An internal dependency may be where only one plumber is available on the construction site. Therefore, each bathroom can only be completed in sequence, unless the company chooses to hire another plumber.

External dependencies are those outside of the project team's control. They are often project activities that have a relationship with non-project activities. External activities could be considered a risk to the project, and if an external dependency is driving the project schedule, the project manager will have to address those kinds of dependencies differently. An example of an external dependency would be any subcontractors used that are not managed by the project team itself.

Class Exercise 6-3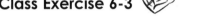

In reviewing the assumptions in the following table, identify which type of dependency each is:

Scenario	Dependency
The training manual can be started about one week after testing of the new system has begun.	
All of the testing cycles need to be completed before the training documentation can be finalized and signed off on.	
The volunteers need to be trained before the team can start setting up all the booths for the event.	
The street sweepers cannot start cleaning the streets until all the cars parked on the street have been moved.	
The golf course superintendent turns on the sprinklers after each hole is fertilized.	
The new product line needs to be available for the spring product launch conference in order to be considered a viable product in the marketplace.	
According to the contract, a go/no-go decision is needed by June 1, 2014.	

Note: one scenario could encompass two different dependencies, one being either discretionary or mandatory and the other being internal or external.

Class Exercise 6-4

Referring to the precedence diagram example completed earlier, do the types of dependencies listed below change anything? Document your thoughts.

_____

_____

_____

_____

_____

_____

_____

WBS ID	Activity Description	Predecessor	Dependency
1.1	Activity A	---	N/A
1.2	Activity B	1.1	Mandatory
1.3	Activity C	1.2	Discretionary
2.1	Activity D	1.2	Discretionary
2.2	Activity E	1.1	Discretionary
3.1	Activity F	2.2, 1.3	Discretionary
4.1	Activity G	2.1	Mandatory
4.2	Activity H	4.1	Discretionary
4.3	Activity I	1.1	Discretionary
4.4	Activity J	4.1, 4.3	Discretionary
5.0	Activity K	4.4, 3.1	External

Case Study 6-3

For the LUV Music project, identify which activities for the project will be considered mandatory, discretionary, internal, or external.

Lags and Leads

Lags and leads are used for two distinct purposes. A lag is used when there is a waiting period between a predecessor and a successor activity. For example, when laying concrete, there is a waiting period between pouring and completion before the next activity can be performed. If the concrete needs to cure for three days before any of the frame of the building can be started, the lag would be depicted as in Figure 6-6 below.

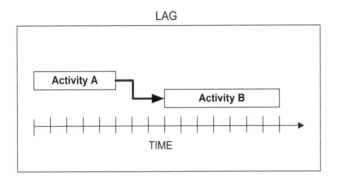

Figure 6-6
Lag

6

A lead is used for a different purpose. Leads are typically used when some acceleration is needed on the project schedule and the project manager is looking for ways to reduce the project schedule without affecting the duration of an activity. For example, when developing software, ideally all training materials should be developed *after* the completion of the software testing in a finish-to-start relationship. To speed up the process, draft training materials *could* be developed before the completion of the software testing. This lead would be depicted as in Figure 6-7 on the following page.

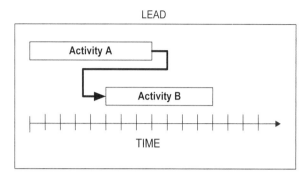

Figure 6-7
Lead

Leads are often used, for example, in building a road. When roads are built, construction companies do not wait for all of the land to be cleared before they start paving the roads. The clearing of the land can happen before paving and can be going on in an overlapping manner.

Class Exercise 6-5

Identify in the chart below if there are any places in the Fundraiser Road Race example in which a lead could be used or a lag should exist?

WBS ID	Activity Name	Lead or Lag	Explanation

Case Study 6-4

Review the LUV Music website project and modify any activities that may require a lag. Also look to see if there may be a way to reduce the overall schedule by two days by implementing a lead.

Updating the WBS Dictionary

At the end of the Sequence Activities process, the project manager should ensure that the WBS dictionary is updated with any modifications through this process. In Figure 6-8 below is an example of a WBS ID for the newspaper advertising activity of the Fundraiser Road Race, a lag of two weeks is needed in order to allow for actual publishing of the newspaper ad.

> **TIP**
> Other project documents that may be updated in the Sequence Activities process include, but are not limited to:
> • Activity lists
> • Activity attributes
> • Milestone lists
> • Risk register

6

WBS ID: 1.3.3.4.1 – Newspaper Advertising
Description: Advertise the Road Race in the local newspaper, both the daily newspaper as well as the weekly entertainment publication. Advertisements in the daily newspaper should begin two months prior to the event and the weekly entertainment publication four months prior to the event.

Responsibility: Marketing – Henry Optimo – Consultant 1

Schedule:
    Milestone: Daily newspaper submission deadlines
                Weekly entertainment newspaper submission deadlines
    Predecessor: Advertising Designs from Marketing Plan
    Successor: Event Date
Schedule Activities:
    1. Request submission packages from local newspaper for both daily and weekly publication
    2. Create advertisement layout
    3. Review layout with sponsor and gain approval
    4. Submit advertisement per submission deadlines
    5. Review publisher proof and approve
    6. Confirm ad published per schedule (Lag of 2 weeks from Review)

Resources Required:
Consultant 1 – Marketing coordinator
Admin 1 – Layout team
Sponsor 1 – Layout review and sign-off

Cost Estimates:
Coordinator (Consultant 1): 20 hours effort
Layout team (Admin): 5 hours effort
Review & sign-off: 4 hours effort

Quality Requirements:
Date, time, location and cost of event must be clearly communicated, including sign-up instructions.

Acceptance Criteria:
Advertisements are published per the agreed-upon schedule.

Figure 6-8
Updated WBS ID

ESTIMATE ACTIVITY RESOURCES PROCESS

The Estimate Activity Resources process includes the effort of estimating the type and quantity of resources that will be needed for the activities. Understanding which activities need to be performed and understanding which resources are available for a project (as indicated by the **resource calendars**) are both critical to determining the resources for each activity. Resources can be people, equipment, or materials.

In addition, most project managers know that resources are usually not plentiful in their organization, and in many cases a project may require that resources outside the organization be utilized. Project managers must understand the policies and procedures regarding staffing within their organization. Some of these policies and procedures could become risks for a project.

The process of estimating activity resources requires that the project manager and project team perform an analysis to determine the resources that are necessary. We will review two commonly used tools and techniques: **alternatives analysis** and **bottom-up estimating**.

The primary outputs of the Estimate Activity Resources process are the actual activity resource requirement, a resource breakdown structure, and updated **project documents** with the resources needed for each work package.

Alternatives Analysis

Alternatives analysis is employed when multiple options exist for utilizing resources and may require the use of **expert judgment**. Not all resources are created equal. There are varying levels of skill and quality that a project team needs to assess.

When an activity is critical to the project schedule, it may be beneficial for the project manager to assign a more experienced resource to that activity to ensure that the activity is performed correctly. Alternatively, if the activity is not on the **critical path**, the activity could be assigned to a less experienced resource and it may not impact the project schedule if the resource takes a little longer than expected to complete activities.

Alternatives analysis also applies to estimating material needs and schedules. Taking into consideration delivery schedules, a project manager may modify the sequence of activities to accommodate multiple deliveries of materials. When taking into consideration the quality and grade of materials (see Chapter 8 on quality management), the project manager may modify the expected output of each activity based on the expected defect rate.

> **TIP**
>
> Many commercial entities, professional societies, and educational institutes routinely publish production rates, unit costs, labor rates, material costs, and equipment costs for many countries and geographic locations.

For our Fundraiser Road Race, four volunteers have been identified as the primary coordinators of the event, along with the consultant that was hired. The resource calendar in Figure 6-9 below gives the availability of resources over the next 12 months.

BEST CONSULTING Fund Raiser Road Race   Project Views ▼   Resources ▼   Reports

Resource Directory

First Name	Last Name	Resource Type/Role Assigned	Other Notes
Volunteer	1	Project Management	Available 5 hours per week. Unavailable July 15 - 21 for vacation.
Volunteer	2	Sponsor Coordination	Available 2 hours per week. On vacation the month of June.
Volunteer	4	Event Logistics	Available 10 hours per week. Not available to work on project until April 15th.
Consultant	1	Marketing	Can start on January 1, 2014. Available for a maximum of 20 hours per week.
Admin	1	Administration	Available only 5 hours per week. Can start on 1/1/14 and work through the duration of the project.
Sponsor	1	Administration	Available as needed. On vacation month of July.
Volunteer	3	Volunteer Coordination	Available 8 hours per week. Not available Nov 6 - 10 and December 15 - 25.

Figure 6-9
Resource
Calendar

Class Exercise 6-6

Based on the resource calendar above, the following assignments have been made (on the next two pages) and added to the activity list. Do you see any issues with the assignments and alternatives?

_____
_____
_____
_____
_____
_____
_____

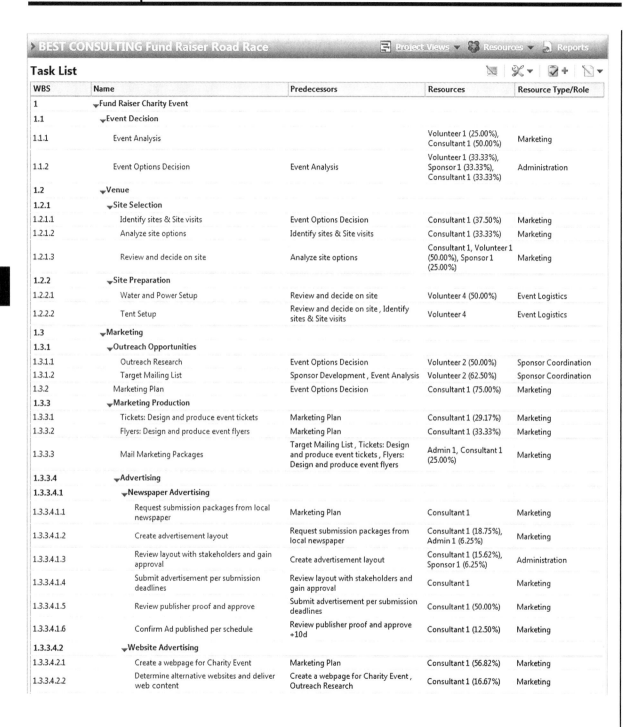

Task List

WBS	Name	Predecessors	Resources	Resource Type/Role
1	Fund Raiser Charity Event			
1.1	Event Decision			
1.1.1	Event Analysis		Volunteer 1 (25.00%), Consultant 1 (50.00%)	Marketing
1.1.2	Event Options Decision	Event Analysis	Volunteer 1 (33.33%), Sponsor 1 (33.33%), Consultant 1 (33.33%)	Administration
1.2	Venue			
1.2.1	Site Selection			
1.2.1.1	Identify sites & Site visits	Event Options Decision	Consultant 1 (37.50%)	Marketing
1.2.1.2	Analyze site options	Identify sites & Site visits	Consultant 1 (33.33%)	Marketing
1.2.1.3	Review and decide on site	Analyze site options	Consultant 1, Volunteer 1 (50.00%), Sponsor 1 (25.00%)	Marketing
1.2.2	Site Preparation			
1.2.2.1	Water and Power Setup	Review and decide on site	Volunteer 4 (50.00%)	Event Logistics
1.2.2.2	Tent Setup	Review and decide on site , Identify sites & Site visits	Volunteer 4	Event Logistics
1.3	Marketing			
1.3.1	Outreach Opportunities			
1.3.1.1	Outreach Research	Event Options Decision	Volunteer 2 (50.00%)	Sponsor Coordination
1.3.1.2	Target Mailing List	Sponsor Development , Event Analysis	Volunteer 2 (62.50%)	Sponsor Coordination
1.3.2	Marketing Plan	Event Options Decision	Consultant 1 (75.00%)	Marketing
1.3.3	Marketing Production			
1.3.3.1	Tickets: Design and produce event tickets	Marketing Plan	Consultant 1 (29.17%)	Marketing
1.3.3.2	Flyers: Design and produce event flyers	Marketing Plan	Consultant 1 (33.33%)	Marketing
1.3.3.3	Mail Marketing Packages	Target Mailing List , Tickets: Design and produce event tickets , Flyers: Design and produce event flyers	Admin 1, Consultant 1 (25.00%)	Marketing
1.3.3.4	Advertising			
1.3.3.4.1	Newspaper Advertising			
1.3.3.4.1.1	Request submission packages from local newspaper	Marketing Plan	Consultant 1	Marketing
1.3.3.4.1.2	Create advertisement layout	Request submission packages from local newspaper	Consultant 1 (18.75%), Admin 1 (6.25%)	Marketing
1.3.3.4.1.3	Review layout with stakeholders and gain approval	Create advertisement layout	Consultant 1 (15.62%), Sponsor 1 (6.25%)	Administration
1.3.3.4.1.4	Submit advertisement per submission deadlines	Review layout with stakeholders and gain approval	Consultant 1	Marketing
1.3.3.4.1.5	Review publisher proof and approve	Submit advertisement per submission deadlines	Consultant 1 (50.00%)	Marketing
1.3.3.4.1.6	Confirm Ad published per schedule	Review publisher proof and approve +10d	Consultant 1 (12.50%)	Marketing
1.3.3.4.2	Website Advertising			
1.3.3.4.2.1	Create a webpage for Charity Event	Marketing Plan	Consultant 1 (56.82%)	Marketing
1.3.3.4.2.2	Determine alternative websites and deliver web content	Create a webpage for Charity Event , Outreach Research	Consultant 1 (16.67%)	Marketing

1.3.3.4.3	▼Magazine Advertising			
1.3.3.4.3.1	Request submission packages from local newspaper	Marketing Plan	Consultant 1 (50.00%)	Marketing
1.3.3.4.3.2	Create advertisement layout	Request submission packages from local newspaper	Consultant 1 (25.00%)	Marketing
1.3.3.4.3.3	Review layout with stakeholders and gain approval	Create advertisement layout	Consultant 1 (15.62%), Sponsor 1 (6.25%)	Administration
1.3.3.4.3.4	Submit advertisement per submission deadlines	Review layout with stakeholders and gain approval	Consultant 1	Marketing
1.3.3.4.3.5	Review publisher proof and approve	Submit advertisement per submission deadlines	Consultant 1 (50.00%)	Marketing
1.3.3.4.3.6	Confirm Ad published per schedule	Review publisher proof and approve	Consultant 1 (12.50%)	Marketing
1.3.4	▼Surveys			
1.3.4.1	▼Pre-Event Survey			
1.3.4.1.1	Create Survey	Marketing Plan	Consultant 1 (33.33%)	Marketing
1.3.4.1.2	Distribute and collect info on PRE-Survey	Create Survey	Volunteer 1 (50.00%)	Project Management
1.3.4.2	▼Post-Event Survey			
1.3.4.2.1	Create Survey	Develop event schedule	Consultant 1 (33.33%)	Marketing
1.3.4.2.2	Distribute and Analyze POST-survey results	Create Survey , Project Management [FF], Setup and takedown of booths and stage	Volunteer 1 (38.46%)	Project Management
1.4	▼Event Logistics			
1.4.1	Food and Drink	Review and decide on site	Volunteer 4 (312.50%)	Event Logistics
1.4.2	▼Booths & Entertainment			
1.4.2.1	Booth & entertainment site map	Review and decide on site	Volunteer 4	Event Logistics
1.4.2.2	Assign sponsors to booths	Booth & entertainment site map , Sponsor Development	Volunteer 4	Event Logistics
1.4.2.3	Determine schedule of booth events and entertainment	Water and Power Setup , Assign sponsors to booths	Volunteer 4 (33.33%)	Event Logistics
1.4.2.4	Setup and takedown of booths and stage	Food and Drink , Volunteer Training: Develop and deliver training for all event day volunteers , Tent Setup	Volunteer 4	Event Logistics
1.4.3	▼Event Schedule			
1.4.3.1	Develop event schedule	Determine schedule of booth events and entertainment , Determine alternative websites and deliver web content , Confirm Ad published per schedule , Mail Marketing Packages , Confirm Ad published per schedule	Volunteer 4 (25.00%)	Event Logistics
1.4.3.2	Assign volunteers to support each event	Volunteers , Develop event schedule	Volunteer 4 (25.00%)	Event Logistics
1.4.4	Volunteer Training: Develop and deliver training for all event day volunteers	Assign volunteers to support each event	Volunteer 3	Volunteer Coordination
1.5	Sponsor Development	Event Options Decision	Volunteer 2 (27.78%)	Sponsor Coordination
1.6	Volunteers	Event Analysis	Volunteer 3 (25.00%)	Volunteer Coordination
1.7	Project Management	Event Analysis	Volunteer 1 (20.83%)	Project Management
		Add Predecessors	Edit Resources	▾

6

Case Study 6-5

Use the resource calendar template below to assign the resources for the LUV Music project to each activity.

Resource	Specialty	Available	Not Available

Bottom-Up Estimating

Bottom-up estimating is used when an activity cannot be estimated with a reasonable degree of certainty. Perhaps the organization doesn't have the expertise, or it may plan on utilizing a vendor for that activity. The project team could still attempt to detail out the type of activities that would be performed without any understanding of sequence. Bottom-up estimating is better than just taking a wild guess since there is a level of thought about the details of the activity.

For example, for the Fundraiser Road Race, the print marketing materials activity is going to be outsourced to XYZ vendor. The following activities are anticipated:
1. Select a printing firm
2. Deliver drafts to printing firm
3. Layout
4. Review and sign-off
5. Machine setup
6. Run proof materials
7. Review and sign-off of proof
8. Print
9. Deliver

A time and resource estimate is created similar to the one in Figure 6-10 below based on our current understanding of the effort. These estimates will be confirmed and refined once an actual vendor is selected.

Task	Resource	Effort
Select printing firm	Consultant, Sponsor	2.0 days
Deliver drafts to printing firm	Consultant	0.5 days
Layout	Printer	1.5 days
Review and sign-off	Printer, Consultant	1 day
Machine setup	Printer	0.25 days
Run proof materials	Printer	0.5 days
Review and sign-off of proof	Printer, Sponsor, Consultant	0.5 days
Print	Printer	1 day
Deliver	Printer	0.25 days
TOTAL		**7.5 days**

Figure 6-10
Time and Resource Estimate

Class Exercise 6-7

You are the project manager on a new product development project, but your organization hasn't performed any product market analysis in the past. You anticipate hiring a consultant organization for this analysis. Use bottom-up estimating to think of the types of activities that may be performed in a product market analysis for either an internal or external solution in the table below:

Activity for Product Market Analysis-Internal	Activity for Product Market Analysis-External

Expert Judgment

Experience in resource-related inputs to a process can help in planning for a project. Find individuals who may have expertise in human resource management or organizational operations. Expert judgment can provide organization-specific productivity data or recommend activity durations from prior similar projects.

Resource Breakdown Structure

Once a determination has been made as to the type of resources that are needed for a project, a resource breakdown structure can be developed. The resource breakdown structure is useful for organizing and reporting project schedule data with resource utilization information.

The resource breakdown structure can identify various categories such as labor, material, equipment, and supplies, and may specify the particular skill or grade required.

Figure 6-11 below shows a resource breakdown structure for the Fundraiser Road Race.

6

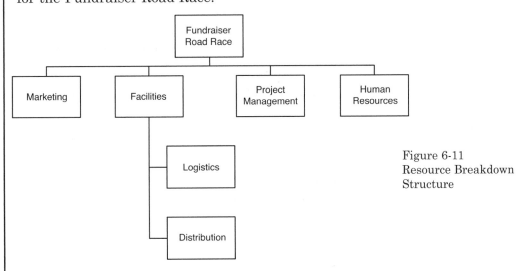

Figure 6-11
Resource Breakdown
Structure

ESTIMATE ACTIVITY DURATIONS PROCESS

As you can probably see, there are really four components of developing a schedule: defining the activities, sequencing the activities, estimating the activity resources, and estimating the activity durations. These four components are, in reality, performed in concert with one another in order to get a full picture of the work that will need to be performed for a project.

6

The Estimate Activity Durations process includes the activities associated with determining how long a specific activity will take to be completed. The information provided in the other three processes is important in the determination of activity durations. Knowing the activity and the specific work to be completed as well as any dependencies on that work helps the project manager determine which resources are needed to successfully complete the project. Understanding the skills of the resources and the number of resources available to work on the activity plays into determining the duration of work to be performed.

In order to identify duration, you must understand the difference between **effort** and **duration** and why utilizing effort in the scheduling process is important.

Effort is the amount of time it would take for a worker to complete the work if all the worker did was work on the activity at hand. Effort does consider the skillset of the worker. An experienced worker should be able to complete an activity with less effort than someone who has less experience.

Duration takes into consideration the worker's availability. Availability is driven by the time the worker may be working on other activities and the worker's down time. Duration strives to find the actual delivery date of an activity.

When scheduling, duration is a more accurate measure. It provides a more realistic estimate of the actual **elapsed time** to deliver a specific activity, as shown in Figure 6-12 below.

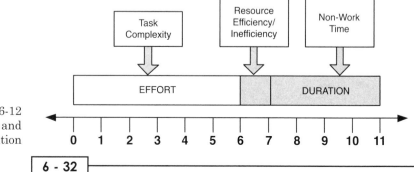

Figure 6-12
Effort and
Duration

The best estimates come from the actual resource performing the work. Early in a project, the project team will usually not have all resources assigned; therefore, it is necessary to use estimating techniques such as **analogous estimating**, **parametric estimating**, or **three-point estimating**.

Analogous Estimates

An analogous estimate utilizes past experience in determining an estimate for a future project activity. In our Fundraiser Road Race, the consultant who was hired determined that it should take two months to develop and implement a marketing campaign for the event. His experience, or **expert judgment**, in assisting organizations in charity events of similar size and goals was used as the benchmark.

Class Exercise 6-8

You are a wedding planner and are trying to estimate the cost for a new client. Most weddings you manage are around 200 people, and the costs tend to run about $40,000 for an average quality wedding. A 25% premium is usually needed if the wedding party wants you to hold the event at a luxury resort. Typically, 50% of the guests will stay at the resort for an extra $300 per guest.

If your client is looking at 250 guests at a luxury resort, what would your cost estimate be using analogous estimating? (Show your work.)

_____
_____
_____
_____
_____
_____
_____
_____
_____
_____
_____
_____

Parametric Estimates

Parametric estimates are more accurate, in general, than analogous estimates. Parametric estimates use data that are more statistically sound. For example, the consultant on the Fundraiser Road Race had historical statistics on the relationship between marketing frequency and participation, as described in Figure 6-13 below.

Figure 6-13
Historical Statistics

Charity Event Attendance with Advertising			
	5 months before event	4 months before event	3 months before event
1 advertisement per month	9,200	8,000	3,800
2 advertisements per month	9,800	8,500	4,200
3 advertisements per month	10,200	9,000	4,800
4 advertisements per month	10,400	9,200	5,000

By understanding this information, the project manager can determine how much time should be spent on advertising the Fundraiser Road Race. Based on the chart above, the Fundraiser Road Race team should plan for a minimum of three advertisements per month.

Class Exercise 6-9

Given the following information regarding costs of building homes in two states, estimate the cost of building a 1,500-square-foot home in California on a ¼-acre lot, including annual taxes, using parametric estimating.

	California	Florida
Building	$300/square foot	$150/square foot
Property	$500,000 per acre	$100,000 per acre
Tax	2% of homesite*	3% of homesite*

*Homesite includes cost of home and land

Three-Point Estimates

Project managers often find it difficult to get team members to provide estimates. When asking for an estimate, you'll find that estimates are based on a set of knowledge and experience that is familiar to that individual. The project manager, when asking the question, is looking for an estimate of what it may typically take, whether the person being questioned will be the performer of the task or not.

One way to improve an estimate when the individual estimator has experience is to use a weighted average. One weighting technique is called beta/PERT, and the formula is:

Estimate = (Optimistic + 4 x Most Likely + Pessimistic) / 6

When an individual is asked to estimate based on what's optimistic, most likely, and pessimistic, the individual can consider various scenarios and skill levels, leading to a better overall estimate.

Activity	Optimistic Estimate	Most Likely Estimate	Pessimistic Estimate	Final Duration Estimate
1.3.2 Marketing Plan	5 days	10 days	15 days	10 days
1.3.4.1 Post-Event Survey—Create	4 days	5 days	12 days	6 days
1.3.4.2 Post-Event Survey—Distribute and Analyze Survey Results	7 days	10 days	31 days	13 days

Figure 6-14
Three-Point
Estimates

For the Fundraiser Road Race, there were no statistics for or experience in the activities above. The team performed an exercise to arrive at a best guess. As the project progresses, the team can reassess these estimates and revise as necessary. These estimates are shown in Figure 6-14 above.

Class Exercise 6-10

Discuss the optimistic, pessimistic and most likely estimates for the following activities. Calculate duration estimates based on the three-point estimating technique. Discuss how this information could be helpful to you.

_____
_____
_____
_____
_____
_____

Activity	Optimistic Estimate	Most Likely Estimate	Pessimistic Estimate	Final Duration Estimate
Driving to work				
Time needed in advance of departure to arrive at the airport to catch a flight				
Reading a 400-page novel				

On the following pages, Figure 6-15, shows a finalized look at the Fundraiser Road Race project with activity durations entered. A variety of estimating techniques were used for this example. Your estimates will most likely differ from this example due to your own experiences and knowledge.

	BEST CONSULTING Fund Raiser Road Race		Project Views ▼	Resources ▼	Reports

Task List

WBS	Name	Predecessors	Duration	hh mm
1	Fund Raiser Charity Event		101d	
1.1	Event Decision		13d	
1.1.1	Event Analysis		10d	
1.1.2	Event Options Decision	Event Analysis	3d	
1.2	Venue		37d	
1.2.1	Site Selection		27d	
1.2.1.1	Identify sites & Site visits	Event Options Decision	10d	
1.2.1.2	Analyze site options	Identify sites & Site visits	15d	
1.2.1.3	Review and decide on site	Analyze site options	2d	
1.2.2	Site Preparation		10d	
1.2.2.1	Water and Power Setup	Review and decide on site	10d	
1.2.2.2	Tent Setup	Review and decide on site , Identify sites & Site visits	3d	
1.3	Marketing		88d	
1.3.1	Outreach Opportunities		57d	
1.3.1.1	Outreach Research	Event Options Decision	10d	
1.3.1.2	Target Mailing List	Sponsor Development , Event Analysis	12d	
1.3.2	Marketing Plan	Event Options Decision	10d	
1.3.3	Marketing Production		49d	
1.3.3.1	Tickets: Design and produce event tickets	Marketing Plan	15d	
1.3.3.2	Flyers: Design and produce event flyers	Marketing Plan	15d	
1.3.3.3	Mail Marketing Packages	Target Mailing List , Tickets: Design and produce event tickets , Flyers: Design and produce event flyers	2d	
1.3.3.4	Advertising		37d	
1.3.3.4.1	Newspaper Advertising		33d	
1.3.3.4.1.1	Request submission packages from local newspaper	Marketing Plan	1d	
1.3.3.4.1.2	Create advertisement layout	Request submission packages from local newspaper	10d	
1.3.3.4.1.3	Review layout with stakeholders and gain approval	Create advertisement layout	8d	
1.3.3.4.1.4	Submit advertisement per submission deadlines	Review layout with stakeholders and gain approval	1d	
1.3.3.4.1.5	Review publisher proof and approve	Submit advertisement per submission deadlines	2d	
1.3.3.4.1.6	Confirm Ad published per schedule	Review publisher proof and approve +10d	1d	
1.3.3.4.2	Website Advertising		37d	
1.3.3.4.2.1	Create a webpage for Charity Event	Marketing Plan	22d	
1.3.3.4.2.2	Determine alternative websites and deliver web content	Create a webpage for Charity Event , Outreach Research	15d	
1.3.3.4.3	Magazine Advertising		24d	
1.3.3.4.3.1	Request submission packages from local newspaper	Marketing Plan	2d	
1.3.3.4.3.2	Create advertisement layout	Request submission packages from local newspaper	10d	
1.3.3.4.3.3	Review layout with stakeholders and gain approval	Create advertisement layout	8d	
1.3.3.4.3.4	Submit advertisement per submission deadlines	Review layout with stakeholders and gain approval	1d	
1.3.3.4.3.5	Review publisher proof and approve	Submit advertisement per submission deadlines	2d	
1.3.3.4.3.6	Confirm Ad published per schedule	Review publisher proof and approve	1d	
1.3.4	Surveys		78d	
1.3.4.1	Pre-Event Survey		11d	
1.3.4.1.1	Create Survey	Marketing Plan	6d	
1.3.4.1.2	Distribute and collect info on PRE-Survey	Create Survey	5d	
1.3.4.2	Post-Event Survey		22d	
1.3.4.2.1	Create Survey	Develop event schedule	6d	

Figure 6-15
Finalized Activity
Durations

1.3.4.2.2	Distribute and Analyze POST-survey results	Create Survey , Project Management [FF], Setup and takedown of booths and stage	13d
1.4	**▾Event Logistics**		**48d**
1.4.1	Food and Drink	Review and decide on site	20d
1.4.2	**▾Booths & Entertainment**		**48d**
1.4.2.1	Booth & entertainment site map	Review and decide on site	4d
1.4.2.2	Assign sponsors to booths	Booth & entertainment site map , Sponsor Development	1d
1.4.2.3	Determine schedule of booth events and entertainment	Water and Power Setup , Assign sponsors to booths	15d
1.4.2.4	Setup and takedown of booths and stage	Food and Drink , Volunteer Training: Develop and deliver training for all event day volunteers , Tent Setup	2d
1.4.3	**▾Event Schedule**		**10d**
1.4.3.1	Develop event schedule	Determine schedule of booth events and entertainment , Determine alternative websites and deliver web content Confirm Ad published per schedule , Mail Marketing Packages , Confirm Ad published per schedule	5d
1.4.3.2	Assign volunteers to support each event	Volunteers , Develop event schedule	5d
1.4.4	Volunteer Training: Develop and deliver training for all event day volunteers	Assign volunteers to support each event	2d
1.5	Sponsor Development	Event Options Decision	45d
1.6	Volunteers	Event Analysis	60d
1.7	Project Management	Event Analysis	90d
		Add Predecessors	
			101d

Level of Effort

Note that in Activity 1.7, Project Management, in the activity durations list above, the duration is for the full duration of the project, or the level of effort. When the work for a particular activity is difficult to estimate and can fluctuate greatly based on the needs of the activity, a level of effort duration can be used.

Case Study 6-6

Review the activities of the LUV Music website project. Use any of the three estimating techniques discussed above—analogous, parametric, or three-point estimating—to determine the duration for each of the activities in the project.

Group Decision Making

In order to improve estimating accuracy and increase the commitment to developed estimates, it is important to involve people. Those who are involved in decision making are more likely to buy in and make a commitment to perform.

Team-based approaches to estimating like **brainstorming**, the **Delphi technique**, or nominal group techniques may harness project participation. These collaborative activities may increase accuracy and commitment to the estimates produced.

Reserve Analysis

The tool and technique of performing a reserve analysis is used when uncertainty exists with the activity duration estimates. A **contingency reserve** is a dollar or time value that is added to the project schedule or budget that reflects and accounts for risk that is anticipated for the project. Reserve analysis determines whether or not some contingency reserves should be added to the durations to accommodate this uncertainty. There are several ways contingency reserves can be applied:

- Add a percentage (%) to all activities
- Add additional tasks to accommodate uncertainty
- Utilize the more pessimistic estimates

A percentage is typically used when uncertainly exists across the entire project before any detailed risk assessment has been performed.

Additional tasks might be added when specific experience and history warrant. For example, in a software development organization, extra testing cycles may be planned because of the assumption that defects will be found in the initial testing of the software.

A more pessimistic estimate may be employed when **resource assignments** have not been finalized, recognizing that the experience levels of the project team members may not be ideal.

These are just a couple of examples of how a reserve analysis can be performed in defining an amount of contingency reserve that can be planned for.

WBS ID: 1.3.3.4.1 – Newspaper Advertising
Description: Advertise the Road Race in the local newspaper, both the daily newspaper as well as the weekly entertainment publication. Advertisements in the daily newspaper should begin two months prior to the event and the weekly entertainment publication four months prior to the event.

Responsibility: Marketing – Henry Optimo – Consultant 1

Schedule:
    Milestone: Daily newspaper submission deadlines
              Weekly entertainment newspaper submission deadlines
    Predecessor: Advertising Designs from Marketing Plan
    Successor: Event Date
Schedule Activities:
1. Request submission packages from local newspaper for both daily and weekly publication (8 hours)
2. Create advertisement layout (15 hours & 5 hours admin)
3. Review layout with sponsor and gain approval (10 hours consultant & 4 hours sponsor)
4. Submit advertisement per submission deadlines (8 hours)
5. Review publisher proof and approve (8 hours)
6. Test the ad out to see if it would compel people to attend
7. Confirm ad published per schedule (1 hour: 2-week lag from review)

Resources Required:
Consultant 1 – Marketing coordinator
Admin 1 – Layout team
Sponsor 1 – Layout review and sign-off

Cost Estimates: (Revised)
Coordinator (Consultant 1): 50 hours effort
Layout team (Admin): 5 hours effort
Review & sign-off: 4 hours effort

Quality Requirements:
Date, time, location and cost of event must be clearly communicated, including sign-up instructions. Desire attendees who like to run, but also have a connection to the charity.

Acceptance Criteria:
Advertisements are published per the agreed-upon schedule.

Figure 6-16
WBS with Added
Activity

At the completion of the Estimate Activity Durations process, the project team should have a complete list of **activities** with **duration estimates**. The information gathered in this process should be captured within each **work package**. An example of a work package for newspaper advertising would be performing some test marketing on the ad created to increase the probability of getting a good turnout for the road race. Figure 6-16 on the previous page shows how such an activity is part of the WBS.

DEVELOP SCHEDULE PROCESS

Once all activities and predecessors are identified and resources and durations determined, the project team can create a formal schedule for a project. The Develop Schedule process addresses the creation of the schedule and determines the critical path of the project.

The **critical path** of a project is the sequence of activities which define the full duration of the project. The activities on the critical path have no opportunity to be delayed because a delay in any of the activities on the critical path will result in an increase in the overall project schedule.

The outcome of the Develop Schedule process is a **project schedule** that reflects an agreed-upon duration to deliver the project and the **schedule baseline**. In many cases, the initial schedule that is developed ends up being longer than the optimal time it should take to deliver.

Tools and techniques covered in this chapter, such as **critical chain**, **schedule compression**, and **resource leveling**, all aid the project manager in developing a comprehensive schedule that meets the objectives of a project.

Schedule Network Analysis

By utilizing the **activity list** with **durations** and the **precedence diagram** previously created, the project manager can perform a schedule network analysis. This analysis employs the tools and techniques below in finalizing the project schedule and the schedule baseline.

The first step of schedule network analysis is to determine the overall duration of the project. That duration is determined by performing "forward pass" and "backward pass" calculations. In order to do that, we must return to the precedence diagram developed previously for our sample project (see page 6-14) and shown below in Figure 6-17.

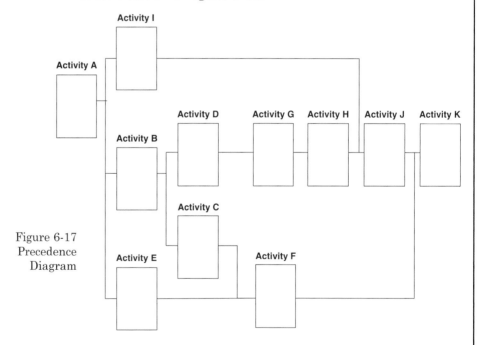

Figure 6-17
Precedence
Diagram

For demonstration purposes, we are going to break down each activity into six specific variables: **duration**, **float**, **early-start**, **early-finish**, **late-start**, and **late-finish**. Each term will be explained as we progress through the schedule development process. We will end up with a table for each activity that looks something like the table in Figure 6-18 on the following page.

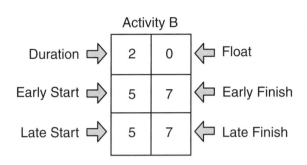

Activity B

Duration ⇨ | 2 | 0 | ⇦ Float

Early Start ⇨ | 5 | 7 | ⇦ Early Finish

Late Start ⇨ | 5 | 7 | ⇦ Late Finish

Figure 6-18
Variables for
Each Activity

The first step in the process of creating a schedule is to utilize the duration for each activity found in the activity list, such as the durations and activity list in Figure 6-19 below.

WBS ID	Activity Description	Predecessor	Duration
1.1	Activity A	---	5 days
1.2	Activity B	1.1	2 days
1.3	Activity C	1.2	4 days
2.1	Activity D	1.2	2 days
2.2	Activity E	1.1	1 day
3.1	Activity F	2.2, 1.3	8 days
4.1	Activity G	2.1	4 days
4.2	Activity H	4.1	3 days
4.3	Activity I	1.1	3 days
4.4	Activity J	4.1, 4.3	5 days
5.0	Activity K	4.4, 3.1	2 days

Figure 6-19
Activities and
Durations

6

From this list of activities, with their dependencies and durations, the network schedule duration value can be completed, as shown in Figure 6-20 on the following page.

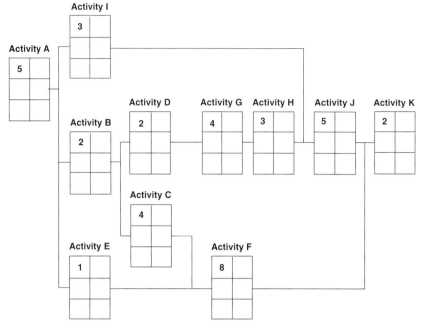

Figure 6-20
Network
Schedule
Durations

Once durations are supplied, the **forward pass** calculation can be performed. This calculation requires the entry of the **early-start** and **early-finish** values for each activity. The starting activity of any network diagram will have an early-start value of 0. The early-finish value is calculated by adding the duration of that activity. For Activity A, early-start = 0 and early-finish = 5 (or 0 + 5).

Once the early-finish value is determined for each predecessor, the early-start value of the successor will be equal to the *largest* value of any preceding early-finish values. For example, the early-start value of Activities I, B, and E will be equal to 5, which is the early-finish value of Activity A. However, for Activity F, the early-start value will be equal to the largest preceding early-finish value of Activities C and E, which is 11.

The creation of the forward pass values demonstrates the *earliest* any activity can start and end throughout the project. For our sample project, the total duration of the project is 23 days, as we can see in Figure 6-21 on the following page.

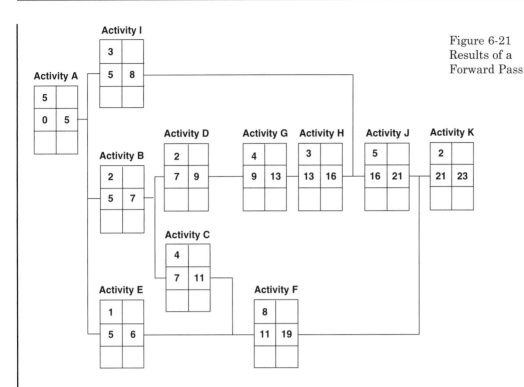

Figure 6-21
Results of a
Forward Pass

Critical Path Method

The critical path method calculates the path within the project that drives the overall duration of the project. Any change to the duration of activities on the critical path *will* change the overall duration of a project.

To determine the critical path, the project manager performs a **backward pass.** To calculate a backward pass, we start with the last activity on the project, Activity K. We set the **late-finish** value to be equal to the duration of the project: 23 days. Then the duration is *subtracted* from the late-finish value to determine the **late-start** value.

As in the **forward pass**, when multiple activities feed into one predecessor, the late-finish value will be equal to the *smallest* late-start value. In our example below, Activity B has two successors, Activities C and D, and the late-finish value is equal to the smaller late-start value of Activities C and D, 7 days.

> **TIP**
>
> There are two approaches to calculating the critical path, one defined here in which you start with zero (0), and the other defined in the *PMBOK® Guide* in which Activity A early-start begins with one (1) instead. Regardless of your chosen approach, the formula for calculating float does not change.

At the end of a backward pass, the first activity, Activity A in our example, should have a late-start value of zero. Figure 6-22 below shows the results of a backward pass.

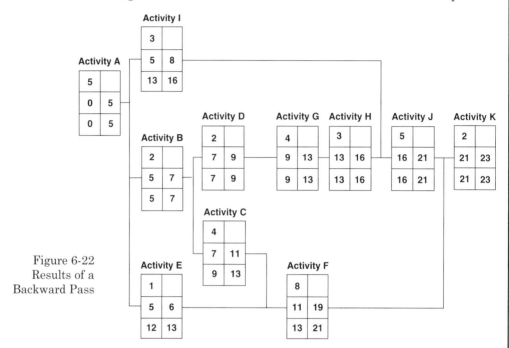

Figure 6-22
Results of a
Backward Pass

The next step is to determine which activities in the network schedule are on the **critical path**. This is determined by calculating the float of each activity. Float is calculated by subtracting early-finish values from late-finish values or by subtracting early-start values from late-start values. The activities with zero float are on the critical path.

In our example in Figure 6-23 on the next page, the critical path is defined as: Activity A, B, D, G, H, J and K. Activities C, E, F, and I all have some float.

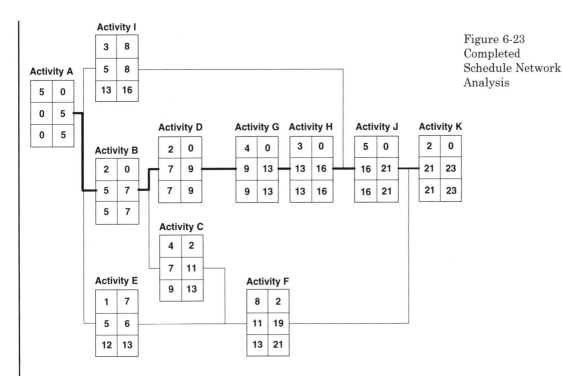

Figure 6-23
Completed
Schedule Network
Analysis

6

Class Exercise 6-11

Based on the durations created and documented on
pages 6-37 and 6-38, create a network diagram for the
Fundraiser Road Race.

Case Study 6-7

Use the activity durations and precedence diagram for
the LUV Music website project to determine the critical
path for the project.

Critical Chain Method

The critical chain method is an alternative to the critical
path method that views the project as a system instead
of as a network of independent tasks. While the critical
path is determined by task-dependency relationships,
the critical chain adds resource dependencies to define a
resource-limited schedule. The longest sequence of
resource-leveled tasks is the critical chain.

The critical chain method requires commitment from management to include appropriate buffers in the project plan and to eliminate scheduling resources for multiple major tasks.

Look at the sample schedules in Figure 6-24 below. In the *before* chart, both Task C and Task E have been identified (by shading) as requiring Resource A. It is not possible for Resource A to simultaneously perform these two tasks, so it is necessary to shift Task E to *after* the completion of Task C.

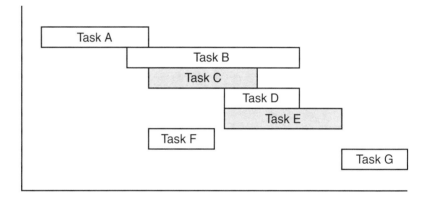

BEFORE

Figure 6-24
Sample Schedules

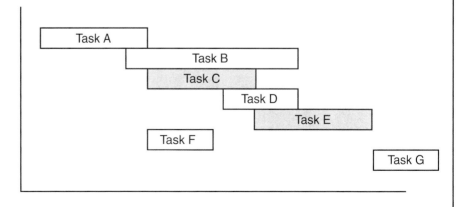

AFTER

In the *after* chart, you will see that the shift in Task E also causes a shift in Task G due to a predecessor dependency, even though Resource A is not required for Task G, causing an overall increase in the project schedule.

This is called a **resource constrained critical path**. The project manager needs to know that, as part of critical chain analysis, he or she may also decide to add some buffers in the project to accommodate resource constraints. If a particular resource isn't expected to be available until a certain date, the project manager may plan for a one-week buffer before the start of that resource to account for any uncertainty in that resource becoming available on the specified date.

Resource Optimization Techniques

Resource leveling and **resource smoothing** are two techniques that can be employed with the project schedule for the over- and under-allocation of resources. There are times when more resources are needed than are available, which may be true for equipment or for people, such as subject matter experts. This need for resources may also cause individual resources to be assigned to one or more tasks during one time period, tasks that together exceed the individual's available time.

Resource smoothing attempts to adjust activities within the existing free and total float, thereby minimizing the potential for affecting the critical path. On the other hand, in resource leveling, the start and finish dates of activities are adjusted based on resource constraints to maintain resources at a constant level, which in many cases causes the critical path to change and the overall project duration to increase.

> **TIP**
> Resource smoothing may not be able to optimize all resources.

Resource usage may be evaluated at the project level by preparing a **resource histogram** to determine total resources used in each time period. Figure 6-25 on the following page demonstrates a resource histogram at the project level. From this diagram, you can see that the project requires more resources than are available during weeks two and six of the project.

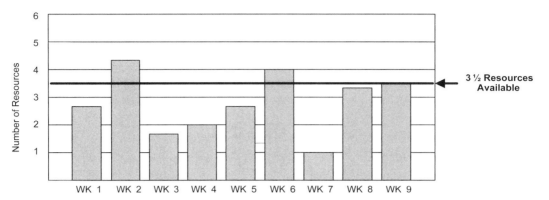

Figure 6-25
Resource Histogram

The project manager may try to eliminate spikes and gaps in total resource usage. Resource leveling is used to reschedule concurrent activities in which individuals have constraints. Resource leveling may result in extending the duration of the project.

There are three common situations that require resource leveling:
- When required resources are only available at certain times
- When required resources are only available in limited quantities
- To keep resource usage at a constant level

In most cases, resource leveling will increase the overall schedule duration.

Schedule Compression

Schedule compression is a tool and technique that is used often both at the beginning of project planning and as changes occur throughout the completion of a project. There are two types of compression techniques: **crashing** and **fast tracking**.

Crashing analyzes options for schedule compression in terms of cost and schedule trade-offs.

Fast tracking identifies activities in the project that are typically performed in sequence and instead causes them to be executed in parallel in order to reduce the overall project schedule.

TIP

When the need to compress a schedule exists, review activity relationships, including leads and lags, to determine if a more appropriate relationship could improve the overall schedule timeline.

For our sample project, you have been asked to reduce the schedule by two days. You reviewed the network diagram on page 6-47 and, based on a discussion with the team, you've identified three options to reduce the schedule. These options are presented in Figure 6-26 below. Which one should you choose and why?

Option	Cost	Risk
Reduce Activity F by 2 days. It has the longest duration and the team feels we wouldn't have to hire an expensive resource, just a junior resource.	$50/day	Low risk. Resource cost is low and complexity of task is low.
Reduce Activity A by 1 day and Activity B by 1 day. Would have to borrow two different resources from another project, but they currently have some availability.	$250/day	Medium risk. Requires two different skill sets to accomplish.
Reduce Activity J by 2 days by replacing the current resource with a more senior resource.	$200/day	High risk. Will cause the project to end up with two critical paths.

Figure 6-26
Schedule
Compression
Options

The best answer would probably be the second option. The first option isn't viable since Activity F isn't on the critical path and reducing it will not reduce the overall schedule. The third option isn't as good as the second in that the risk is higher. This third solution is to reduce Activity J, which is the second to last activity in the entire project. It is always better to focus on earlier tasks to allow for and respond to additional requests for schedule compression that may be made.

It is important to note that for crashing and fast tracking, schedule compression only occurs if the activities being affected impact the critical path of the project.

Class Exercise 6-12

For the Fundraiser Road Race, we are trying to reduce the schedule by one week. List three options the project team may have. Which option would you choose?

Option	Cost	Schedule	Risk

Creating a Schedule

Once the network analysis is complete, a schedule can be created. The most common form of schedule presentation is a **Gantt Chart**. A Gantt chart is a type of network schedule, but in a bar-chart format. To create a Gantt chart, start with the network diagram and align the start dates of each activity, similar to the one below in Figure 6-27 for our sample project.

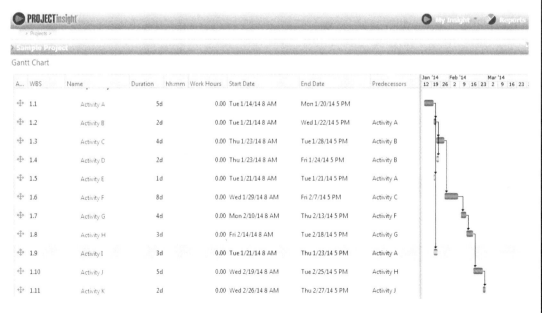

Figure 6-27
Gantt Chart

Class Exercise 6-13

Create a Gantt chart for the Fundraiser Road Race project.

Case Study 6-8

Create a Gantt chart for the website project for the LUV Music project.

Schedule Baseline

A final step of the Develop Schedule process is to update any work packages that may have been impacted by the schedule network analysis techniques.

The schedule baseline consists of an approved version of the schedule that is based on a network schedule analysis. Any assumptions made in creating the schedule baseline should be documented within each of the associated WBS dictionaries.

CONTROL SCHEDULE PROCESS

Control Schedule is the process of monitoring the results of activities being completed as they relate to the original plan and responding to any changes as they occur. In order to successfully manage a schedule, timely information on the completion or delay of activities is imperative.

The outputs of the Control Schedule process include **work performance information** and **change requests**.

Performance Reviews

Every project should have regular reporting on work performance. Performance reviews involve an analytical process of measuring, comparing, and analyzing performance in relation to the project schedule. The results of performance reviews should assist the project manager in determining if action is needed by the project manager or project team.

TIP

Using computer-based scheduling tools to calculate activity start and finish dates that are based on defined dependencies can facilitate the identification of scheduling issues.

6

TIP
Trend analysis examines project performance over time to determine if performance is improving or deteriorating.

Trend analysis, the **critical path method**, the **critical chain method**, and **earned value management** (EVM) are modeling techniques frequently used in assembling performance reviews.

Comparing actual performance to planned performance is critical in monitoring and controlling all aspects of project work. Chapter 7 on cost management covers the tool and technique of earned value management in detail. There are a few concepts of EVM that are particularly important to know for the purposes of time management.

Regarding time management, it is important to know how to calculate the schedule variance and the schedule performance index.

A **schedule variance** (SV) occurs when the expected or **planned value** (PV) differs from the performed or **earned value** (EV).

Consider an activity which is planned to take 10 days at a cost of $100 per day. It is expected that the resource will spend 5 hours each day. The total cost of the activity is planned at $1,000.

After 3 days, the resource has only spent 10 hours and therefore only earned $200 worth of performance.

The formula for schedule variance is EV − PV. For this particular example, the schedule variance is a negative $100. After 3 days, the resource only earned $200 worth of performance and should have achieved $300 worth.

Negative schedule variances mean that an activity is behind schedule while positive schedule variances reflect that performance is ahead of schedule.

TIP
All earned value measures are in terms of dollars.

Schedule variance calculations can be applied to an individual activity or accumulated to reflect the overall schedule variance of a project.

A **schedule performance index** (SPI) is slightly different from the schedule variance in that it reflects the performance trend and can be used for forecasting. The SPI is calculated by dividing earned value (EV) by planned value (PV).

In the example just discussed, the SPI is $200 / $300, or 0.667. Numbers less than one reflect an activity or project behind schedule, while numbers greater than one reflect the activity or project being ahead of schedule.

SPI is typically calculated on the entire project, and the project manager can use this calculation to determine if the project will continue to perform in the same way.

> **TIP**
>
> Project management software facilitates the tracking of planned versus actual dates, as well as any variance in project performance.

Class Exercise 6-14

Below is a sample progress report which identifies work performance information on the Fundraiser Road Race. Review the information provided and determine if there are any concerns about the project status. If there are, what would be a proposed response to the variance?

Performance Report

Project Name: Fundraiser Road Race
Date: 2/2/14
Internal Project Status Meeting

Tasks Completed:	Planned Hrs	Actual Hrs
Event Analysis	60	65
Event Options Decision	24	28
Identify Sites & Site Visits – Requires Sign-off	30	20

Issues:

No site found that would donate facility for FREE.

Tasks Not Started:	Planned Start Date	Planned Hrs to Date
Volunteers	01/15	40
Outreach Research	01/20	40
Marketing Plan	01/20	60
Sponsor Development	01/20	20
Analyze Site Options	02/03	0
Create Pre-Event Survey	02/03	0
Request Submission Package from Local Newspaper	02/03	0
Request Submission Package from Magazines	02/03	0
Create Webpage for Charity Event	02/03	0

PROFESSIONAL RESPONSIBILITY

Schedule management is about accurately reflecting the time it will take to complete work. When considering the four aspects of professional responsibility—responsibility, respect, fairness, and honesty—the project manager must keep certain things in mind at all times:

- Don't artificially add hours to cover costs from another project
- Don't assume that resources are always available because assumptions increase the risk of double booking resources
- Don't ignore the fact that people go on vacation

It is the project manager's responsibility to provide accurate, unbiased information regarding the project schedule.

KEY INTERPERSONAL SKILLS FOR SUCCESS

The interpersonal skill highlighted in this chapter is:

Conflict Management

Because of the challenges of managing projects, conflict is expected at some time during the project life cycle. Conflict may arise from differences over schedules, technical requirements, cost, personalities, organizational challenges, management, the customer or end user, and a wide variety of other causes.

Project managers who successfully lead teams find ways to encourage conflict when it can lead to better project decisions and to resolve conflict when necessary to create a collaborative approach among team members. Managing conflict requires that the project manager find a way to build and maintain a trusting relationship among team members and others associated with a project.

Much of the effort in developing a detailed and comprehensive schedule will inevitably cause conflict within the team and especially with the customer. Initial expectations of project duration are generally too optimistic. Detailing out a schedule usually requires that these expectations be modified.

BE A BETTER PROJECT MANAGER

Exercise: getting team members to follow the project schedule.

Purpose: getting team members to understand the dependencies developed within the project schedule.

Anyone who has managed projects for any length of time knows that we continually get frustrated when a project schedule is developed and then, as the project progresses, it appears that no one is following the schedule. We find ourselves constantly at battle regarding task sequence.

Steps:

1. Recognize that *most* project team members look at a schedule and don't understand how to read it.
2. Realize that *you* must be the interpreter of the schedule.
3. Ensure that anyone performing a particular task is aware of the inputs needed, the expected output, and the recipient of any given task.
4. Project managers *must* use the schedule as *their* tool to ensure that activities are assigned in a timely manner. Review daily or weekly the activities that:
   - Have been accomplished
   - Are in process and being worked on
   - Are next up in the project schedule (say, 2 weeks out)
5. Document and communicate these three states of activities to team members regularly.

SAMPLE CAPM EXAM QUESTIONS ON TIME MANAGEMENT

1. An organizational process asset that can influence the Control Schedule process may be:

   a) WBS templates
   b) Cost control guidelines
   c) Monitoring and reporting methods
   d) Quality assurance policies

2. A tool and technique of the Control Schedule process is:

   a) The schedule management plan
   b) Schedule compression
   c) Work performance data
   d) Project baseline

3. As a project is carried out and float time is consumed on individual activities, the float left over for the remaining activities is:

   a) Insignificant
   b) Reduced
   c) Unchanged
   d) Increased

4. Which activity in the table below is on schedule?

Activity	PV	AC	EV
Survey	500	2,000	400
Remove Debris	2,000	3,500	2,000
Dig Hole	3,000	2,000	2,800
Emplace Forms	1,200	1,000	1,100
Pour Concrete	5,000	3,000	2,500

   a) Dig Hole
   b) Remove Debris
   c) Survey
   d) Emplace Forms

5. The planning effort that precedes the work performed in the Plan Schedule Management process is called:

   a) Develop WBS
   b) Develop Project Management Plan
   c) Create Schedule
   d) Define Activities

6. Identifying and documenting the work necessary to complete the project deliverables is part of the _____ process.

   a) Sequence Activities
   b) Define Activities
   c) Plan Schedule Management
   d) Estimate Activity Resources

7. Work effort that is required to complete a WBS component is called a:

   a) Work package
   b) Schedule activity
   c) Rolling wave plan
   d) Decomposition

8. A key benefit of the Sequence Activities process is that it:

   a) Shows the logical dependencies among activities
   b) Is the basis for estimating, scheduling, and controlling project work
   c) Provides guidance on how the schedule will be managed
   d) Depicts a schedule that shows planned dates for completion of activities

Notes:

9. In the precedence diagramming method, common logical relationships or dependencies include:

   a) Start-to-node
   b) Finish-to-start
   c) Arrow-on-node
   d) Start-to-finish

10. What is the activity that logically comes before a dependent activity?

    a) Activity
    b) Mandatory dependency
    c) Predecessor
    d) Successor

11. When an activity is not detailed enough to have a reasonable level of confidence in the estimate, it may be necessary to:

    a) Use a project management scheduling tool
    b) Look for published estimating data
    c) Perform a parametric estimate
    d) Decompose the activity into more detail

12. _____ estimating is a tool and technique of the Estimate Activity Durations process that is useful when there is a limited amount of detailed information available about a project.

    a) Parametric
    b) Statistical sampling
    c) Analogous
    d) Monte Carlo simulation

Notes:

6

13. Mary drives six miles to work and passes through thirteen traffic lights. Optimistically, she could get all green lights and make it to work in ten minutes. However, she could also hit all red lights, taking her twenty-three minutes to get to work. Most often, it takes Mary fourteen minutes to drive to work because she usually only hits five red lights. Using the beta/PERT concept for the expected duration of a activity, what is the expected value duration (in minutes) for Mary's drive?

a) 7.9
b) 14.8
c) 15.7
d) 29.2

14. The amount of time that a schedule activity can be delayed after the early-start date without delaying the project finish date is called the:

a) Duration
b) Total float
c) Free float
d) Critical path

Notes:

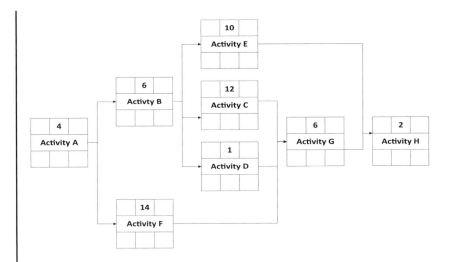

15. What is the critical path of the network diagram above?

a) A-F-G-H
b) A-B-D-G-H
c) A-B-E-G-H
d) A-B-C-G-H

ANSWERS AND REFERENCES FOR SAMPLE CAPM EXAM QUESTIONS ON TIME MANAGEMENT

Section numbers refer to the *PMBOK® Guide.*

1. **C** **Section 6.7.1.6 – Monitoring and Controlling**
   A) is an organizational process asset used to develop the WBS; B) focus on cost, not schedule; D) focus on quality, not schedule. Make sure you are clear about what the question is asking.

2. **B** **Section 6.7.2 – Monitoring and Controlling**
   A), C), and D) are inputs to the Control Schedule process.

3. **B** **Section 6.7.2.1 – Monitoring and Controlling**
   As slack is consumed, there is less slack available for the remaining noncritical activities.

4. **B** **Section 7.4.2.1 – Monitoring and Controlling**
   For the activity of removing debris, schedule variance = EV – PV = 2000 – 2000 = 0. Zero variance indicates that an activity is on schedule or has been completed.

5. **B** **Section 6.1 – Planning**
   The scope baseline is part of the project plan that is an input to the Plan Schedule Management process. The scope baseline includes the project scope statement, WBS, and WBS dictionary. B) is a more complete answer than A), which produces the WBS alone.

6. **B** **Section 6.2 – Planning**
   WBS work packages are further decomposed into activities.

7. **B** **Section 6.2 – Planning**
   A) is the lowest level in the WBS; B) is a subset of work packages and is defined as the work to be performed in order to produce the deliverables; C) is another form of progressive elaboration; D) is a tool and technique used in order to define work packages and schedule activities.

8. **A** **Section 6.3 – Planning**
   B) is a benefit of the Define Activities process;
   C) is a benefit of the Plan Schedule Management
   process; D) is a benefit of the Develop Schedule
   process.

9. **B** **Section 6.3.2.1 – Planning**
   The precedence diagramming method is an example of a schedule networking technique. Start-to-
   finish is not commonly used.

10. **C** **Section 6.3.2.1 – Planning**
    The successor cannot start until the predecessor
    has finished in a tradition finish-to-start relation-
    ship. The successor is dependent on the predeces-
    sor.

11. **D** **Section 6.4.2.4 – Planning**
    A) and B) are tools of the Estimate Activity
    Resources process; C) is a technique in the
    Estimate Activity Durations process.

12. **C** **Section 6.5.2.2 – Planning**
    A), B), and D) require a significant amount of
    information.

13. **B** **Section 6.5.2.4 – Planning**
    Expected value of duration (weighted average) =
    [Optimistic + 4(Most Likely) + Pessimistic] / 6
    = (10 + 4(14) + 23) / 6 = 14.8 minutes

14. **B** **Section 6.6.2.2 – Planning**
    Total float focuses on the project finish date; free
    float focuses on flexibility before an activity's ear-
    ly-start date.

15. **D** **Section 6.6.2.2 – Planning**
    The critical path is the path with no float.

ANSWERS TO CLASS EXERCISES

You may not agree with these answers. Responses do depend on the situations that you yourself have experienced.

Class Exercise 6-1: Logical Relationship/ Dependency

Scenario	Logical Relationship/ Dependency
The training manual can be started about one week after testing of the new system has begun.	Start-to-start
All of the testing cycles need to be completed before the training documentation can be finalized and signed off on.	Finish-to-finish
The volunteers need to be trained before the team can start setting up all the booths for the event.	Finish-to-start
The street sweepers cannot start cleaning the streets until all the cars parked on the street have been moved.	Finish-to-start
The golf course superintendent turns on the sprinklers after each hole is fertilized.	Finish-to-start

Class Exercise 6-2: Precedence Diagram (see top of next page)

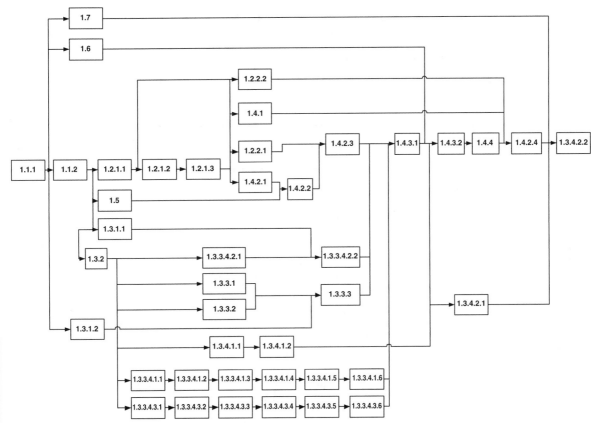

Class Exercise 6-3: Types of Dependencies

Scenario	Dependency
The training manual can be started about one week after testing of the new system has begun.	Discretionary and Internal
All of the testing cycles need to be completed before the training documentation can be finalized and signed off on.	Discretionary and Internal
The volunteers need to be trained before the team can start setting up all the booths for the event.	Discretionary and Internal
The street sweepers cannot start cleaning the streets until all the cars parked on the street have been moved.	Mandatory and External
The golf course superintendent turns on the sprinklers after each hole is fertilized.	Discretionary and Internal
The new product line needs to be available for the Spring product launch conference to be considered viable in the marketplace.	Mandatory and External
According to the contract, a go/no-go decision is needed by June 1, 2014.	Mandatory and External

Class Exercise 6-4: Evaluating Dependencies

WBS ID	Activity Description	Predecessor	Dependency
1.1	Activity A	---	N/A
1.2	Activity B	1.1	Mandatory
1.3	Activity C	1.2	Discretionary
2.1	Activity D	1.2	Discretionary
2.2	Activity E	1.1	Discretionary
3.1	Activity F	2.2, 1.3	Discretionary
4.1	Activity G	2.1	Mandatory
4.2	Activity H	4.1	Discretionary
4.3	Activity I	1.1	Discretionary
4.4	Activity J	4.1, 4.3	Discretionary
5.0	Activity K	4.4, 3.1	External

Depending on the situation, these dependencies may not make any difference. Noting that Activities B and G are mandatory means that Activity B can only start after Activity A, and Activity G can only start after Activity D finishes. That does increase the importance of completing Activities A and D in a timely manner.

The external dependency on Activity K means that either Activity J or F is being performed by an outside group.

Class Exercise 6-5: Leads and Lags

WBS ID	Activity Name	Lead or Lag	Explanation
1.2.2.2	Tent Setup	Lead	Tent setup doesn't have to wait until the water and power are in place and ready.
1.3.4.1	Create Post-Survey	Lag	The dependency to 1.4.3 can have a lag of several weeks. It just depends on how tight the schedule is.
1.3.3.4.3.6	Review Publisher Proof and Approve	Lag	Usually there is a waiting period while publishers perform their function.

Class Exercise 6-6: Alternatives Analysis

Not much can be determined yet. You may be somewhat concerned over the sheer number of activities assigned to the consultant for marketing with *only* twenty hours per week available. That may not be enough later in the project.

An alternative may be to get Volunteer 2 involved since he or she is coordinating the sponsors.

Class Exercise 6-7: Bottom-Up Estimating

The chart below is an example of using bottom-up estimating to determine activities in a product market analysis if an external vendor is chosen.

Activity for Product Market Analysis-External	Comments
Identify several marketing firms specializing in our industry.	
Research the success of potentially selected firms.	
Analyze, research, and select a firm.	
Complete a contract with a firm.	
Have selected firm complete marketing analysis.	

The next chart lists activities that may be performed if the task is kept internal.

Activity for Product Market Analysis-Internal	Comments
Identify target markets.	
Determine what the product is and how it can help the particular market.	
Create a market research survey.	
Perform a market survey.	
Analyze the results of the survey.	
Create a prototype.	
Test market the product.	
Gather conclusions.	

Class Exercise 6-8: Analogous Estimating

Old project:
$40,000 / 200 attendees = $200 / attendee

New project:

250 attendees x $200 / attendee =	$50,000
Luxury resort premium (+ 25%) =	$12,500
Hotel cost at resort 125 x $300 =	$37,500
Total Cost:	$100,000

Class Exercise 6-9: Parametric Estimating

Formula:
1,500 x $300 = $450,000 (Building cost)
$500,000 x 0.25 = $125,000 (Land cost)
$575,000 x 1.02 = $586,500 (Total cost)

	California	Florida
Building	$300/square foot	$150/square foot
Property	$500,000 per acre	$100,000 per acre
Tax	2% of homesite	3% of homesite
Total	**$586,500**	

Class Exercise 6-10: Three-Point Estimating

A class discussion alone is enough to answer this class exercise. Each student will have different experiences with regard to driving to work, arriving at an airport, or reading a book.

If using this book as a self-study, practice calculating the weighted three-point estimate.

Class Exercise 6-11: Network Diagram

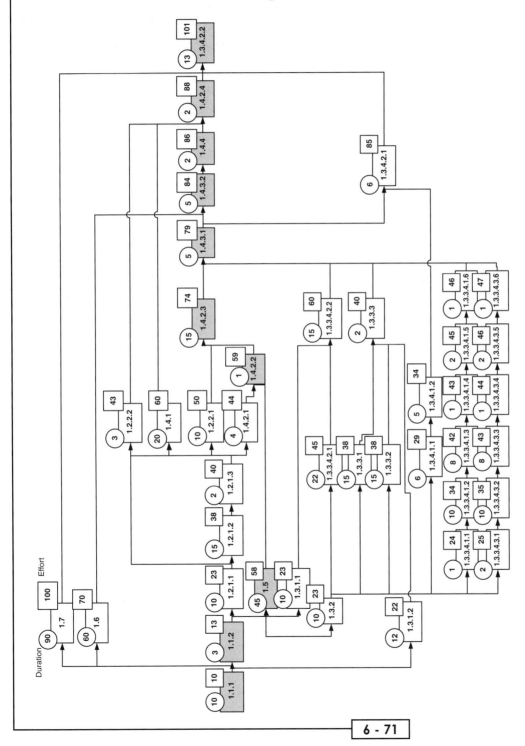

Class Exercise 6-12: Schedule Compression

Option	Cost	Schedule	Risk
Activity 1.3.4.2.2—Distribute and analyze post-survey results (13-day activity)	Low cost impact	Reduce by 7 days	High—may not be feasible to remove 7 days and have enough time to get back the results.
Activity 1.5—Sponsor development (45-day activity)	Low cost impact	Reduce by 7 days	Medium—may require resource to spend more time earlier in the project and may not provide results.
Activity 1.4.2.3—Determine schedule of booth events and entertainment (15-day activity)	Medium cost impact	Reduce by 7 days	Medium—will have to add another resource who may not be as familiar with the project objectives.

Class Exercise 6-13: Gantt Chart

BEST CONSULTING Fundraiser Road Race

WBS	Name	Duration	Start Date	End Date
1	Fundraiser Charity Event	101d	1/1/2014 8:00 AM	5/21/2014 5:00 PM
1.1	Event Decision	13d	1/1/2014 8:00 AM	1/17/2014 5:00 PM
1.1.1	Event Analysis	10d	1/1/2014 8:00 AM	1/14/2014 5:00 PM
1.1.2	Event Options Decision	3d	1/15/2014 8:00 AM	1/17/2014 5:00 PM
1.2	Venue	37d	1/20/2014 8:00 AM	3/11/2014 5:00 PM
1.2.1	Site Selection	27d	1/20/2014 8:00 AM	2/25/2014 5:00 PM
1.2.1.1	Identify sites & Site visits	10d	1/20/2014 8:00 AM	1/31/2014 5:00 PM
1.2.1.2	Analyze site options	15d	2/3/2014 8:00 AM	2/21/2014 5:00 PM
1.2.1.3	Review and decide on site	2d	2/24/2014 8:00 AM	2/25/2014 5:00 PM
1.2.2	Site Preparation	10d	2/26/2014 8:00 AM	3/11/2014 5:00 PM
1.2.2.1	Water and Power Setup	10d	2/26/2014 8:00 AM	3/11/2014 5:00 PM
1.2.2.2	Tent Setup	3d	2/26/2014 8:00 AM	2/28/2014 5:00 PM
1.3	Marketing	88d	1/20/2014 8:00 AM	5/21/2014 5:00 PM
1.3.1	Outreach Opportunities	57d	1/20/2014 8:00 AM	4/8/2014 5:00 PM
1.3.1.1	Outreach Research	10d	1/20/2014 8:00 AM	1/31/2014 5:00 PM
1.3.1.2	Target Mailing List	12d	3/24/2014 8:00 AM	4/8/2014 5:00 PM
1.3.2	Marketing Plan	10d	1/20/2014 8:00 AM	1/31/2014 5:00 PM
1.3.3	Marketing Production	49d	2/3/2014 8:00 AM	4/10/2014 5:00 PM
1.3.3.1	Tickets: Design and produce event tickets	15d	2/3/2014 8:00 AM	2/21/2014 5:00 PM
1.3.3.2	Flyers: Design and produce event flyers	15d	2/3/2014 8:00 AM	2/21/2014 5:00 PM
1.3.3.3	Mail Marketing Packages	2d	4/9/2014 8:00 AM	4/10/2014 5:00 PM
1.3.3.4	Advertising	37d	2/3/2014 8:00 AM	3/25/2014 5:00 PM
1.3.3.4.1	Newspaper Advertising	33d	2/3/2014 8:00 AM	3/19/2014 5:00 PM
1.3.3.4.1.1	Request submission packages from local newspaper	1d	2/3/2014 8:00 AM	2/3/2014 5:00 PM
1.3.3.4.1.2	Create advertisement layout	10d	2/4/2014 8:00 AM	2/17/2014 5:00 PM
1.3.3.4.1.3	Review layout with stakeholders and gain approval	8d	2/18/2014 8:00 AM	2/27/2014 5:00 PM
1.3.3.4.1.4	Submit advertisement per submission deadlines	1d	2/28/2014 8:00 AM	2/28/2014 5:00 PM
1.3.3.4.1.5	Review publisher proof and approve	2d	3/3/2014 8:00 AM	3/4/2014 5:00 PM
1.3.3.4.1.6	Confirm Ad published per schedule	1d	3/19/2014 8:00 AM	3/19/2014 5:00 PM
1.3.3.4.2	Website Advertising	37d	2/3/2014 8:00 AM	3/25/2014 5:00 PM
1.3.3.4.2.1	Create a webpage for Charity Event	22d	2/3/2014 8:00 AM	3/4/2014 5:00 PM
1.3.3.4.2.2	Determine alternative websites and deliver web content	15d	3/5/2014 8:00 AM	3/25/2014 5:00 PM
1.3.3.4.3	Magazine Advertising	24d	2/3/2014 8:00 AM	3/6/2014 5:00 PM
1.3.3.4.3.1	Request submission packages from magazines	2d	2/3/2014 8:00 AM	2/4/2014 5:00 PM
1.3.3.4.3.2	Create advertisement layout	10d	2/5/2014 8:00 AM	2/18/2014 5:00 PM
1.3.3.4.3.3	Review layout with stakeholders and gain approval	8d	2/19/2014 8:00 AM	2/28/2014 5:00 PM
1.3.3.4.3.4	Submit advertisement per submission deadlines	1d	3/3/2014 8:00 AM	3/3/2014 5:00 PM
1.3.3.4.3.5	Review publisher proof and approve	2d	3/4/2014 8:00 AM	3/5/2014 5:00 PM
1.3.3.4.3.6	Confirm Ad published per schedule	1d	3/6/2014 8:00 AM	3/6/2014 5:00 PM
1.3.4	Surveys	78d	2/3/2014 8:00 AM	5/21/2014 5:00 PM
1.3.4.1	Pre-Event Survey	11d	2/3/2014 8:00 AM	2/17/2014 5:00 PM
1.3.4.1.1	Create Survey	6d	2/3/2014 8:00 AM	2/10/2014 5:00 PM
1.3.4.1.2	Distribute and collect info on Pre-Survey	5d	2/11/2014 8:00 AM	2/17/2014 5:00 PM
1.3.4.2	Post-Event Survey	22d	4/22/2014 8:00 AM	5/21/2014 5:00 PM
1.3.4.2.1	Create Survey	6d	4/22/2014 8:00 AM	4/29/2014 5:00 PM
1.3.4.2.2	Distribute and Analyze Post-survey results	13d	5/5/2014 8:00 AM	5/21/2014 5:00 PM
1.4	Event Logistics	48d	2/26/2014 8:00 AM	5/2/2014 5:00 PM
1.4.1	Food and Drink	20d	2/26/2014 8:00 AM	3/25/2014 5:00 PM
1.4.2	Booths & Entertainment	48d	2/26/2014 8:00 AM	5/2/2014 5:00 PM
1.4.2.1	Booth & entertainment site map	4d	2/26/2014 8:00 AM	3/3/2014 5:00 PM
1.4.2.2	Assign sponsors to booths	1d	3/24/2014 8:00 AM	3/24/2014 5:00 PM
1.4.2.3	Determine schedule of booth events and entertainment	15d	3/25/2014 8:00 AM	4/14/2014 5:00 PM
1.4.2.4	Setup and takedown of booths and stage	2d	5/1/2014 8:00 AM	5/2/2014 5:00 PM
1.4.3	Event Schedule	10d	4/15/2014 8:00 AM	4/28/2014 5:00 PM
1.4.3.1	Develop event schedule	5d	4/15/2014 8:00 AM	4/21/2014 5:00 PM
1.4.3.2	Assign volunteers to support each event	5d	4/22/2014 8:00 AM	4/28/2014 5:00 PM
1.4.4	Volunteer Training: Develop and deliver training for all event day volunteers	2d	4/29/2014 8:00 AM	4/30/2014 5:00 PM
1.5	Sponsor Development	45d	1/20/2014 8:00 AM	3/21/2014 5:00 PM
1.6	Volunteers	60d	1/15/2014 8:00 AM	4/8/2014 5:00 PM
1.7	Project Management	90d	1/15/2014 8:00 AM	5/20/2014 5:00 PM
		101d	1/1/2014 8:00 AM	5/21/2014 5:00 PM

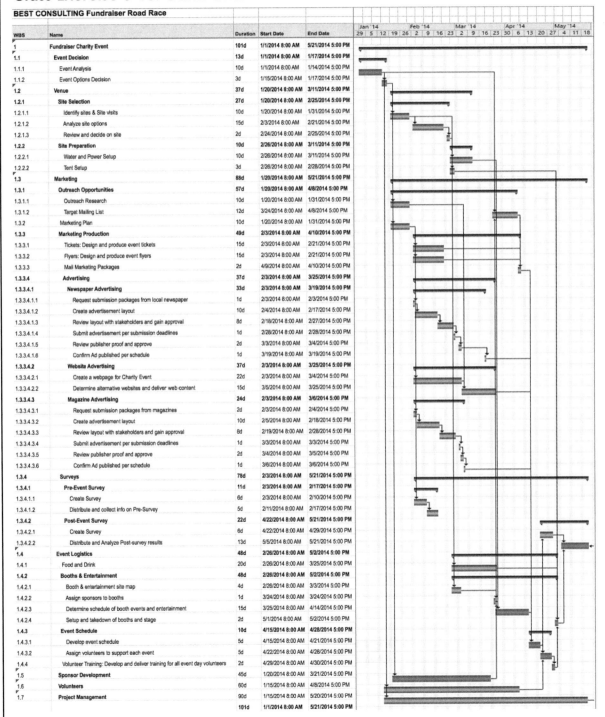

6

6

Class Exercise 6-14: Earned Value
Based on the total planned hours of 274 hours, earned value was *only* 113 (there were no partially completed tasks). The schedule variance on the project is $113 - 274 = <161>$ indicating that the project is significantly behind schedule.

There are two other observations from a scheduling perspective.

1. There is a significant issue on the identification of the site that needs to be addressed.
2. There are four tasks that should have started by 2/2, but have not yet.

As the project manager, you must understand the reasons these tasks are in trouble and take action where warranted.

ANSWERS TO CASE STUDIES CAN BE FOUND IN THE WAV™ FILES

This book has free material available for download from the Web Added Value™ resource center at *www.jrosspub.com*.

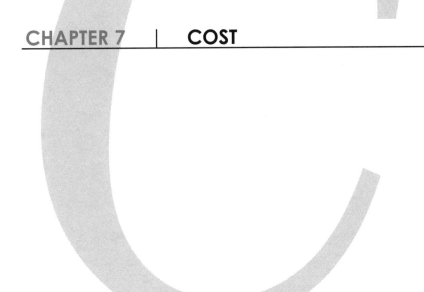

COST

7

COST MANAGEMENT

The Cost Management knowledge area focuses on defining the detailed costs of the work to be performed in order to meet project objectives. Cost management requires input from **scope management** in the context of the work to be performed and **time management** in terms of the effort it will take to perform the work. In addition to labor costs, all resource costs must be considered, including materials. Similar to the other knowledge areas discussed so far, managing and controlling the costs of a project are integral to the success of the project.

Many challenges exist for the project manager in dealing with cost management. Costs of a project are the most difficult aspect to control; once costs begin to shift out of control, it is extremely difficult, if not impossible, to bring a project's costs back in line with the original project cost objectives. Depending on the type of organization, the cost management functions a project manager employs can range dramatically. It is important for the project manager to understand all the tools available and leverage them appropriately for the project being worked.

One key technique that is discussed within the context of cost management is **earned value**. Earned value is applicable to several of the knowledge areas, but it will be addressed thoroughly within this chapter.

Knowledge Area Processes

Within the cost management knowledge area there are four processes within two process groups.

Planning	Monitoring and Controlling
Plan Cost Management Estimate Costs Determine Budget	Control Costs

Key Definitions

Budget at completion (BAC): the sum of all budgets established for the work to be performed.

Contingency reserve: budget within the cost baseline or performance measurement baseline that is allocated for identified risks that are accepted and for which contingent or mitigating responses are developed.

Crashing costs: costs incurred as additional expenses above the normal estimates to speed up an activity.

Estimate to complete (ETC): the estimated additional costs to complete activities or the project.

Management reserve: a dollar value, not included in the project budget, that is set aside for unplanned changes to project scope or time that are not currently anticipated.

Percent complete: the amount of work completed on an activity or WBS component.

Rough order of magnitude estimate (ROM): an estimate with a range of −25% to +75% often used during project initiation.

PLAN COST MANAGEMENT PROCESS

Plan Cost Management is the process that establishes the policies, procedures, and documentation for planning, managing, expending, and controlling costs. Planning for cost management is important as an input to the overall **project management plan**.

The key benefit of this process is that it directs how project costs will be managed throughout a project. Project costs are extremely hard to control, so having a structure around the approach to cost control is imperative.

Expert Judgment, Meetings, and Analytical Techniques

Expert judgment, meetings, and analytical techniques are the three tools and techniques used in the Plan Cost Management process.

The only output of the Plan Cost Management process is the **cost management plan**. One thing to note for the cost management plan is that the details included in this plan can vary greatly from company to company and project to project. For example, some projects may be very cost driven while others may not. Consider projects in your organization that are internal projects. Are the costs managed differently from costs that are directly related to a client engagement? Figure 7-1 below shows a sample schedule and cost management plan.

Schedule and Cost Management Plan

Project Name: Fundraiser Road Race

Date: 2/2/14

Any issues identified through normal communication channels must be presented to the Project Manager for review and determination of priority. Once prioritized, they will be incorporated into the overall schedule.

Project Insight will be the tool of choice for maintenance of the project schedule and work-package assignments.

Some items will not be considered a priority, however they will be recorded as such for consideration at a later time. These un-prioritized items will be retained in an excel spreadsheet table and will be reviewed periodically for prioritization.

As progress is reported based on work-package completion, there may be either co-dependencies affected—positively or negatively—and/or availability of resources will become a critical path item. The Project Manager's role will be to continuously monitor those dependencies and either address them directly or work with Sr. management to ensure any risks are minimized.

Figure 7-1
Schedule and Cost
Management Plan

Since costs and schedule are tied so closely together, the project manager chose to combine the management plan for both.

ESTIMATE COSTS PROCESS

The Estimate Costs process is the process of determining the costs associated with delivering a project. Costs include the costs of labor as well as the costs of materials needed to complete all the schedule activities on the project.

TIP

In long-duration projects or those dealing with a variety of currencies, the "cost of capital" must be addressed by the project management team.

The Estimate Costs process includes many of the same tools and techniques employed under the Estimate Activity Durations process, such as expert judgment, **analogous estimates**, **parametric estimates**, **three-point estimates**, and **reserve analysis**, as well as **bottom-up estimates**, but with a focus on estimating the cost of schedule activities.

The results of the Estimate Costs process are **activity cost estimates** and a **basis of estimate** which should be included in each **WBS dictionary**.

Analogous Estimates

Analogous estimating is an estimate that compares to past experience. For the Fundraiser Road Race project, the consultant has worked on over twenty road races in the past five years. With a most recent road race, he had the following experience:

Attendance	1,500
Costs of advertising	$20,000
Costs of site	$6,000
Costs of giveaways	$9,000

Figure 7-2
Prior Road Race
Expenditures

Based on what is known so far about the project, an initial estimate of costs based on 2,000 attendees is:

Attendance	2,000
Costs of advertising	$20,000
Costs of site	$6,000
Costs of giveaways	$12,000

Figure 7-3
Estimated Road Race
Expenditures

Since the estimated number of attendees is 33% more than the consultant's experience, the costs of giveaways have increased proportionately. The other two components—costs of advertising and costs of site—may not vary significantly based on the attendance volume; therefore, the consultant feels confident that those numbers could stay the same.

Parametric Estimates

As discussed in Chapter 6, parametric estimates can also be used for cost estimates.

Parametric estimates are based on specific "parameters" or metrics that can be used to predict costs and are typically more accurate than analogous estimates.

In addition to attendee information, the consultant for the Fundraiser Road Race also has statistics on the costs of magazine advertisements that have been used in determining the overall advertising costs, as shown in Figure 7-4 below.

According to this information, if the road race team determines that it wants to run an advertisement four times per month for four months, the estimated costs of advertising would be:

Magazine Advertising Costs			
	5 months before event	4 months before event	3 months before event
1 advertisement per month	10% discount per ad	5% discount per ad	$800 per ad per month
2 advertisements per month	10% discount per ad	5% discount per ad	$700 per ad per month
3 advertisements per month	10% discount per ad	5% discount per ad	$500 per ad per month
4 advertisements per month	10% discount per ad	5% discount per ad	$350 per ad per month

Figure 7-4
Magazine
Advertising Costs

- 16 advertisements x $350 per ad per month = $5,600 in advertising
- Since they will run the ads for four months, a 5% discount will apply = $280
- The total estimated cost for advertising is: $5,600 − $280 = $5,320

Three-Point Estimating

As we know, it is difficult to get exact estimates early on in a project since information regarding the details of a project is not yet known. A way to obtain more accurate estimates of costs is to request specific estimates from the people or organizations that are going to perform the work based on a set of specifications. To do this early on in the project may be unrealistic. The use of three-point estimating can alleviate this concern because it builds in a level of risk based on past experiences.

The formula for these estimates is:
Estimate = (Optimistic + 4 x Most Likely + Pessimistic) / 6

Requesting most likely, pessimistic, and optimistic estimates establishes a range which aids in assessing the risk of delivering the estimated activity.

> **TIP**
>
> Merely averaging the optimistic, pessimistic, and most likely estimates does not emphasize the most frequent occurrence.

Activity	Optimistic Cost Estimate	Most Likely Cost Estimate	Pessimistic Cost Estimate	Final Cost Estimate
1.3.3.4.1 Newspaper Advertising	$400	$500	$750	$525
1.3.3.4.2 Website Advertising	$1,000	$1,200	$2,500	$1,383
1.3.3.4.3 Magazine Advertising	$2,000	$5,000	$8,000	$5,000

Figure 7-5
Range of Estimates

In Figure 7-5 above, knowing the most likely estimates for advertising could aid the project team in communicating to sponsors the expected costs. Since the Fundraiser Road Race is expected to obtain donations for all its costs, having a reasonable estimate is important.

For those activities that are time driven, weighted three-point estimating can be used to determine an appropriate **labor rate**. Assuming you have a choice ranging from using a very experienced worker to using a student intern, the actual cost of performing the work can change. You may choose to use a "blended" rate based on the weighted three-point estimating formula. For each of the resources listed in Figure 7-6 below, a blended labor rate will be used against the hours estimated in time management. With this information, the costs of each activity can be determined.

Activity	Resource Type	Optimistic Estimate (Intern)	Most Likely Estimate (Industry Average)	Pessimistic Estimate (Expert)	Blended Labor Rate
A	Engineer	$45.00/hour	$60.00/hour	$150.00/hour	$72.50/hour
B	Administrator	$10.00/hour	$25.00/hour	$45.00/hour	$25.83/hour
C	Technician	$20.00/hour	$35.00/hour	$95.00/hour	$42.50/hour

Figure 7-6
Blended
Labor Rates

This tool of weighted three-point estimating can also be applied to material costs for any activity. Some materials can vary in unit cost or in quality, which could impact the overall cost of the activity, as shown in Figure 7-7.

Activity	Resource Type	Activity Effort Estimate	Final Labor Rate Estimate	Total Activity Costs for Labor
A	Engineer	$10.00/hour	$72.50/hour	$725.00
B	Administrator	$5.67/hour	$25.83/hour	$146.46
C	Technician	$9.83/hour	$42.50/hour	$417.78

Figure 7-7
Total Costs for
Labor

Bottom-Up Estimates

Bottom-up estimating is a tool and technique that takes the costs at the lowest level of detail available and rolls those costs up to a high level for reporting and tracking purposes. Ideally, if costs are captured at the activity or work package level, the overall budget of the project is as accurate as possible.

Class Exercise 7-1

Assuming the following effort, labor rates, and material costs for Activity E and I, determine the bottom-up estimate for our sample project (see page 6-43).

WBS ID	Activity Name	Predecessor	Effort	Duration	Labor Rate	Cost
1.1	Activity A	--	10 hours	5 days	$72.50/hour	
1.2	Activity B	1.1	5.67 hours	2 days	$25.83/hour	
1.3	Activity C	1.2	9.83 hours	4 days	$42.50/hour	
2.1	Activity D	1.2	3 hours	2 days	$42.50/hour	
2.2	Activity E	1.1	6 hours	1 day	$42.50/hour	+$300 materials
3.1	Activity F	2.2, 1.3	25 hours	8 days	$72.50/hour	
4.1	Activity G	1.3	10 hours	4 days	$42.50/hour	
4.2	Activity H	4.1	2 hours	3 days	$42.50/hour	
4.3	Activity I	4.2	10 hours	3 days	$25.83/hour	+$1,000 materials
4.4	Activity J	4.3	20 hours	5 days	$72.50/hour	
5.0	Activity K	4.4, 3.1	5 hours	2 days	$72.50/hour	

Case Study 7-1

For the LUV Music website project, see the various tools and techniques for estimating activity costs and update the activity spreadsheet with cost estimates.

Reserve Analysis

Similar to the discussion of reserve analysis within time management, reserve analysis is a tool and technique that can be employed within cost management to address uncertainty and risk within a project. Again, there are several ways to apply contingency to the costs of a project, including:
- Adding a percentage (%) to all activities
- Using the more pessimistic estimates

You might want to add additional dollars to an estimate when specific experience and history warrant. For example, suppose you anticipate inflation to impact the cost of a project. If the inflation rate is expected to grow by 0.5% annually, it would be appropriate to apply this rate to labor and material costs across the project. This kind of contingency reserve could be applied to single tasks as well.

A more pessimistic estimate may be used when resource assignments have not been finalized, recognizing that the experience level of project team members may not be ideal. The use of a weighted three-point estimate, as described above, would be a method of applying contingency reserves when the actual resources are unknown.

For our Fundraiser Road Race project, for example, if you determine that costs are based on actual costs from five years ago, you may determine that you must consider the cost of inflation, and add 10% to all estimates.

At the completion of the Estimate Costs process, the project team should have cost estimates for *all* activities on the activity list. The information gathered and decided in this process should be captured within each of the **work packages**.

Now you can probably see a pattern coming. After all activity cost estimates have been determined, the results of all analyses need to be captured in the **WBS dictionary** for each work package.

Within the WBS dictionary, the **basis of estimate** should be defined. It is always helpful for project managers to document their thought process and rationale as estimates are created to eliminate any confusion and incorrect assumptions that might be made later in the project. Figure 7-8 on the following page shows an example of a WBS dictionary with cost estimates included.

WBS ID: 1.3.3.4.1 – Newspaper Advertising

Description: Advertise the Road Race in the local newspaper, both the daily newspaper as well as the weekly entertainment publication. Advertisements in the daily newspaper should begin two months prior to the event and the weekly entertainment publication four months prior to the event.

Responsibility: Marketing – Henry Optimo – Consultant 1

Schedule:
  Milestone: Daily newspaper submission deadlines
           Weekly entertainment newspaper submission deadlines
  Predecessor: Advertising Designs from Marketing Plan
  Successor: Event Date

Schedule Activities:
  1. Request submission packages from local newspaper for both daily and weekly publication (8 hours)
  2. Create advertisement layout (15 hours & 5 hours admin)
  3. Review layout with sponsor and gain approval (10 hours for consultant & 4 hours for sponsor)
  4. Submit advertisement per submission deadlines (8 hours)
  5. Review publisher proof and approve (8 hours)
  6. Confirm ad published per schedule (1 hour: 2 week lag from review)

Resources Required:
Consultant 1 – Marketing coordinator
Admin 1 – Layout team
Sponsor 1 – Layout review and sign-off

Cost Estimates: *(Assumes coordinator: $100/hr for Sponsor; $70/hr for Consultant; $20/hr for Admin; average knowledge)*

Coordinator (Consultant 1): 50 hours	$3500	
Layout team (Admin): 5 hours	$ 100	
Review & sign-off (Sponsor): 4 hours	$ 400	
Total costs:	$4000 – No material costs	

Quality Requirements:
Date, time, location and cost of event must be clearly communicated, including sign-up instructions.

Acceptance Criteria:
Advertisements are published per the agreed-upon schedule.

Figure 7-8
WBS with Cost
Estimates

Cost of Quality

Quality is discussed in Chapter 8 of this study guide and the *PMBOK® Guide*; however, quality must be discussed briefly here in the context of cost estimates. Every project is unique and must address the quality expectations of the customer. Depending on the expectations for quality, the cost estimates and activity durations, which are also estimated, may vary. For example, if you are the project manager on a medical device project, the cost of quality may be higher than if you are managing the Fundraiser Road Race project.

The project manager and project team must weigh the costs and benefits of any activity as they relate to quality.

Group Decision Making

Just as with scope and time management, group decision making assists in building commitment and accountability for project costs. The more you involve team members in defining costs estimates, the more committed they are to meeting project targets.

Case Study 7-2

For the LUV Music website project, identify any schedule activities to which you may want to add additional work or time in order to ensure that the deliverable quality is improved. Adjust the costs of those activities accordingly.

DETERMINE BUDGET PROCESS

The Determine Budget process brings everything together that we've discussed so far under scope, time, and cost management. The ultimate result is a **cost baseline** that reflects the scope of work to be performed, the approved schedule to be met, and the costs necessary to deliver the work.

The ultimate objective of this process is to create a final authorized **time-phased budget** for the project that provides a plan for how funds will be spent during the execution of the project (as outlined in the **funding requirements**). This cost baseline will be used to monitor project performance during the execution of the project. The cost baseline is the approved version of the time-phased budget, excluding any management reserves.

TIP
Know the difference between budget and cost baselines. See Figure 7-8 in the *PMBOK®* *Guide*.

Cost Aggregation

Cost aggregation is the act of rolling up all the costs defined for each work package to create a total dollar amount for the entire project over time. Consider the Fundraiser Road Race. Each of the work packages is associated with a different period of time. If costs are distributed equally in each time period, a matrix similar to the one in Figure 7-9 on the following page is created.

	Dur.	Total Budget Labor	Total Budget Materials	Day 1	Day 2	Day 3	Day 4	Day 5	Day 6	Day 7	Day 8	Day 9	Day 10	Day 11	Day 12	Day 13	Day 14	Day 15	Day 16	Day 17	Day 18	Day 19	Day 20	Day 21	Day 22	Day 23
Activity A	5	725.00		145	145	145	145	145																		
Activity B	2	146.46							73	73																
Activity C	4	417.78									104	104	104	104												
Activity D	2	127.50									64	64														
Activity E	1	255.00	300						255																	
									300																	
Activity F	8	1812.50													227	227	227	227	227	227	227	227				
Activity G	4	425.00											106	106	106	106										
Activity H	3	85.00															28	28	28							
Activity I	3	258.30	1000						86	86	86															
									1000																	
Activity J	5	1450.00																		290	290	290	290	290		
Activity K	2	362.50																							181	181
TOTAL		$ 6,065.04	$1,300.00	145	145	145	145	145	1714	159	254	168	211	211	333	333	255	255	255	517	517	517	290	290	181	181
Cumulative Total				145	290	435	580	725	2439	2599	2853	3021	3232	3443	3775	4108	4363	4618	4873	5389	5906	6423	6713	7003	7184	7365

Figure 7-9
Cost Matrix

Once the cost per day is determined, a cumulative cost can be derived, resulting in a **cumulative cost curve** or **S-curve**, such as the sample S-curve shown in Figure 7-10 below.

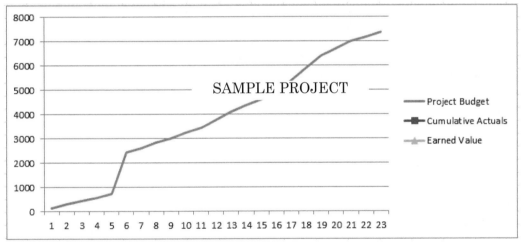

Figure 7-10
Sample
Project
S-Curve

An S-curve gets its name from the general shape a typical time-phased budget will form when graphed over time. The spike in the Sample File curve is due to the material expense required for Activity I.

For the Fundraiser Road Race, although all the primary participants except the consultant are volunteers, we assumed the rates of labor in Figure 7-11 below in order to capture the overall cost of our fundraiser.

Resource Type	Budget Labor Rate
Consultant	$70.00/hour
Sponsor	$100.00/hour
Administration	$20.00/hour
Volunteers 1, 2, 3 and 4	$25.00/hour

Figure 7-11
Rates of Labor

Following the rates of labor are a summary of the **budget at completion** (Figure 7-12) and, on the following page, the **cumulative cost curve (cost baseline)** (Figure 7-13) for the Fundraiser Road Race.

STATUS COMMENTS	SCORECARD	MORE DETAILS	**BUDGET**	PERFORMANCE	RESOURCES

Earned/planned values calculated through 11/24/2013 Calculate Now

	Cost/Actual:
Planned Value (PV):	$0.00
Earned Value (EV):	$0.00
Work Total:	$71,070.00
Actual Total (AC):	$0.00
Work Estimate To Complete:	$71,070.00
Work Estimate At Completion:	$71,070.00
Work Estimate At Completion (CPI):	$71,070.00
Target Budget:	
Est. Total / Prop. Total:	$23,700.00
Invoiced Total:	

Figure 7-12
Budget at
Completion

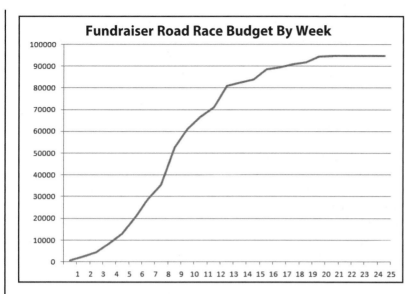

Fundraiser Road Race Budget By Week

Figure 7-13
Cumulative
Cost Curve

Case Study 7-3

Use the schedule developed for the LUV Music website project to create a time-phased budget.

Reserve Analysis

Reserve analysis has been discussed in several places already. The reason it is mentioned here, with the Determine Budget process, is that once the budget is aggregated, the project manager and potentially project stakeholders need to determine if any additional contingency reserves or management reserves are needed for the project as a whole.

Contingency reserves are dollars set aside to address the risk of the planning process having omitted activities that are necessary for in-scope items. Such reserves are allowances for unplanned changes which are necessary to deliver on the **project objectives**. These reserves can be reflected as part of each **activity** or as part of the project as a whole and should be included in the project **cost baseline**.

TIP

Contingency reserves are usually managed by the project manager.

TIP

Know the differences between activity contingency, contingency reserves (at the control account level), and management reserves.

In our Fundraiser Road Race marketing efforts, if the project management team identifies that it has missed a critical task that would be necessary to ensure that the advertising successfully draws enough people to the event, contingency reserves should be used to fill in that gap. The project manager usually has the discretion to use this type of reserve.

Management reserves are budget reserves for unplanned changes to project scope and cost. These reserves are still associated with managing the known scope of the project; however, these dollars are *not* included in the cost baseline that is developed from aggregating the activity costs. Management reserves are usually tightly controlled by the project owner or sponsor and not easily accessible to the project team.

Funding Limit Reconciliation

Most projects have limits on committing funds. These limits mean that a certain amount of funds is available for a certain period or through a certain milestone. Only activities up to that funding limit should be funded. If there are limits defined for a project, the project manager must be concerned with ensuring that the right activities are performed in order for the project to meet its **milestones** within the funding limits provided.

Class Exercise 7-2

In our Sample Project budget on page 7-13, the following expenditures are needed to support project efforts:

Days 1 to 5:	$725.00
Days 6 to 10:	$2507.00
Days 11 to 15:	$1386.00
Days 16 to 20:	$2095.00
Days 21 to 23:	$653.00

After reviewing the time-phased budget on page 7-13, what can you do if you can *only* spend $2,000 every five days?

CONTROL COSTS PROCESS

The Control Costs process is about monitoring the status of a project against the project budget and cost baseline. As in prior discussions on monitoring and controlling, having timely information is critical to the project manager's ability to respond to changes and issues with the current plan in a timely manner.

The intended outputs of the Control Costs process include **work performance information**, **change requests**, and **cost forecasts**.

Earned Value Management

Earned value management (EVM) is a tool and technique for measuring performance that eliminates bias. When only using actual cost to planned performance, actual performance can appear positive when in actuality it is negative. The basic dimensions of EVM are:
- **Planned value (PV)**: the sum of the approved cost estimates for activities scheduled to be performed during a given period
- **Actual cost (AC)**: the amount of money actually spent in completing work in a given period
- **Earned value (EV)**: the sum of the approved cost estimates for activities completed during a given period

There are four basic formulas to calculate variance on a project using EVM:
- **Cost variance (CV)** is earned value (EV) minus actual cost (AC); it is the difference between the budgeted cost of the work completed and the actual cost of completing the work, so a negative number means the project is over budget
  - $CV = EV - AC$
- **Schedule variance (SV)** is earned value (EV) minus planned value (PV); it represents the difference between what was accomplished and what was scheduled; a negative number means the project is behind schedule
  - $SV = EV - PV$

- **Cost performance index (CPI)** is earned value (EV) divided by actual cost (AC); it is the ratio of what was completed to what it cost to complete it, so values less than 1.0 indicate we are getting less than a dollar's worth of value for each dollar we have actually spent; CPI measures cost efficiency
  - CPI = EV / AC
- **Schedule performance index (SPI)** is earned value (EV) divided by planned value (PV); it is the ratio of what was actually completed to what was scheduled to be completed in a given period, so a values less than 1.0 mean the project is receiving less than a dollar's worth of work for each dollar we were scheduled to spend; SPI measures schedule efficiency
  - SPI = EV / PV

Earned value can be calculated at an individual activity level or for the overall project. While cost and schedule variances (CPI and SPI) are useful in controlling individual activity costs, the two indices are most useful for trend analysis of work accomplished.

Figure 7-14
Sample Earned
Value Calculation

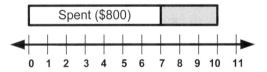

Let's take an activity in which you expect to spend $1,000 in a 10-day period, as depicted in Figure 7-14 above. You are now at day 7, and you have spent $800 so far. Are you where you should be for the activity? Now consider that you expected to spend $100 per day, but you really only completed about 60% of the work you expected. Where do you stand now?

Earned value is about providing you a more objective look at the state of your activity.

For this example, the following is true after 7 days:
   Actual Costs (AC) = $800
   Planned Value (PV) = $700, or $100 per day
   Earned Value (EV) = $600, or 60% of work completed

Based on this information, you can calculate the following:
   Schedule Variance (SV) = $600 − $700 = <$100>
   Cost Variance (CV) = $600 − $800 = <$200>

If you remember that negative numbers are "bad" for this particular activity, you are both behind schedule by one day's worth of work and over budget by $200.

The SPI and CPI are indices that can be used in forecasting future costs. They can be calculated at the activity or project level. In our example above, the CPI = $600 / 800 or 0.75, which means that for every dollar spent, the project is only getting $0.75 of value.

Would this be beneficial to know when asked for a projection of future costs?

Class Exercise 7-3

Using the chart below, calculate the cost and schedule variance for each activity and for the overall project, then answer the following questions:
   Which activities are behind schedule?
   Which activities are ahead of schedule?
   Is the project over or under budget?

Activity	Budget at Completion	Planned Value	Actual Costs	Earned Value	Cost Variance	Schedule Variance
A	$1,000	$1,000	$1,200	$1,000		
B	$500	$500	$400	$400		
C	$2,000	$1,500	$1,200	$1,000		
D	$4,000	$2,000	$2,200	$2,500		
E	$1,000	$0	$100	$100		
Total	$8,500	$5,000	$5,100	$5,000		

Class Exercise 7-4

What is the overall SPI and CPI for the Sample Project from Exercise 7-3?

Class Exercise 7-5

Look at the S-curve below for the Fundraiser Road Race. Calculate SV, CV, SPI, and CPI. AC = 26,000, PV = 21,000, and EV = 18,000.

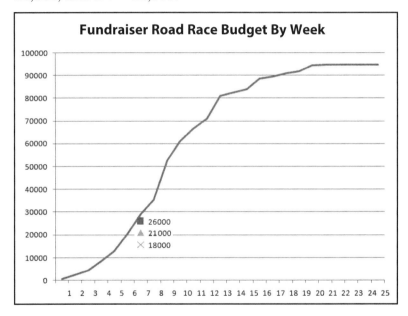

Forecasting

As a project progresses, changes to the project activities, whether in time or cost, are inevitable. No estimate is 100% accurate, and it is the project manager's role to understand what has occurred on the project and the impact of project developments on the anticipated total cost of the project.

Forecasting is the tool and technique that provides a mathematical estimate of what the future costs of a project will be based on the past activity of the project.

The goal of forecasting is to determine the **estimate at completion** (EAC) for the project. There are several ways to determine EAC. The EAC is the amount we expect the total project to cost on completion. The S-curve in Figure 7-15 below shows the various earned value formulas with the EAC depicted.

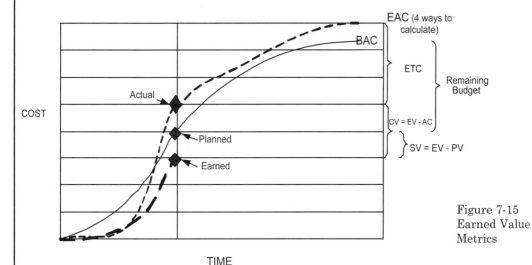

Figure 7-15
Earned Value
Metrics

There are four methods listed in the *PMBOK® Guide* for computing EAC. Three of these methods use a formula to calculate EAC. Determining which formula to use will depend on the individual situation and the credibility of the actual work performed compared to the planned budget.

- A **new estimate** is most applicable when the actual performance to date shows that the original estimates were fundamentally flawed or when they are no longer accurate because of changes in conditions relating to the project
  - EAC = AC + New Estimate for Remaining Work
- The **original estimate** formula is most applicable when actual variances to date are seen as being the exception, and the expectations for the future are that the original estimates are more reliable than the actual work effort efficiency to date
  - EAC = AC + (BAC − EV)

- The **performance estimate low** formula is most applicable when future variances are projected to approximate the same level as current variances
    - EAC = AC + (BAC – EV) / CPI

  A shortcut version of this formula is:
    - EAC = BAC / CPI
- The **performance estimate high** formula is used when the project is over budget and the schedule impacts the work remaining to be completed
    - EAC = AC + (BAC – EV) / (CPI x SPI)

Class Exercise 7-6

The following S-curve was created for our Sample Project, with an overall project CPI of 0.78125. As the project manager, you know that Activities A and B got off to a bad start. Once the kinks were worked out, all subsequent activities to date were performing as planned. What formula should you use to calculate EAC and why?

Note that AC = 3,200, EV 2,500, and PV = 2,853.

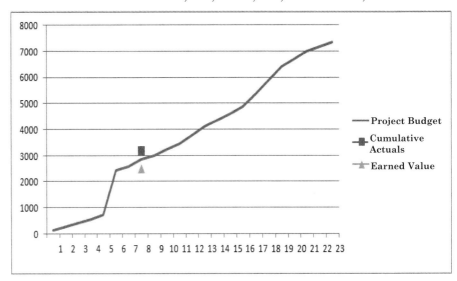

To Complete Performance Index (TCPI)

Another technique for forecasting is to determine the cost performance that must be attained to meet the BAC or EAC. Based on the BAC, the formula is:
- $TCPI = (BAC - EV) / (BAC - AC)$

If the EAC has been approved, it will be used instead of the BAC. The formula based on the EAC is:
- $TCPI = (BAC - EV) / (EAC - AC)$

Class Exercise 7-7

Regarding Class Exercise 7-6, if a new EAC is not viable for the Fundraiser Road Race, what is the TCPI necessary to perform in order to stay on the original budget? (Show your work.)

_____
_____
_____

Performance Reviews

Performance reviews involve collecting cost and performance information over time and comparing that information to baselines. **EVM** is one method of determining variance from plan.

If EVM is being used, three specific pieces of information can be determined. **Variance analysis** explains the reasons for the variances. **Trend analysis** provides information on performance improvement or deterioration. And **earned value performance** compares actual performance to the documented schedule and cost baselines.

Figure 7-16 on the following page an example of a report of performance in terms of earned value.

The project manager continuously monitors variances to the plan. Assessing the degree of variance and determining whether **corrective action** or **preventive action** may be needed is a key project manager role.

Figure 7-16
Road Race Snapshot

Figure 7-16 below shows a snapshot of the Fundraiser Road Race at the beginning of the project. As work is performed, actual hours and variances will be monitored.

Performance Hours

	Planned Hours (PVH)	Accomplished Hours (EVH)	Actual Hours (AH)	Accomplished Hours Variance (AHV)	% Accomplished Hours Variance	% Accomplished Hours Variance (EVH)	Scheduled Hours Variance (SHV)	% Scheduled Hours Variance	Accomplished Hours Performance Index	Scheduled Hours Performance Index
Work Hours	0.00	0.00	0.00	0.00			0.00			
Billable Work Hours	0.00	0.00	0.00	0.00			0.00			

Billable Gross Profit Analysis

Invoice Analysis

	Hours	Rate	Expense	Total
Billable	0.00	$0.00		$0.00
Invoiced	0.00	$0.00	$0.00	$0.00
Actual	0.00	$0.00		$0.00
Invoiced - Billable Variance	0.00	$0.00	$0.00	$0.00
Invoiced - Actual Gross Profit	0.00	$0.00	$0.00	$0.00

Estimates To/At Completion

	Estimate To Complete (Remaining Work)	Estimate At Completion (Actuals/Billables Plus Remaining Work)	Estimate At Completion (CPI) (Actuals/Billables Plus Remaining Work divided by the Performance Index)
Work Hours	1,833.00	1,833.00	1,833.00
Work Total	$71,070.00	$71,070.00	$71,070.00
Billable Work Hours	1,833.00	1,833.00	1,833.00
Billable Work Total	$0.00	$0.00	$0.00

Class Exercise 7-8

Based on reading this report for the Fundraiser Road Race, does anything on the project require corrective action or preventive action?

_____
_____
_____

Reserve Analysis

Once an assessment has been made regarding performance, adjustments to planned reserves can be made. If planned risk events do not occur, the unused contingency can be removed, or if additional risks are anticipated, reserves can be increased.

7

PROFESSIONAL RESPONSIBILITY

Cost management is about accurately reflecting the costs of a project and delivering accurate forecasts of anticipated project costs. When considering the four aspects of professional responsibility—responsibility, respect, fairness, and honesty—the project manager must keep certain things in mind at all times:

- Don't shift dollars to make things look better
- Don't pull from reserves or contingencies inappropriately
- Don't lie to a customer to create a change request to cover other mismanagement; lead by example by being open and honest about assumptions and expectations; project team members and owners and sponsors are influenced by such behavior

It is the project manager's responsibility to provide accurate, unbiased information regarding project costs.

7

BE A BETTER PROJECT MANAGER

Exercise: facilitating better estimates.

Purpose: people are generally lousy estimators. They typically don't consider all the activities necessary to deliver a deliverable. When asking team members for their duration or cost estimates, the following questions would be helpful.

Steps: Ask the following questions as appropriate.

1. Does your estimate include time and dollars for any review efforts? Or are reviews spelled out separately in the schedule for these activities?
2. If the activity being estimated requires review, which resource is needed?
3. Are there any other people, training, or materials you need to complete your task(s)?
4. Do you trust the estimates? Use a three-point estimate to identify negative and positive risks associated with pessimistic and optimistic estimates.

7

SAMPLE CAPM EXAM QUESTIONS ON COST MANAGEMENT

1. Which process provides guidance on how project costs will be managed during a project?

   a) Control Costs
   b) Determine Budget
   c) Estimate Costs
   d) Plan Cost Management

2. Which of the following cost management processes are planning processes?

   a) Control Costs, Plan Cost Management
   b) Estimate Activity Resources, Estimate Costs
   c) Estimate Costs, Determine Budget
   d) Plan Cost Management, Estimate Activity Resources

3. Why should you consider stakeholder requirements when managing cost?

   a) Stakeholders have differing views on when costs are expended
   b) Stakeholders are interested in whether external resources have the appropriate skill sets
   c) Stakeholders have expectations about what should be included in the scope of a project
   d) Stakeholders will review the schedule to determine when resources will be needed

4. An estimate that has a range of -25% to +75% is called:

   a) Definitive
   b) Rough order of magnitude
   c) Budget
   d) Baseline

Notes:

5. Parametric cost estimating involves:

   a) Using the WBS to do bottom-up estimates
   b) Defining the parameters of the life cycle
   c) Calculating individual estimates of work packages
   d) Using a statistical model to estimate costs

6. As the project manager on a medical device project, you are asked to put together a budget for the project. Considering various costing alternatives is part of the _____ process.

   a) Estimate Costs
   b) Determine Budget
   c) Control Costs
   d) Plan Cost Management

7. The _____ process involves aggregating the costs of individual schedule activities to establish a cost baseline.

   a) Control Costs
   b) Plan Cost Management
   c) Determine Budget
   d) Estimate Costs

8. The difference between the project budget and the cost baseline is _____.

   a) Management reserves
   b) Expected cash flows
   c) Residual funds
   d) Change requests

9. Contingency reserves can be used:

   a) Only upon formal request
   b) Only for schedule activities that utilize people resources
   c) At the discretion of the project manager
   d) Only for schedule activities that utilize material resources

Notes:

7

10. What is the key benefit of the Control Costs process?

    a) It determines how much the project will cost
    b) It provides guidance on how funds will be spent
    c) It creates a cost baseline used to measure performance against
    d) It allows you to determine whether or not variances require corrective action

11. Use the following chart for the next question:

Task	PV	AC	EV
1	95	100	95
2	150	130	110
3	130	130	130
4	80	60	70

Which task is on schedule and within budget?

    a) Task 1
    b) Task 2
    c) Task 3
    d) Task 4

12. Based on the table below, what is the cost variance for case 9?

Case	PV	AC	EV
1	10,000	10,000	10,000
2	10,000	8,000	10,000
3	10,000	8,000	8,000
4	9,000	12,000	10,000
5	10,000	12,000	12,000
6	10,000	10,000	12,000
7	12,000	12,000	10,000
8	10,000	8,000	9,000
9	12,000	10,000	11,000

    a) <$1,000>
    b $1,000
    c) <$2,000>
    d) $2,000

Notes:

13. The cost performance index is computed as:

a) Earned value divided by actual cost
b) Earned value minus actual cost
c) Earned value minus planned value
d) Earned value divided by planned value

14. Use the following table for the next question:

Task	PV	AC	EV
1	10,000	8,000	9,000
2	12,000	10,000	11,000

What is the cost variance for task 2?

a) $1,000
b) $2,000
c) <$1,000>
d) <$2,000>

15. Information about the costs of activities that have been authorized and incurred would be found in the _____.

a) Work performance data
b) Enterprise environmental factors
c) Cost baselines
d) Organizational process assets

7

ANSWERS AND REFERENCES FOR SAMPLE CAPM EXAM QUESTIONS ON COST MANAGEMENT

Section numbers refer to the *PMBOK® Guide.*

1. **D** **Section 7.1 – Planning**
    A) in this process, expenditures and changes to the cost baseline are monitored; B) in this process, costs are aggregated and a cost baseline is established; C) in this process, cost amounts are determined.

2. **C** **Section 7.1 – Planning**
    Be familiar with the relationship between knowledge areas, process groups, and processes. The Estimate Activity Resources process is a planning process in the time management knowledge area.

3. **A** **Section 7.1 – Planning**
    Differences may occur among stakeholders who have differing expectations for quality, which may have differing costs. Note that the accounting department views money spent when a product has been received or services have been performed, while the finance department views money spent when payment is made.

4. **B** **Section 7.2 – Planning**
    A) a definitive estimate typically ranges from -5% to +10%; C) and D) there are no generally accepted ranges for a budget or baseline.

5. **D** **Section 7.2.2.3 – Planning**
    Parametric estimates use a model of statistical relationships among variables and rely on verified historical information.

6. **A** **Section 7.2 – Planning**
    Estimate Costs is the process of determining the monetary amounts necessary to complete all project activities.

7. **C** **Section 7.3 – Planning**
The Determine Budget process is a planning process within the project cost management knowledge area.

8. **A** **Section 7.3.3.1 – Planning**
The project budget is the sum of the cost baseline and management reserves.

9. **C** **Section 7.3.3.1 – Planning**
A) is part of the project budget; a formal request is not required although it may be customary in some organizations; B) and D) contingency reserves can be used for both human resources and material resources.

10. **D** **Section 7.4 – Planning**
A) is a benefit of the Estimate Costs process; B) is a benefit of the Plan Cost Management process; C) is a benefit of the Determine Budget process.

11. **C** **Section 7.4.2.1 – Monitoring and Controlling**
SPI = 1, CPI = 1

12. **B** **Section 7.4.2.1 – Monitoring and Controlling**
Cost Variance (CV) = EV – AC
CV = $11,000 – $10,000 = $1,000

13. **A** **Section 7.4.2.1 – Monitoring and Controlling**
CPI = EV / AC

14. **A** **Section 7.4.2.1 – Monitoring and Controlling**
CV = EV – AC
CV = $11,000 – $10,000 = $1,000

15. **A** **Section 7.3.1 – Planning**
Work performance data is an input to the Control Costs process. The key word here is incurred.

ANSWERS TO CLASS EXERCISES

Class Exercise 7-1: Bottom-Up Estimate

WBS ID	Activity Name	Predecessor	Effort	Duration	Labor Rate	Cost
1.1	Activity A	--	10 hours	5 days	$72.50/hour	$725.00
1.2	Activity B	1.1	5.67 hours	2 days	$25.83/hour	$146.46
1.3	Activity C	1.2	9.83 hours	4 days	$42.50/hour	$417.78
2.1	Activity D	1.2	3 hours	2 days	$42.50/hour	$127.50
2.2	Activity E	1.1	6 hours	1 day	$42.50/hour	$255.00 + $300 materials
3.1	Activity F	2.2, 1.3	25 hours	8 days	$72.50/hour	$1,812.50
4.1	Activity G	1.3	10 hours	4 days	$42.50/hour	$425.00
4.2	Activity H	4.1	2 hours	3 days	$42.50/hour	$85.00
4.3	Activity I	4.2	10 hours	3 days	$25.83/hour	$258.30 + $1,000 materials
4.4	Activity J	4.3	20 hours	5 days	$72.50/hour	$1,450
5.0	Activity K	4.4, 3.1	5 hours	2 days	$72.50/hour	$362.50
	Total		106.5 hours			$7,365.04

Class Exercise 7-2: Cost of Quality

1) You can purchase the materials for Activity I sooner during days 1 thru 5.
2) For days 6 thru 10, you can delay some of the work on Activity J and back load the activities.

Class Exercise 7-3: Earned Value Management

Activities B and C are behind schedule. Activities D and E are ahead of schedule. The project is over budget.

Activity	Budget at Completion	Planned Value	Actual Costs	Earned Value	Cost Variance	Schedule Variance
A	$1,000	$1,000	$1,200	$1,000	<$200>	0
B	$500	$500	$400	$400	0	<$100>
C	$2,000	$1,500	$1,200	$1,000	<$200>	<$500>
D	$4,000	$2,000	$2,200	$2,500	$300	$500
E	$1,000	$0	$100	$100	0	$100
Total	$8,500	$5,000	$5,100	$5,000	<$100>	$800

Class Exercise 7-4: Earned Value Management

SPI = 4,800 / 4,000 = 1.2 (ahead of schedule)
CPI = 4,800 / 4,900 = 0.98 (over budget)

Class Exercise 7-5: Earned Value Management

SV = 18,000 – 21,000 = <3,000>
CV = 18,000 – 26,000 = <8,000>
SPI = 18,000 / 21,000 = 0.86
CPI = 18,000 / 26,000 = 0.69

Class Exercise 7-6: Forecasting

You should use the formula that uses the remaining budget, the original estimate formula.

EAC = AC + (BAC – EV)
3,200 + (7,365 – 2,500) = 8,065

Class Exercise 7-7: To Complete Performance Index

TCPI = (BAC – EV) / (BAC – AC)
(7,365 – 2,500) / (7,365 – 3,200)
4,865 / 4,165 = 1.17

7

Class Exercise 7-8: Variance Analysis

****For Class Discussion Only****

ANSWERS TO THE CASE STUDIES CAN BE FOUND IN THE WAV™ FILES

This book has free material available for download from the
Web Added Value™ resource center at *www.jrosspub.com*.

QUALITY

CHAPTER 8 | **QUALITY**

8

QUALITY MANAGEMENT

The quality management knowledge area emphasizes customer satisfaction and continuous improvement. Key to understanding quality in the context of PMI is considering the differences between **project quality** and **product quality**. This chapter focuses primarily on project quality, but its applicability can be leveraged in a product quality environment as well.

The project manager is responsible for ensuring that the project meets the quality objectives laid out within the **project charter** and **project management plan**. Quality will vary greatly from project to project and from company to company depending upon many factors. It is the project manager's responsibility to ensure that the appropriate level of quality is delivered to ensure a successful completion of the project and a satisfied customer.

Knowledge Area Processes

8

Within the quality management knowledge area there are three processes within three process groups.

Planning	Executing	Monitoring and Controlling
Plan Quality Management	Perform Quality Assurance	Control Quality

Key Definitions

Accuracy: an assessment of correctness in which the closer a result is to a specified value, the more accurate the result.

Capability maturity model integration (CMMI): defines the essential elements of effective processes. It is a model that can be used to set process improvement goals and provide guidance for quality processes.

Grade: a category that differentiates items with the same functional use but not the same characteristics.

Malcolm Baldrige award: the national quality award given by the U.S. National Institute of Standards and Technology. Established in 1987, the award program recognizes quality in business and other sectors. It was inspired by Total Quality Management (TQM).

Organizational project management maturity model (OPM3®): focuses on an organization's knowledge, assessment, and improvement elements.

Precision: a measure of exactness based on the interval of measurement. The smaller the interval, the more precise the measurement.

Process quality: specific to the type of product or service being produced and the customer expectations, the level of process quality will vary. Organizations strive to have efficient and effective processes in support of the product quality expected. For example, the processes associated with building a low-quality, low-cost automobile can be just as efficient as, if not more efficient than, the processes associated with building a high-quality, high-cost automobile.

Product quality: specific to the type of product produced and the customer requirements, product quality measures the extent to which the end products of the project meet the specified requirements. Product quality can be expressed in terms that include, but are not limited to, performance, grade, durability, support of existing processes, defects, and errors.

Project quality: typically defined within the project charter, project quality is usually expressed in terms of meeting stated schedule, cost, and scope objectives. Project quality can also be addressed in terms of meeting business objectives that have been specified in the charter. Solving the business problems for which the project was initiated is a measure of quality for the project.

Quality: the degree to which a set of inherent characteristics satisfies the stated or implied needs of the customer. To measure quality successfully, it is necessary to turn implied needs into stated needs via project scope management.

Quality policy: a statement of principles indicating what the organization defines as quality.

Six Sigma: an organized process that utilizes quality management for problem resolution and process improvement. It seeks to identify and remove the causes of defects.

Warranty: assurance that products are fit for use or the customer receives compensation. Warranties could cover downtime and maintenance costs.

PLAN QUALITY MANAGEMENT PROCESS

Planning for quality requires the discipline to focus on meeting the objectives of the project. Managing projects requires that the objectives laid out in the **project charter** are achieved through the careful planning and execution of the overall **project plan**.

The measurement of quality must be defined by the recipient of the project (the customer), and a plan must be put in place to ensure compliance with the agreement about the level of quality that is acceptable. All of this takes place within the Plan Quality Management process.

There are two aspects of quality that must be addressed in any project: **project quality** and **product quality**. Project quality is ensuring that the **constraints** of the project are addressed and planned around.

8

For example, a project is expected to be delivered on time, within a certain budget, utilizing certain resources, delivering certain scope deliverables, and addressing and responding to certain risks. These are all components of project quality that constrain what a project can do. These constraints are given in Figure 8-1 below.

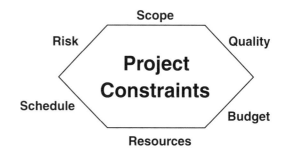

Figure 8-1
Project
Constraints

Product quality is the measurement of how well the deliverables have met the requirements of the project. For example, if the project is to create a cell phone that is supposed to have a mean-time-between-failure (MTBF) of 15 months, then the ultimate measure of quality must quantify that the phones being produced meet this requirement.

The primary outputs of the Plan Quality Management process are the **quality management plan**, a **process improvement plan**, **quality metrics**, and **quality checklists**. A sample quality management plan is provided in the **WAV™ files**.

The Plan Quality Management process incorporates all the activities needed to understand what quality is for the project and to identify how the achievement of quality will be validated.

Cost-Benefit Analysis

Projects do not have unlimited funds, so evaluating the cost of quality is critical in determining the appropriate quality level for the project. Most people think of a cost-benefit analysis as a means to justify an overall project. For example, if a project is proposed, and a cost-benefit analysis determines that it will save the organization $2 million, that project should be funded. However, cost-benefit analyses can also be used to determine the level of quality needed for a project.

Let's use our example of the cell phone again. In producing cell phones, organizations have choices with regard to the type of materials and processes used to deliver a cell phone to certain specifications. Circuit boards that are used in cell phones can be produced with varying levels of quality, which usually translate to a lower or higher price. If a typical circuit board has a MTBF of ten months, the cell phone company may have to purchase a more expensive circuit board to meet the 15 month MTBF requirement. A simple cost-benefit analysis for circuit board costs might be:

Cost-Benefit Analysis of Circuit Board Costs					
Circuit Board Analysis	5-month MTBF	10-month MTBF	15-month MTBF	20-month MTBF	25-month MTBF
Vendor Cost	$10/100 circuits	$40/100 circuits	$120/100 circuits	$200/100 circuits	$500/100 circuits
All Other Phone Costs	$30	$50	$80	$80	$80
Anticipated Sale Price of Phone	$50	$100	$150	$200	$210
Anticipated Sales in Units	100,000	80,000	40,000	10,000	8,000
Profit per Unit	$19	$46	$68	$100	$80
Total Profitability	$1,900,000	$3,680,000	$2,720,000	$1,000,000	$640,000

In this example, if the organization is required to meet or exceed the 15-month MTBF, then the profitability expectations should be set at $2.7 million. If the project is expected to exceed 15-month MTBF, then the organization can choose between the 20- or 25-month MTBF. The organization should NEVER choose the 5- or 10-month options, even though the 10-month option shows the greatest profit, because doing so would cause the project to not meet the product quality expectations.

TIP

Less rework, higher productivity, lower costs, increased stakeholder satisfaction, and increased profitability are major benefits of performing cost-benefit analyses.

Class Exercise 8-1

The CEO of BEST CONSULTING is wondering if it might be better to hire an organization to find sponsors for the Fundraiser Road Race event or to have volunteers perform that function. What should be considered in making a decision to hire or to use volunteers?

1. _____
2. _____
3. _____
4. _____
5. _____

Cost of Quality

Based on the decisions made to support the objectives of the project, there is a quantifiable measure of quality that can be made. Quality costs can be divided into two categories: the **cost of conformance** and the **cost of non-conformance** to quality standards.

The cost of conformance to quality standards means that there is a proactive decision to eliminate errors from a project and product. Effort must be expended within the project budget in order to ensure conformance. There are two types of costs of conformance: **prevention** and **appraisal**.

Examples of prevention costs could include:
- Costs due to increasing the number of training days to ensure that users understand a system thoroughly
- Costs due to developing a regression test plan to ensure that new enhancements do not impact prior functionality

Examples of appraisal costs could include:
- Costs due to increasing the percentage of product inspected to reduce or eliminate defective parts, thereby keeping them from reaching the customer
- Costs due to purchasing state-of-the-art equipment that automates a very labor-intensive, manual process

TIP

Quality management today increasingly emphasizes the importance of prevention over inspection. It is better to build in the appropriate quality than respond to poor quality.

Costs of non-conformance to quality standards include the costs that organizations incur after a project has been completed and are paid for by the operations of the business. There are two types of costs of non-conformance: **internal failure** and **external failure**.

Examples of costs of internal failure could include:
- Costs incurred once inspection of the final product has been performed and any defective products have been thrown away

Examples of costs of external failure could include:
- Costs due to the increase in warranty work if inferior components are used in a product
- Costs incurred when customers are lost due to their dissatisfaction with a project's product, whether it is an actual physical product or simply a new process
- Costs incurred from an increase in lawsuits due to a product that causes harm

Costs of non-conformance to **quality standards** should be considered when determining the appropriate quality level for a project.

<table><tr><td>**TIP**
The concept that "quality is free" results from transferring costs of non-conformance to costs of conformance, which are usually less expensive.</td></tr></table>

Class Exercise 8-2

In the table below, identify whether the type of cost of each item results from whether the item conforms or doesn't conform to quality standards.

Scenario	Conformance/Non-Conformance
Add additional testing cycles	
Modify warranty repair agreement to allow returns up to 90 days	
Increase defects detected through process automation	
Implement a repair program for the shoe department at all retail stores	
Reduce the costs of production by purchasing lower grade materials	
Send the entire project team to a project management class	

Seven Basic Quality Tools

As part of the Plan Quality Management process, the project team should determine how it will measure adherence to quality.

There are several types of quality tools that can help identify when things are not preforming to expectations. The seven that are specifically mentioned in the *PMBOK® Guide* are:
- Cause and effect diagrams
- Flowcharts
- Checksheets
- Pareto diagrams
- Histograms
- Control charts
- Scatter diagrams

Cause and effect diagrams are graphical tools used to help determine the cause of an issue. They are also known as **Ishikawa diagrams** or **fishbone diagrams**. Often, problems or issues are identified based on a series of symptoms. Addressing these symptoms themselves may not translate into solving an actual problem because a symptom itself isn't a **root cause**. The purpose of cause and effect diagrams is to determine the root cause of a problem.

The sample cause and effect diagram in Figure 8-2 on the next page shows how a problem is identified (the central line describes the issue). By a process of asking a series of "Why?" questions, the participants in this exercise can identify the root cause of the issue.

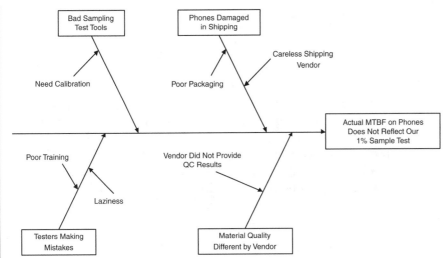

Figure 8-2
Sample Cause and
Effect Diagram

Flowcharts are tools that can be used to improve communication and identify potential problems within a new system or business process. Flowcharting is used frequently in documenting **business processes** and determining areas for **improvement** or articulating the business process so that it can be automated through technology. A sample flowchart is given in Figure 8-3 below.

TIP

Flowcharts are also known as process maps or SIPOC (Supplier, Input, Process, Output, Customer) models.

8

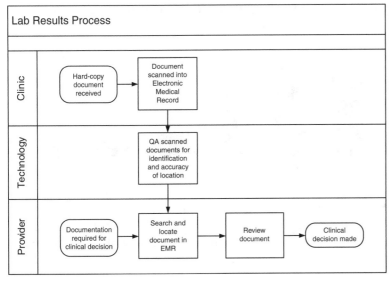

Figure 8-3
Sample
Flowchart

Class Exercise 8-4

Create a flowchart for how you get up in the morning to get ready for your day.

Checksheets, also called data tables or tally sheets, are typically used to gather data. Checksheets are helpful in ensuring that all data needed is gathered consistently in order to perform analysis. Once gathered, data within checksheets may be displayed in other ways, such as in Pareto diagrams and other histograms. A sample checksheet is given in Figure 8-4 below.

Problem	Month			
	1	2	3	Total
A	II	II	I	5
B	I	I	I	3
C	THL	II	THL	12
Total	8	5	7	20

Figure 8-4
Sample
Checksheet

Pareto diagrams are a type of histogram in which the information is sorted by frequency, as in the sample Pareto diagram in Figure 8-5 below. If a Pareto diagram is used to sort those issues that occur with the greatest frequency, they can help an organization identify and focus on those issues first.

> **TIP**
> The concept of "Pareto optimo" is also called the 80/20 rule because 20% of defects account for 80% of costs.

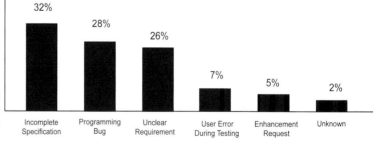

Figure 8-5
Sample Pareto
diagram

Histograms are good visual tools to identify frequency of occurrence. In the chart in Figure 8-6 on the facing page, issue #8 has the highest frequency of occurrence and issue #2 the lowest.

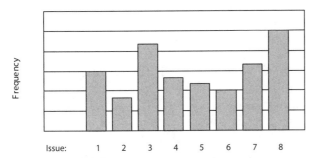

Figure 8-6
Sample
Histogram

Control charts are great tools to monitor performance within acceptable upper and lower boundaries. In the cell phone example, the project team has tracked the MTBF of a sampling of phones and created the control chart in Figure 8-7 below.

TIP
Control charts are useful in identifying when processes require attention.

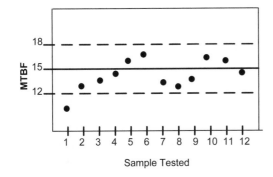

Figure 8-7
Sample
Control Chart

8

Scatter diagrams are useful if the variable being measured doesn't trend but rather is grouped or patterned; scatter diagrams show a correlation between variables, as in the sample in Figure 8-8 below.

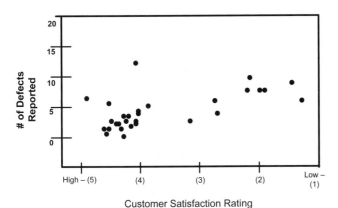

Figure 8-8
Sample Scatter
Diagram

TIP

There are many quality planning tools. See Figure 8.1.2.7 of the *PMBOK® Guide* for additional examples. The key here is to determine which tools will help you best manage your project and provide information on its performance.

In addition to the quality tools defined in the *PMBOK® Guide*, there are two other tools to highlight.

Run charts show trending. If the objective of a project is to see an increase or decrease in a variable, then a run chart may be an appropriate measurement tool. A sample run chart is given in Figure 8-9 below.

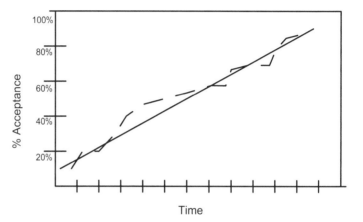

Figure 8-9
Sample Run
Chart

Gantt charts are mostly used to measure the progress of a project, typically to evaluate project quality as it relates to schedule. (A sample Gantt chart can be found in Chapter 6, page 6-52.)

Class Exercise 8-3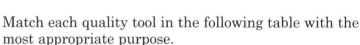

Match each quality tool in the following table with the most appropriate purpose.

Chart	Purpose
A. Gantt chart	Compare frequency of occurrence at a point in time
B. Scatter diagram	Demonstrate priorities
C. Upper/lower control chart	Show project progress
D. Pareto diagram	Show trends
E. Histogram	Show patterns
F. Run chart	Identify when defects exceed expectations

Benchmarking

Benchmarking is a technique that can be used when the comparison of future data to past data is necessary. Benchmarking is often used when organizations are improving a process. The benchmark may be described in terms of widgets per day, output per hour, average call time, etc. Benchmark information provides the project team a "steady state."

In our cell phone example, for instance, let's say current cell phone production processes typically produce 100 cell phones per day per person on the assembly line. A project to improve the efficiency of the manufacturing process would be expected to increase the number of cell phones that can be produced per day per person. The benchmark to be measured against will be the 100 cell phones per day per person.

Design of Experiments

Design of experiments is a structured, organized technique for determining the relationship between different factors affecting a process and the output of that process. Design of experiments defines a set of experiments in which relevant factors are varied systematically. The results of these experiments help identify optimal conditions because they identify those factors that most influence the output and those that have less influence.

Statistical Sampling

Statistical sampling is a very common technique for determining how well a project is performing compared to the quality standards set. Sampling is less costly than 100% inspection and generally provides enough information for a project team's needs.

An example of statistical sampling would be running 1% of all cell phones produced through an automated testing machine that simulates 20 months of usage. The results of this sampling should give the project team an

8

indication of whether or not the 15-month MTBF will be achieved. An upper/lower control chart could be a useful tool to validate results.

The primary output of the Plan Quality Management process is the **quality management plan**. The quality management plan indicates how the project defines and performs quality. Care must be taken to determine the appropriate tools to measure both **project quality** and **product quality**. The quality management plan may include quality metrics and a checklist as depicted in Figure 8-10 below for our Fundraiser Road Race project.

Quality Management Plan

For the Fundraiser Road Race, the following objectives have been defined:
- Raise $300,000 for the local Children's Charity in this first event.
- Raise awareness within the state about the Children's Charity.
- Develop a core staff of volunteers that will participate in this fund raising event and become the leaders of any future charitable events that the organization wishes to support.
- Develop a repeatable process for planning and executing charitable events.

Quality Metrics:
In order to satisfy the objectives, the project team has identified that the following will be developed in order to effectively measure the success of the project:
1. The Road Race should deliver $300,000 in donations +/- 10% to be considered a success.
2. An evaluation of who in the community knows about the Children's Charity and the kinds of services it provides to the needy. It would be acceptable to see an increase in awareness by 10% based on a random sample of people living in the community within a 30 mile radius of the location of the event.
3. Procedures must be documented and available for reuse at the kickoff of the next charitable event.

Quality Checklist:
In order to deliver on these requirements, the following must be attained:
1. Collect and store the funds that are received from all sources. Compare funds collected to the targets defined in the Quality Metrics.
2. Perform a pre- and post-survey to determine awareness before and after the event. Evaluate the change from the pre-survey results to the post-survey results and determine if the Quality Metric has been attained.
3. Confirm that a single procedure document has been produced and delivered to senior management by the conclusion of the Road Race.

Figure 8-10
Quality
Management
Plan

Case Study 8-1

For the LUV Music website project, identify three quality tools or techniques that can be used to measure the successful delivery of the project objectives. Identify what information is needed to be captured in order to successfully monitor these metrics, and also identify how this measurement should be represented.

PERFORM QUALITY ASSURANCE PROCESS

The Perform Quality Assurance process ensures that the **quality standards** that have been defined are used. One key concept to remember here is that in order to receive accurate data from the Control Quality process, an organization's **quality procedures** must be performed consistently and accurately.

Quality assurance is the mechanism to determine the consistent and accurate application of quality procedures. Typically quality assurance is performed by specialized teams, who do not perform the work being evaluated, or by specialists who are not part of the project team.

When organizations have a haphazard approach to quality, the information received will be inaccurate and can lead to poor decision making and additional costs to the organization.

The key output of the Perform Quality Assurance process are **change requests** and various updates to project documentation. In addition to the quality tools previously described, both **quality audits** and **process analysis** are tools organizations can use to determine if quality processes are working as expected.

> **TIP**
>
> Know the definitions of each of the Quality Management knowledge area quality tools. See Sections 8.1.2.3, 8.1.2.7, 8.2.2.1, and 8.3.2.1 of the *PMBOK® Guide*.

8

TIP

Quality audits may be conducted by outside agencies like the International Organization for Standardization (ISO).

Quality Audits

Quality audits are structured reviews of project activities. A person performing a quality audit is looking to determine if the project team is following the policies, processes, and procedures laid out in the **quality management plan**.

Process Analysis

Process analysis is a tool that can be used to identify where **improvement** is needed. For our cell phone scenario, in the context of quality assurance, the quality audit may require that the process itself be analyzed to determine why the testing results consistently do not reflect the defect rate experienced in the field.

For example, let's say that the field experience shows a 12-month MTBF for cell phones, but the sampling process showed an 18-month MTBF. An internal analysis of what occurs in the testing process would need to be performed. The objective of this analysis would be to determine why there is such a great discrepancy between what is occurring in the marketplace and what is occurring within the testing process.

The results of **quality audits** or process analyses may include recommendations to:
- Modify existing organizational process assets
- Initiate a change request to address a deficiency identified
- Update the project management plan or any other project documents to reflect the findings

On the facing page, Figure 8-11 shows an example of a change request that may be initiated as a result of a quality audit.

CHANGE REQUEST

Project Name: Fundraiser Road Race

Date: 2/15/14

Project Manager: Henry Optimo

Requestor Name: H. Optimo

Request Decision: Approve [ ] Reject [ ]

Date Reviewed:

Priority:

[X] High – Mission Critical, Urgent

[ ] Medium

[ ] Low

Reason for Priority:
Impact on success of Road
Race Project

Business Problem: [to be filled out by Requestor]
The target mailing list that was developed by the marketing group only provided a list of 1000 targets.

Business Implications: [to be filled out by Requestor]
The development of a target mailing list may not provide the expected results anticipated for the Fund Raiser Road Race. The expectation is to raise over $300,000 for the Children's Charity.

Requirements and Options: [to be filled out by Business Analyst]
Must have a minimum of 10,000 targets based on standards provided by American Marketing Association. 10,000 targets should gross a minimum of 2500 participants in the road race.

Current Process Impacts: [to be filled out by Business Analyst]
Will require marketing department to perform additional searches for sources not currently available to them.

System Implications: [to be filled out by Business Analyst & Technical Architect, if applicable]
None known at this time

Proposed Changes: [to be filled out by Business Analyst & Technical Architect, if applicable]
Increase search to include as many sources of targets that would provide a 10,000 target mailing list.

Risks:

Recommendation:

Approved By:
Business Representative   _____
Project Manager   _____
Project Sponsor   _____

Figure 8-11
Change Request

CONTROL QUALITY PROCESS

The Control Quality process includes the actual work of capturing information and measuring that information against the **metrics** that have been defined in the Plan Quality Management process. Typically, quality control is performed by a team of individuals who specialize in monitoring results. The results captured must be relevant to the project and measured against what has been defined in the quality management plan.

As the project manager, you need to know what metrics should be measured to ensure quality on the project, and you need to ensure that the quality control team is measuring the appropriate metrics.

As you plan for quality in your project, keep in mind the differences between these pairs of terms.

prevention versus **inspection**
attribute sampling versus **variables sampling**
tolerances versus **control limits**

8

TIP
The standards against which a deliverable is inspected are those that are defined in the project documents that address performance, grade, durability, support of existing processes, defects, and errors.

The tools and techniques used in the Control Quality process are the same tools and techniques available in the Plan Quality Management and Perform Quality Assurance processes. Basically, the tools and techniques the project team plans to use should be the tools and techniques actually used when measuring performance.

The difference is that the outputs of the Control Quality process are the **quality control measurements**, **work performance information**, **validated deliverables**, **validated changes**, and **change requests**.

Class Exercise 8-5

You are the manager of a call center, and you would like to find out the causes of customer dissatisfaction. Perform a cause and effect analysis using a fishbone diagram to answer the question: Why are customers irritated when calling into a 1-800 call center?

Inspection

The tools and techniques for the Control Quality process are the same as those discussed for the Plan Quality Management process, the seven basic **quality tools** and **statistical sampling**. Inspection is an additional tool under the Control Quality process. Inspection is a physical examination of the deliverables of a project to determine if they meet acceptable standards. Inspections can be performed throughout the project life cycle to aid in determining **conformance to quality**.

Class Exercise 8-6

Using the template below, identify three ways for the Fundraiser Road Race team to use inspection to determine quality.

Inspection	Explanation of Inspection Process
1	
2	
3	

The Perform Quality Control process is critical to ensuring that the project has met the expectations of the organization as described in the **project charter**.

Case Study 8-2

Based on the quality metrics defined in Case Study 8-1, create an inspection process that will be used to validate at least one deliverable of the LUV Music website project.

8

PROFESSIONAL RESPONSIBILITY

Quality management is about accurately capturing and reporting on the deliverables of a project. Quality is a perception that can only be approved by the customer of the project. When considering the four aspects of professional responsibility—responsibility, respect, fairness, and honesty—the project manager must keep certain things in mind at all times:

- Define quality metrics that are achievable and realistic
- Report results accurately and without bias
- Respond appropriately when the metrics show the process is out of control

It is the project manager's responsibility to provide accurate, unbiased information regarding a project's quality.

8

KEY INTERPERSONAL SKILLS FOR SUCCESS

The interpersonal skill highlighted in this chapter is:

Coaching

Project managers will be more successful if they help their team members become successful. One way to accomplish this is for the project manager to work with the team members or individuals to help them build new skills or expand existing skills.

In this chapter we discuss many different quality tools, techniques, and approaches. We stated earlier that quality does not just happen because a plan exists. It is up to the project manager and the project team to commit to the level of quality that is expected. The project team members may or may not have experience with each tool and therefore may not be aware that a more appropriate tool exists. The project manager may need to coach the team on the creation and usefulness of the tools that are chosen in order to ensure the highest quality.

8

BE A BETTER PROJECT MANAGER

Exercise: selecting quality measures

Purpose: although measuring quality is important to every project, it may not be necessary or feasible to measure too many things. When presented with a large volume of recommended measures, discuss the following as a team to narrow down the efforts associated with measuring quality.

Steps:

1. What are the first three key indicators of project success?
2. What are the first three key indicators of product success?
3. Do we have the ability to track these measures? If not, can we start to track them? What would the effort be to do so?
4. Create a shortened list of measures and review with client.
5. Obtain approval and add necessary steps to the project schedule.

SAMPLE CAPM EXAM QUESTIONS ON QUALITY MANAGEMENT

1. What is the main value of the Perform Quality Assurance process?

   a) Helps the team improve quality processes
   b) Guides the project manager on how quality will be managed throughout the project
   c) Identifies causes of poor product quality
   d) Validates that project work meets the stakeholders' requirements

2. Which of the following are inputs to the Perform Quality Assurance process?

   a) Work performance information, quality control measurements, and change requests
   b) Stakeholder register, enterprise environmental factors, and organizational process assets
   c) Quality metrics, quality control measurements, and project documents
   d) Change requests and organizational process assets updates

3. As a project manager, you should have a working knowledge of statistical control processes, which may be used in the _____ process.

   a) Perform Integrated Change Control
   b) Manage Project Team
   c) Control Quality
   d) Direct and Manage Project Work

4. Which of the following are organizational process assets that are inputs to the Control Quality process?

   a) Work performance data and deliverables
   b) Quality metrics and checklists
   c) Quality audit reports and quality process documentation
   d) Quality standards and issue and defect reporting procedures

5. Modern quality management recognizes the importance of _____.

   a) Tools and techniques
   b) Quality audits
   c) Inputs and outputs
   d) Prevention over inspection

6. Who has the primary responsibility for quality management in a project?

   a) Project manager
   b) Management
   c) Quality manager
   d) Project engineer

7. When a process is considered to be out of control, it:

   a) Will have variances which are outside acceptable limits
   b) May not be changed to provide improvements
   c) Shows differences caused by expected events or normal causes
   d) Should not be inspected or reworked for any reason

8. In order to ensure a project will satisfy the needs for which it was undertaken, project managers will utilize:

   a) The Control Quality process
   b) Project Quality Management
   c) The Perform Quality Assurance process
   d) The Plan Quality Management process

Notes:

9. The process in which the project manager identifies the quality standards that are relevant to the project is...

   a) The Project Quality Management process
   b) The Plan Quality Management process
   c) The Control Quality process
   d) The Perform Quality Assurance process

10. The difference between grade and quality is that:

   a) Grade is concerned with the attributes of the product, whereas quality is concerned with how well the product meets requirements
   b) Grade is concerned with fitness-for-use, while quality is concerned with how well the product meets requirements
   c) Grade is concerned with the cost to conform to specific requirements, while quality is concerned with the cost of non-conformance
   d) Grade and quality are actually synonymous and have no real difference on projects

11. Another term for the cost of poor quality is:

   a) Sunk costs
   b) Defects
   c) Failure costs
   d) Contract termination

12. A/An _____ is a bar chart that shows a distribution of values.

   a) Control chart
   b) Histogram
   c) Ishikawa diagram
   d) Flowchart

Notes:

8

13. The output of the Control Quality process that determines the correctness of deliverables is called:

a) Recommended defect repair
b) Quality control measures
c) Validated defect repair
d) Verified deliverables

14. A category or rank used to distinguish items that have the same functional use but differing technical characteristics is called:

a) Grade
b) Precision
c) Functional specifications
d) Quality

15. Monitoring and recording results of executing quality activities to assess performance is part of:

a) Quality planning
b) Quality assurance
c) Quality control
d) Total quality management

8

Notes:

8

ANSWERS AND REFERENCES FOR SAMPLE CAPM EXAM QUESTIONS ON QUALITY MANAGEMENT

Section numbers refer to the *PMBOK® Guide*.

1. **A** **Section 8.2 – Executing**
   B) occurs in the Plan Quality Management process; C) and D) occur in the Control Quality process.

2. **C** **Section 8.2.1 – Executing**
   A) are outputs of the Control Quality process; B) are inputs to the Plan Quality Management process; D) are outputs of the Perform Quality Assurance process.

3. **C** **Section 8.3 – Monitoring and Controlling**
   A working knowledge of statistical quality control tools is important to help evaluate outputs to the Control Quality process.

4. **D** **Section 8.3.1.8 – Monitoring and Controlling**
   A) Performance data collected from other controlling processes; B) output of Plan Quality Management; C) output of Perform Quality Assurance Project documents.

5. **D** **Section 8.0 – Planning**
   The disciplines of both Project Management and Quality Management recognize the importance of prevention over inspection, management responsibility, customer satisfaction, and continuous improvement.

6. **A** **Section 8.0 – Planning**
   Ultimately the project manager is responsible for project quality; management is responsible for providing proper resources to achieve the desired quality.

7. **A** **Section 8.1.2.3 – Monitoring and Controlling**
   Control charts are excellent tools to utilize when trying to determine if a process is performing within or outside acceptable limits.

8. **B** **Section 8.0 – Planning**
Control Quality, Perform Quality Assurance, and Plan Quality Management are processes in the Project Quality Management knowledge area.

9. **B** **Section 8.1 – Planning**
A) Project Quality Management is the knowledge area; C) Control Quality monitors specific project results; D) Perform Quality Assurance ensures that the project employs all necessary processes.

10. **A** **Section 8.0 – Planning**
During project planning, it is important to understand the expected levels of grade and quality that are needed. This understanding will help in determining the level of quality control that will be required on the project.

11. **C** **Section 8.1.2.2 – Planning**
A) are expended costs; B) are the results of poor quality; D) poor quality may cause contract terminations of poor performing vendors.

12. **B** **Section 8.1.2.3 – Planning**
A) compares data measurements to control limits; C) is a fishbone or cause and effect diagram; D) is a graphical representation of a process.

13. **D** **Section 8.3.3 – Monitoring and Controlling**
In addition to verified deliverables, an output of the Control Quality process is validated change requests.

14. **A** **Section 8.0 – Planning**
High and low grade items may both have high quality (for the technical characteristics present).

15. **C** **Section 8.3 – Planning**
Know the difference between quality assurance and quality control. The Perform Quality Assurance process is the process of auditing to determine that the quality standards are used and are appropriate.

ANSWERS TO CLASS EXERCISES

Class Exercise 8-1: Cost-Benefit Analysis

Possible considerations are:
1. How much experience do volunteers have?
2. How much experience do vendors have?
3. Does BEST CONSULTING already know what the expected amount of sponsorship is and how difficult the team feels it will be to achieve?
4. Will the cost of a vendor impact the ability of the team to reach its charity contribution goal? Without this expertise, will the team be able to achieve its goal?
5. Is there value in using a vendor, especially if BEST CONSULTING wants to hold regular events?

Class Exercise 8-2: Cost of Quality

Scenario	Conformance/Non-Conformance
Add additional testing cycles	Conformance
Modify warranty repair agreement to allow returns up to 90 days	Non-conformance
Increase defects detected through process automation	Conformance
Implement a repair program for the shoe department at all retail stores	Non-conformance
Reduce the costs of production by purchasing lower grade materials	Non-conformance
Send entire project team to a project management class	Conformance

Class Exercise 8-3: Quality Tools

Chart	Purpose
A. Gantt chart	Compare frequency of occurrence at a point in time **(E)**
B. Scatter diagram	Demonstrate priorities **(D)**
C. Upper/lower control chart	Show project progress **(A)**
D. Pareto diagram	Show trends **(F)**
E. Histogram	Show patterns **(B)**
F. Run chart	Identify when defects exceed expectations **(C)**

Class Exercise 8-4: Flowchart

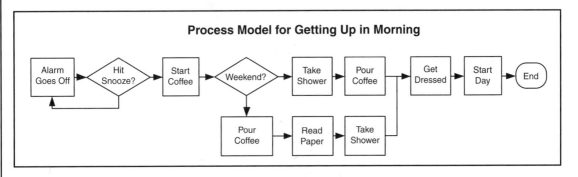

Process Model for Getting Up in Morning

8

Class Exercise 8-5: Cause and Effect Diagram

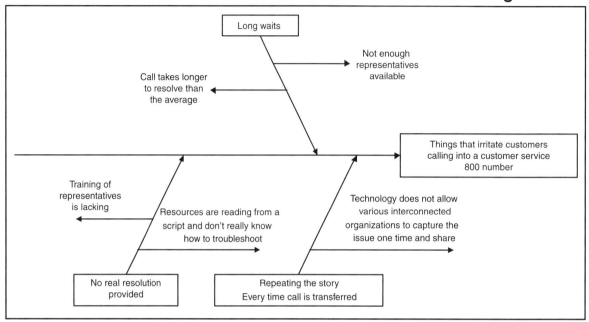

Class Exercise 8-6: Inspection

The chart below provides a couple of examples of inspection processes that could be implemented for the Fundraiser Road Race.

Inspection	Explanation of Inspection Process
1	Test each tent to confirm that electrical is set up correctly
2	Count/collect all tickets at gate to confirm attendance
3	Review flyer materials prior to sending them out to mailing list

ANSWERS TO THE CASE STUDIES CAN BE FOUND IN THE WAV™ FILES

Web Added Value™

This book has free material available for download from the Web Added Value™ resource center at *www.jrosspub.com*.

CHAPTER 9 | **HUMAN RESOURCES**

9

9

HUMAN RESOURCES MANAGEMENT

The human resources management knowledge area is directed at the project manager's ability to build, develop, and manage a project team. It is the one knowledge area that does not have any monitoring and controlling processes. The focus of this chapter is understanding **organizational structures** and their impact on project success as well as the **general business skills** and **interpersonal skills** a project manager must possess to succeed.

> **TIP**
> It is important to read Appendix G in the *PMBOK® Guide*.

A project manager needs to understand that his or her role is not an administrative one. Project managers are general managers of a project and in that context must wear many hats and adapt to the needs of a project, especially the needs of the project team, to succeed.

Knowledge Area Processes

Within the human resources management knowledge area, there are four processes within two process groups.

Planning	Executing
Plan Human Resource Management	Acquire Project Team Develop Project Team Manage Project Team

Key Definitions

Authority: the right to make decisions necessary for the project or the right to expend resources.

Colocation: project team members are physically located close to one another in order to improve communication, working relations, and productivity.

Leadership: the ability to get an individual or group to work toward achieving an organization's objectives while accomplishing personal and group objectives at the same time.

Multi-criteria decision analysis: this technique utilizes a decision matrix to provide a systematic analytical approach for establishing criteria such as risk levels, uncertainty, and valuation to evaluate and rank many ideas.

Organizational breakdown structure (OBS): a type of organizational chart, different from a responsibility assignment matrix (RAM), in which work package responsibility is related to the organizational unit responsible for performing that work. It may be viewed as a very detailed use of a RAM with work packages of the work breakdown structure (WBS) and organizational units as its two dimensions.

Power: the ability to influence people in order to achieve needed results.

Resource calendar: a calendar that documents the time periods in which project team members can work on a project.

Responsibility assignment matrix (RAM): a structure that relates project roles and responsibilities to the project scope definition.

Team building: the process of getting a diverse group of individuals to work together effectively. Its purpose is to keep team members focused on the project goals and objectives and to understand their roles in the big picture.

Virtual teams: groups of people with shared objectives who fulfill their roles with little or no time spent meeting face to face.

PLAN HUMAN RESOURCE MANAGEMENT PROCESS

The human resource plan is a subsidiary plan of the project management plan. Planning the resources for a project includes not only managing the project team, but also obtaining the correct skill sets and documenting the **roles and responsibilities** of those resources, their **reporting relationships**, and any efforts that are necessary to ensure that the project team can perform at the appropriate level, such as training.

The output of the Plan Human Resource Management process is the **human resource plan** itself. It includes three primary components:
- Roles and responsibilities of the project team
  - Roles of team members
  - Authority of team members
  - Responsibility of team members
  - Competency of team members
- Project organization charts
- Staffing management plan
  - Staff acquisition plan
  - Resource calendar
  - Staff release plan
  - Concurrent assignments and priorities
  - Training needs
  - Recognitions and rewards
  - Compliance with roles
  - Safety policies and procedures

Some of the tools a project manager needs in order to develop a comprehensive human resource plan include **organization charts**, **networks**, and an understanding of **organizational theory**. An example of a human resource plan for the Fundraiser Road Race can be found in Figure 9-1 on the following page.

9

Human Resources Management Plan
Project Name: Fundraiser Road Race
Date: 2/2/14

This project is expected to be executed with volunteer employees of BEST CONSULTING.

VOLUNTEERS:
BEST CONSULTING's policy regarding employee volunteers is as follows:

1) All volunteers must sign a waiver stating that they will not hold BEST CONSULTING liable for any injuries incurred during the volunteer event.
2) Volunteers must not be asked to spend more than 10 hours per week on a volunteer effort.

EXTERNAL RESOURCES:
If external resources are needed to execute on the project, Mary Urbanski will be the HR representative for acquiring appropriate staffing. No paid resources can be hired without Ms. Urbanski's review and approval.

BONUS' and REWARDS:
Participation in the fundraiser project does not qualify for service rewards.

Figure 9-1
Human
Resource Plan

TIP
Organizational structures may change during the course of a project, affecting team members' responsibilities.

Organization Charts and Position Descriptions

Organization charts come in many forms, the most common of which is a hierarchical chart similar to the one in Figure 9-2 below.

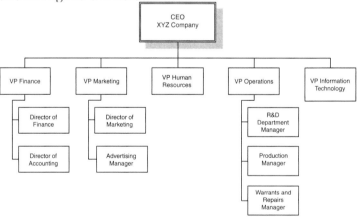

Figure 9-2
Organizational
Chart

Organization charts show a reporting relationship between individuals or departments within an organization, describing the areas of responsibility covered. For any project, an organization chart can be developed showing the relationship of team members to each other based on their individual contributions to the project and their unique skill sets.

An organization chart is different from a responsibility chart, which relates individuals to responsibilities rather than showing reporting relationships.

Networking

Networking is a technique that project managers can employ to gain an understanding of an organization, a client, and the political environment that can impact the effectiveness of staffing options. It is critical to understand the environment in which a project will operate. A project manager that does not consider a project's environment will ultimately have difficulty succeeding.

In addition, project team members can be extremely effective when using internal networks to "give" and "get" necessary information in order to successfully perform their jobs.

Organizational Theory

Organizational theory looks at the way people, teams, and organizations interact. Understanding the dynamics of varying organizational structures, realms of influence, and ways in which people work can provide the project manager additional insight into team dynamics and make the project manager more effective in dealing with **conflict**, **politics**, and **project issues** in general.

Expert Judgment

Expert judgment within human resources management can be applied in many ways to improve human resource planning. Some examples include:
- Assess roles needed for projects based on standardized organization role descriptions
- Determine preliminary effort levels and the needed number of resources
- Provide guidelines for how long it might take to staff a project based on market experience and project conditions
- Identify risks of staff acquisition, retention, and release planning

> **TIP**
> Networking is an activity that can energize collaboration within a project or between project participants and other stakeholders.

> **TIP**
> The project manager must consider the pros and cons of each organization structure—functional, matrix, or projectized—as a project moves from one phase to the next.

9

Class Exercise 9-1

Given the scenarios described below, discuss an approach the project manager should take.

Scenario	Recommended Approach
You are a project manager in a functional organization. Two of your key resources work for a manager who is constantly pulling these resources for production issues. These constant interruptions on work necessary for the project are now approaching an urgent level.	
The sponsor of a program is a very outspoken individual and always feels that he is right. His best friend is the CEO of the company so people try to accommodate his wishes as much as possible. This past week, he asked the project team to implement a change that is out-of-scope in the team's mind, but he is adamant that it is part of the scope.	
You are a project manager in a strong matrix organizational structure. A key resource has had a family emergency that will take her away from the office for at least three weeks.	

Case Study 9-1

By answering the questions below, create a human resource plan for the LUV Music website project.

1) What type of resources does the project require in terms of skill set and competency?
2) Will the project team acquire project resources internally or externally?
3) Will the project team be able to train current staff if ideal resources are not available?
4) What will the project organization chart look like?

ACQUIRE PROJECT TEAM PROCESS

The Acquire Project Team process involves determining the availability needs of the project resources and actually obtaining the resources to complete the project work defined. In other words, it indicates when resources are going to be needed and which resources are going to be obtained.

Acquiring project team members occurs throughout the project life cycle. In some cases, project team members are assigned to projects in advance of the project starting (this is called project **pre-assignment**). Or a project may acquire project team members through external organizations, such as consultants or staff augmentation firms. The decision to use internal or external resources is defined within the **staff management plan**.

In this chapter, we focus on two tools and techniques available to the project manager in acquiring project team members: **negotiation** and **virtual teams**.

The two primary outputs of the Acquire Project Team process are the **project staff assignments** and a **resource calendar**. The creation of a staff assignment plan and a resource calendar is an ongoing effort.

Projects are generally made up of individuals who can be categorized by five distinct characteristics:
- Assigned full time to the duration of a project
- Assigned part time to the duration of a project
- Assigned full time to a portion of a project or phase
- Assigned part time to a project and bringing a specific, urgent, or important skill
- Assigned part time to a project performing standardized, routine tasks

Understanding the types of resources assigned will aid the project manager in managing and motivating team performance.

Pre-assignment

When project participants are selected in advance, they are considered pre-assigned. Often, pre-assignment will be used as part of a competitive proposal if a project award is dependent upon having specific expertise on a project.

Negotiation

A project manager will often need to use negotiating skills to acquire the appropriate resources. Negotiation is a necessary skill for project managers for a variety of reasons. The project manager interacts with all levels of an organization—senior management, functional management, customers, and team members. It is unlikely that all parties the project manager works with are aligned with the goals and objectives of the project. The ability to successfully negotiate with people is critical to the successful delivery of a project.

Negotiation can range from informal to formal. What people think of when they think of negotiation is two parties working to close a contractual deal. This is an example of a formal form of negotiation. Informal forms of negotiation occur more frequently. An example of informal negotiation would be a project manager discussing with a functional manager the unique skill sets and availability of staff members to determine the appropriate resource for a project.

The *PMBOK® Guide* advocates a "win-win" approach to negotiation. This means that both parties who are negotiating reach an agreeable conclusion based on a perceived mutual benefit.

Acquisition

When needed resources are not available within the performing organization, acquiring resources from outside sources may be necessary. Acquiring such resources may involve hiring resources or subcontracting out for the necessary expertise on a temporary basis.

TIP

Multi-criteria decision analysis in selecting project team members may include one or more of the following factors:
- Availability
- Cost
- Experience
- Ability
- Knowledge
- Skills
- Attitude
- International concerns

Acquisition is a special type of procurement. It is indeed a type of procurement, but it is often handled through a human resource department or organization rather than a procurement department or organization.

Class Exercise 9-2

Review the situations below. Is each an example of a "win-win" or a "win-lose" scenario? Describe what you would do differently, if anything.

Scenario	Win-Win or Win-Lose?	What would you do differently?
The functional manager of the development department has pulled the lead developer from your project without asking for your permission. You go to your sponsor and ask for a three-way conference call with the functional manager. Prior to the meeting, you prepare your sponsor to communicate to the functional manager that your project is the most important project in the organization and that nothing should be distracting the lead developer from the project.		
The project manager for the vendor was due to deliver a design of a new amusement park ride on July 1st. It is now July 2nd, and you have not heard from the vendor, so you send off a scathing email to the vendor's superiors stating that you feel that their organization does not live up to its commitments.		

Virtual Teams

In today's environment, technology has provided organizations with a way to reach and utilize skilled resources without **colocating** those resources. For the project manager, this is both a benefit and a risk to the project.

Using virtual teams makes it much easier to acquire resources (and sometimes at a lower cost than might otherwise have been available) and is a great benefit to a project that requires unique skills. There are many benefits of using virtual teams.

> **TIP**
> Be sure to know the various benefits of virtual teams. See Section 9.2.2.4 of the *PMBOK® Guide*.

TIP

Often at issue are the ethnic, linguistic, or technological misunderstandings and conflicts when communicating effectively in a virtual environment.

On the other hand, managing virtual teams is more difficult and can increase the cost of a project. When people are not colocated, increased communication efforts are necessary to ensure that communication is effective.

Resource Calendars and Project Staff Assignments

Figure 9-3 below is a resource calendar for our Fundraiser Road Race project. A resource calendar shows the availability of each resource. This availability may or may not align with the needs of the project. Staff assignments are developed from the project schedule and show when a particular resource or type of resource is required.

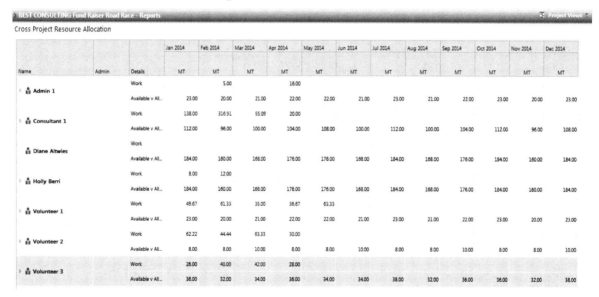

Figure 9-3
Resource
Calendar

Comparing the resource calendar and project schedule allows the project manager to determine if there are any gaps in resource needs, which would warrant the execution of a staff augmentation plan or additional training for existing staff.

Class Exercise 9-3

Using the resource calendar defined above for the Fundraiser Road Race, determine if there are any gaps in staff assignments.

DEVELOP PROJECT TEAM PROCESS

The Develop Project Team process allows the project manager to focus on how to get the most out of the project team. In an ideal world, the project manager would be given every resource that has been requested with the best possible skill set and a team that works cohesively as a unit. This is unfortunately unrealistic.

As the project manager develops the **resource calendar** and **staff assignments**, there will be gaps identified that the project manager will have to address. The Develop Project Team process ensures that team members have the appropriate skills to perform their jobs; the team interacts effectively and the team environment is conducive to success when all members are prepared for the work they will need to perform.

The output of this process consists of regular assessments of the team (**team performance assessments**). As you can see, this process relies heavily on good general management skills such as setting clear ground rules for the project team and effectively utilizing **interpersonal skills** and **team-building skills**.

The steps a project manager uses to develop the team must be included in the **WBS dictionary** as a **basis of estimate** of costs and in the project as work to be performed.

> **TIP**
> One cost of not colocating virtual teams arises from the requirement for greater formality and specificity of direction. For instance, clear WBS dictionaries and subsidiary project plans are much more important with virtual teams.

Interpersonal Skills for Developing a Team

Interpersonal skills are generally known as "soft skills." Utilizing these soft skills provides a positive working environment for the project team. In the context of the Develop Project Team process, some examples of these skills include, but are not limited to:
- Influence
- Empathy
- Creativity
- Group facilitation

Class Exercise 9-4

Read the following situations for our Fundraiser Road Race. Determine which kind of interpersonal skill you might use to address each scenario.

Scenario for Developing a Team	Recommended Interpersonal Skill
Your lead quality assurance analyst on the software development project has just gotten word that a close family member has become gravely ill and, in fact, is not expected to survive more than three months. There are some key deliverables coming up in the next couple of weeks.	
You are the project manager on a construction project for your local church. Most of your workers are volunteers. As the building is being raised, one of the volunteers notices that one wall of the building without any windows faces a highly trafficked walking path. The volunteer asks if something could be done with that wall.	
You walk into a meeting with all the volunteers for an event. The room is rather chaotic, and one volunteer looks rather stressed. She explains that no one likes the assignments they have been given for the road race, and they all want to change assignments.	

Training

When projects have limited access to a specialized skill set or "ideal" resources, the project manager may anticipate the need to provide additional training for select project team members.

Team Building

One of the key concepts that the *PMBOK® Guide* stresses is that *every* project is *unique*. Uniqueness is expected because every project comes with its own set of variables. A key variable is the people and the personalities that make up the project team. In a perfect world, everyone gets along and marches to the same goals and objectives. The reality is that all teams go through a developmental process from **forming**, to **storming**, to **norming**, to **performing**, and finally to **adjourning**. All teams go through this process. The difference is the amount of time it takes a team to move into the performing stage.

Throughout the various states of team development, the project manager's role as leader will change. Figure 9-4 below demonstrates the stages of a team and the types of leadership skills a project manager may need.

TIP
The project manager should plan different team building activities for the core project management team and other project participants.

Figure 9-4
Leadership
Roles

Stage	Role as Leader
Forming	• Help members get to know each other • Provide clear direction and purpose • Involve members in developing plans, clarifying roles, and establishing ways of working together • Provide the information the team needs to get started
Storming	• Resolve issues of power and authority • Develop and implement agreements about how decisions are made and who makes them • Adapt the leadership role to allow the team to become more independent • Encourage members to take on more responsibilities
Norming	• Fully utilize team members' skills, knowledge, and experience • Encourage and acknowledge members; encourage respect for one another • Encourage members to "roll up their sleeves" and work collaboratively
Performing	• Update the team's methods and procedures to support cooperation • Help the team understand how to manage change • Represent and advocate for the team with other groups and individuals • Monitor work progress and celebrate achievements
Adjourning	• Facilitate project team members moving to other projects • Ensure that work is completed • Assess overall project performance

One reason some teams take longer to attain high performance is that **communication** is not an exact science, and what is written and spoken can be misinterpreted, causing individuals to veer off course.

The longer the project timeline is, the more chance there is for team members to stray off course and to lose focus on the project objectives.

In order to keep project teams focused, motivated, and enthusiastic, the project manager will employ various **team building activities**. In addition, communication effectiveness may be impacted by changes in team member assignments or organizational relationships.

Depending on the phase or deliverables of a project, different skills may be required of the project team members. The project manager must continue to assess the needs of the team and include the appropriate project team members as the needs of the project change.

Ground Rules

Establish clear expectations of acceptable behavior for project team members. Clear guidelines decrease misunderstanding and increase productivity. This is especially critical when colocation synchronization is needed or cultural variances are present.

Colocation

Colocation, in the context of the Develop Project Team process, is a tool that can be used to increase team performance. Teams that are colocated interact differently from those that are not. Teams that are colocated tend to resolve **conflict** more easily and perform at higher levels because **communication** is enhanced by having physical contact with other team members.

TIP

When only a portion of the team is colocated, be aware that the benefits of informal collaboration for the group that is colocated could be a barrier or conflict for others who may be working remotely.

A project manager may have to use colocation as a tool if he or she finds that a **virtual team** environment increases the project risk beyond what is acceptable. Be conscious that when dealing with a virtual team environment, the organizational relationships may vary in formality and motivation.

Recognition and Rewards

People are motivated in different ways. The project manager wants to ensure that team members exhibit desirable behavior. One way to reinforce desirable behavior is to reward positive actions. Penalizing undesirable behavior is not recommended, since rewarding positive behavior can be more effective.

The project manager must provide an environment in which the team members feel compelled to perform their best. **Ground rules** and expectations for performance should be defined within the **human resource plan** and be shared with the project team. Rewards and recognition should be provided when team members go beyond what is expected of them to ensure project success. In this kind of environment, the team works more cohesively and effectively, with everyone striving for the same objectives.

> **TIP**
> Different people respond differently to different recognition and reward options. These differences could come from a diversity in skill or ethnic background.

> **TIP**
> If undesirable conduct is severe enough, it may require mangerial corrective action.

9

Class Exercise 9-5

Given the following scenarios, what approach(es) might the project manager use to develop the project team?

Scenario	Recommended Approach
For your project, all of your team members are located in Des Moines, Iowa, except for yourself and the training resource, who will be critical during the implementation phase of the project. Travel resources are limited for this project, so you can only plan four trips during the course of the six-month project.	
As the project manager, you are responsible for managing the costs of the project as well as the schedule. The company you are working for has never had any sort of time sheet process in order to capture the actual costs of a project. The sponsor has been very supportive in implementing a time sheet process. Unfortunately, in the first month of the project, very few people have been tracking their time well.	

MANAGE PROJECT TEAM PROCESS

Assessments of the project team's performance from the Develop Project Team process are a key input to the Manage Project Team process. The Manage Project Team process is the response to the results provided in the **team performance assessment**.

This process is considered an executing process in that the project manager is managing how the team is performing; it is *not* considered a monitoring and controlling process since it does not look at monitoring and controlling project performance. Team performance and project performance are two separate things, even though they are interrelated. The Manage Project Team process focuses on team performance and the improvement of that performance.

> **TIP**
> Know the differences between personal assessment tools and team performance assessments.

Similar to the Develop Project Team process, many **general management skills** are necessary in the Manage Project Team process in order for the project manager to succeed. The project manager must continuously observe the project team and assess the environmental state of the project. **Observation** and **conversation** are used to stay in touch with the work and attitudes of project team members.

To insure that a project performs well, project managers also have to address team members' performance. Project managers are generally responsible for delivering informal or formal **performance appraisals** on the project team's performance. **Conflict management** and additional **interpersonal skills** are desirable for a project manager to positively evolve a team.

Successfully managing and leading a project team require that project managers use **influencing** skills as well as abide by the professional and ethical behavior standard set forth by PMI's *Code of Ethics and Professional Conduct*.

The outputs of the Manage Project Team process are less tangible than those of many of the other knowledge areas within the *PMBOK® Guide*. Most of the outputs focus on the outcome of an assessment and a determination as to whether anything needs to change. Changes can come in the form of updates to **enterprise environmental factors**, **organizational process assets**, and the **project management plan**, and may warrant a **change request**.

Issue Log

If you agree that the project manager must continuously assess the environment and state of a project, you see that capturing issues and their associated resolutions on a regular basis can provide the project manager with invaluable information about the activities of a project.

An issue log is a document generally accessible to all project participants that captures activities and concerns that the project team members have experienced during the course of the project as well as the actual resolution of issues. It is very useful to ensure that lessons learned are followed though on and applied during and subsequent to the project.

> **TIP**
> Issue resolutions could be part of ongoing team building for the project management team or project team.

9

Figure 9-5 below shows a sample issue log for our Fundraiser Road Race.

Issue #	Description	Initiator	Responsible Person	Target Date/ Priority	Resolution	Completion Date
1	In searching for a location to hold the race, the team only found one venue that was willing to donate the space. However, the race would have to be run on a very hilly terrain, which may deter attendance. There were other locations that were asking for a $500 fee to fund the cleanup.	Consultant 1				
2	Volunteer 2 has identified over 100 corporate outreach options and doesn't have the time to investigate them all.	Volunteer 2	Sponsor	1/22/14 HIGH	Focus on companies that have sponsored events like this in the past.	1/22/14

Figure 9-5
Issue Log

There are several components that should be mandatory to consider in any issue log.

- Issue description—it is important to completely describe the situation that is of concern, the more detailed, the better; this description will allow someone to review the issue at a later date and get a good sense of the situation that caused the issue
- Initiator—knowing the person who raised the issue is important if more detail is needed for the resolution
- Responsible person—each issue ultimately needs to be resolved in some manner; assigning a responsible person for each resolution provides accountability to the project team
- Target date for completion—not all issues are created equal; some issues or concerns may have a very low priority, while others may be critical to the project, so it is important for the project team to assess the priority of an issue when assigning a target date; focusing team members on low-priority issues takes them away from delivering work that is already scheduled

- Resolution explanation—once an issue has been resolved, it is important to document the resolution, even if it is to "do nothing;" again, the project manager can use this tool as a way to assess what is transpiring or has transpired on a project
- Actual completion date—bringing an issue to closure means that there is an actual completion of the resolution; it is important to close any loops and document when an issue has been resolved

Conflict Management

Conflicts are unavoidable on projects due to their temporary nature. Conflict are inevitable whenever change occurs, and projects always involve some change. Conflicts can arise from:

- Projects being carried out in high-stress environments
- Roles and responsibilities being unclear or ambiguous
- The multiple-boss syndrome in which the priority of work becomes an issue
- Technologies being new or complex
- Teams being brought together for the first time

The *PMBOK® Guide* considers schedule issues, priority of work issues, people resource issues, technical options, and performance trade-off issues as being the most likely to cause tension in project environments.

Ways to Manage Conflict

The contemporary view of conflict management is that conflict can have a positive or negative impact on a project and organization. Conflict can and should be managed. Whether it is beneficial or detrimental to the project depends on the source of the conflict and the way it is handled by the project manager. Conflict is also a natural result of change and is inevitable among people working together. Should a disruptive conflict continue or escalate, the project manager must become involved and help find a satisfactory solution to the conflict. In a matrix organizational structure, managing the conflict of work priorities for team members is generally the responsibility of the project manager. The project manager needs to apply various motivational techniques to overcome any such issues.

Conflict resolution is situational. While there are preferred forms, project managers may handicap themselves by using a single resolution method in all circumstances. Some ways to manage conflict are:

- **Problem solving** (**confrontation**): the project manager directly addresses the disagreement and gets all parties to work together to solve the problem; once the problem is defined, information is collected, alternatives are identified, and the most appropriate solution is selected; this method is considered win-win and is recommended for long-term resolution; **collaboration** is a form of problem-solving
- **Compromising**: various issues are considered toward an agreed-upon solution that brings some degree of satisfaction to the conflicting parties, so both parties give up something that is important to them; this method is considered lose-lose and is likely to be temporary
- **Forcing**: one person's viewpoint is accepted at the expense of another party; this method is considered win-lose and can build antagonism and cause additional conflicts, so it is appropriate primarily in low-value situations
- **Smoothing**: the opposing party's differences are de-emphasized while commonalities are emphasized on the issue in question; this way of resolving conflict keeps the atmosphere friendly but does not resolve the conflict, it only delays it; smoothing could be used with one of the three methods above
- **Withdrawal**: retreating from the actual or potential issue or conflict situation; this method is appropriate only for situations in which a cooling-off period is needed; withdrawal does not resolve the conflict but only delays it

TIP

Smoothing acknowledges the fact that not all problems need to be resolved.

Project Performance Appraisals

Task, budget, schedule, scope, and quality performance assessment is a continuous process of documenting individual, team, and vendor performance. This ongoing assessment can trigger action by the project team members.

Documenting performance, identifying and deciding how to resolve (or not to resolve) issues, as well as monitoring team conflict will help the project manager. Diligence here can ensure the project manager is responding in a timely matter to any issues that come up in a proactive, rather than reactive, manner.

Class Exercise 9-6

When managing project teams, common problems such as the ones described below will occur. Discuss what can or should be done if the following situations arise.

Common Problems	What to Do
Floundering	
Dominating or overbearing participants	
Reluctant participants	
Feuding team members	
Unquestioning acceptance of opinions and facts	
Rush to accomplishment	
Wanderlust, digression, and tangents	

Interpersonal Skills for Managing a Team

Using "soft" interpersonal skills provides a positive working environment for the project team. In the context of the Manage Project Team process, some examples of these skills include, but are not limited to:
- Leadership
- Influencing
- Effective decision making

There are many interpersonal skills and **general management skills** that project managers can employ in various situations during a project. Knowing when to use any of them is a matter of experience and assessing the project environment, which includes an understanding of the project stakeholders, team members, and political environment.

A project manager is a leader. As a leader, he or she must look at things in a different way from the project team. Figure 9-6 below highlights some of the differences between a leader and a project team member. Where do you stand?

Figure 9-6
Leaders and
Team Members

Leader	Team Member
Ensures team goals are achievable but challenging enough to meet organizational needs and provide a sense of accomplishment	Helps establish performance goals and standards for individual team performance
Helps balance the complexity of measures and controls with value received	Develops methods to measure results and checkpoints for control purposes
Participates with the team to test the action plan's validity against other alternatives	Outlines the actions required to accomplish goals and standards
Reviews what cooperation and support are required and helps obtain them if required	Specifies participation required from colleagues or other units within the organization
Follows the progress of the work, reinforces achievement, assists in problem solving when indicated, and ensures targets are met or are modified if circumstances so indicate	Reports progress as work is performed, seeks guidance and assistance when needed, and adjusts plan as required

Adapted from Maddux, Robert B.

9

Class Exercise 9-7

Read the following situations. Determine which kind of interpersonal skill you might use to address the concern.

Scenario	Recommended Interpersonal Skill
You are the project manager on a new development project. Your project team is typically working on several projects at once. Your lead business analyst just received word that she has three new projects that need to get started, but in order for those projects to start, she needs to hire more analysts. This happens at the same time the current project is at a critical testing juncture. She walks into your office with a look of sheer panic.	
The architect on a new community hospital construction project has expertise in designing premier facilities for communities that have an extensive budget. He has won numerous awards and takes great pride in his work. Your project is lucky enough to have this same architect working on it due to his friendship with the state assemblyman. This project has a limited budget, but when the initial design is received, the initial projected cost is twice what the community is prepared to spend.	

PROFESSIONAL RESPONSIBILITY

Human resource management is about accurately and effectively determining what necessary resources are and ensuring that those resources are employed appropriately and effectively on a project. When considering the four aspects of professional responsibility—responsibility, respect, fairness, and honesty—the project manager must keep certain things in mind at all times:

- Use negotiating and influencing skills with integrity, looking for a "win-win" situation
- Use the conflict resolution technique most effective in the particular situation
- Work ethically and hold the project team to professional and ethical behavior
- Fairly recognize and reward positive behaviors
- Resolve conflict appropriately and allow all parties to communicate their sides

It is the project manager's responsibility to demonstrate the behaviors that he or she desires in the team.

9

BE A BETTER PROJECT MANAGER

Exercise: team building through group conversations

Purpose: getting to know your team

When project teams are first formed, it is highly likely that there are people in the group who do not know one another. As a project manager, getting your team members to feel comfortable with one another is a key way to move them to a performing developmental state quickly.

Here's one way to do that.

Steps: at your next project team meeting, use one of the following conversational topics. Go around the room and allow each team member to express his or her thoughts and opinions on the topic.

Topic ideas:
1. Anybody will work hard if . . .
2. People who run things should be . . .
3. I would like to be . . .
4. One thing I like about myself is . . .
5. Nothing is so frustrating as . . .
6. Ten years from now, I . . .
7. Every winning team needs . . .
8. I take pride in . . .
9. If you want to see me get mad . . .
10. A rewarding job is one that . . .

After the conclusion of the exercise, ask your project team members what they learned about other team members that was surprising or that they had in common. This exercise will build bonds between team members.

You'll be surprised by what you learn!

9

SAMPLE CAPM EXAM QUESTIONS ON HUMAN RESOURCES MANAGEMENT

1. The process that addresses how to obtain the human resources necessary for a project is the _____ process.

   a) Manage Project Team
   b) Develop Project Team
   c) Plan Human Resource Management
   d) Acquire Project Team

2. Two objectives of the Develop Project Team process are:

   a) Achieve high performance as a team and meet project objectives
   b) Improve networking skills and relationships
   c) Gain consensus on project deliverables and improve relationships
   d) Improve cohesiveness of the team and increase face-to-face interactions

3. Influencing team behavior, resolving issues, and appraising the performance of individual team members is a key benefit of which process?

   a) Acquire Project Team
   b) Plan Human Resource Management
   c) Develop Project Team
   d) Manage Project Team

4. Inputs to the Acquire Project Team process include which of the following?

   a) Project staff assignments, resource calendars, and project management plan updates
   b) Human resource documentation, personnel administration policies, and location of resources
   c) Negotiation, multi-criteria decision analysis, and acquisition
   d) Virtual teams, pre-assignment, and costs of adding a team member

Notes:

5. Teams that perform the majority of their work together without interacting face to face is an example of _____ teams.

   a) Functional
   b) Virtual
   c) Collocated
   d) Technical

6. A key output of the Acquire Project Team process is:

   a) Roles and responsibilities
   b) Updates to the human resource plan
   c) The staffing management plan
   d) The project organization chart

7. The five stages of team development occur in the following order:

   a) Storming, norming, forming, performing, adjourning
   b) Forming, storming, norming, performing, adjourning
   c) Norming, forming, storming, performing, adjourning
   d) Forming, norming, storming, performing, adjourning

8. Team performance assessments that show the team is improving can include:

   a) Improvements in individual skills or competencies
   b) Increased staff turnover rate
   c) Additional storming behaviors
   d) Missing schedule deadlines

Notes:

9

9. Positive work relationships between team members can be enhanced through successful:

   a) Negotiation
   b) Succession plans
   c) Outsourcing
   d) Conflict management

10. The key skills a project manager must have in order to successfully develop the project team are _____ skills.

   a) Planning
   b) Organizing
   c) Interpersonal
   d) Formal authority

11. PMI's *Code of Ethics and Professional Conduct* requires that all project managers should follow _____ behavior.

   a) Influential
   b) Formal
   c) Acceptable
   d) Ethical

12. Training needs, recognition, rewards, and _____ are inputs to the staffing management plan.

   a) Organizational theory
   b) Safety
   c) Networking
   d) Position descriptions

Notes:

9

13. The main benefit of documenting project roles and responsibilities in a responsibility assignment matrix is that it:

    a) Increases negative risks (threats) on the project due to resource utilization

    b) Helps the project manager make sure that stakeholder expectations are met

    c) Clarifies and communicates who is contributing to and responsible for the project activity

    d) Can be used as an input to planning the procurement of resources

14. Which of the following are outputs of the Plan Human Resource Management process?

    a) Project staff assignments, resource calendars, and project management plan updates

    b) Organizational theory, expert judgment, and meetings

    c) Project management plan, organizational process assets, and activity resource requirements

    d) Roles and responsibilities, project organization charts, and staffing management plan

15. In selecting resources for your project, you must share the resource pool with other project teams. Your project requires a critical technical skill that only one resource possesses—Jack! In planning, you:

    a) Request Jack for 100% of the time for the full project duration

    b) Request Jack 100% for the design and execution phases even though you only have half-time work for him

    c) Talk to each of the other project managers and determine which project needs Jack the most, and then adjust schedules accordingly

    d) Take Jack out to dinner and explain how critical this project is and how working on the project will be good for his career

Notes:

ANSWERS AND REFERENCES FOR SAMPLE CAPM EXAM QUESTIONS ON HUMAN RESOURCES MANAGEMENT

Section numbers refer to the *PMBOK® Guide*.

1. **D** **Section 9.2 – Executing**
   A) and B) occur after human resources are acquired; C) defines human resources required.

2. **A** **Section 9.3 – Executing**
   B) While networking skills may be important for team members, improving them is not an objective of Develop Project Team; C) the team must gain consensus on project deliverables among many stakeholders; this occurs during Define Scope and Create WBS; D) face-to-face interactions may help team member cohesiveness but they are not objectives of Develop Project Team.

3. **D** **Section 9.4 – Executing**
   A) helps guide the selection of appropriate resources; B) defines roles and responsibilities; C) focuses on teamwork and building competencies.

4. **B** **Section 9.2.1 – Executing**
   These are all enterprise environmental factors that may influence which team members are acquired; A) are outputs of the Acquire Project Team process; C) and D) are tools and techniques of the Acquire Project Team process.

5. **B** **Section 9.2.2.4 – Executing**
   Virtual teams allow project managers new possibilities when acquiring project team members.

6. **B** **Seaton 9.2.3 – Executing**
   A), C), and D) are all components of the Plan Human Resource Management process.

7. **B** **Section 9.3.2.3 – Executing**
   The five stages of team development are forming, storming, norming, performing, and adjourning.

8. **A Section 9.3.3.1 – Executing**
   Assessing team performance can be informal or
   formal. Effective team development activities will
   increase team performance. B), C), and D) indicate that team performance is getting worse.

9. **D Section 9.4.2.3 – Executing**
   Conflict is inevitable in any project and skillful
   project managers build positive relationships
   between team members by learning effective conflict management techniques.

10. **C Section 9.4.2.4 – Executing**
    A) and B) are important in project management,
    but interpersonal skills are most useful in
    developing the team; D) is not a skill.

11. **D Section 1.1 – Initiating**
    PMI's *Code of Ethics and Professional Conduct*
    requires that all project managers subscribe to
    acting ethically in all project activities.

12. **B Section 9.1 – Planning**
    A), C), and D) are all tools and techniques of the
    Plan Human Resource Management process.

13. **C Section 9.1 – Planning**
    A) typically, risk is reduced if a RAM is used;
    B) indirectly, a RAM may help ensure that
    stakeholder expectations are met by having the
    right people in the job, but this is not the best
    answer; D) usually, a RAM will be prepared after
    the make versus buy decision is made.

14. **D Section 9.1 – Planning**
    A) are outputs of the Acquire Project Team pro-
    cess; B) are tools and techniques of the Plan
    Human Resource Management process; C) are
    inputs to the Plan Human Resource Management
    process.

15. **C Section 9.2.2 – Planning and Section 5.3.1 of
    the *Code of Ethics and Professional Conduct***
    The *Code of Ethics and Professional Conduct* does
    not condone deceit. Competition must consider the
    needs of the organization.

ANSWERS TO CLASS EXERCISES

Class Exercise 9-1: Planning Human Resources Management

Scenario	Recommended Approach
You are a project manager in a functional organization. Two of your key resources work for a manager who is constantly pulling these resources for production issues. These constant interruptions on work necessary for the project are now approaching an urgent level.	In this situation it is important for the project manager to have a great working relationship with the functional managers. Find out what is going on within that department and weigh the urgency of the departmental issues against the urgency of the project. It is equally important to understand the workload of your resources because they may work for other project managers or functional managers.
The sponsor of a program is a very outspoken individual and always feels that he is right. His best friend is the CEO of the company, so people try to accommodate his wishes as much as possible. This past week, he asked the project team to implement a change that is out-of-scope in the team's mind, but he is adamant that it is part of the scope.	There are a couple of things that can be done here. If you have a good relationship with the sponsor, you may choose to approach him directly to determine why he believes the change is within scope and to negotiate with him. If you do not have a good relationship with the sponsor, you may want to get the support of the CEO first and then ask the CEO to negotiate on the team's behalf.
You are a project manager in a strong matrix organizational structure. A key resource has had a family emergency that will take her away from the office for at least three weeks.	In a strong matrix environment, you have more authority. Most likely you will be able to acquire the appropriate resource for your project yourself. Key person unavailability is an appropriate risk event to be identified, qualitatively assessed, and dealt with throughout a project.

Class Exercise 9-2: Negotiation

Scenario	Win-Win or Win-Lose	What would you do differently?
The functional manager of the development department has pulled the lead developer from your project without asking for your permission. You go to your sponsor and ask for a three-way conference call with the functional manager. Prior to the meeting, you prepare your sponsor to communicate to the functional manager that your project is the most important project in the organization and that nothing should be distracting the lead developer from the project.	Win-Lose	Ideally you, the sponsor, and the functional manager should discuss why the resource is needed by the functional manager and work together for an agreeable solution that allows both efforts to succeed.
The project manager for the vendor was due to deliver a design of a new amusement park ride on July 1st. It is now July 2nd, and you have not heard from the vendor, so you send off a scathing email to the vendor's superiors stating that you feel that their organization does not live up to its commitments.	Win-Lose	You should never send off an email to anyone's superior without collecting all the facts. There is a lot of information you do not know here, such as how big a client you are to this vendor, if the project manager is out sick, or if you can still deliver the design on the critical path. Your first course of action should be to try to reach the vendor's project manager in person.

Class Exercise 9-3: Staff Assignments

In reviewing the resource calendar defined for the Fundraiser Road Race, there are several things that jump out as issues.

1. The consultant is overextended in February. There are more activities planned for him than he has time to accommodate.
2. In March, the third volunteer is also overextended.
3. In general, each of the volunteers has only a handful of hours a week to allocate to the project, which may not be enough to support the project.

Class Exercise 9-4: Interpersonal Skills

Scenario for Develop Project Team Process	Recommended Interpersonal Skill
Your lead quality assurance analyst on the software development project has just gotten word that a close family member has become gravely ill and, in fact, is not expected to survive more than three months. There are some key deliverables coming up in the next couple of weeks.	Empathy—work out a plan to allow your lead analyst to take the time necessary and still deliver on the project. In addition, if this is a critical staff resource, you may have to reference the risk register for the recommended risk mitigation plan.
You are the project manager on a construction project for your local church. Most of your workers are volunteers. As the building is being raised, one of the volunteers notices that one wall of the building without any windows faces a highly trafficked walking path. The volunteer asks if something could be done with that wall.	Creativity—you may want to have a contest for the team to see what could be done with the wall.
You walk into a meeting with all the volunteers for an event. The room is rather chaotic, and one volunteer looks rather stressed. She explains that no one likes the assignments they have been given for the road race, and they all want to change assignments.	Group facilitation—you may want to postpone the meeting and then strategize with this volunteer about how to explain to the others how the assignments were made.

Class Exercise 9-5: Develop Project Team

Scenario	Recommended Approach
For your project, all members of your team are located in Des Moines, Iowa, except for yourself and the training resource who will be critical during the implementation phase of the project. Travel resources are limited for this project, so you can only plan four trips during the course of the six-month project.	Since the training resource is critical during implementation of the project, it may make sense to colocate the trainer with the team approximately one month before members go live and keep the training resource there one month after they go live.
As the project manager, you are responsible for managing the costs of the project as well as the schedule. The company you are working for now has never had any sort of time sheet process in order to capture the actual costs of a project. The sponsor has been very supportive in implementing a time sheet process. Unfortunately, in the first month of the project, very few people have been tracking their time well.	You may want to work with the sponsor on a reward or recognition program for the people who complete their time sheets in a timely manner during the course of the project.

Class Exercise 9-6: Manage Conflict

Common Problems	What to do
Floundering	Floundering is when team members just can't seem to get the task at hand accomplished. You need to tackle the reason for not completing the work.
Dominating or overbearing participants	You have two choices here: get the overbearing participants to subside or get those who are being subordinate to speak up. This usually requires some one-on-one time with both sides.
Reluctant participants	Reluctant participants need encouragement that their ideas are as important as anyone else's. Determine if there is a perception that participation in the project can affect career advancement.
Feuding team members	This conflict needs to be addressed quickly. Negotiating tactics and influence are both critical in getting to consensus with the feuding parties.
Unquestioning acceptance of opinions and facts	You may think this isn't a problem, but it is. You want "good" conflict on your project. You want the team members to challenge each other to come up with optimal results.
Rush to accomplishment	Just because you get the project done on time doesn't mean that the project achieved the stated objectives. Constantly challenge the team to validate that the objectives of the project are going to be met.
Wanderlust, digression, and tangents	When project team members are allowed to dissent or wander off course, the objectives of the project will not be realized. Keep the project team focused on the goals and regularly measure the attainment of deliverables and objectives.

9

Class Exercise 9-7: Interpersonal Skills

Scenario	Recommended Interpersonal Skill
You are the project manager on a new development project. Your project team is typically working on several projects at once. Your lead business analyst just received word that she has three new projects that need to get started, but in order for those projects to start, she needs to hire more analysts. This happens at the same time the current project is at a critical testing juncture. She walks into your office with a look of sheer panic.	A combination of leadership and decision making will be needed here. As the project manager, you need to help your team in problem solving. This doesn't mean that you resolve the problem yourself; you need to work with the business analyst's manager to identify alternatives and then facilitate discussion as to which alternative can provide the optimal solution.
The architect on a new community hospital construction project has expertise in designing premier facilities for communities that have an extensive budget. He has won numerous awards and takes great pride in his work. Your project is lucky enough to have this same architect working on it due to his friendship with the state assemblyman. This project has a limited budget, but when the initial design is received, the initial projected cost is twice what the community is prepared to spend.	Influencing skills will be needed here. You want the community to have a hospital with the prestige associated with this well-renowned architect, but you don't want to insult him by asking that he reduce the design costs by 50%. This is a clear example of a resource that has not provided an outcome with explicit or implicit constraints. The project manager has the responsibility to raise this issue with the architect.

ANSWERS TO THE CASE STUDY CAN BE FOUND IN THE WAV™ FILES

This book has free material available for download from the Web Added Value™ resource center at *www.jrosspub.com*.

CHAPTER 10 | **COMMUNICATIONS**

10

10

COMMUNICATIONS MANAGEMENT

Communications management is about *all* the communications a project manager has to address: communication directed to the team, to senior management and stakeholders, as well as to functional levels, peers, and external entities. Since projects are about getting work done with resources that include people, it is imperative to ensure excellent communication within the project environment to maximize everyone's time and effort associated with delivering the activities required to meet a project's objectives. A lack of communication and inappropriate or excessive communication will circumvent the efforts a project manager puts into clearly defining scope, schedule, and budget.

Good communications are probably the most important skill a project manager can have. Communications come in many different forms. A project manager must understand the tools available in order to select the appropriate communication method for a project.

Here are some aspects of communications any project manager should know:
- Send messages in terms the receiver understands
- Provide examples to improve the clarity of complex information
- Use repetition to reinforce key concepts
- Organize messages before transmitting them
- Ask the receiver to report what he or she has heard
- Concentrate on the sender and what is being said
- Suspend judgment until the sender finishes the message
- Ask questions when you don't understand
- Maintain good eye contact
- Minimize distractions

10

Knowledge Area Processes

Within the communications management knowledge area there are three processes within three process groups.

Plan Communications Management	Manage Communications	Control Communications

Key Definitions

Acknowledge: indicates receipt of a message by a receiver, but does not indicate that the receiver understood or agreed.

Active listening: the receiver confirms listening by nodding, eye contact, and asking questions for clarification.

Decode: the term for the receiver translating a message into an idea or meaning.

Effective listening: the receiver attentively watches the sender to observe physical gestures and facial expressions. In addition, the receiver contemplates responses, asks pertinent questions, repeats or summarizes what the sender has sent, and provides feedback.

Encode: the term for the sender translating an idea or meaning into a language for sending.

Feedback: affirming understanding and providing information.

Noise: anything that compromises the original meaning of a message.

Non-verbal communication: about 55% of all communication, based on what is commonly called body language.

Paralingual communication: optional vocal effects or the tone of voice that may help communicate meaning.

Transmit message: the term for using a communication method to deliver a message.

Work performance data: the raw observations and measurements identified during activities being performed to carry out project work.

Work performance information: the performance data collected from various controlling processes, analyzed in context, and integrated based on relationships across areas.

Work performance reports: the physical or electronic representation of work performance information compiled in project documents and intended to generate decisions, actions, or awareness.

> **TIP**
> Know the differences between work performance data, work performance information, and work performance reports.

PLAN COMMUNICATIONS MANAGEMENT PROCESS

Once a project has been initiated, the project manager must understand the informational needs of each stakeholder. Not all stakeholders are created equal, and the project team must not assume that one method of communicating will work for every stakeholder.

The Plan Communications Management process addresses, for each stakeholder:
- Who needs what information?
- When will they need it?
- How will it be given to them?
- Who will give it to them?
- How will information be stored and retrieved?

10

In the *PMBOK® Guide*, communicating is the primary role of the project manager. Lack of communication, miscommunication, and incorrect communication are all contributors to project failure.

A stakeholder register is a primary input to planning for communications. In Chapter 13 of this book we will discuss the creation of this tool, but for our discussion here, we provide you a brief introduction to it. Figure 10-1 provides an example of a stakeholder register with all but the communications requirements column filled in.

A **communications management plan** is the primary output of the Plan Communications Management process. A communications management plan expands on what is documented in the stakeholder register and adds the communication requirements needed for each stakeholder.

Figure 10-1 on the following page gives an example of a communications management plan for the Fundraiser Road Race, as well as a stakeholder register used to identify the communications requirements of each stakeholder.

10

Communications Management Plan

Project Name: Fundraiser Road Race

Date: 2/2/14

Regular communications between all stakeholders and project team members are imperative to the success of the overall plan. Due to the limited resources initially on the project, many of the internal communications will be performed during the weekly project reviews.

Below is the Stakeholder Register that will be used to capture our communication requirements for all external stakeholders.

Figure 10-1
Communications
Management Plan
and Stakeholder
Register

Stakeholder Register					
Stakeholder	**Identification Information**	**Assessment Information**	**Stakeholder Classification**	**Communications Requirements**	**Risk Tolerance**
Sponsor: Tom Wang	VP of Product Development and Sales	A successful event is one in which all four objectives are met or exceeded	Internal supporter		
Participants in the event	Anyone who attends the event, such as a runner, a volunteer, or someone interested in the particular charity	Wants a fun time and maybe to win some prizes; do not want to be stressed	Neutral participant		
Children's Charity	The recipient of the proceeds of the event; will be able to do more for the patients and community when donations are received	Mostly interested in the outcome of the project; will participate in the event by providing an information book and a place for individuals to make donations at the event	External supporter		

10

Communication Requirements Analysis

Just as it performs a stakeholder analysis, the project team should perform a communication requirements analysis. This analysis looks at the communication needs of every stakeholder listed in the stakeholder register and, based on the information provided, the team makes a determination regarding the type and format of communications to be used with each stakeholder.

When analyzing communications, the project manager must consider:
- Communication channels
- Communication technology
- Communication models
- Communication methods (forms and format)

Communication Channels

Communication channels are one-to-one communications that exist for a team. The more channels, the more complex the communications analysis. Figure 10-2 below shows communication channels for five team members.

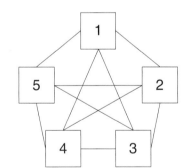

Figure 10-2
Communication
Channels

The formula to determine the number of communications channels that exist on a project is:

(n[n − 1]) / 2 where n indicates the number of people

For example, if five people work on a project, n = 5, and the number of communications channels = 5(4) / 2 = 10.

With seven people, n = 7, and the number of channels = 7(6) / 2 = 21. The number of channels has more than doubled with just two additional team members.

Communication Technology

Methods to transfer information can vary greatly from project to project based on the uniqueness of the project. What one set of stakeholders requires on a project does not mean that the next set of stakeholders will require the same.

It is important to look at several factors when determining the technology to be used for your project communications:

- Urgency: determines the frequency and format of the information being communicated
- Availability of technology: technology must be compatible, available, and accessible to all stakeholders throughout the project's duration
- Ease of use: communication technology must be suitable to project participants; training in appropriate use and any special needs of individuals must be accommodated
- Project environment: issues of colocation, multiple locations, time zones, language, and other cultural environmental factors that may be present must be considered
- Sensitivity and confidentiality of information: issues of transmission and storage security as well as backup and recovery must be dealt with

Some examples of communication technology may be email, shared network drives, or secured phone line.

10

Communication Models

The *PMBOK® Guide* emphasizes the basic communication model that consists of the following components: a sender, a receiver, a medium through which messages are sent and received, noise, and feedback. Some communication models may be different or more complex, but this basic model is by far the most common. Figure 10-3 below illustrates this basic communication model.

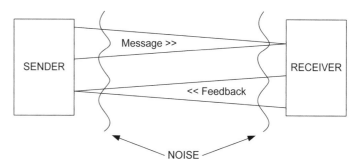

Figure 10-3
Communication
Model

The sender encodes a message, chooses the medium by which to send the message, and attaches symbols, gestures, or expressions to confirm that the message has been understood. As the message passes through the medium, it encounters "noise" that interferes with transmission and meaning. The receiver decodes the message based on his or her background, experience, language, and culture. The receiver sends a feedback message through the medium to the sender, which may be an acknowledgment of receipt or a response indicating understanding.

Communication Methods

Communications methods (both forms and formats) may be broadly classified into three categories:
- **Interactive Methods** of communicating include meetings, phone calls, and video conferencing
  - **Formal verbal** communication such as presentations and speeches should be used when persuading people to accept ideas and products

- **Informal verbal** communication such as meetings, conversations, humor, and inquiries is used for small informal groups, team building, and day-to-day communications
- **Push methods** of communicating include letters, memos, reports, emails, faxes, etc. that are sent to stakeholders
  - **Formal written** communication should be used for key documents such as project plans, the project charter, communicating over long distances, complex problems, legal documents, and long or technical situations for a wide and varied audience
  - **Informal written** communication should be used for status updates, information updates, and day-to-day communications
- **Pull methods** of communicating include intranet sites and knowledge repositories and are more likely to use formal written methods

> **TIP**
> Special care needs to be taken when deciding to use social media to communicate because they are informal, not widely used, and have privacy issues.

Choosing between the forms and formats of communications can seem like a daunting task. The best source in determining the appropriate form and format of communications is each individual stakeholder.

Meetings

Discussion and dialog with project team members to determine appropriate ways to update and communicate project information is critical to effective communication. Several situations are best dealt with in meetings:
- Resolving problems
- Making decisions
- Communicating decisions
- Building relationships

10

Who	What	When	By Whom	How
Tom Wang	Status report; identify potential participants and sponsor opportunities, cost issues, and donation tally	Weekly	Project Manager	Email or face-to-face
Participants	Date and times of event	Weekly	Project Manager	Web, newspapers, and magazines
Charity	Overall project milestones and donation tally	Monthly; more frequently in last month prior to event	Project Manager	Email

Figure 10-4
Communications
Requirements

The Figure 10-4 above was put together for the Fundraiser Road Race. As you can see, detailing out the requirements for each stakeholder can help you determine the communications requirements for each.

Class Exercise 10-1

Fill out the communications requirements column of the stakeholder register on the following page with information on the who, what, when, by when, and how of the communications requirements for each stakeholder listed, as well as the anticipated level of detail and responsible person.

10

Stakeholder Register					
Stakeholder	**Identification Information**	**Assessment Information**	**Stakeholder Classification**	**Communications Requirements**	**Risk Tolerance**
Sponsor: Tom Wang	VP of Product Development and Sales	A successful event is one in which all four objectives are met or exceeded	Internal supporter		
Participants in the event	Anyone who attends the event, such as a runner, a volunteer, or someone interested in the particular charity	Wants a fun time and maybe to win some prizes; do not want to be stressed	Neutral participant		
Children's Charity	The recipient of the proceeds of the event; will be able to do more for the patients and community when donations are received	Mostly interested in the outcome of the project; will participate in the event by providing an information book and a place for individuals to make donations at the event	External supporter		

The **communication management plan** is the key output of the Plan Communications Management process. It includes information on how communications will be managed for the project. A variety of information can be included in a communications management plan as described within the *PMBOK® Guide*. See especially section 10.1.3.1 on page 296.

Case Study 10-1

For the LUV Music website, use the template on the following page to identify the communications requirements for each stakeholder.

Communications Requirements				
Who	What	When	By Whom	How

10

MANAGE COMMUNICATIONS PROCESS

The Manage Communications process is an executing processes. It is the act of delivering on the communications management plan.

When performing this process, the person responsible must understand and utilize appropriate, available **communication technology, communication models,** and **communication methods** accordingly. Lack of appropriate communications will more than likely cause issues and conflict within a project.

Communication Technology

The communication technologies chosen within the Plan Communications process can vary from project to project and also throughout the life of a project. The focus must be to ensure that the choice of technology for communicating, a choice made in an earlier process, is appropriate to the information or action to be communicated. As a project progresses, the appropriate technology could change.

Communication Models

During the Manage Communications process, the project manager should focus on ensuring that the choice of communication model is appropriate to the project and barriers to communication are identified and managed.

Communication Methods

Communication methods are ways in which communications can be delivered. During the Plan Communications Management process, the project team determines which methods can be used for each stakeholder. The Manage Communications process is the executing process that actually delivers the communications in the way described in the communications plan.

10

Choose a method to ensure information created and distributed has been received and understood to enable response and feedback.

Performance Reporting

The Managing Communications process is the executing process within the Communications knowledge area. Performance reporting is a big part of what project managers do within this process. Performance reporting is the act of collecting and distributing performance information and must be appropriate for each stakeholder. Performance reports should show the status of a project. They may include additional information based on the stakeholder, such as:
- Analysis of past performance
- Analysis of project forecasts
- Current status of risks and issues
- Work completed during the period
- Work to be completed in the next period
- A summary of changes approved in the period

Class Exercise 10-2

Use the communications plan created in Class Exercise 10-1 for the Fundraiser Road Race project, and determine the best communication technology and method for the situations listed below.

Communications Requirement	Technology and Method
As the project manager, you need to keep the Children's Charity informed of the progress on meeting the $300,000 goal.	
Since having sponsors for the event is critical to meeting the objective that the event does not cost anything, you need to keep the project sponsor informed as to the progress of obtaining sponsors.	
You need to inform participants in the event.	

10

CONTROL COMMUNICATIONS PROCESS

The Control Communications process monitors and controls communication throughout the project life cycle.

As stated earlier, stakeholders come with various needs and expectations. Project performance may need to be communicated through a variety of methods in order to facilitate understanding and to provide appropriate information to the person or organization receiving the communication. Work performance data and issue logs are critical in the process of controlling communications.

The primary output of the Control Communications process is the **work performance information** for the project.

To facilitate the control of communication, **information management system**, **expert judgment**, and **meetings** are used regularly by the project team.

Activities in the Control Communications process can trigger an iteration of the Plan Communications Management and the Manage Communications processes.

Information Management Systems

An information management system provides a set of standard tools for the project manager to capture, store, and distribute information to stakeholders about project cost, schedule progress, and performance. Monitoring all the available information allows for a timely response to issues that arise.

TIP
Information management systems are a tool and technique for housing different types of project documentation and information.

10

Expert Judgment

A project team often relies on expert judgment to asses the impact of communication, need for action or intervention, actions to be taken, and the time frame for taking action. Experience with the best methods of communicating with stakeholders in similar situations and on similar projects can be helpful in keeping a project under control, especially when dealing with problems or issues in communicating.

Meetings

Regularly scheduled meetings with stakeholders, from sponsors to vendors, is important to ensure that communication is received and understood. Face-to-face meetings are always more effective than virtual meetings, in that all parties can see both verbal and non-verbal forms of communication.

10

PROFESSIONAL RESPONSIBILITY

Within the communications management knowledge area, the project manager has the responsibility to keep everyone informed of the project status and to keep the lines of communication open between project participants and stakeholders.

Using a variety of communication methods such as interactive, push, or pull methods can improve success. However, assuming that each participant will go out and search for his or her own information is not an excuse for miscommunication. The project manager must regularly assess the quality of the communication method used within the project and adjust as necessary.

KEY INTERPERSONAL SKILLS FOR SUCCESS

The interpersonal skill highlighted in this chapter is:

Communication

Communications management focuses on managing information from its creation, flow, and ultimate archiving or disposition. There is an explicit acknowledgment that a project manager's personal skill at communicating is vital to a project's success. The project manager must work to understand others and their personal communication styles, cultural norms that affect communications, and their own relationships with others. Active listening techniques help a project manager build other interpersonal skills such as negotiating and influencing.

One of the project manager's primary responsibilities on a project is to ensure information is being used appropriately. The project manager must make sure that all of the following are documented, shared, and reviewed by all appropriate stakeholders:
- Project vision
- Schedules
- Stakeholder expectations
- Acceptance criteria
- Project status

10

BE A BETTER PROJECT MANAGER

Exercise: project status reports

Purpose: develop project status reports that share information

A project status report is a tool that should be leveraged to provide information to and from many stakeholders. It is important that status reports convey progress as well as concerns and issues. The project manager must understand which activities have been completed and which require more scrutiny. Status reports can be used to highlight concerns about issues that have occurred or have the potential to occur.

The table below lists several *dos* and *don't*s of status reporting.

Bad Status Reports	Good Status Reports
Describe all project issues without prioritizing them	Highlight key areas requiring attention or action
Are too wordy	Clearly articulate actions to be taken and by whom
Duplicate other reports	Outline issues that affect project outcomes
Have a lack of focus	Suggest actions to resolve issues
Don't connect the issue to the impact on the project	Name the person responsible for an action item
Fail to tie to an objective or show when an objective is not being met	List the potentially harmful risks
Don't focus on delivery of objectives	Detail recent accomplishments
	Suggest next steps

10

SAMPLE CAPM EXAM QUESTIONS ON COMMUNICATIONS MANAGEMENT

1. A breakdown in communication _____ impacts a project.

   a) Usually positively
   b) Sometimes
   c) Always
   d) Usually negatively

2. In which process is project information collected, distributed, and stored?

   a) Report Information
   b) Control Communications
   c) Manage Communications
   d) Plan Communications Management

3. A key input to the Control Communications process is:

   a) The communication model
   b) Stakeholder communication requirements
   c) The staff management plan
   d) Resolved issues

4. Status review meetings are an example of a tool and technique within the _____ process.

   a) Plan Stakeholder Engagement
   b) Manage Project Team
   c) Plan Communications Management
   d) Control Communications

5. An email is an example of which form of communication?

   a) Pull communication
   b) Interactive communication
   c) Push communication
   d) Formal communication

Notes:

6. Noise can impact communication because it:

   a) Interferes with understanding a message
   b) Is too loud for stakeholders to hear well
   c) Distracts the sender
   d) Is usually deliberate

7. The _____ process is a project
   communications management process in the
   executing process group.

   a) Identify Stakeholders
   b) Control Communications
   c) Plan Communications Management
   d) Manage Communications

8. Using email to send a project status report is an
   example of a technique in which process?

   a) Manage Communications
   b) Distribute Information
   c) Control Communications
   d) Plan Communications Management

9. Using the communication links formula, how many
   communication links are there when the team
   size is 8?

   a) 8
   b) 28
   c) 16.6
   d) 32

10. A communication skill that project managers should
    develop to clarify and confirm understanding is:

    a) Facilitating
    b) Listening
    c) Presentation
    d) Meeting management

Notes:

10

11. The act of collecting and distributing status reports, progress measurements, and forecasts is:

    a) Communication requirements analysis
    b) Modeling interpersonal communications
    c) Using information management systems
    d) Performance reporting

12. A key benefit of the Control Communications process is that it:

    a) Ensures that information is flowing to all project stakeholders
    b) Identifies and documents the approach to communicate
    c) Ensures that the project manager is following the plan
    d) Allows an efficient flow of communications

13. The process of monitoring and controlling communications to make sure stakeholders have the information they need is:

    a) Manage Stakeholder Engagement
    b) Control Communications
    c) Control Stakeholder Engagement
    d) Manage Communications

14. Work performance information includes:

    a) Information management systems to store and distribute information
    b) Meetings to determine ways to respond to stakeholder requests
    c) Expert judgment from customers and end users
    d) Status and progress information on the project

Notes:

15. Throughout the project life cycle, communicating to meet stakeholders' information needs takes place during which process?

    a) Control Communications
    b) Manage Communications
    c) Plan Communications Management
    d) Manage Stakeholder Engagement

Notes:

10

ANSWERS AND REFERENCES FOR SAMPLE CAPM EXAM QUESTIONS ON COMMUNICATIONS MANAGEMENT

Section numbers refer to the *PMBOK® Guide.*

1. **D Section 10.3 – Monitoring and Controlling**

2. **C Section 10.2 – Executing**
   The Manage Communications process is performed throughout a project.

3. **B Section 10.3.1.1 – Monitoring and Controlling**
   A) is a technique used in the Plan Communications process; B) are part of the project management plan; C) is part of the human resources management plan and focuses on acquiring team members; D) would not require additional communication control.

4. **D Section 10.3.2.3 – Monitoring and Controlling**
   Status review meetings are a communication tool used to exchange and analyze information about a project.

5. **C Section 10.1.2.4 – Planning**
   Understand the differences in types of communication and when each is used.

6. **A Section 10.1.2.3 – Planning**
   Noise in this context does not mean the loudness of the sound. It can be a distraction the receiver is experiencing and is usually not deliberate.

7. **D Section 10.2 – Executing**
   Communicating is a general management skill that includes planning, executing, and monitoring and controlling processes.

8. **A Section 10.2.2.3 – Executing**
   Electronic communication and conferencing tools are all tools for managing communications; B) is no longer a process name.

9. **B** **Section 10.1.2.1 – Planning**
The communication links formula is:
$(n(n-1)) / 2$
$(8(8-1)) / 2 = 28$

10. **B** **Section 10.2. – Executing**
A) brainstorming, conflict resolution, problem solving, and meeting management are facilitation techniques; C) abilities to tailor the material, maintain energy and interest, and engage the audience are key presentation skills; D) the ability to balance the need for thorough discussion without getting off topic is a key meeting management skill.

11. **D** **Section 10.2.2.5 – Executing**
A) is a technique in the Plan Communications Management process to determine the information needs of stakeholders; B) models typically include senders, receivers, and how messages are transmitted but are not the transmission of information; C) information management systems are a tool used in the Manage Communications process which may include managing hard copies, electronic communications, and project management tools.

12. **A** **Section 10.3 – Monitoring and Controlling**
B) is part of the Plan Communications Management process; C) there are no processes that ensure the project manager is following a plan; D) is part of the Manage Communications process.

13. **B** **Section 10.3 – Monitoring and Controlling**
A) focuses on stakeholder communications and addressing issues; C) focuses on first monitoring and then adjusting strategies related to stakeholders; D) focuses on everything to do with information creation, collection, distribution, storage, etc.

14. A **Section 10.3.3.1 – Monitoring and Controlling**
A), B), and C) are all tools and techniques of the Control Communications process.

15. A **Section 10.3 – Monitoring and Controlling**
As part of the Control Communications process, the project manager should know how resources are being utilized in order to complete work that is scheduled.

10

ANSWERS TO CLASS EXERCISES

Class Exercise 10-1: Communications Requirements

Stakeholder Register					
Stakeholder	**Identification Information**	**Assessment Information**	**Stakeholder Classification**	**Communications Requirements**	**Risk Tolerance**
Sponsor: Tom Wang	VP of Product Development and Sales	A successful event is one in which all four objectives are met or exceeded	Internal supporter	*Must* know if the event is getting the "buzz." Keep him abreast of potential participants, sponsorship opportunities, cost coverage, and donation tally. Regular communication in the form of a status report with key indicators will be required.	
Participants in the event	Anyone who attends the event, such as a runner, a volunteer, or someone interested in the particular charity	Wants a fun time and maybe to win some prizes; do not want to be stressed	Neutral participant	Tell potential participants early enough in the process to allow time to put the event on their calendars. Communications will be via web, newspapers, and magazines. Communication will start once a date is set and we are within five months of the event.	
Children's Charity	The recipient of the proceeds of the event; will be able to do more for the patients and community when donations are received	Mostly interested in the outcome of the project; will participate in the event by providing an information book and a place for individuals to make donations at the event	External supporter	At fairly infrequent intervals, at a very minimum on a monthly basis, communicate to the Children's Charity with information on overall project milestones. More frequent communications will be provided within one month of the event to provide insight into the size of the potential donation.	

Class Exercise 10-2: Technology and Method

Communications Requirement	Technology and Method
As the project manager, you need to keep the Children's Charity informed of the progress on meeting the $300,000 goal.	Monthly status reports Weekly email communications within one month of the event
Since having sponsors for the event is critical to meeting the objective that the event does not cost anything, you need to keep the project sponsor informed as to the progress of obtaining sponsors.	Weekly project metrics will be emailed to the Tom Wang on the following metrics: • # of sponsors • $ per sponsor • Costs to date
You need to inform participants in the event.	Marketing materials will be distributed via websites, newspapers, and magazines within X months of the event. The number of months will be based on an optimal number of participants for a reasonable cost.

ANSWERS TO THE CASE STUDY CAN BE FOUND IN THE WAV™ FILES

WAV Web Added Value™

This book has free material available for download from the Web Added Value™ resource center at *www.jrosspub.com*.

RISK

R

11

RISK MANAGEMENT

The risk management knowledge area is a critical knowledge area for project managers. The identification, assessment, and strategies for managing and controlling risk can make or break a project's success. Projects, by their very nature, are inherently risky. No one knows all the risks associated with a project early on, and no one can predict what may happen in the future that could impact the success of a project. This knowledge area focuses on providing several tools and techniques for assessing and controlling risk on projects. In some cases, the tools are simple and easily implemented. In others, they are very complex.

Project managers must make risk management a part of their everyday thought process and formalize it when necessary within their projects. Depending on many factors, a project manager must determine what level of risk management must be adhered to. Selecting an inappropriate level of diligence regarding risk management quickly impacts a project manager's ability to deliver a project successfully.

Knowledge Area Processes

Within the risk management knowledge area, there are six processes within two process groups.

Planning	Monitoring and Controlling
Plan Risk Management Identify Risks Perform Qualitative Risk Analysis Perform Quantitative Risk Analysis Plan Risk Responses	Control Risks

11

Key Definitions

Contingency plan: a response to a risk event that will be implemented only if the risk event occurs.

Contingency reserve: budget within the cost baseline or performance measurement baseline that is allocated for identified risks that are accepted and for which contingent or mitigating responses are developed.

Decision theory: a technique for assisting in reaching decisions under uncertainty and risk. It points to the best possible course, whether or not the forecasts are accurate.

Fallback plan: a response plan that will be implemented if the primary response plan is ineffective.

Issue: a risk event that has occurred.

Opportunities: risk events or conditions that are favorable to a project.

Residual risk: the risk that cannot be eliminated in implementing a risk response plan.

Risk: an uncertain event or condition that could have a positive or negative impact on a project's objectives.

Risk appetite: the degree of uncertainty an entity is willing to take on in anticipation of a reward.

Risk threshold: the measures, along the level of uncertainty or the level of impact, at which a stakeholder may have a specific interest. Risk will be tolerated under the threshold and not tolerated over the threshold.

Risk tolerance: the degree, amount, or volume of risk that an organization or individual will withstand.

Secondary risk: when implementing a risk response, a new risk that is introduced as a result of the response.

Threat: a risk event or condition that is unfavorable to a project.

Workarounds: unplanned responses to risks that were previously unidentified or accepted.

PLAN RISK MANAGEMENT PROCESS

The Plan Risk Management process defines how an organization will conduct risk management efforts for the project. Every project brings with it a level of risk. Some risks are acceptable, while other risks are not. The project team, and especially the project manager, needs to continuously assess the needs of the project and the potential risk events and determine when to act.

Project risk also evolves over time. Depending on the stage of a project, the number and types of risk events can change or be closed. For example, when the Mars rover successfully landed in August, 2012, the project manager stated, "We have retired a lot of risk today."

The primary output of the Plan Risk Management process is the creation of the **risk management plan**. The activities that typically lead up to the definition of the risk management plan are various **analytical techniques** and **planning meetings**. A sample risk management plan for the Fundraiser Road Race is given in Figure 11-1 below.

11

Risk Management Plan

Project Name: Fundraiser Road Race

Date: 2/2/14

Each BEST CONSULTING project is required to review and plan for risks. If an existing risk register template does not exist for this type of project, the project manager will facilitate an initial risk identification and strategy meeting.

Additionally, a stakeholder register must be created and stakeholder risk tolerances defined.

As the fundraiser road race project plan is developed and execution of that plan commences, new risks and opportunities will arise. Each work package will address expected risks, which will be prioritized. As risks become apparent, it is the entire team's responsibility to raise the issues during regular project team meetings or sooner if a risk impact is imminent.

Figure 11-1
Risk
Management
Plan

Analytical Techniques

In developing the risk management plan, several things should be considered: **risk categories, stakeholder tolerances**, and **probability and impact definitions** and **matrices**. **Stakeholder risk profile analyses** and **strategic risk scoring sheets** can be used to summarize and understand the overall risk management context of the project.

Risk Categories

Organizations that routinely deliver similar projects will have similar risks that may occur from project to project. These types of risks, or categories, can be reused by project teams to ensure that risks are adequately addressed in each project.

A tool that can be used to help project teams review the probable risks is a **risk breakdown structure** (RBS). An RBS can provide the project team with a structured approach to reviewing typical risks by category and subcategory.

Risk categories can also be used to define stakeholder risk, such as an uncooperative or unsupportive stakeholder.

Stakeholder Tolerances

Just as we discussed earlier regarding communications management, stakeholders have different needs and desires. They also have different risk tolerances. That is, project stakeholders have varying **risk appetites**. Some stakeholders are afraid of risks (they are risk averse), while others are not (they are risk seekers), and still others are neutral. **Risk tolerance** is measured in terms of "perceived" utility or value. For example, one person may be willing to invest $10,000 in a start-up company knowing that there is a possibility that all of the money invested may be lost, but the trade-off is a ten-fold increase in the investment if the company is successful. Another person might *only* invest $10,000 if he or she

knows there is a guaranteed return of 3%. The first person is a risk seeker, while the second is risk averse. These differing levels of tolerance are depicted in Figure 11-2 below.

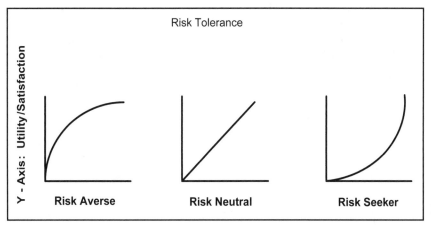

Figure 11-2
Risk Tolerance

Understanding the types of stakeholders that are involved in a project in terms of risk will help the project team determine how to respond to potential risk on a project. Stakeholder tolerances can be captured within the stakeholder register already discussed.

For example, if a project sponsor considers a project critical to the organization, and the project team *must* deliver within budget, the tolerance for budget risk will be very low. The project manager may consider incorporating more budget reserves within the project tasks to increase the probability of staying within budget.

Class Exercise 11-1

Enhance the stakeholder register from Class Exercise 10-1 with the anticipated risk tolerance for each stakeholder. Document your reasons that you consider stakeholders risk averse, risk neutral, or risk seeking.

> **TIP**
> Analytical techniques such as a risk profile analysis of stakeholders may help in determining each individual's risk appetite and risk tolerance. Strategic risk scoring sheets may also be used to provide high-level assessments of overall project risk exposure.

11

Probability and Impact Decision Chart

Every organization considers risk differently. Making decisions about which risks to address and which to ignore is a challenge for all organizations. What you want to avoid is spending an inappropriate amount of time resolving a risk that has very little impact on an organization or a project. Developing a probability and impact decision chart such as the one in Figure 11-3 below is one way to keep the discussions on risk management appropriate to the project at hand.

Figure 11-3
Decision Chart

	Low Risk	Medium Risk	High Risk
Scope	Cannot achieve $300,000 donation goal (+/- 5%).	Cannot achieve $300,000 donation goal (+/- 10%).	Cannot achieve $300,000 donation goal (+/- 15%).
Schedule	Initial event cannot be scheduled until late summer.	Initial event cannot be scheduled before late fall.	Initial event cannot be held before year's end.
Cost	Costs more than $5,000 over the cost of the consultant.	Costs more than $15,000 over the cost of the consultant.	Costs more than $25,000 over the cost of the consultant.
Quality	A core volunteer team is in place, but written documented procedures are only in draft form.	A core volunteer team is in place, but written documented procedures are not available.	A core volunteer team is not in place and documented procedures are not available.

Meetings

Risk management planning meetings can be formal or informal. Most often, risks are discussed throughout the project life cycle. The project team may meet specifically on the topic of risk management; however, the project manager and project team need to ensure that risk is discussed and addressed.

As projects progress, risks will change, and in order to effectively respond to risk, risk management needs to be regularly included in discussions.

Expert Judgment

Since risks can have a significant impact on a project, it is important to leverage expert judgment in identifying risks. Individuals or groups familiar with similar projects should be consulted to ensure that a team is considering all things that could impact a project's overall success.

IDENTIFY RISKS PROCESS

The Identify Risks process involves collecting information from the various stakeholders regarding potential risks that can occur. Gathering information from a variety of sources, including the **risk breakdown structure (RBS)**, the **stakeholder register**, **enterprise environmental factors**, and the various subsidiary management plans, the project team can compile a comprehensive list of potential risks for a project.

The output of the Identify Risks process is the **risk register**. The risk register is a comprehensive document which defines the possible risks for a project. Early in the planning phase of a project, the risk register is just a skeletal document. As the project progresses and discussions ensue in various other knowledge areas, the risk register evolves into a comprehensive tool which defines project risks and strategies for managing risks if they occur.

Risks can negatively or positively impact a project and stakeholder. Most consider risks as negative events, but depending on the **stakeholder risk tolerance**, some risks can truly be positive. For example, the stakeholder who is willing to invest $10,000 in the start-up business may think about his or her investment: "With the right guidance, my investment of $10,000 will increase to $100,000 within two years." This upside, or positive, risk may be thought of as stakeholder's appetite for an event with a positive outcome.

> **TIP**
> The issue log is an important document to regularly review for additional risk identification opportunities. Risks that have occurred as an issue may trigger subsequent risks.

11

There are several pieces of information that should be captured for any risk:
- **Risk events**
- **Risk categories**
- **Risk owners**
- **Risk triggers**
- **Risk responses**
- **Risk appetites**

Consider a fire drill. Every organization that operates within a building must have some fire exit strategy. A fire exit strategy is a form of risk response. The risk event is that if a fire occurs, the employees of the organization would be placed in danger. Obviously, this is a negative external risk that organizations want to mitigate. One way to mitigate the risk of anyone being hurt in a fire is to create a fire drill evacuation plan.

Usually, someone within the organization, or in a particular area of the building, is put in charge of ensuring that all of the employees who work in that building or area are evacuated safely; this person is the risk owner. The risk trigger could be a fire alarm ringing. Once the risk has been triggered, there are specific procedures or responses that the owner follows, and if employees are not accounted for, the appropriate parties are contacted immediately. A risk register for this event is given in Figure 11-4 below.

Risk Register			
Risk Event	Risk Category	Risk Owner	Risk Trigger
If a fire occurs, the employees of the organization would be placed in danger	Employee Safety	John Smith	Fire alarm sounds

Figure 11-4
Risk Register

Many tools can be used to aid the project manager and project team in the creation of the risk register. These tools include **documentation reviews**, **information gathering techniques**, **checklist analysis**, **assumptions analysis**, **diagramming techniques**, **SWOT analysis**, and **expert judgment**.

Documentation Reviews

Reviewing documentation that may be available for a project will help the project team identify risks. For example, if a contract is signed to initiate a project, there are probably key points in the contract that can cause risk for the project. A typical contract risk may be a clause imposing penalties if a project is not delivered by a certain date.

> **TIP**
> Project managers should read all contracts associated with a project. Requirements may be stated in a contract that are not documented in any other place.

Class Exercise 11-2

Review the precedence diagram discussed in Class Exercise 6-4, page 6-20 and the activity dependencies (mandatory or discretionary) for our sample project. Then create a risk statement for Activity K.

Class Exercise 11-3

Based on the documentation already produced for the Fundraiser Road Race, where else might you look to identify potential risk events?

Information Gathering Techniques

There are some ways the project team can identify risks for a project that require little effort on the part of the project team.

Brainstorming is a technique that allows the project team members to state what is on their minds based on some kind of stimulus. This stimulus could simply be asking questions or having an ongoing discussion, but brainstorming is a free flow of ideas in which no idea is considered "bad." The intent of brainstorming is to allow for a flow of information.

11

The **Delphi technique** is a form of expert judgment. A facilitator solicits ideas on project risk from individuals who are considered experts on some aspect of a project. The results are continuously refined for further comment, with the outcome being a consensus on key project risks.

Interviewing is a technique commonly used to solicit information from individuals who may have an interest in the project, such as project stakeholders, or experience in similar projects.

Root cause analysis is a technique that focuses the project team on addressing the underlying causes of risks rather than the symptoms. For example, a car manufacturer can address the mean-time-between-failure of a car engine by planning for a replacement part program or can address the issue by identifying a root cause, which may be the engine design itself.

Class Exercise 11-4

Individually or in groups, use an information gathering technique to identify, in the table on the following page, five to ten risks for the Fundraiser Road Race and determine the category in which each risk falls, such as marketing, financial, etc.

Risk Event	Risk Category

Checklist Analysis

Checklists are often based on historical source documents of risks that have been previously encountered. They may be augmented by review of the **risk breakdown structures** of similar projects.

Assumptions Analysis

Risks may go unidentified if assumptions made at all levels of project participants remain unvoiced. The many information gathering techniques can identify assumptions made so they can be made explicit and given careful consideration. It can be difficult to validate and analyze assumptions because they are often influenced by experiences and may not even be consciously held.

> **TIP**
> Always question assumptions in order to flesh out any inaccuracy, instability, or inconsistency in them and to determine if any assumptions are incomplete.

11

Diagramming Techniques

Diagramming techniques are more visual than information gathering techniques. These visual techniques enable participants to think through the risks in a different way. Some visual techniques include **cause and effect diagrams**, **process flowcharts**, and **influence diagrams**, all of which have been discussed in prior chapters.

Diagramming techniques guide participants through the process in a logical way to ensure that processes and steps are not missed. In comparison, a brainstorming session may not ensure that participants cover the entire business process.

Influence diagrams offer an intuitive way to identify and display the essential elements of a project, including decisions, uncertainties, and objectives, and how each influences the others.

The simple influence diagram in Figure 11-5 below shows how decisions about marketing budget and product price influence expectations about a product's market size and market share. These, in turn, influence unit sales, which in turn influence costs and revenues, which affect the overall profit.

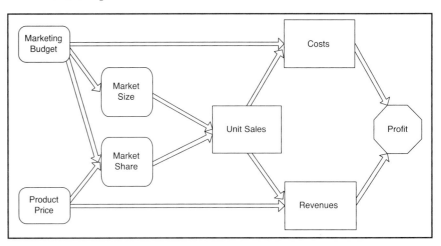

Figure 11-5
Influence Diagram

SWOT Analysis

A SWOT analysis is a specific technique that focuses on strengths, weaknesses, opportunities, and threats for a project in order to prompt discussion and thought regarding risks. This type of technique gives equal discussion to both positive and negative risks and is typically presented in a grid format.

Class Exercise 11-5

For the Fundraiser Road Race project, develop a SWOT analysis in the grid provided below.

Strengths	Weaknesses

Opportunities	Threats

Expert Judgment

The experience of the project team as well as the knowledge of other people involved in a project, including others within an organization and external sources, can be harnessed by involving such people in periodic reviews of project risks.

Writing a Risk Statement

Once a risk has been identified, it is important to write it down in a format that is easy to read. For instance, it is not appropriate to state that a risk is a "contract risk" because that is a category of risk. It is more appropriate to define risk in terms of an "if-then" statement. For example:

"If the project is not delivered on or before 12/31/16, then the project will begin to incur penalties of 1% of the total project cost each month the project goes undelivered."

Stating the risk in these terms makes it clear to the stakeholders what the risk is and what the effect is if the risk is realized.

Class Exercise 11-6

Below is a risk register template for the Fundraiser Road Race project. Practice writing good risk statements. Use the results from Class Exercise 11-4 and identify three new risks that may be applicable to the project or rewrite the risks previously identified. Identify the risk owner and trigger.

Note: Do not fill in the Risk Response column at this time.

Risk Category	Risk Statement	Owner	Trigger	Risk Response

Case Study 11-1

Create a risk register for the LUV Music website project. List at least five risks.

PERFORM QUALITATIVE RISK ANALYSIS PROCESS

The Perform Qualitative Risk Analysis process takes all the information from the Identify Risks process and prioritizes the risks based on the probability and impact of each occurring. The primary tool and technique used in this process is the **probability and impact analysis**. Once completed, any outputs of this process are used to update the **risk register**.

Risk Probability and Impact Analysis

Within the **risk management plan**, probability and impact definitions were created. These definitions are used to help determine which risks will be responded to based on the priority of each risk.

A probability and impact analysis utilizes all the risks defined in the risk register. The objective of this analysis is to assess the probability of a specific risk occurring and the impact on the project if the risk does occur. Once probability and impact are defined, risks can be prioritized.

> **TIP**
> Risk priority is based on the product of the probability and impact and can aide the project manager in acquiring scarce project resources. On projects with high risk, the project manager can better negotiate for the best resources.

11

Probability and Impact Matrix

Both the probability and impact values must be defined separately using a rating system, such as one to five. For each risk, multiply the probability and impact values to determine the qualitative risk score. Once the score is determined, review the matrix to determine the priority of a risk. The higher the score, the higher the priority of the risk, as demonstrated in Figure 11-6 below.

Probability & Impact Score for a Risk						
Probability	Risk Score = P X I					
5	5	10	15	20	25	HIGH
4	4	8	12	16	20	
3	3	6	9	12	15	MED
2	2	4	6	8	10	
1	1	2	3	4	5	LOW
	1	2	3	4	5	
	Impact (Ratio Scale)					

Figure 11-6
Probability and
Impact Matrix

Those risks that fall into the definitions requiring action (a high enough priority) will be addressed by the project team. Those risks that fall into the risk definitions that do not require action will be captured on a watchlist and the risk will simply be accepted rather than explicitly dealt with.

The project manager should have the informed consent of the project sponsor, based on the results of the qualitative risk analysis, and understand the sponsor's risk tolerance.

TIP

The project manager must have the informed consent of the project sponsor that the risks with a lower priority will not be dealt with in risk quantification.

Class Exercise 11-7

Review the risks identified in the risk register for the Fundraiser Road Race project from both Class Exercise 11-4 and 11-6, and determine the probability and impact score using the probability and impact grid on page 11-16. In the space below, list the top five risks warranting action with their probability and impact scores.

Risk	Probability	Impact

Risk Data Quality Assessment

While it may not take significant time and resources, scrutinizing the quality of the risk data is a vital step in assuring that risk issues will be appropriately addressed. The project sponsor, members of the project management team, and project or program management resources should be used in this assessment.

Risk Categorization

Previously, we identified various categories of risk. Each risk event was associated with a specific risk category. Once the project team has a complete understanding of the risks associated with a project, team members can determine if any particular risk category of the project has greater risk exposure than other risk categories.

It is possible that a particular risk category does not include any risks that are considered high probability and high impact, but the volume of risks identified in that particular category could still warrant action.

Evaluating risks based on their categories can provide the project team information that would not have been identified otherwise.

Risk Urgency Assessment

Another consideration when evaluating risks is the urgency of the situation. Some risks may have a high probability and high impact, but may not need to be addressed immediately. Others may not have as high a risk score, but should be addressed in advance of the risk that scored the highest.

Figure 11-7 below shows two risks that have been identified for our Fundraiser Road Race project.

Risk	Probability	Impact
If the road race location is not chosen within the first month of the project, the team will be unable to ensure that marketing materials are delivered early enough to ensure enough participants in the race.	6	10
If the food and drink vendors aren't selected two months before the road race, the t-shirts they will be giving away to all participants will not be able to be delivered the week before the race.	8	8

Figure 11-7
Identified Risks

In this example, the team has identified that the risk score of the second risk is 64, while the risk score of the first risk is 60. However, since the impact of the first risk is very high, and the urgency is greater, the first risk should be addressed prior to addressing the second risk.

Expert Judgment

Fresh eyes are essential to ensure that project sponsorship, project management, and critical project participants do not minimize or exaggerate the risks for a project. Risks must be properly quantified before they are quantitatively analyzed.

Class Exercise 11-8

Re-evaluate the risk scores of the risks that did not make the top five in Class Exercise 11-7 for the Fundraiser Road Race project. Are there other situations in which a risk with a lower risk score would need to be addressed earlier than one with a higher score?

PERFORM QUANTITATIVE RISK ANALYSIS PROCESS

The Perform Quantitative Risk Analysis process focuses on numerically assessing risk for a project, rather than relying on estimates or opinions based on past performance or expertise. For example, we stated previously that if the race site isn't determined within one month of the project start date, the chance of the road race attracting enough people will be impacted. Quantitative risk analysis attempts to determine how much the project will be impacted.

There are many tools that can be used to quantify risk for a project. The simplest tools include talking to experts (expert judgment) to obtain their relative insight into the risks being analyzed and the expected outcomes, as well as **interviewing** and **probability distribution** that provide historical data from which determinations can be made. Two additional tools are **quantitative risk analysis** and **modeling techniques**.

> **TIP**
>
> One consequence of the Perform Qualitative Risk Analysis process may be a determination that the scope of a project cannot be achieved with the expected level of quality because doing so may be unfeasible or unaffordable.

11

Quantitative Risk Analysis and Modeling Techniques

These tools provide the user with a way to simulate various alternatives in order to understand the possible outcomes of risk. The *PMBOK® Guide* outlines a couple of modeling techniques. We will review **expected monetary value** (EMV) analysis here.

EMV is used to determine the average outcomes of a specific scenario. EMV for a project is calculated by multiplying the value of each possible outcome by its probability of occurrence and adding the products together.

For our Fundraiser Road Race, the following determination has been made:
- There is a 20% chance that it will rain on the day of the road race if it is held in September, and a 5% chance of rain in any other month.
- If there is rain on the day of the road race, there will be approximately 3,000 fewer people in attendance; if it doesn't rain, we anticipate 9,000 attendees
- If there is rain on the day of the road race, we will have to purchase additional materials costing an additional $5,000
- Each attendee will be charged $10 at the door; historically, participants usually donate an additional $25 while at the event

Figure 11-8 on the following page shows a sample expected monetary value analysis for the Fundraiser Road Race.

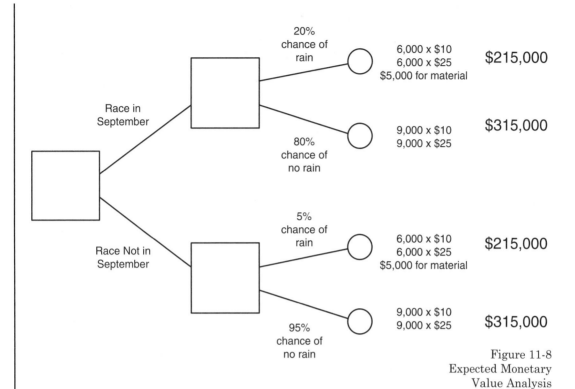

20%
chance of
rain

6,000 x $10
6,000 x $25
$5,000 for material

$215,000

Race in
September

9,000 x $10
9,000 x $25

$315,000

80%
chance of
no rain

5%
chance of
rain

6,000 x $10
6,000 x $25
$5,000 for material

$215,000

Race Not in
September

9,000 x $10
9,000 x $25

$315,000

95%
chance of
no rain

Figure 11-8
Expected Monetary
Value Analysis

A **sensitivity analysis** helps determine risk with the
highest potential impact on a project, while **modeling**
or **simulations** can translate specified uncertainties of a
project into their potential impact on project objectives.

Expert Judgment

Experts with current applicable experience in identifying
potential cost, quality, and schedule impacts on project
outcomes are vital to the interpretation of risk data, given
project capabilities and culture.

Class Exercise 11-9

Using EMV, evaluate the risk of death or injury to a
participant or volunteer during the Fundraiser Road
Race.

> **TIP**
> A tornado diagram displays
> the results of a sensitivity
> analysis, comparing the
> relative importance of
> variables to the impact of
> those variables.

11

PLAN RISK RESPONSES PROCESS

The Plan Risk Responses process is a critical planning process because it puts in place the approach to handling risks if they occur. As we discussed earlier, not all risks need to be addressed. Developing responses is a conscious analysis to determine if the project team needs to proactively address a risk or not.

Risks are events that have a possibility of occurring, but have not yet occurred. A risk becomes an issue when there is a trigger that causes the risk event to occur.

There are strategies for handling both positive and negative risks.

Project teams must assess each risk based on the priorities defined earlier and determine if action needs to be taken. The outputs of the Plan Risk Responses process are an updated **risk register** and any **contract decisions** that may have been made as a result of the risk analysis.

Strategies for Negative Risks or Threats

Figure 11-9
Strategies for
Negative Risks

Figure 11-9 below outlines the four strategies for negative risks or threats and gives an example of each strategy for the Fundraiser Road Race.

Strategy	Definition	Example
Avoid	Change the project management plan to eliminate the threat entirely.	Since there may not be enough tents on the day of an event and BEST CONSULTING wishes to hold these events annually, tents could be purchased to eliminate the risk.
Transfer	Shift all or some of the risk to a third party.	Purchase insurance, so that if the event is cancelled, the charity will still get its money.
Mitigate	Reduce the probability and/or impact of an adverse risk event.	Set a rain date and publish it in all of the marketing materials.
Accept	Take no action as part of the planning process.	Do nothing.

Strategies for Positive Risks or Opportunities

Outlined below in Figure 11-10 are the four strategies for positive risks or opportunities, with an example for our Fundraiser Road Race.

Figure 11-10
Strategies for
Positive Risks

Strategy	Definition	Example
Exploit	Ensure that the opportunity is realized.	Find one sponsor that is willing to donate $300,000.
Share	Allocate ownership to a third party who may best be able to capture the opportunity.	Hire a consultant knowledgeable in raising funds.
Enhance	Increase the probability and/or impact of the opportunity.	Mandate that all the employees of BEST CONSULTING participate in the event.
Accept	Take no action as part of the planning process.	Do nothing.

Contingent Response Strategies

When a risk is low enough to not warrant any response, the strategy should be to accept that the risk could occur and do nothing. Sometimes the steps taken to respond to a risk may leave either **residual risks** or **secondary risks**. Planning a response that will be executed under certain predefined conditions is a contingent response strategy.

When risks are determined to require action, any necessary updates to the **WBS**, **schedule**, **budget**, etc. should be made, and the **project management plan** should be updated accordingly.

Expert Judgment

Experts internal or external to a project may be involved for certain specified and defined risk events. These experts may be drawn from internal or external sources as needed.

11

Figure 11-11
Strategies for
Negative Risks

Probability & Impact Score for Negative Risk			
High	Mitigate/ Transer	Mitigate/ Avoid	Mitigate/ Avoid
Medium	Accept	Mitigate/ Transfer	Mitigate/ Avoid
Low	Accept	Mitigate/ Accept	Mitigate/ Transfer
Probability	Low	Med	High
	Impact (Ratio Scale)		

Figure 11-11 above describes the Fundraiser Road Race approach to addressing risks that are defined. Based on the probability and impact score, the organization has recommended these approaches to managing negative risks.

Once each risk that warrants a strategy has been evaluated, the **risk register** should be updated with information from the strategy decision. Figure 11-12 on the following page is an example of an updated risk register for the Fundraiser Road Race project.

Risk Category	Risk Statement	Owner	Trigger	Risk Response
Marketing	If the road race location is not chosen within the first month of the project, the team will be unable to ensure that the marketing materials are delivered early enough to ensure enough participants in the race.	Consultant 1	1 month milestone	Mitigate by having a checkpoint with the marketing team one week prior to the target date. *Add a review meeting to the project schedule.*
Marketing	If the food and drink vendors aren't selected two months before the road race, the t-shirts that will be given away to all participants by the vendors will not be able to be delivered the week before the race.	Volunteer 4	2 month milestone	Mitigate by setting the target date for a decision 3 months prior to the road race. *Add a review meeting to the project schedule.*
Financial	If it rains on the day of the event and tents are not available, fewer than 5,000 people will attend.	Volunteer 4	Rain forecast greater than 30% on the day of the event	Avoid by purchasing tents.

Figure 11-12
Updated Risk
Register

If the project team determines that the risk of rain warrants action, the project schedule would be updated as identified in Figure 11-13 below with a new task for purchasing tents.

WBS	Name	Predecessors	Duration	hh mm
1	Fund Raiser Charity Event		101d	
1.1	Event Decision		13d	
1.1.1	Event Analysis		10d	
1.1.2	Event Options Decision	Event Analysis	3d	
1.2	Venue		37d	
1.2.1	Site Selection		27d	
1.2.1.1	Identify sites & Site visits	Event Options Decision	10d	
1.2.1.2	Analyze site options	Identify sites & Site visits	15d	
1.2.1.3	Review and decide on site	Analyze site options	2d	
1.2.2	Site Preparation		17d	
1.2.2.1	Water and Power Setup	Review and decide on site	10d	
	Purchase Tents	Identify sites & Site visits +10d		
1.2.2.2	Tent Setup	Review and decide on site , Identify sites & Site visits	3d	

BEST CONSULTING Fund Raiser Road Race — Project Views — Resources — Reports

Task List

Figure 11-13
Updated
Schedule

Class Exercise 11-10

Using the risks you identified in Class Exercise 11-6, add a risk response to each of the risks listed. Consider the following questions:
- Is there any residual or secondary risk as a result of the risk response you've chosen?
- Are there any positive risks for the Fundraiser Road Race?

CONTROL RISKS PROCESS

Risks need to be regularly reviewed and assessed in order for the benefits of risk planning to be realized. The Control Risks process does not occur only once. It is an ongoing effort to continuously assess risks for a project. Project managers must ensure that when a risk trigger occurs, the risk response plan is carried out. Consider any residual risk that may linger as risks are addressed and identify new risks that may impact the project as the project progresses.

The outputs of the Control Risks process are any necessary updates or additions to the **risk register** as well as potential **change requests**.

Risk Reassessment

Project team members who make risk management a part of their daily activities improve their chances for success. One way to make reassessment a part of the project management processes is to set aside time at **status meetings** to review key risks and determine if anything has changed, warrants change, or should be retired, and if any risk is new.

Risk Audits

Audits are necessary to evaluate the effectiveness of any process. A risk audit is no different. Since risk is a projection of what could happen, it is useful to assess:
- How well the team anticipated a risk
- How effective the response was when a risk occurred
- How effective a response strategy was in reducing the probability of a risk occurring

Risk audits can be scheduled at any time; however, it is extremely important to ensure that the goals of the audit are clearly defined before conducting an audit.

Variance and Trend Analysis

Variance analysis and trend analysis tools are helpful in identifying if risk response strategies are working. These tools can also identify additional areas for which risk assessment may be necessary.

For example, if a project team has implemented a risk mitigation effort to reduce the probability of a particular task going over budget, then as the performance metrics are captured, the project team can determine if the variances experienced or the trends being seen are an indication of risk strategy effectiveness or not. If the cost variances for the budget are staying within expected levels, then one can deduce that the mitigation efforts—in terms of risks to the project's cost—have been successful.

> **TIP**
>
> Every risk accepted as a priority risk should have a risk owner. The owner should be responsible for providing the status of the risk situation at review meetings.

11

Class Exercise 11-11

An organization is considering using a higher-cost 20-month mean-time-between-failure (MTBF) cell phone circuit to reduce the risk of cell phone failure. In order to determine if the organization should purchase the more expensive cell phone circuit, the company ran a sample test of each of the products simulating 15 months and 20 months of usage. The two control charts below display the results. Should the organization purchase the more expensive component, the 20-month MTBF? Would the information provided warrant a change request and increase in budget?

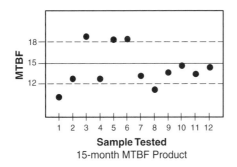

Sample Tested
15-month MTBF Product

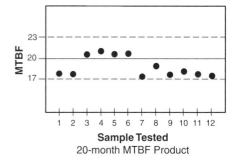

Sample Tested
20-month MTBF Product

Technical Performance Measurement

Technical performance measurement speaks directly to the achievement of objectives, *not* just the achievement of project performance. Quantifiable measurements of technical performance are things like throughput, system response time, defect rates, and durability.

Reserve Analysis

Budget and schedule **contingency reserves** are determined based on the amount of risk anticipated for a project. Performing a reserve analysis regularly and comparing the remaining contingency to the expected future risk of a project is important in order to keep the overall project in control.

Seeing a large portion of project budget or schedule contingency utilized early in the project should alert the project manager to the fact that **risk strategies** may not be effective and should trigger additional risk management efforts.

Meetings

A simple but key tool and technique to keeping risk in check during a project's execution is to make risk a regular conversation during status meetings. The more the concepts of managing risk are discussed and followed up on, the more likely all team members will start participating. The key here is not to have risk management be the job of the project manager; rather, it should be the job of the entire project team.

Throughout a project, the project manager and the project team need to continuously update the **risk register** as risks are closed, triggered, or identified. In doing so, project teams will function with the most up-to-date information and will be able to work effectively in a "risky" environment.

TIP
Risks that have been retired as part of the execution of a project should be closed but not eliminated Retired risks may be retained in an appendix to the risk register.

TIP
Project risk management should be on the agenda of all scheduled and adhoc meetings.

11

PROFESSIONAL RESPONSIBILITY

Risk management is about effectively identifying, planning for, and responding to risks when they occur. When considering the four aspects of professional responsibility—responsibility, respect, fairness, and honesty—the project manager must keep certain things in mind at all times:

- Don't ignore risks that could impact a project, even if the news is not well received by all stakeholders
- Honestly assess all risks that are identified
- Work on risks that are identified as the most important to a project and not those risks that you personally believe should be addressed

It is the project manager's responsibility to make risk management a continuous part of the project life cycle.

11

KEY INTERPERSONAL SKILLS FOR SUCCESS

The interpersonal skill highlighted in this chapter is:

Influencing

Project managers need to build strong influencing skills since they frequently lack legitimate authority to manage team members. Influencing means the project manager gains the cooperation of stakeholders without traditional reward and penalty motivations. Project managers often accomplish such cooperation by practicing fairness, honesty, and respect, and also by taking responsibility for the actions of themselves and the project team.

When evaluating risks, people will have differing views of the probability and impact of each risk. Keen influencing skills can help others gain consensus to move the project forward and not get stuck in "analysis paralysis."

11

BE A BETTER PROJECT MANAGER

Exercise: where are our risks?

Purpose: identify risks more thoroughly by using experts within your own organization.

Steps: everyone knows "that" person who is the squeaky wheel, "that" person who is fast to say, "I told you so." Just as in contract development, not everyone enjoys talking about things that can go wrong, except for "that" person. We'll call that person the negativity expert.

Embrace the negativity expert when it comes to identifying risks. This is the opportunity for him or her to feel special, to be heard, and to make a difference in the organization and the project.

Allow the negativity expert the podium to brainstorm the risks that he or she sees.

The only ground rules that must be set are:
- The negativity expert must understand that the team will review, assess, and prioritize each risk
- Such expert must agree that not all risks warrant action and be willing to let go of those that have a low probability and low impact, or whichever other criteria your organization uses

SAMPLE CAPM EXAM QUESTIONS ON RISK MANAGEMENT

1. One of the main goals of project risk management is to:

   a) Decrease the likelihood and impact of positive events
   b) Minimize the probability and consequences of adverse project events
   c) Minimize the probability and consequences of opportunities
   d) Increase the likelihood and impact of negative events

2. To be successful, an organization should be committed to manage risk _____.

   a) When schedules are in danger of being overrun
   b) When costs spiral out of control
   c) Proactively and consistently
   d) During the planning and monitoring and controlling process groups

3. The degree, amount, or volume of risk that an organization or individual will withstand is called risk:

   a) Attitude
   b) Appetite
   c) Tolerance
   d) Threshold

4. Deciding how to plan and execute risk management events for a project is the objective of the _____ process.

   a) Plan Risk Management
   b) Executing Process Group
   c) Identify Risks
   d) Monitor and Control Risks

5. The risk register:

    a) Identifies schedule activities for resources that are estimated
    b) Is created early in a project and rarely updated
    c) Documents results of project activities
    d) Documents the outcomes of risk management planning

6. Which of the following is an output of the Identify Risks process?

    a) Enterprise environmental factors
    b) Project scope statement
    c) Roles and responsibilities
    d) Risk register

7. _____ risk analysis is a cost-effective tool for prioritizing risks on a project.

    a) Quantitative
    b) Qualitative
    c) Quality
    d) Cause and effect

8. Which process helps project managers focus on high priority risks?

    a) Plan Risk Management
    b) Identify Risks
    c) Perform Qualitative Risk Analysis
    d) Perform Quantitative Risk Analysis

9. The Perform Quantitative Risk Analysis process is usually:

    a) Performed on all risks identified in the risk register
    b) Performed on risks prioritized during qualitative risk analysis
    c) A cost-effective tool for determining risk priorities
    d) An input to the risk management plan

Notes:

11

10. A charity event party is to be held that will cost $10 per person:

> If the party is held inside, 150 people are likely to attend.
> If the party is held outside, 200 people are likely to attend.
> There is a 20% chance of rain on the date of the party.
> If it rains and the party is held inside, only 100 people will attend.
> If it rains and the party is held outside, only 80 people will attend.

In the example above, if the goal of the project is to maximize revenue, which of the two options maximizes revenue and why:

a) Held inside because the expected monetary value is $1,200
b) Held inside because the expected monetary value is $1,400
c) Held outside because the expected monetary value is $1,400
d) Held outside because the expected monetary value is $1,760

11. The key benefit of planning risk responses is that it:

a) Allows the project team to add needed resources to the budget or schedule
b) Helps the project team determine which are high priority risks that should be addressed
c) Provides a guideline for how risk management will be handled on a project
d) Defines a large number of risks that may have an impact on a project

Notes:

12. Which of the following are strategies to manage threats?

    a) Avoid, transfer, exploit
    b) Mitigate, accept, enhance
    c) Share, transfer, accept
    d) Avoid, transfer, mitigate

13. When a project management team updates a risk breakdown structure template based on the results of a current project, the team is updating a(n):

    a) Organizational process asset
    b) Enterprise environmental factor
    c) Risk response plan
    d) Probability and impact matrix

14. Overall project risk represents:

    a) Risks that have been identified
    b) The sum of all individual risks
    c) The effect of risks on a project as a whole
    d) The impact of negative risks to a project

15. The following are Perform Quantitative Risk Analysis process tools and techniques:

    a) Decision tree and sensitivity analysis
    b) Risk attitude assessment and meetings
    c) Mitigation and contingency responses
    d) Risk reassessment, risk audits, and reserve analysis

Notes:

11

ANSWERS AND REFERENCES FOR SAMPLE CAPM EXAM QUESTIONS ON RISK MANAGEMENT

Section numbers refer to the *PMBOK® Guide*.

1. **B** **Section 11.0 – Planning**
   The answers to this question require careful reading; make sure you understand what the correct combination is.

2. **C** **Section 11.0 – Planning**
   Although all six of the risk management processes are in the planning and monitoring and controlling process groups, C is the better answer because it indicates planning ahead for what might happen and not ignoring risk.

3. **C** **Section 11.0 – Planning**
   A) is the overall perspective on the level of risk that an individual or organization is willing to take; B) is the degree of uncertainty offset by the anticipation of a reward; D) is the dividing line between accepting or not accepting risk.

4. **A** **Section 11.1 – Planning**
   The risk management plan is integrated within the overall project management plan.

5. **D** **Section 11.2 – Planning**
   The risk register should be reviewed and updated regularly throughout a project's entire life.

6. **D** **Section 11.2 – Planning**
   Identified risks are documented in the risk register.

7. **B** **Section 11.3 – Planning**
   A) quantitative analysis typically requires more complex and costly tools; C) & D) a root cause or cause-and-effect analysis doesn't focus on prioritization.

8. **C** **Section 11.3 – Planning**
   A) helps the project manager determine the type and nature of risk management that will be performed; B) risks must be identified before the

team can determine which are high priority;
D) usually occurs after identifying high-priority
risks to quantify their probability and impact.

9. **B Section 11.4 – Planning**
A) the Perform Quantitative Risk Analysis pro-
cess is not performed on *all* risks; C) occurs in the
Perform Qualitative Risk Analysis process; D) the
risk management plan is an input to the Perform
Quantitative Risk Analysis process.

10. **D Section 11.4 – Planning**
The party should be held outside because the
expected monetary value for holding it outside is
$1,760, which is greater than $1,400 if it is held
inside. There are only two choices: hold inside or
outside; you cannot choose whether it rains or not.

11. **A Section 11.5 – Planning**
B) occurs during qualitative analysis; C) occurs
during risk management planning; D) occurs
when identifying risk.

12. **D Section 11.5 – Planning**
Exploit, enhance, and share are all strategies for
opportunities or positive risks.

13. **A Section 11.6 – Monitoring and Controlling**
Maintaining organizational templates with
experiences learned after each project is
considered a best practice.

14. **C Section 11.0 – Planning**
Overall project risk represents the effect of risks
on the project as a whole.

15. **A Section 11.4 – Planning**
B) are tools for risk planning; C) are part of the
Plan Risk Responses process; D) are tools and
techniques of the Monitor and Control Risks process.

ANSWERS TO CLASS EXERCISES

Class Exercise 11-1: Risk Tolerances

Stakeholder Register					
Stake-holder	Identification Information	Assessment Information	Stakeholder Classification	Communications Requirements	Risk Tolerance
Sponsor: Tom Wang	VP of Product Development and Sales	A successful event is one in which all four objectives are met or exceed-ed	Internal supporter	*Must* know if the event is getting the "buzz." Keep him abreast of potential participants, sponsorship opportunities, cost coverage, and donation tally. Regular communication in the form of a status report with key indicators will be required.	Risk seeker. Tom is the VP of product development and is always looking for new opportunities to try.
Participants in the event	Anyone who attends the event, such as a runner, a volunteer, or someone interested in the particular charity	Want a fun time and maybe to win some prizes; do not want to be stressed	Neutral participant	Tell potential participants early enough in the process to allow them time to put the event on their calen-dars. Communication will be via web, newspapers, and magazines. Communication will start once a date is set and we are within five months of the event.	Risk neutral. Participants generally want to have a nice event, but they typically don't worry about the risks that can occur.
Children's Charity	The recipient of the proceeds of the event; will be able to do more for the patients and community when donations are received	Mostly interested in the outcome of the project; will participate in the event by providing an information book and a place for individuals to make donations at the event	External supporter	At fairly infrequent intervals, at a very minimum on a monthly basis, communicate to the Children's Charity with information on overall project milestones. More frequent communications will be provided within one month of the event to provide insight into the size of the potential donation.	Risk averse. The charity won't spend any money it doesn't have.

Class Exercise 11-2: Identify Risks

If the vendor does not deliver on time, the project will *not* be able to be completed on time.

Class Exercise 11-3: Identify Risks

****For Class Discussion Only****

Class Exercise 11-4: Information Gathering Techniques

Risk	Risk Category
If volunteers will be required to put in more hours than they have available, the morale of the team will be impacted.	Resource
If we are unable to shift some of the work from the consultant in February, there will be some activities that will miss their scheduled target dates.	Resource
If we are unable to obtain another volunteer in the month of March, then Volunteer 4 will not be able to deliver on the scheduled activities.	Resource
If we only plan on getting 8,000 people to the event, the chance of reaching our $300,000 donation goal will be at risk.	Financial
If we schedule the event in September, the chance of rain occurring on the event date will increase.	Environment or Scheduling

11

Class Exercise 11-5: SWOT

Strengths	Weaknesses
Has a strong advocate in the sponsor, Tom Wang. He is very influential in the community. Henry Optimo is a strong project manager and has worked on projects like this for ten years.	BEST CONSULTING has never hosted an event like this before. The Children's Charity is not well known within the state.

Opportunities	Threats
The Children's Charity is well known within the local community.	The economy is causing everyone to watch more closely where they spend funds. Weather could be a factor in the fall.

Class Exercise 11-6: Risk Statements

Risk Category	Risk Statement	Owner	Trigger	Risk Response
Marketing	If the road race location is not chosen within the first month of the project, the team will be unable to ensure that the marketing materials are delivered early enough to ensure enough participants in the race.	Consultant 1	1-month milestone	
Marketing	If the food and drink vendors aren't selected within two months of the road race, the t-shirts that will be given away to all participants by the vendors will not be able to be delivered the week before the race.	Volunteer 4	2-month milestone	
Financial	If it rains on the day of the event and tents are not available, fewer than 5,000 people will attend.	Volunteer 4	Rain forecast greater than 30% on event day	

Class Exercise 11-7: Probability and Impact

**** For Class Discussion Only****

Class Exercise 11-8: Risk Urgency

**** For Class Discussion Only****

Class Exercise 11-9: Quantitative Risk Analysis

**** For Class Discussion Only****

For your discussion, you may want to consider the following facts:
- There is a 95% chance of obtaining insurance; liability insurance against death or injury to a participant costs $1,000
- There is a 5% chance of not being able to obtain insurance, which means you will have to self-insure for a cost of $20,000

Class Exercise 11-10: Risk Response Strategies

**** For Class Discussion Only****

Class Exercise 11-11: Variance and Trend Analysis
**** For Class Discussion Only****

For your discussion, consider that the component with the 20-month MTBF has a more reliable result than the 15-month one. If the organization is interested in achieving that level of quality consistently, then it may consider the additional costs. Review the project charter and stakeholder risk tolerances to aid in your decision making.

ANSWERS TO THE CASE STUDY CAN BE FOUND IN THE WAV™ FILES

Web
Added
Value™

This book has free material available for download from the
Web Added Value™ resource center at *www.jrosspub.com*.

11

PROCUREMENT

CHAPTER 12 | **PROCUREMENT**

12

12

PROCUREMENT MANAGEMENT

The procurement management knowledge area is focused on the knowledge and skills a project manager must have in order to successfully manage external entities as deliverers of specific project deliverables. Not all projects utilize resources that are readily available within an organization. More often than not, resources—both individual and corporate—are engaged to facilitate a project's delivery. Project managers conversant in good procurement processes can effectively leverage resources outside of their direct control.

According to the *PMBOK® Guide*, project managers are not expected to be procurement specialists; procurement organizational units do that. However, project managers must understand the basics of **contracting**, **negotiating**, and **contract administration** to succeed. In addition, knowing the procurement processes helps project managers who manage **subprojects** for other buyers.

Projects that have procurement arrangements become more complex in that they involve additional entities. That does not mean that the project is riskier, just more complex. In many cases, organizations procure items to reduce risk.

Knowledge Area Processes

Within the procurement management knowledge area there are four processes within four process groups.

Planning	Executing	Monitoring and Controlling	Closing
Plan Procurement Management	Conduct Procurements	Control Procurements	Close Procurements

Key Definitions

Agreements: any documents or communications that define the initial intentions of a project. They can take the form of a contract, memorandum of understanding (MOU), letter of agreement, verbal agreement, email, etc.

Bidder conference: the buyer and potential sellers meet prior to the contract award to answer questions about the scope of work and clarify requirements; the intent is for all sellers to have equal access to the same information.

Buyer: the performing organization, client, customer, contractor, purchaser, or requester seeking to acquire goods and services from an external entity (the seller). The buyer becomes the customer and key stakeholder.

Commercial-off-the-shelf (COTS): a product or service that is readily available from many sources; selection of a seller is primarily driven by price.

Contract: the binding agreement between a buyer and seller.

Letter contract: a written preliminary contract authorizing the seller to begin work immediately; it is often used for small-value contracts.

Letter of intent: this is *not* a contract, but simply a letter without legal binding that says the buyer intends to hire the seller.

Point of total assumption: in a fixed price contract, the point above which the seller will assume responsibility for all costs; it generally occurs when the contract ceiling price has been exceeded.

Privity: the contractual relationship between the two parties of a contract. If party A contracts with party B and party B subcontracts to party C, there is no privity between party A and party C.

Seller: the bidder, contractor, source, subcontractor, vendor, or supplier who will provide the goods and services to the buyer. The seller generally manages the work as a project, utilizing all processes and knowledge areas of project management.

Single source: selecting a seller without competition. This may be appropriate if there is an emergency or prior business relationship.

Sole source: selecting a seller because it is the only provider of the needed product or service.

PLAN PROCUREMENT MANAGEMENT PROCESS

The Plan Procurement Management process is the only procurement process that will always be performed in every project. This is because every project manager must determine if there is anything that can or should be purchased. The Plan Procurement Management process encompasses all the efforts needed to determine what will be procured for a project. It includes analysis of what to purchase, criteria on how to select vendors, actual statements of work for items determined to be purchased, as well as a procurement plan regarding how procurements will be managed throughout the project.

The primary outputs of the Plan Procurement Management process are the **make or buy decision**, **source selection criteria**, **procurement SOW**, and **procurement management plan**. A sample procurement management plan is shown in Figure 12-1 below.

12

Procurement Management Plan

Project Name: Fundraiser Road Race
Date: 2/2/14

At present there are no expectations of any items that need to be procured for the fundraiser road race project.

If items are identified as part of executing the project, the following process will be followed:

1) All procurement requests will be directed to Sue Flanders, Procurement Specialist
2) All procurement requests must comply with standard procurement policies
3) The project sponsor must sign-off on all procurement requests over $2,500.
4) For purchases over $10,000, a competitive bid process must be initiated.

Figure 12-1
Procurement
Management Plan

Make or Buy Analysis

Determining whether to make or buy items for a project is a **general management technique**. In many cases, this determination includes analyzing the costs and benefits of purchasing rather than making. Some of the reasons for deciding to purchase versus make a product are given in Figure 12-2 below.

Reasons to Make	Reasons to Buy
• Cost	• Cost
• Integration of operations	• Supplier expertise
• Idle existing capacity	• Small-volume costs too high
• Direct control or customization	• Limited capacity or time
• Proprietary design	• Augment labor force
• Poor supplier experiences	• Maintain multiple sources or reduce risk
• Stabilize work force	• Indirect control is acceptable

Figure 12-2
Reasons to
Make or Buy

Make or buy decisions are not always financially motivated. Often, a decision to purchase is driven by the expertise (**expert judgment**) of the organization or is based on the risk presented. For example, organizations may choose to contract for personnel with a specific skill set because the particular skill set is not something that the organization would require full-time. In this case, a contract relationship may be the best alternative regardless of the cost.

Similarly, an organization may choose to buy from multiple sources. For example, if a project relies heavily on having materials available in order to succeed, the organization may choose to use multiple vendors for the same product to ensure that the materials are always available. Relying on only one vendor would be too risky in this case.

Expert Judgment

An organization's purchasing unit is an excellent resource for the project manager. Leveraging such expertise when purchasing decisions are needed can significantly reduce risk on a project. Purchasing departments can provide a range of expertise, from service level agreements to intellectual property protection.

When make or buy decisions are made, the **WBS** and **project management plan** must be updated, as well as any other planning documents developed to this point.

Class Exercise 12-1

A cell phone company determines that the vendor costs are too high to achieve the appropriate 15-month mean-time-before-failure (MTBF) and wants to explore developing the phone circuits itself. It has the manufacturing facility but has only produced circuits for larger telephone switchboards.

The information in the table below was pulled together by the finance department in order to help make a decision. Perform a make or buy analysis and answer the following questions.

Should the company produce the circuits itself or hire a vendor? What other considerations are there in making this decision?

	Make	**Buy**
Number of units needed	40,000	40,000
Cost of materials	$0.50/unit	$120/100 units
Labor rate	$8.50/hour	Not applicable
Productivity expectations	10 units/hour for first 10,000 units 30 units/hour for remaining 30,000 units	Not applicable
Scrap rate	10%	99% acceptance rate
Setup fee	$10,000	Not applicable

Market Research

The procurement organization may lack expertise and the relationships needed if the project is a new innovation, providing entry into a new market, or leveraging new technologies. Market research can provide the project manager and the procurement team the needed information to search out appropriate vendors to fulfill the project's requirements.

12

Meetings

Collaborating with potential bidders through meetings may identify additional project opportunities and clarification of component systems and processes.

Procurement Management Plan

TIP
Know the various components that can be included in a procurement management plan. See the *PMBOK® Guide* Section 12.1.3.1.

As the primary output of the Plan Procurement Management process, the procurement management plan documents how the procurement processes will be managed, from developing procurement documents through contract closure. Many organizations already have procurement departments, and often, this kind of plan is part of standard operating procedures.

Procurement Statement of Work

Another result of the make or buy analysis is the procurement statement of work. This document will be provided to any potential vendors as information for preparing formal proposals. A procurement statement of work is very similar to a project charter document. It details the project scope of work and any assumptions, constraints, and other pertinent details a vendor team will need in order to estimate the work to be performed.

Source Selection Criteria

As the result of a make or buy analysis, it is typical to identify specific criteria for selecting a vendor once the proposals have been received. The criteria will be used to rate, or score, potential sellers. Objective criteria are ideal for facilitating a contract selection process.

Contract Types

The primary objective of contract type selection is to have risk distributed between the buyer and seller so that both parties have motivation and incentive for meeting the contract goal. If the product or service is not well defined, both the buyer and seller are at risk.

The following factors may influence the type of contract selected:
- Overall degree of cost and schedule risk
- Type/complexity of requirement
- Extent of price competition
- Cost/price analysis
- Urgency of requirement/performance period
- The level of detail in the statement of work
- Frequency of expected changes
- Industry standards for types of contracts used

There are three general types of contracts:

- **Fixed price** (FP) or lump sum contracts involve a predetermined fixed price for a product; it is the preferred type of contract in many situations and is used when the product is well defined
- **Cost reimbursable** (CR) or **cost plus** contracts involve payment based on the seller's actual costs, a fee, and a potential incentive for meeting or exceeding project objectives; it may be easier to initiate but requires more oversight by the buyer
- **Time and material** (T&M) contracts (sometimes called **unit price** contracts) contain characteristics of both FP and CR contracts and are generally used for small dollar amounts; these contracts may be priced on a per-hour or per-item basis (like fixed price contracts) but the total number of hours or items is not determined (open-ended cost-type arrangements like CR contracts)

Fixed Price Contracts

In fixed price contracts, the seller is paid an agreed-upon price for the work to be performed which must include the seller's profit and any necessary contingencies. Therefore, the seller bears a higher burden of the cost risk than the buyer. Typical types of fixed price contracts are:

- **Firm-fixed price** (FFP): also called a lump sum contract, in which the seller bears the greatest degree of risk; this is a common type of contract when the seller agrees to perform a service or furnish supplies at an established contract price

  One example of an FFP contract:

Contract price	$100,000
Seller's actual cost	$70,000
Buyer's total payments	$100,000

  The seller's actual cost is usually not disclosed in this type of contract; the seller's profit is $30,000 in this example

  Another example of an FFP contract:

Contract price	$100,000
Seller's actual cost	$130,000
Buyer's total payment	$100,000

  The seller loses $30,000 on this contract

- **Fixed price incentive fee** (FPIF): a complex type of contract in which the seller bears a higher burden of risk, but the purpose of the incentive is to shift some of the risk back to the buyer; typically, for every dollar the seller reduces cost below the target, the cost savings are split between the buyer and seller based on the share ratio (a ceiling price is established so the buyer does not pay more than the ceiling price; therefore, if costs exceed the ceiling, the seller receives no additional payments)

  One example of an FPIF contract:

Target cost	$100,000
Target profit	$10,000
Contract price value	$110,000
Ceiling price	$120,000
Share ratio (buyer/seller)	80-20
Seller's actual cost	$80,000
Difference	$20,000

TIP

Contracts are formal agreements between the buyer and seller.

12

Profit calculation:

Seller's share of difference (20%)	$4,000
Target profit	$10,000
Total profit	$14,000

Total calculation:

Actual cost	$80,000
Total profit	$14,000
Buyer's total payment	$94,000

Another example of an FPIF contract: same targets and ceiling as above; if the project's actual cost increases to $130,000, the buyer pays the seller $120,000 (the ceiling amount) and the seller receives no additional payments, which means the seller may have no profit on the product or service sold

- **Fixed price with economic price adjustment (FP-EPA):** this contract may be used when the term of the contract spans multiple years; it provides for adjustment to the contract prices when specified economic events occur and is intended to reduce the seller's risk of price changes of purchased items

An example of an FP-EPA contract: contract price is $100,000 for each of three years; if a commodity used in the production of the product or service increases due to inflation, the contract price will be increased

TIP

The type of contract used may be driven by your organization. Check with your procurement department for guidance.

12

Cost Reimbursable Contracts

In this type of contract, the buyer and seller agree to the costs to be reimbursed and to the amount of profit. Therefore, the buyer bears the highest cost risk. Common forms of cost reimbursable contracts include:

- **Cost plus fixed fee** (CPFF): this is a common form of cost reimbursable contract in which the buyer bears the burden of the cost risk because the buyer pays all costs; the seller's fee, or profit, is fixed at a specific dollar amount and may be a percent of the original estimated cost; this type of contract is often used in research projects and projects in which the scope of work lacks clear definition

   One example of an CPFF contract:

Estimated cost	$100,000
Fixed fee	$10,000
Contract value	$110,000
Seller's actual cost	$150,000
Fixed fee	$10,000
Buyer's total payment	$160,000

   Another example of a CPFF contract may be when the fee is renegotiated at the time that a buyer approves changes that increase or decrease the scope of the project.

Estimated cost:	$100,000
Fixed Fee:	$10,000
Contract value:	$110,000
Approved scope changes of	$20,000
New Estimated cost:	$120,000
Renegotiated Fee:	$12,000
New Contract value:	$132,000

- **Cost plus incentive fee** (CPIF): in this type of contract, risk is shared by the both buyer and seller, and the seller is paid for agreed to, allowable costs plus an agreed upon fee, and an incentive that is both specific and measurable; if the final costs are less than the expected costs, both the buyer and seller benefit by splitting the cost savings on a prenegotiated sharing formula; this type of contract is used for long performance periods.

  The difference between FPIF and CPIF contracts is that FPIF contracts include a ceiling, above which the seller will not recover any cost; CPIF contracts do not have a ceiling on cost, but they often have maximum and minimum fees

  An example of a CPIF contract:

Target cost	$100,000
Target fee	$10,000
Maximum fee	$15,000
Minimum fee	$7,000
Share ratio (buyer/seller)	80-20
Seller's actual cost	$120,000
Difference (over target cost)	($20,000)

  Profit calculation:

Target profit	$10,000
Seller's share of overage (20%)	$4,000
Calculated profit	$6,000
Minimum profit	$7,000

  Total calculation:

Actual cost	$120,000
Total profit	$7,000
Buyer's total payment	$127,000

- **Cost plus award fee** (CPAF): a contract in which an award pool is created and managed by an award committee; subjective judgments are used to determine the award, giving the buyer more flexibility than in a CPIF contract; administrative costs are high

12

Time and Material Contracts

Time and material contracts are generally used when requirements are not well defined. Often they are used for efforts such as research and development, feasibility, or consultation.

A **purchase order** is a simple form of a time and material contract that is often used for buying commodities. It is a unilateral contract and only signed by one party, rather than a bilateral contract that is signed by both parties.

- An example of a T&M contract: in anticipation of a hurricane forecast for the site of a construction job, the buyer's project manager asks the contractor to prepare for high winds on a time and materials basis to be invoiced after the work is completed; the seller buys 20 8x4-foot plywood panels for a total of $1,000 and hires local labor for 15 hours at $10 per hour for a total of $150; the seller submits an invoice for $1,150

Class Exercise 12-2

Answer the following questions. Show your work in the space provided.

Situation 1:

Contract Type:	FFP
Contract Price:	$450,000
Seller Cost:	$400,000

What is the seller's profit?

_____

_____

_____

_____

Situation 2:

Contract Type:	FP-EPA
Contract Duration:	3 years
Annual Contract Price:	$50,000
Estimated Annual Inflation:	5%

What is the buyer's cost?

_____
_____
_____
_____

Situation 3:

Contract Type:	CPIF
Seller Actual Cost:	$140,000
Seller Target Cost:	$150,000
Target Incentive Fee:	$ 40,000

($10,000 to $50,000; gets max if under cost)
Share Ratio: 80/20 (buyer/seller)

What is the seller's revenue?

_____
_____
_____
_____

Case Study 12-1

For the LUV Music website project, use the template below to identify criteria that may be important if your organization determines that the website might best be developed by an external development firm. What considerations would you have in a make or buy decision?

Criteria	Expected Results or Considerations

CONDUCT PROCUREMENTS PROCESS

The Conduct Procurements process includes all activities associated with searching out and selecting **vendors**. In the Plan Procurements Management process, project managers identify what items are going to be purchased, if any, the type of contract, and any **selection criteria** that may have been agreed upon.

The tools and techniques useful in the Conduct Procurements process include **bidder conferences**, **advertising**, **proposal evaluation techniques**, and **procurement negotiations**. As in many of the previous chapters, **expert judgment** and **independent estimates** can always be utilized.

The outputs of the Conduct Procurements process are **selected sellers** and **agreement(s)**.

Bidder Conferences

Once bidders have been identified, bidder conferences are used to allow potential bidders to meet with buyers prior to the submission of any proposal. Bidder conferences are held after the procurement statement of work has been distributed. These conferences provide a forum for questions and answers and allow all potential bidders to hear the questions as well as the answers buyers give in response at the same time. The purpose of bidder conferences is to ensure that no preferential treatment is given to any particular vendor. They also simplify the communication of questions and answers to all bidders simultaneously.

Proposal Evaluation Techniques

A formal proposal evaluation technique is a structured process for evaluating the **criteria** that have been defined within the Plan Procurement Management process. Criteria for selection should be objective and measurable whenever possible. In some cases, a weighting may be added to the selection criteria to provide a more equitable value to those criteria that are more important to the success of the project.

Criteria	Expected Response Satisfy = 100 Partially Satisfy = 50 Does Not Satisfy = 0	Weight	Score
Vendor must have been in the business of designing and manufacturing cell phone circuits for more than 8 years.		40% of score	
Product must perform at 15-month MTBF for 99% of an applicable sample test. Vendor must provide demonstrated proof of achievement of this quality standard.		50% of score	
Vendor must not use subcontractors for manufacturing of circuits.		5% of score	
Vendor is a certified small business.		5% of score	

Above is an example of weighted selection criteria for our cell phone circuit purchase. Weighting is typically applied as a multiplier factor.

Case Study 12-2

Using the selection criteria defined in Case Study 12-1, incorporate a weighting for each criterion that you feel is appropriate.

Expert Judgment

Expertise can be useful in evaluating received proposals. Experts may be an individual or a multi-disciplinary team that has expertise in evaluating proposals and assessing the overall score of each.

Advertising, Independent Estimate, and Analytical Techniques

There are many types of tools organizations can use to find, evaluate, and select potential sellers.

Advertising and internet searching can help organizations reach out and find potential vendors. Organizations can use various media to request bids from vendors, including websites, newspapers, trade organizations, and professional organizations.

Estimates provided by an independent entity can be used to objectively compare bids to a benchmark. And other analytical techniques may be used in bidder evaluations to assure that prospective bidders have relevant experience in fulfilling similar deliverables.

Procurement Negotiations

Once seller(s) are selected, a negotiation process will ensue. The purpose of negotiation is to reach an agreement on the overall scope of the procurement. Because contracts are **legally binding agreements** between buyer and seller, the project manager is typically not the person responsible for these processes. Experts in the procurement processes are more likely given the responsibility of ensuring that contracts are negotiated and appropriately documented. The project manager may provide expert knowledge about the project and its objectives, but he or she performs a more supportive role in procurement negotiation efforts.

Negotiation is a **general management skill** that comes up frequently in project management. Although the primary objective of negotiation is to reach agreement on a fair and reasonable price, product, and delivery, the *PMBOK® Guide* advocates the importance of a **win-win** situation in which a good relationship is developed with the seller. A **win-lose** situation may result in contract issues and problems for either the buyer or the seller, or both.

Some of the key issues to be considered in negotiation are:
- Roles and responsibilities of negotiating parties
- Technical and business management approaches and methodologies
- The party that has final authority in the negotiation
- Any applicable laws
- Pricing
- Contract financing and payment terms

> **TIP**
>
> The project manager's role in the procurement management processes is to represent the project sponsor's interests and to gain his or her informed consent.

Negotiation Tactics

There are several negotiation tactics (adapted from *Principles of Project Management* by PMI), including:

- **Imposing a deadline**: a powerful tactic since it emphasizes the schedule constraints of the project and implies a possible loss to both parties
- **Surprises**: one party springs a surprise on the other, such as a change in dollar amount
- **Stalling**: one party claims it does not have the authority, that the person with authority is not available, or that it needs more information
- **Fair and reasonable**: one party claims the price is equitable because another organization is paying it
- **Delays**: necessary when arguments are going nowhere, tempers are short, or one party goes off on a tangent
- **Deliberate confusion**: either distorting facts and figures or piling on unnecessary details to cloud the issues
- **Withdrawal**: either the negotiator is so frustrated that he or she does not continue or one side makes an attack and then retreats
- **Arbitration**: a third party is brought in to make decisions, including decisions on final outcomes
- **Fait accompli**: one party claims "What is done is done and cannot be changed"

The outcome of negotiations is a signed contract with the selected seller or vendor. In most cases, an organization will negotiate with the "winner" of the bid based on the selection criteria evaluation. As contract negotiations progress, there is always the possibility of not reaching an agreement. If that occurs, organizations should have a fall-back plan for the vendor next on the list.

> **TIP**
>
> If the contract relationship warrants a different change control system than you have in your organization, that fact should be documented in the project management plan.

12

Class Exercise 12-3

Read the situations below and identify the negotiation tactic being used.

Situation	Negotiation Tactic
Two CEOs have been in negotiations to buy one of the companies for the past three months and are nearing contract closure. The company being bought is in a dire financial position. The potential buyer has not answered the calls of the seller in the last week.	
You are very frustrated with a key vendor for your project. You have experienced poor quality of the materials provided and have asked repeatedly for the vendor to fix the problem. Your contract administrator sent a letter last week stating that the problem must be fixed by the end of the month or you will be forced to use a different vendor.	

CONTROL PROCUREMENTS PROCESS

Once a contract is signed, the management of the contract relationship is performed in the same way as a project. Both the buyer and seller administer their obligations in the procurement contract with their best interests involved.

The outputs of the Control Procurements process are **work performance information**, **change requests**, and any updates to **project documents**, **organizational process assets**, or the **project management plan**.

Contract Change Control System

Just as in projects, not everything is known at the time a contract is signed. Change is inevitable, even if the change is a clarification to the procurement documents. In many cases, the project itself causes changes in the relationship between buyer and seller and can impact the contract terms, such as quantities or delivery dates. Some situations that may warrant a change to the contract include:

- A gap in project requirements that affects the deliverables of the seller
- A new feature or change request approved for the project that impacts the vendor's deliverable

A change control system defines the process of modifying a contract. In most cases, organizations already have in place a contract change control process and projects will use this existing organizational process asset.

Procurement Performance Reviews

Just as with project performance reviews, procurement relationships can also be reviewed. It is good practice to evaluate vendors' progress in delivering to the contract terms. Ideally, these reviews should be part of the project activities throughout the execution phase of the contract delivery. These reviews can be informal or formal, but the results should be incorporated into the regular project reporting performed by the project manager and should be included in the **WBS** as work to be performed within the project.

Inspections and Audits

Inspections and audits are similar to procurement performance reviews; however, they are more formal in nature and more than likely are looking closely at the vendor's internal processes. Whereas procurement performance reviews report on contract progress, inspections and audits look more at compliance in terms of product quality or process quality.

Performance Reporting

Sellers' work performance reports and data should be evaluated against agreed-upon requirements. The vendor performance should be compared to agreed-upon performance and management actions can be taken as necessary.

12

CUSTOMER SERVICE

Claims Administration

Claims administration is the act of responding to conflict between buyer and seller. Whenever a disagreement occurs between buyer and seller in terms of a claim, dispute, or appeal that cannot be resolved mutually, a claims administration function will be triggered. Many contracts have language within them that addresses how these claims, disputes, or appeals will be handled, such as **arbitration**.

Payment Systems and Records Management Systems

> **TIP**
> A payment system ensures that all seller payments are made and documented in agreement with contract terms.

Payments to sellers should always be preceded by certification of satisfactory work for the project. Criteria for certification should be documented in the terms of the contract. Records management systems archive the documentation of the contract activity for the project. Proper functioning of this system permits informed, timely payment, delivery, and closure of a vendor relationship. It also provides documentation of poor performance and allows for timely action to remedy issues and support needed litigation or other actions.

CLOSE PROCUREMENTS PROCESS

> **TIP**
> Contract documents, correspondence, and related material are archived through a records management system.

The Close Procurements process brings an individual agreement to completion and ties up any loose ends that are necessary to ensure that the obligations spelled out in the contract are fulfilled and accepted by the buyer.

Similar to the Close Project or Phase process, verification of the contract work is the key output in the form of a **closed procurement**.

12

Procurement Audits

As we've discussed before, audits are structured reviews. In the context of procurements, audits are a structured review of the entire procurement management process. The purpose of these audits is to evaluate how well the processes have been performed and evaluate the results for improvement later.

Sometimes the results of these audits help to enhance the various organizational process assets, such as the change control process or contract templates.

Procurement Negotiations

When contracts have claims, disputes, or appeals, contracts cannot be officially closed until all such claims, disputes, or appeals have been brought to settlement. The claims administration technique described above can result in a negotiated settlement or **legal agreement**.

TIP

Early termination of a contract is a special case of procurement closure.

12

PROFESSIONAL RESPONSIBILITY

Procurement management is about conducting procurement relationships with professionalism and fairness. When considering the four aspects of professional responsibility—responsibility, respect, fairness, and honesty—the project manager must keep certain things in mind at all times:

- Always strive for a win-win result in contract negotiations
- Manage vendor relationships as a part of the project team and do not look for a scapegoat
- Provide transparency of information between the buyer and seller
- Provide constructive feedback to the vendor to help improve the buyer-seller relationship

It is the project manager's responsibility to ensure the success of a project. When procurements are included in the project, the project manager's responsibility includes ensuring that the vendor has every opportunity to succeed.

KEY INTERPERSONAL SKILLS FOR SUCCESS

The interpersonal skill highlighted in this chapter is:

Negotiation

Project managers need to develop negotiation skills because it's likely that some stakeholders will have competing interests and objectives for some aspects of any project. The goal is to reach an agreement that all parties can accept and support, even if they don't agree with every aspect of it.

The skills needed to successfully negotiate overlap with other interpersonal skills such as conflict management, communication, trust building, influencing, and leadership. Project managers need good analytical skills that will help them focus on the issues, distinguish between wants and critical needs, and discover what is most important to each party. Listening and not taking situations personally are vital. In addition, the PMI *Code of Ethics and Professional Conduct* requires fair dealing with all parties.

BE A BETTER PROJECT MANAGER

Exercise: managing vendor relationships

Purpose: don't put yourself and your company at risk with vendors

Steps: most project managers can recite a horror story with a vendor that caused chaos on a project; not every project manager has a contract administrator on which to rely

Here are several best practices that you can use for most procurement relationships:

1. Be as diligent with your vendor requirements as you would like your clients to be with you.
2. Communicate regularly with vendors; don't think that just because vendors have a statement of work, they can work without some interaction with you.
3. If the vendor's deliverable covers more that one month of work, ensure that the milestones the vendor is expected to deliver are set and incorporated into your project schedule.
4. Get to know your vendors. Networking with vendors is just as important as, if not more important than, networking with sponsors. It is a great way to have some influence over the vendors.
5. Don't do your vendors' job. Hold them accountable. You are hiring them for their expertise. Your job is to monitor and control, not to do their work.
6. Business practices may vary in your industry or country. There are federal laws that prohibit practices that may be accepted or legal in other countries or cultures.

SAMPLE CAPM EXAM QUESTIONS ON PROCUREMENT MANAGEMENT

1. The document that describes and provides guidance as to how the project team will manage multiple suppliers is called the:

   a) Project management plan
   b) Procurement management plan
   c) Procurement statement of work
   d) Request for proposal

2. A contract that typically includes unit labor or material rates is considered a _____ contract.

   a) Time and materials
   b) Cost plus incentive fee
   c) Cost plus fixed fee
   d) Firm fixed fee

3. A key input to the Plan Procurement Management process is/are the:

   a) Sellers' proposals
   b) Requirements documentation
   c) Schedule leveling guidelines
   d) Selected sellers

4. Which of the following is part of the Control Procurements process?

   a) Answering questions of potential sellers
   b) Developing a request for proposal
   c) Negotiating a contract
   d) Confirming that changes to the contract are made

Notes:

5. The Control Procurements process is responsible for:

   a) Clarifying the structure and requirements of the contract
   b) Obtaining seller responses and awarding a contract
   c) Completing the project and documenting the work
   d) Managing the contractual relationship and performance of the work

6. What is a key benefit of the Control Procurements process?

   a) Assuring that buyer and seller both meet requirements specified in the contract
   b) Requiring only the seller to meet all the terms of the agreement
   c) Providing a vehicle to determine which seller should be selected
   d) Defining which project needs should be made by purchasing outside the organization

7. Outputs of the Close Procurement process include updates to which organizational process assets?

   a) Issue log and work performance data
   b) Work performance information and change requests
   c) Procurement file and lessons learned documentation
   d) Procurement audits and records management system

8. A procurement audit is a technique used in which closing process?

   a) Monitor and Control Project Work
   b) Close Procurements
   c) Direct and Manage Project Work
   d) Close Project or Phase

Notes:

12

9. Finalizing open claims, collecting final results, and documenting results in the archives takes place in which process?

    a) Close Procurements
    b) Control Communications
    c) Close Project or Phase
    d) Verify Scope

10. Documenting agreements for future reference is a key benefit of which process?

    a) Close Procurements
    b) Control Communications
    c) Close Project or Phase
    d) Control Stakeholder Engagement

11. The process of obtaining responses from prospective vendors is:

    a) Conduct Procurements
    b) Close Procurements
    c) Plan Procurements
    d) Control Procurements

12. A key output of the Conduct Procurements process is:

    a) Selected sellers
    b) Change requests
    c) A procurement management plan
    d) Risk register updates

13. The bidder's conference is a part of which process?

    a) Plan Procurements
    b) Conduct Procurements
    c) Control Procurements
    d) Select Procurements

Notes:

12

14. If the project team determines that a component of the project will be purchased:

    a) The work is removed from the WBS
    b) A contract administrator must be assigned to the team
    c) The processes in project procurement management will be performed
    d) That portion of scope is no longer the project team's responsibility

15. Which of the following are outputs of the Control Procurements process?

    a) Approved change requests and procurement documents
    b) Work performance data and agreements
    c) A records management system and inspections
    d) Updates to schedule and cost baselines

Notes:

12

12

ANSWERS AND REFERENCES FOR SAMPLE CAPM EXAM QUESTIONS ON PROCUREMENT MANAGEMENT

Section numbers refer to the *PMBOK® Guide*.

1. **B** **Section 12.1 – Planning**
   A) includes the procurement management plan as a subsidiary plan, but B) is a better answer; C) defines what scope will be included in the purchase; D) defines what is needed and will be sent to potential sellers.

2. **A** **Section 12.1 – Planning**
   Time and materials contracts base the total cost of the contract on specified labor and material rates that typically include all overhead and profit for a project.

3. **B** **Section 12.1 – Planning**
   A) are inputs to the Conduct Procurements process; C) is a technique for the Control Schedule process; D) are outputs of the Conduct Procurements process.

4. **D** **Section 12.3 – Monitoring and Controlling**
   A) is part of the Conduct Procurements process; B) is part of the Plan Procurement Management process; C) is part of the Conduct Procurements process.

5. **D** **Section 12.3 – Monitoring and Controlling**
   A) is part of the Plan Procurement Management process; B) is part of the Conduct Procurements process; C) is part of the Close Procurements process.

6. **A** **Section 12.3 – Monitoring and Controlling**
   B) both buyers and sellers must meet the terms of an agreement; C) is part of the Conduct Procurements process; D) is part of the Plan Procurement Management process.

7. **D** **Section 12.4.3 – Closing**
   A) Inputs to Control Communications; B) outputs of Control Procurements; C) inputs to Close Procurements.

8. **B** **Section 12.4 – Closing**
A procurement audit is a structured review of the procurement processes

9. **A** **Section 12.4 – Closing**
Know the differing activities that take place during the Close Procurements and Close Project or Phase processes; the Close Procurements process focuses on external agreements.

10. **A** **Section 12.4 – Closing**
Final documentation of scope completion, total project cost, lessons learned, etc. are needed to effectively close a procurement.

11. **A** **Section 12.2 – Executing**
B) occurs when the seller completes contract deliverables; C) during this process, prospective sellers are identified; D) the main focus of this process is managing agreements between the buyer and seller.

12. **A** **Section 12.2 – Executing**
Although change requests and updates to the project management plan may be outputs of the Conduct Procurements process, the selection of the seller is a key output and therefore the best answer.

13. **B** **Section 12.2 – Executing**
The bidders conference is used to help all sellers have the same understanding of the proposal requirements.

14. **C** **Section 12.1 – Planning**
A) the team is likely to keep the items on the WBS at a higher level; B) typically, contract administrators are not team members; D) the project manager is still responsible, but purchasing a component of the project may reduce some of the performance risk.

15. **D** **Section 12.3 – Monitoring and Controlling**
A) and B) are inputs to the Control Procurements process; C) are tools and techniques.

12

ANSWERS TO CLASS EXERCISES

Class Exercise 12-1: Make or Buy

Buy Decision:
   Material costs = $400 x $120 = **$48,000**

Make Decision:
   Total production = 40,000 + 10% (scrap) = 44,000
   Material cost of goods = 44,000 x $0.50 = $22,000
   Labor costs
      1st 10,000 units = 1,000 hours x $8.50 = $8,500
      Remaining 34,000 units = 1,133 hours x 8.50 =
         $9,631
   Production setup costs: $10,000
   Total Costs to Make: **$50,131**

Therefore, the company should buy the circuit.

Other considerations include:
   • There are different risks to taking on the
     responsibility of manufacturing, such as legal
     or environmental risks
   • Will the 15-month MTBF be achievable if the
     circuit is built in-house?
   • These numbers do not consider the cost of
     rework
   • These numbers do not reflect the possibility that
     a more important project for the organization
     may be affected by a potential decision to build
     the circuits in-house

Class Exercise 12-2: Contracts

Situation 1:
   $450,000 – $400,000 = $50,000

Situation 2:
   $50,000 + ($50,000 x 1.05) + (($50,000 x 1.05) x 1.05)
   $50,000 + $52,500 + $55,125 = $157,625

Situation 3:

Seller gets paid cost: $140,000

Incentive fee is: 50,000 x 0.20 = $10,000

Total revenue = $150,000

Class Exercise 12-3: Negotiating

Situation	Negotiation Tactic
Two CEOs have been in negotiations to buy one of the companies for the past three months and are nearing contract closure. The company being bought is in a dire financial position. The potential buyer has not answered the calls of the seller in the last week.	Could be either delaying or withdrawal; there is not enough information to know for sure
You are very frustrated with a key vendor for your project. You have experienced poor quality of the materials provided and have asked repeatedly for the vendor to fix the problem. Your contract administrator sent a letter last week stating that the problem must be fixed by the end of the month or you will be forced to use a different vendor.	Imposing a deadline

ANSWERS TO THE CASE STUDIES CAN BE FOUND IN THE WAV™ FILES

Web Added Value™

This book has free material available for download from the Web Added Value™ resource center at *www.jrosspub.com*.

STAKEHOLDERS

CHAPTER 13 | **STAKEHOLDERS**

13

13

STAKEHOLDER MANAGEMENT

Project success may be determined by meeting the needs and expectations of stakeholders more than by any other factor. While project teams may focus on bringing in the scope of a project with the appropriate quality on time and on budget, the knowledge area of stakeholder management has taken on a new importance in successfully managing projects. This knowledge area has a general focus on stakeholders outside the project team.

Stakeholder management isn't just about communicating better with stakeholders. As you deepen your understanding of these concepts, you will begin to see the complexities of successfully managing stakeholders. An analysis of stakeholders will identify the relationships and competing interests that must be resolved for projects to deliver what is desired.

Stakeholder identification has become more important because even the smallest projects often have an impact on a wide range of stakeholders, and those stakeholders may have an unexpected effect on a project. Part of identifying stakeholders includes determining a stakeholder's attitudes about a project, the product of the project, the team, and management. Add to that mix a stakeholder's ability to influence the project, either formally or informally, and this situation can create potent opportunities and threats for project managers.

Analyzing stakeholders to plan how to engage them in a project is likely to require discretion on the part of the project manager and team. Implementing the stakeholder management plan and controlling stakeholder engagement will include a variety of communication strategies and interpersonal skills. Issues related to stakeholders will challenge even the most experienced project managers.

Knowledge Area Processes

Within the stakeholder management knowledge area there are four processes within four process groups.

Initiating	Planning	Executing	Monitoring and Controlling
Identify Stakeholders	Plan Stakeholder Management	Manage Stakeholder Engagement	Control Stakeholder Engagement

Key Definitions

Affiliation power: power that results from whom you know or whom an individual has access to.

Change log: a comprehensive list of changes made during a project.

Expert power: power that results from an individual's knowledge, skills, and experience.

Legitimate power: formal authority that an individual holds as a result of his or her position.

Penalty (coercive, punishment) power: power that results from an ability to take away something of value to another.

Referent (charisma) power: power that results from a project manager's personal characteristics.

Reward power: power that results from an ability to give something of value to another.

Stakeholder: an individual, group, or organization who may affect, be affected by, or perceive itself to be affected by a decision, activity, or outcome of a project.

Stakeholder register: a project document that includes the identification, assessment, and classification of project stakeholders.

Virtual team: a group of people with shared objectives who fulfill their roles with little or no time spent meeting face to face.

IDENTIFY STAKEHOLDERS PROCESS

Every project will affect something or someone. The Identify Stakeholders process focuses on determining who those stakeholders are and how they are impacted by a project's delivery. The Identify Stakeholders process is one of only two processes that are included in the initiating process group—highlighting the importance of understanding the project's stakeholders as early as possible.

The principal tool and technique of the Identify Stakeholders process is a **stakeholder analysis** and the primary output is a **stakeholder register**.

Stakeholder Analysis

A stakeholder analysis includes gathering and evaluating information regarding the people or organizations impacted by a project. In many cases, the project manager will seek **expert judgment** in order to analyze stakeholders. Stakeholders can impact a project and can themselves be impacted positively or negatively. The results of the stakeholder analysis provide the project manager and the project team insight into the needs and desires of the stakeholders, which in turn will be useful in determining the appropriate methods of communication for each specific stakeholder.

Some of the categories to be analyzed include stakeholder:
- **Interests**—what is important to the stakeholder?
- **Expectations**—what is the end product that the stakeholder would like to see?
- **Influence**—how can the stakeholder impact the project?
- **Power**—how much authority does the stakeholder have?

> **TIP**
> Interests and expectations should include the perceived benefit or threat of a project to a stakeholder. If there is opposition or hostility to a project, it should be explicitly stated in the risk management plan.

13

Figure 13-1
Power and
Interest Grid

	Low	High
High **Power** **Low**	High Power Low Interest	High Power High Interest
	Low Power Low Interest	Low Power High Interest

Low   Interest   High

A power/interest grid, as depicted above in Figure 13-1, is useful in assessing stakeholders. This kind of analysis is helpful in determining who will support the project, ignore the project, and potentially detract from the project.

Stakeholder	Interests	Expectations	Influence	Power
Sponsor, Tom Wang, VP Business Development and Sales	Very interested in ensuring this project is a success and lays the groundwork for future events	Would like to raise a minimum of $300,000	Extremely influential in the organization; has helped the organization grow to what it is today	Key decision maker in the organization
Participants in the event	Not overly concerned with the success of the event	Want to have a fun event and a good time	Without participants, the event will not occur	No power in the success of the immediate event, but more so in the success of any future events
Children's Charity	Appreciates any level of contribution BEST CONSULTING can provide	Any charitable donation	None	None

Figure 13-2
Stakeholder
Analysis

Figure 13-2 above is a stakeholder analysis developed by the project manager for the Fundraiser Road Race for several key stakeholders.

Class Exercise 13-1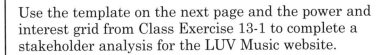

Plot the stakeholders listed for the Fundraiser Road Race on the power and interest grid below. Then assess how each of the stakeholders would respond to the following situation:

- The project team has determined that it cannot obtain the necessary sponsorship to cover all the project costs

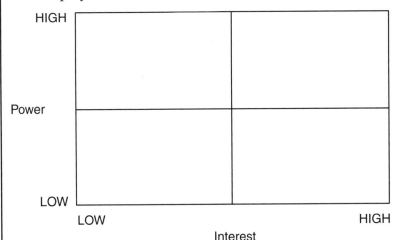

Case Study 13-1

Use the template on the next page and the power and interest grid from Class Exercise 13-1 to complete a stakeholder analysis for the LUV Music website.

13

Stakeholder Analysis				
Stakeholder	Interests	Expectations	Influence	Power

Expert Judgment

Managing stakeholders, especially external stakeholders, can be one of the most challenging tasks for a project manager. When starting a project, seek out others within the organization who may already have a relationship with the key stakeholders of the project. Use their experience and advice in putting together your stakeholder register.

Meetings

In the Identify Stakeholder process, it is important to spend time meeting with various people, both stakeholders and others who have insight about and experience with the stakeholders in order to develop an understanding of the major project stakeholders. These meetings help facilitate the exchange and analysis of information regarding roles, interest, and other knowledge that may be helpful in managing the stakeholders. Sometimes this is called a profile analysis meeting.

Stakeholder Register

The only output to the Identify Stakeholders process is the stakeholder register. Once the analysis of each stakeholder is complete, a stakeholder register can be developed. The purpose of a stakeholder register is to summarize the analytical efforts above and provide direction to the team on how to communicate with each stakeholder; it can be used in conjunction with the **stakeholder analysis** to develop a **stakeholder management plan** as part of the Plan Stakeholder Management process.

The stakeholder register can include a variety of types of information. In general, there are three components to the stakeholder register:

1) Identification information: name, position, location, and role are typical data elements captured.
2) Assessment information: this is where the information on the stakeholder analysis is summarized.
3) Stakeholder classification: identifying if each stakeholder is internal or external to the organization, and if each is perceived as a supporter, neutral, or resistant to a project.
4) Additional information on communication needs and risk tolerances will be added as part of the communications knowledge area and risk knowledge area processes.

13

Class Exercise 13-2

Take the information provided in the stakeholder analysis and create a stakeholder register in the template below. Do not fill in the columns Stakeholder Classification, Communications Requirements, or Risk Tolerance yet.

Stakeholder Register					
Stakeholder	Identification Information	Assessment Information	Stakeholder Classification	Communications Requirements	Risk Tolerance

Case Study 13-2

Utilizing the same template above, and your stakeholder analysis from Case Study 13-1, create a Stakeholder Register for the LUV Music website.

PLAN STAKEHOLDER MANAGEMENT PROCESS

Following the identification and analysis of stakeholders, the project manager needs to decide how to deal with the stakeholders. The stakeholder management plan should document actions that engage stakeholders, manage their expectations, and maintain relationships between team members and other stakeholders.

The **stakeholder register** and **project management plan** are main inputs to this process, along with enterprise environmental factors and organizational process assets. From the project management plan, the defined scope, human resource requirements, and communication techniques will have an impact on how the project team plans for stakeholder management.

Analytical Techniques

Understanding that stakeholder engagement is critical to the success of a project during the Plan Stakeholder Management process, the project team should evaluate the level of stakeholder engagement that exists and compare that to the level of stakeholder engagement that is necessary for success. Any gaps will need to be planned for as part of the stakeholder management plan.

There are 5 basic classifications of stakeholder engagement:
- Unaware
- Resistant
- Neutral
- Supportive
- Leading

Just as project team members may have differing levels of work during a project, stakeholders may also need to have different levels of involvement throughout the life of a project. A **stakeholder engagement assessment matrix** is one tool for defining the current state (C) and desired state (D). See Figure 13-3 below for an example.

Figure 13-3
Stakeholder
Engagement
Matrix

Stakeholder	Role	Unaware	Resistant	Neutral	Supportive	Leading
Jackie K	Sponsor				D C	
Henry W	PM					D C
Kat R	Designer		C			D
Maria G	Implementer		C		D	
Lou B	Implementer			C	D	

13

Engagement levels will vary from stakeholder to stakeholder and from project to project. Engagement levels can range from unaware (not connected to the project and not understanding the project's potential impacts) to leading (totally aware of the project and its potential impacts, and actively engaged in the project). Defining stakeholders' engagement levels can significantly improve communication and, ultimately, the project's success.

Expert Judgment

Determining the level of engagement required at each stage of the project for each stakeholder is an important function of the Plan Stakeholder Management process. Using existing expertise and relationships within your organization can reduce the risk of miscommunication with stakeholders and unnecessary conflict on the project.

Meetings

Similar to the Identify Stakeholder process, internal meetings are helpful in improving the understanding of stakeholders and discussing approaches to best manage these relationships within the Plan Stakeholder Management process.

Class Exercise 13-3

Create a stakeholder engagement assessment for the Fundraiser Road Race and then update the Stakeholder Classification column for your stakeholder register.

Stakeholder Management Plan

Outputs of the Plan Stakeholder Management process are project document updates and a stakeholder management plan. The stakeholder management plan includes:
- Engagement levels (both current and desired)
- Impacts (effects of scope changes on stakeholders)
- Relationships and overlap among stakeholders
- Communications requirements

- Information on the format and content of communications
- Need for and reason for communication
- Timing of information distribution

A stakeholder management plan will take into consideration other components of the project management plan such as the **communications management plan**. Below in Figure 13-4 are a sample stakeholder management plan and stakeholder register.

Figure 13-4
Stakeholder
Management
Plan and
Stakeholder
Register

Stakeholder Management Plan

Project Name: Fundraiser Road Race

Date: 2/2/14

The fundraiser road race project has a few key stakeholders that will need to be managed throughout this project.

- The sponsor, our VP of Business Development and Sales, Tom Wang
- The participants in the event
- The community who will benefit from the funds raised

The chart below outlines information provided to date on the needs of each stakeholder.

Stakeholder	Engagement Level	Relationship	Communications Requirements	Communication Plan
Tom Wang	Supportive and very interested in seeing a successful event.	Vice President of Business Development & Sales and Sponsor of the project	Financial progress on meeting the expected numbers of the project	Weekly management calls scheduled
The Participants	Supportive and looking forward to a fun event.	Indirect relationship to the project team Many participants may actually be the volunteers on the project and their family and friends	Keep the potential participants informed on date and time of the event through marketing efforts	Monthly advertising to start and more frequent communications within 1 month of the event
The Community	Supportive because they will be the recipients of the funds raised.	Indirect relationship The community will benefit based on the efforts of the Children's Charity.	Communicate the ending results of the efforts and who contributed to the success of the event	Monthly communication on progress of event and anticipated funds raised

13

Case Study 13-3

For the LUV Music website, use the template below to create a project stakeholder management plan. Leverage the work you did in both the communication knowledge area and risk knowledge area chapters of this book to summarize stakeholders for this project.

Stakeholder Management Plan				
Stakeholder	Engagement Levels	Relationships	Communications Requirements	Communication Plan

MANAGE STAKEHOLDER ENGAGEMENT PROCESS

Managing stakeholder engagement means ensuring that all communications and interactions between the project team and the various stakeholders are clear and unambiguous. Proactively communicating with stakeholders allows the project manager and the project team to set the correct expectations with each stakeholder, reducing the risk of misunderstanding and conflict.

Effectively managing stakeholder expectations takes much effort. Recognizing that each stakeholder potentially has unique needs and expectations, the project manager and project team must always consider the information gathered in the **stakeholder management plan** and the **communications management plan** when opening any communication with a stakeholder. These requirements should be updated when their perceived effectiveness changes or explicit preferences change.

When proactive communications falter, conflict arises. Clarifying and resolving issues in a timely manner also contributes to effectively managing stakeholder expectations.

The primary outputs of the Manage Stakeholder Engagement process include the creation and constant updating of **issue logs** and **change requests**.

Communication Methods

Communication methods are addressed again here within the Manage Stakeholder Expectations process. All of the methods described within the communication management knowledge area are also available to the project manager in this process.

> **TIP**
> A key benefit of the Manage Stakeholder Engagement process is increased support of stakeholders and minimized resistance to a project.

13

Interpersonal Skills

Interpersonal skills are addressed in several places in the *PMBOK® Guide*. The stakeholder management knowledge area requires that project managers have a firm understanding of the various interpersonal skills needed to succeed. There are eleven key skills the project manager must have in order to succeed:

- Leadership
- Team building
- Motivation
- Communications
- Influencing
- Decision-making
- Political and cultural awareness
- Negotiation
- Trust building
- Conflict management
- Coaching

In managing stakeholder expectations, most, if not all, of these skills will be utilized.

Management Skills

Management skills, as they relate to stakeholder management, include, but are not limited to, facilitation, speaking, and negotiating. If the goal is to reduce the risk of miscommunication, the project manager must be able to clearly articulate a situation, result, or resolution effectively. Project managers with limited management skills will increase the risk of a project failing.

TIP

In section 13.3.2.3 of the *PMBOK® Guide*, the management skill "modify organizational behavior to accept the project outcomes" relates directly to the intent that a project's objectives be met within the receiving organization. A project that is not successfully adopted by the receiving organization should be considered a failure even if delivered on time and on budget.

13

Class Exercise 13-4

Read the statements in the chart below. Define what is unclear and recommend alternative wording to increase understanding.

Example	What Is Unclear?	Recommended Alternative Wording
Project Manager to Customer: "The development of the new system will be ready on Friday."		
Customer to Project Team: "This project is critical to our business success. It will significantly increase our competitiveness in the marketplace."		
Project Manager to Sponsor: "The project is on schedule to be delivered by the end of the year. We are working through a couple of issues the client asked us for, but we should have them resolved. Worst case is that we will be slightly over budget."		

CONTROL STAKEHOLDER ENGAGEMENT PROCESS

The Control Stakeholder Engagement process focuses on maintaining stakeholder engagement throughout a project by monitoring relationships and revising strategies for managing stakeholders when needed.

The **issue log**, **work performance data**, and project documents are inputs to this process that help the project manager determine what is happening with stakeholders in addition to some of the specific elements in the project management plan. These inputs include the plans to accomplish work, managing all the core project team members, supporting team members (and others who are doing the work of the project), and the **change management process**.

As the project manager uses the stakeholder management plan to monitor stakeholder activities and engagement, he or she will also link this plan to the scope of work completed, verification of quality, and validation of scope. Any discrepancies may be identified for corrective or preventive actions.

Work performance information and **change requests** are typical outputs of the Control Stakeholder Engagement process.

Information Management Systems

Just as in the Control Communications process, information management systems are key in providing a central way to capture, store, and distribute information in the Control Stakeholder Engagement process.

Expert Judgment

We all know things change on projects, including changes to who the stakeholders are and in their interest and involvement with a project. Ongoing assessments with knowledgeable people can reduce the risk of miscommunication and conflict as a project progresses.

Meetings

Be sure to use status meetings with stakeholders to keep them informed, but also to communicate internally any changes to stakeholder engagement.

PROFESSIONAL RESPONSIBILITY

Stakeholder management is about effectively communicating with stakeholders and providing accurate information regarding a project's status. When considering the four aspects of professional responsibility—responsibility, respect, fairness, and honesty—the project manager must keep certain things in mind at all times:

- Always communicate to stakeholders with their needs in mind
- Do not lie to stakeholders
- Be realistic when evaluating variances, and provide quality information to stakeholders to ensure good decision making

It is the project manager's responsibility to provide accurate, unbiased information regarding a project's status.

13

KEY INTERPERSONAL SKILLS FOR SUCCESS

The interpersonal skills highlighted in this chapter are:

Political Awareness

Project managers must learn how to navigate organizational politics, which are always present. Politics in an organization are established by norms of behavior, communication, how power is used, etc. Politics affect how the project management processes are carried out, and project managers need to find appropriate ways to work within the system and, potentially, when to go outside the system.

For example, the basic assumptions driving business changed during the 1990s. Before, what was discussed were things like continuity, planning, diversification, scale, security, uninformed customers, and national borders as driving business factors. Now, the discussion is about how change, coping with the unexpected, focus, segmentation, flexibility, responsiveness, speed, demanding customers, and freedom of movement are the most prevalent factors driving business.

Culture

Culture is an important concept in stakeholder management. In today's society, the global economy is influencing more and more organizations, and it is important for a project manager to understand how culture can impact a project and what can be done to ensure success in a multicultural project environment.

Culture is everything that people have, think, and do as members of their society (that is, everything that is shared by at least one other person). It is important to understand that culture is learned; it is not bred into a particular group. Culture is a cluster of related values that individuals have in common and believe in. Can people's beliefs be influenced? Of course they can. What an individual believes in his or her childhood is influenced by experiences and encounters throughout his or her life, which will shape that person's value system. Culture is very complex yet dynamically stable. In other words, culture evolves over time. Cultural changes do not happen overnight; they are adaptations to human learning, environmental conditions, and the interactions between people's learning and conditions.

Cultures are integrated in that a particular value may be related to other values within a culture; cultures are not random assortments of values.

Cultural differences require different management approaches by the project manager. Knowing the values of each project participant will greatly improve the project manager's overall effectiveness. Cultural differences should also be considered a value-add to a project. Diversity provides an opportunity for new solutions to old problems. Do not shy away from a culturally diverse project. You may learn a lot!

Trust Building

Trust is the foundation of effective teamwork. Without trust, it's difficult for teams to be honest and share their ideas and opinions. Without trust, it is more difficult for teams to make decisions, hold each other accountable, and measure progress and accomplishment accurately. Project managers must make the effort to build trust among core team members as well as key project stakeholders and influencers.

BE A BETTER PROJECT MANAGER

Exercise: communicating bad news to stakeholders

Purpose: change is inevitable on any project, and the project manager will be presented with situations from time to time that may be considered bad news to certain stakeholders.

Do not hide the bad news or lie. A surprise is much more detrimental to trust than being up front and sharing the information.

You may have to hold an internal meeting to strategize ways in which to deliver the bad news and ideally a plan for remediation. Your message must be clear.

Sharing and working through issues together with stakeholders increases rapport and long-term trust.

13

SAMPLE CAPM EXAM QUESTIONS ON STAKEHOLDER MANAGEMENT

1. The ability of stakeholders to influence a project is highest during:

    a) The initial stages
    b) Planning processes
    c) The progression of a project
    d) Executing processes

2. Which of the following processes provide inputs to the Manage Stakeholder Engagement process?

    a) Direct and Manage Project Work
    b) Perform Integrated Change Control
    c) Control Communications
    d) Manage Project Team

3. Tools and techniques used in the Manage Stakeholder Engagement process include:

    a) Resolved issues and approved change requests
    b) Interpersonal skills and communication methods
    c) Team building activities and colocation
    d) Weekly status meetings and active listening

4. The main output of the Identify Stakeholders process includes which items?

    a) Stakeholder demographics and classification
    b) Assessment information and a communication plan
    c) Stakeholder management plan and an action plan
    d) Identification information and a stakeholder management plan

5. Which of the following processes provide inputs to the Identify Stakeholders process?

    a) Define Scope
    b) Collect Requirements
    c) Plan Communications Management
    d) Develop Project Charter

Notes:

13

6. A salience model is a combination of which stakeholder characteristics?

   a) Power, interest, involvement
   b) Influence, impact, interest
   c) Power, influence, impact
   d) Urgency, power, legitimacy

7. The benefit of monitoring stakeholder relationships is that stakeholders will be engaged more effectively. This is accomplished in which process?

   a) Identify Stakeholders
   b) Plan Stakeholder Management
   c) Manage Stakeholder Engagement
   d) Control Stakeholder Engagement

8. Which of the following are outputs of the Control Stakeholder Engagement process?

   a) Organizational process assets updates and meetings
   b) Work performance information and change requests
   c) Issue log and project management plan
   d) Project documents and expert judgment

9. Which of the following organizational process assets updates are outputs of the Control Stakeholder Engagement process?

   a) Stakeholder notifications and project records
   b) Stakeholder register and issue log
   c) Schedule and cost management plans
   d) Stakeholder management plan and human resources management plan

10. Determining the information needs of the project stakeholders is part of the _____ process.

   a) Plan Stakeholder Management
   b) Define Scope
   c) Manage Communications
   d) Manage Stakeholder Engagement

Notes:

13

11. Defining a clear plan of action is a valuable outcome of which process?

   a) Identify Stakeholders
   b) Plan Stakeholder Management
   c) Manage Stakeholder Engagement
   d) Control Stakeholder Engagement

12. Activities that take place during the Manage Stakeholder Engagement process include:

   a) Gaining commitment from stakeholders
   b) Analyzing the impact a stakeholder could have
   c) Identifying who has the ability to influence the project
   d) Determining that a stakeholder is uninterested

13. Which of the following organizational process assets are most likely to affect the Identify Stakeholders process?

   a) Organizational culture and regional practices
   b) Stakeholder analysis and industry standards
   c) Templates for the stakeholder register and lessons learned
   d) Product life cycle and quality policies

14. The Control Stakeholder Engagement process provides an input to which of the following processes?

   a) Direct and Manage Project Work
   b) Perform Integrated Change Control
   c) Manage Project Team
   d) Control Communications

15. When there are major disagreements on a project's deliverables, which technique would most increase the effectiveness of stakeholder engagement activities?

   a) Reviewing the issue log
   b) Holding face-to-face meetings
   c) Using the information management system
   d) Using the expertise of an external consultant

Notes:

13

ANSWERS AND REFERENCES FOR SAMPLE CAPM EXAM QUESTIONS ON STAKEHOLDER MANAGEMENT

Section numbers refer to the *PMBOK® Guide*.

1. **A** Section 13.3 – Executing

   In the initial stages of a project, little money has been spent and there have been few deliverables completed.

2. **B** Section 13.3.1 – Executing

   Inputs to the Manage Stakeholder Engagement process are a stakeholder management plan (from the Plan Stakeholder Management process), communications management plan (from the Plan Communications Management process), change log (from the Perform Integrated Change Control process), and organizational process assets such as organizational communications requirements and procedures to manage issues and change.

3. **B** Section 13.3.2 – Executing

   A) would be part of a closing process, not an executing process; C) are techniques used in the Develop Project Team process, but many stakeholders will not be team members; D) many stakeholders will not attend weekly status meetings; active listening is a good technique to use for stakeholders.

4. **A** Section 13.1 – Initiating

   B), C), and D) are outputs of the Plan Stakeholder Management process.

5. **D** Section 13.1.1 – Initiating

   A) scope is defined after requirements are collected; for B) and C), the stakeholder register (an output of the Identify Stakeholders process) is an input to the Collect Requirements and Plan Communications Management processes.

6. **D** Section 13.1.2.1 – Initiating

   All of the answers are classification models for stakeholder analysis. The salience model classifies stakeholders according to urgency, power, and legitimacy.

7. **D** **Section 13.4 – Monitoring and Controlling**
Look for key words that help identify the correct answer. Monitoring activities occur during control processes.

8. **B** **Section 13.4.2 – Monitoring and Controlling**
A) organizational process assets are an output and meetings are techniques in the Control Stakeholder Engagement process; C) these are both inputs to the Control Stakeholder Engagement process; D) expert judgment is a technique in the Control Stakeholder Engagement process.

9. **A** **Section 13.4.3 – Monitoring and Controlling**
B) are both project document updates; C) and D) are all project management plan updates.

10. **A** **Section 13.2 – Planning**
B) focuses on the project, service, or result boundaries, not stakeholders' information needs; C) involves collecting, distributing, and storing information which would occur after stakeholder needs are planned for; D) the Manage Stakeholder Engagement process involves communicating to stakeholders to meet their needs, which would also occur after stakeholders' needs are planned for.

11. **B** **Section 13.2 – Planning**
The word "plan" in the question should guide you to an answer with a planning process.

12. **A** **Section 13.2.2.1 - Planning**
While all of these actions could take place during the Manage Stakeholder Engagement process, B), C), and D) should take place during the Identify Stakeholders process.

13

13. C Section 13.3.1.4 – Executing

A) are enterprise environmental factors, as are industry standards in B; B) stakeholder analysis is a tool of the Identify Stakeholders process; D) are organizational process assets, but they are not as influential as answer C.

14. B Section 13.4.4 – Executing

To answer this question, it's important to know flows among processes.

15. B Section 13.4.2.3 – Monitoring and Controlling

A) an issue log is an input to the Control Stakeholder Engagement process; B), C), and D) are tools and techniques of the same process, but major disagreements are usually resolved best with a face-to-face discussion.

13

ANSWERS TO CLASS EXERCISES

Class Exercise 13-1: Power and Interest

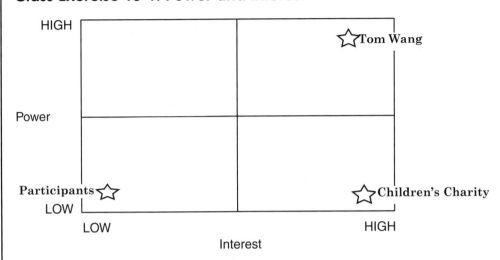

Class Exercise 13-2: Stakeholder Register

Stakeholder Register					
Stakeholder	**Identification Information**	**Assessment Information**	**Stakeholder Classification**	**Communications Requirements**	**Risk Tolerance**
Sponsor: Tom Wang	VP of Product Development and Sales	A successful event is one in which all four objectives are met or exceeded			
Participants in the event	Anyone who attends the event, such as a runner, a volunteer, or someone interested in the particular charity	Want a fun time and maybe to win some prizes; do not want to be stressed			
Children's Charity	The recipient of the proceeds of the event; will be able to do more for the patients and community when donations are received	Mostly interested in the outcome of the project; will participate in the event by providing an information book and a place for individuals to make donations at the event			

13

Class Exercise 13-3: Stakeholder Engagement Assessment and Stakeholder Register

Stakeholder	Role	Unaware	Resistant	Neutral	Supportive	Leading
Tom Wang	Project Sponsor				C	D
Participants in the event	Participants			C D		
Children's Charity	Customer				C D	

Class Exercise 13-4: Skillful Communication

Example	What Is Unclear?	Recommended Alternative Wording
Project Manager to Customer: "The development of the new system will be ready on Friday."	What will be ready on Friday? Will it be the prototype or a fully tested system?	"The development of the new system will be ready for user acceptance testing on Friday."
Customer to Project Team: "This project is critical to our business success. It will significantly increase our competitiveness in the marketplace."	The project may be critical to the customer's business, but what is it to the organization delivering the project? Do you understand what "competitiveness" means to your customer?	"This project is critical to our business success. This is a new product that will allow us to compete with new entrants to our market. The delivery of this project in a timely manner is crucial. There are significant incentives to the project delivery organization to deliver the project on time."
Project Manager to Sponsor: "The project is on schedule to be delivered by the end of the year. We are working through a couple of issues the client asked us for, but we should have them resolved. Worst case is that we will be slightly over budget."	Not much is said here about what the "issues" are. As the sponsor, I'd be suspicious.	"The project is on schedule to be delivered by the end of the year as planned. The client has asked us for a few minor adjustments to the training materials that are certainly within the scope of the project. However, the time spent on putting these materials together was underestimated by 10%."

ANSWERS TO THE CASE STUDIES CAN BE FOUND IN THE WAV™ FILES

Web Added Value™

This book has free material available for download from the Web Added Value™ resource center at *www.jrosspub.com*.

FINAL EXAM

E

14

14

SAMPLE FINAL EXAM

You should spend 62 minutes answering these 50 sample questions. This timing is similar to the average time per question used in the actual exam. The mix of questions presented in this sample final exam is representative of that in the CAPM exam. A passing score is 70%, or 35 correct answers.

1. Which of the following enterprise environmental factors can influence the Manage Communications process?

    a) Choice of media and writing style
    b) Meeting management and facilitation techniques
    c) Organizational culture and government standards
    d) Templates and lessons learned

2. Which of the following is an output of the Control Communications process?

    a) Policies and standards
    b) Information management systems
    c) Updated report formats
    d) Meetings

3. Defining a communication approach is part of the _____ process.

    a) Identify Stakeholders
    b) Plan Communications Management
    c) Control Communications
    d) Manage Communications

Notes:

14

Activity	PV	AC	EV
Requirements	200	150	200
Design	500	540	490
Development	850	750	250
Testing	400	300	200

4. In the above table for a software development project, which task has been completed?

   a) Requirements
   b) Design
   c) Development
   d) Testing

5. As project manager, you need to let your team know how it is doing on the project schedule overall. Of the three activities in progress to date—planning, testing, and design—you calculate planned value and earned value as shown in the table below.

Activity	PV	AC	EV
Planning	$20,000	$25,000	$25,000
Testing	$17,000	$20,000	$15,000
Design	$34,000	$45,000	$42,000
Totals	**$71,000**	**$90,000**	**$82,000**

As a whole, your project is roughly:

   a) Behind schedule
   b) Ahead of schedule
   c) Tracking exactly to schedule
   d) Cannot determine

14

Notes:

6. Which of the following elements of the project management plan are inputs to the Plan Cost Management process?

   a) Organizational process assets
   b) Enterprise environmental factors
   c) Scope and schedule baselines
   d) Project charter

7. A key benefit of the Estimate Costs process is that it:

   a) Determines how much a project will cost
   b) Provides guidance on how funds will be spent
   c) Creates a cost baseline against which performance is measured
   d) Allows you to determine whether or not variances require corrective action

8. The process mainly concerned with obtaining human resources for a project is the _____ process.

   a) Develop Project Team
   b) Acquire Project Team
   c) Estimate Activity Resources
   d) Plan Procurement Management

9. Accommodating as a means of managing conflict is a tactic in which:

   a) The person retreats from the conflict situation
   b) A viewpoint is exerted at the potential expense of the other party
   c) Both parties give up something to get to an acceptable form of resolution
   d) Areas of agreement are emphasized rather than areas of difference

Notes:

14

10. Tracking team member performance and providing feedback to enhance project performance is part of the _____ process.

   a) Manage Communications
   b) Manage Project Team
   c) Control Communications
   d) Develop Project Team

11. Conflict resolution techniques that may be used on a project include:

   a) Compromising, smoothing, forcing, and withdrawing
   b) Controlling, directing, forcing, and negotiating
   c) Compromising, controlling, organizing, and directing
   d) Confronting, smoothing, forcing, and listening

12. A grid that shows the project resources assigned to each work package is a:

   a) Stakeholder engagement assessment matrix
   b) Probability and impact matrix
   c) Responsibility assignment matrix
   d) Power and interest grid

13. A primary output of the Close Project or Phase Process is a/an:

   a) Project management plan
   b) Final result transition
   c) Accepted deliverable(s)
   d) Contract documentation

14. Overall management of project work is a benefit of activities that take place in which process?

   a) Direct and Manage Project Work
   b) Control Scope and Control Schedule
   c) Manage Project Team
   d) Manage Stakeholder Engagement

Notes:

15. When segmenting a project into logical subsets, each subset will have a distinct focus, a unique set of controls, and a hand-off of work produced. This is called a:

a) Portfolio
b) Phase
c) Project
d) Program

16. Results of project iterations should always be documented as updates to:

a) The project management plan
b) The project statement of work
c) The communication matrix
d) The risk register

17. The knowledge area that includes all the processes and activities needed to identify, define, combine, unify, and coordinate project management activities is:

a) Project scope management
b) Executing process group
c) Project integration management
d) Project schedule management

18. _____ are often used to assess the inputs needed to develop the project charter.

a) Experts' judgments
b) Make-or-buy decision criteria
c) Historical information and a lessons learned analysis
d) A risk register and response plan

19. Factors that are considered to be true, real, or certain without proof or demonstration are:

a) Constraints
b) Estimates
c) Assumptions
d) Deadlines

Notes:

14

20. A performance domain:

    a) Describes the processes required to ensure that the various elements of a project are properly coordinated
    b) Is a category of projects that have common components significant in such projects, but are not needed or present in all projects
    c) Contains tasks, knowledge, skills, and cross-cutting knowledge and skills required to competently perform project management tasks
    d) Is a logical grouping of project management inputs, tools and techniques, and outputs

21. Reviewing, analyzing, and approving change requests is an activity within which of the following processes:

    a) Monitor and Control Project Work
    b) Control Communications
    c) Manage Communications
    d) Perform Integrated Change Control

22. An enterprise environmental factor which can influence the development of the project management plan is:

    a) A project management information system
    b) Expert judgment
    c) Organizational process assets
    d) Historical information

23. A procurement audit is a:

    a) Complete set of indexed records to be included in the final project files
    b) Structured review of the compliance with organizational policies and procedures
    c) Structured review of the procurement process from planning through closing
    d) Process to assess the magnitude of any change requests to the seller

Notes:

24. During which step of the procurement processes will contract negotiations occur?

   a) Conduct Procurements
   b) Close Procurements
   c) Plan Procurements
   d) Control Procurements

25. The Plan Procurement Management process identifies:

   a) Which project needs can be best met by buying products
   b) What sellers propose as a solution to a request
   c) How payments will be scheduled for a contract
   d) What contract change control system will be used

26. The contract type in which the seller is paid only the contract amount is:

   a) Firm fixed price
   b) Fixed price incentive fee
   c) Time and materials
   d) Cost reimbursable

27. Process analysis is a tool and technique within the _____ process.

   a) Collect Requirements
   b) Perform Quality Assurance
   c) Control Quality
   d) Plan Quality Management

28. A quality control tolerance:

   a) Is seen from a stakeholder perspective
   b) Determines if a characteristic is present or not
   c) Is a specified range of acceptable results
   d) Keeps errors out of the process

Notes:

14

29. Environmental factors that may affect quality planning are:

    a) Schedule and cost baselines
    b) Risks documented in the risk register
    c) Historical databases of lessons learned
    d) Government regulations

30. Monitoring and controlling risks often results in _____ being identified that weren't considered important earlier in the project.

    a) Deliverables
    b) New risks
    c) Environmental factors
    d) Organizational process assets

31. When managing a project which has multiple phases, it is likely that risks will:

    a) Be different in each phase
    b) Stay consistent from phase to phase
    c) Be resolved at the end of a phase
    d) Have residual risks

32. The risk management plan includes information regarding:

    a) How often risk management activities will be performed throughout a project
    b) Using the Delphi technique to reach a consensus on risks
    c) The effect of interactions among various risk events
    d) Which risks are most important to address for the project

Notes:

33. Which of the following statements is true regarding project risk?

    a) Risks are primarily related to negative impacts on at least one project objective
    b) Project risk is something that has already happened
    c) Risks may have positive or negative outcomes
    d) Project risk should include the chance of a unique event such as a tsunami

34. Given the information provided below, which option should be chosen if the goal is to maximize revenue?

    If a party is held inside, 100 people can attend at $10 each
    If a party is outside, 200 people can attend at $10 each
    There is a 40% chance of rain on the date of the party
    If it rains and the party is held inside, only 80 people will attend
    If it rains and the party is held outside, only 100 people will attend.

    a) Held inside because expected monetary value is $1,800
    b) Held inside because expected monetary value is $920
    c) Held outside because the expected monetary value is $3,000
    d) Held outside because the expected monetary value is $1,600

35. A risk should be managed aggressively if:

    a) The probability of occurrence and impact are low
    b) The probability of occurrence is high and impact is low
    c) The risk is determined to be long term rather than short term
    d) The probability of occurrence and impact are high

Notes:

14

36. Which is an output of the Validate Scope process?

   a) Work results
   b) Accepted deliverables
   c) Scope changes
   d) Deliverables

37. A technique for determining the cause of differences between the baseline and actual performance is:

   a) An organizational process asset
   b) Variance analysis
   c) Earned value
   d) A quality metric

38. The work breakdown structure represents the:

   a) Work specified in the approved project scope statement
   b) Dependencies between schedule activities on a project
   c) Calculated critical path of the project
   d) Project organizations it relates to work packages

39. Which of the following tools and techniques are commonly used in the Define Scope process?

   a) Work breakdown structure templates and decomposition
   b) Alternatives generation and facilitated workshops
   c) Product and benefit/cost analysis
   d) Expert judgment and inspection

40. To document how specific requirements meet the business need of a project, the team would use the:

   a) Project management plan
   b) Requirements documentation
   c) Requirements traceability matrix
   d) Project scope statement

Notes:

41. Providing a road map for how scope will be managed throughout a project is a key benefit of which process?

    a) Plan Scope Management
    b) Collect Requirements
    c) Define Scope
    d) Create WBS

42. The _____ process will assist the project manager in minimizing resistance to a project.

    a) Identify Stakeholders
    b) Plan Stakeholder Management
    c) Manage Stakeholder Engagement
    d) Control Stakeholder Engagement

43. Identifying the influence a stakeholder has on a project is typically recorded in the _____.

    a) Stakeholder register
    b) Risk register
    c) Stakeholder management strategy document
    d) Project charter

44. The primary purpose of identifying stakeholders is to:

    a) Get their help in developing the WBS
    b) Create a project organization chart
    c) Update organizational process assets
    d) Analyze their expectations of the project

45. Why should a project manager spend time identifying and classifying stakeholders early in a project?

    a) To assure ease of approvals from the regulators
    b) To understand a stakeholder's ability to influence the project
    c) To monitor stakeholder engagements efficiently
    d) To minimize resistance to the project

Notes:
_____
_____
_____
_____
_____
_____
_____
_____
_____
_____
_____
_____
_____
_____
_____
_____
_____
_____
_____
_____
_____
_____
_____
_____
_____

14

46. The _____ process provides inputs to the Control Stakeholder Engagement process?

    a) Direct and Manage Project Work
    b) Perform Integrated Change Control
    c) Control Quality
    d) Manage Project Team

47. To assess how involved a stakeholder might be in a project, you should use which of the following tools?

    a) Responsibility assignment matrix
    b) Stakeholder register
    c) Stakeholders engagement assessment matrix
    d) Requirements traceability matrix

48. The measure used to assess the magnitude of project schedule variations is:

    a) The Cost Performance Index (CPI)
    b) The Schedule Performance Index (SPI)
    c) Earned Value (EV)
    d) Cost Variance (CV)

49. A key benefit of the Estimate Activity Resources process is that it:

    a) Develops more accurate cost and duration estimates
    b) Is the basis for estimating, scheduling, and controlling project work
    c) Provides guidance on how the schedule will be managed
    d) Depicts a schedule that shows planned dates for completion of activities

Notes:

14

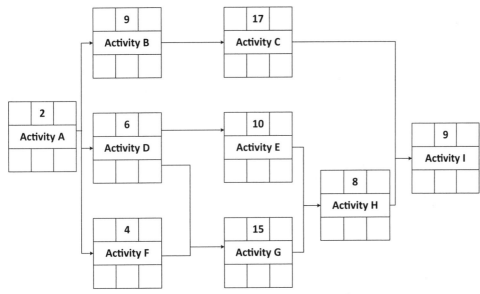

50. What is the total duration of the project in the chart above?

a) 31 weeks
b) 34 weeks
c) 40 weeks
d) 54 weeks

SAMPLE FINAL EXAM ANSWERS

with explanations and references can be found in Chapter 15, Appendix B.

Web Added Value™

This book has free material available for download from the Web Added Value™ resource center at *www.jrosspub.com*.

APPENDICES

APPENDIX A

SAMPLE ASSESSMENT EXAM ANSWERS AND REFERENCES
Section numbers refer to the *PMBOK® Guide*.

1. **A** **Section 10.2 – Communications Management – Executing**
   B) is true of the Plan Communications Management process; C) may be true, but is not the best answer; D) is part of the Control Communications process.

2. **C** **Section 10.3.1.5 – Communications Management – Monitoring and Controlling**
   A) are basic communication skills; B) are environmental enterprise factors; D) information management systems are environmental enterprise factors, and listening techniques are basic communication skills.

3. **B** **Section 10.0 – Communications Management – Planning**
   Communication technology deals with how information is transferred among stakeholders.

4. **D** **Section 7.4.2.1 – Cost Management – Monitoring and Controlling**
   $CV = EV - AC$; $CV = \$10,000 - \$7,500 = \$2,500$; when doing such calculations, always start with EV; C) is the CPI.

5. **B** **Section 7.4.2.1 – Cost Management – Monitoring and Controlling**
   $SV = EV - PV = \$1300 - \$1200 = \$100$

6. **A** **Section 7.0 – Cost Management – Planning**
   B) generally, the cost of acquiring the project team is measured by time spent by the project manager or PMO, unless a specialized resource must be purchased; C) subcontracted items should be addressed in managing cost; D) costs of ongoing operations are not included in project cost management.

7. **D Section 7.2.2.2 – Cost Management – Planning**
While parametric and three-point estimates might rely on historical information, the analogous estimate is useful as a top-down approach when there is little detailed information and the projects are very similar.

8. **C Section 7.3 – Cost Management – Planning**
A) occurs in the Estimate Costs process; B) occurs in the Plan Cost Management process; C) occurs in the Determine Budget process; D) occurs in the Control Costs process.

9. **A Section 9.2 – Human Resources Management – Executing**
Acquiring the project team is made easier if you have documented the project roles, responsibilities, and skills in the human resources plan.

10. **B Section 9.3 – Human Resources Management – Executing**
Understanding the competencies needed and the actual competencies of the project team are both critical in knowing what skills to develop.

11. **A Section 9.4.2 – Human Resources Management – Executing**
While all of these may influence how you manage a team, communication is the most vital.

12. **B Section 9.3 – Human Resources Management – Executing**
Team members are accountable to both the functional manager and the project manager in a matrix organization.

13. **C Section 4.6 – Integration Management – Closing**
A) adds objectivity to acceptance of project deliverables; B) the benefit of this process is determining what causes poor quality and validating that deliverables meet requirements.

14. **A Section 3.7 – Integration Management – Closing**
This is the definition of the closing processes group.

15. **C Section 4.3 – Integration Management – Executing**
Know the differences between corrective action, preventive action, and defect repair.

16. C **Section 3.8 – Integration Management – Executing**
Know the difference between data and information; data is typically an input to many processes and information is typically an output.

17. A **Section 4.0 – Integration Management – Initiating**
B) defines how projects should be managed; C) defines the project life cycle; D) is the focus of the initiating process group.

18. C **Section 4.1.3 – Integration Management – Initiating**
A) defines the project deliverables and the work required to create those deliverables; B) the project SOW is an input to the charter; D) a contract can define the SOW, which in turn is an input to the project charter and subsequently the scope statement.

19. C **Section 1.2 – Integration Management – Initiating**
Review the PMI *Code of Ethics and Professional Conduct*.

20. D **Section 4.5.2.2 – Integration – Monitoring and Controlling**
Meetings are used in every knowledge area for all kinds of decision making, option evaluation, or information exchange. Because this question specifically asks about change requests, D) is the best answer.

21. B **Section 4.2 – Integration Management – Planning**
A) the *PMBOK® Guide* is a standard for good practices in project management; the project management plan and subsidiary plans are recommended, but not mandatory; C) the project manager is responsible for the development of the project management plan and its subsidiary plans; D) project plans vary depending on the application area and complexity of a project.

22. D **Section 2.4.2.3 – Integration Management – Planning**
Iterative or incremental life cycles include a set of deliverables at the end of each iteration.

15

23. B   Section 3.4 – Scope Management – Planning
It is the planning process group that enables progressive elaboration in order to obtain that specificity. Planning is performed throughout the project duration, allowing ever-increasing understanding of the requirements.

24. B   Section 12.4 – Procurement Management – Closing
The Close Procurements process supports the Close Project or Phase process.

25. D   Section 12.2 – Procurement Management – Executing
Keep in mind that proposals are prepared by the prospective sellers.

26. B   Section 12.3 – Procurement Management – Monitoring and Controlling
The Control Procurements process also includes managing process relationships and making changes to contracts as appropriate.

27. D   Section 12.1 – Procurement Management – Planning
These are also called "cost plus" contracts.

28. A   Section 8.2.2.2 – Quality Management – Executing
B) quality tools such as histograms or cause and effect diagrams are used to measure performance; C) is out because flowcharting helps analyze how problems occur; D) the objective of process analysis is to identify needed improvements based on problems experienced.

29. C   Section 8.3.1.4 – Quality Management – Monitoring and Controlling
Work performance data are used to produce project quality performance metrics.

30. B   Section 8.1 – Quality Management – Planning
A) includes the overall benefits of planning, performing quality assurance, and controlling quality; C) the main benefit of the Perform Quality Assurance process is to improve quality processes; D) the main benefit of the Control Quality process is to identify poor processes or quality and to validate deliverables.

31. D **Section 11.6.2.5 – Risk Management – Monitoring and Controlling**
A) is a comparison made in a risk audit; B) is a comparison made in analogous estimating; C) is a comparison made in the Control Schedule process.

32. C **Section 11.1 – Risk Management – Planning**
A) are tools and techniques of the Identify Risks process; B) are tools and techniques of the Perform Quantitative Risk Analysis process; D) are tools and techniques of the Perform Qualitative Risk Analysis process.

33. A **Section 11.3 – Risk Management – Planning**
A) risk impacts may be called consequences, results, or outcomes.

34. D **Section 11.4 – Risk Management – Planning**
A) is a benefit of the Identify Risks process; B) is a benefit of the Perform Qualitative Risk Analysis process; C) describes the response strategy of avoidance.

35. B **Domain IV – Scope Management – Monitoring and Controlling**
Maximizing team performance, measuring performance to identify variances, and implementing approved changes are tasks from the executing performance domain III.

36. D **Section 5.1.1.4 – Scope Management – Planning**
A) occurs during executing, monitoring, and controlling; B) and C) are enterprise environmental factors.

37. C **Section 5.2 – Scope Management – Planning**
A), B), and D) all focus on project scope, not stakeholder needs. In the Collect Requirements process, the team will determine how to meet stakeholder needs based on the documentation obtained in the Plan Stakeholder Management process.

38. C **Section 5.3 – Scope Management – Planning**
A) the benefit of this process is that it directs how scope will be managed; B) helps the team manage project and product scope; D) breaks the work down into manageable pieces.

15

39. A **Section 5.4 – Scope Management – Planning**
B) the procurement statement of work is an output of the Plan Procurement Management process, and the project statement of work is an input to the Develop Project Charter process; D) product analysis is a technique of the Define Scope process.

40. C **Domain V – Task 7 – Stakeholder Management – Closing**
Measuring customer satisfaction and getting customer feedback should be performed at the close of every project to enhance customer relationships.

41. C **Section 13.3 – Stakeholder Management – Executing**
A) at this point, the team has identified and categorized stakeholders; B) planning for how to interact with stakeholders should help, but the main goal of managing stakeholders is to get feedback and determine if the project deliverables will meet stakeholders' needs.

42. B **Section 13.3.2 – Stakeholder Management – Executing**
These are all tools and techniques used in Project Stakeholder Management: A) are part of the Plan Stakeholder Management process; C) are part of the Control Stakeholder Engagement process; D) are part of the Identify Stakeholders process.

43. B **Section 13.3.3 – Stakeholder Management – Executing**
The project management plan is updated to reflect any changes to the communications management plan. Organizational process assets are inputs, and updates to organizational process assets are outputs for many of the processes throughout the *PMBOK® Guide.*

44. A **Section 13.1 – Stakeholder Management – Initiating**
B) the main benefit of this process is to have a defined plan for dealing with stakeholders; C) the main benefit of this process is to increase support for the project's goals; D) the main benefit is to maintain stakeholder engagement as the project progresses and changes.

45. D **13.4.1 – Stakeholder Management – Monitoring and Controlling**
A) expert judgment is a technique in the Control Stakeholder Engagement process; B) an organizational process asset is an output and meetings are techniques in the Control Stakeholder Engagement process; C) are both outputs of the Control Stakeholder Engagement process.

46. A **Section 6.7.2.1 – Time Management – Monitoring and Controlling**
B) determines where there is flexibility in the schedule; C) focuses on dealing with resource constraints; D) can be analyzed to determine trends, but A) is a better answer.

47. A **Section 6.1.1.3 – Time Management – Planning**
B), C), and D) are organizational process assets.

48. C **Section 6.5.1.4 – Time Management – Planning**
Resource skill and availability are major factors in activity durations.

49. C **Section 6.6.3.1 – Time Management – Planning**
A) defines how the schedule of the project will be managed; B) provides information on competed and unfinished schedule activities; D) is a tool and technique of the Control Schedule process.

50. D **Section 6.4 – Time Management – Planning**
A) puts activities in order based on dependency; B) breaks the WBS components into smaller units; C) estimates calendar time for each activity.

APPENDIX B

SAMPLE FINAL EXAM ANSWERS AND REFERENCES
Section numbers refer to the *PMBOK® Guide*.

1. **C** **Section 10.2.1.3 – Communications Management – Executing**
   A) and B) are basic communications skills; D) are organizational process assets.

2. **C** **Section 10.3.3 – Communications Management – Monitoring and Controlling**
   A) is an input to the Control Communications process; B) and D) are tools of the Control Communications process.

3. **B** **Section 10.1 – Communications Management – Planning**
   It is important to the success of any project to plan how you will communicate.

4. **A** **Section 7.4.2.1 – Cost Management – Monitoring and Controlling**
   For Requirements, the schedule variance = earned value – planned value = 200 – 200 = 0. Zero schedule variance means that a task is complete.

5. **B** **Section 7.4.2.1 – Cost Management – Monitoring and Controlling**
   SV = EV – PV = \$82,000 – \$71,000 = \$11,000; the schedule variance is positive which means more work has been accomplished than planned and the project is ahead of schedule.

6. **C** **Section 7.1.1 – Cost Management – Planning**
   A), B), and D) are not elements of the project management plan.

7. **A** **Section 7.2 – Cost Management – Planning**
   B) is part of the Plan Cost Management process; C) is part of the Determine Budget process; D) is part of the Control Costs process.

8. B   **Section 9.2 – Human Resources Management – Executing**
        A) strives to improve the competencies and interactions of team members to enhance project performance; C) is a time management process that includes more than human resources, such as materials, equipment, supplies, etc.; D) may be executed if any team members are contract resources, and typically, B) would happen before D).

9. D   **Section 9.4.2.3 – Human Resources Management – Executing**
        A) is a withdrawal/avoid (nothing solved) negotiation tactic; B) is a force/direct (win-lose) negotiation tactic; C) is a compromise/reconcile (lose-lose) negotiation tactic.

10. B   **Section 9.4 – Human Resources Management – Executing**
        A) focuses on how to collect and share information about project performance; B) the Manage Project Team process involves the comprehensive coordination for the entire team; C) the focus is on making sure stakeholders have the information they need; D) the Develop Project Team process focuses on what each individual needs to be effective.

11. A   **Section 9.4.2.3 – Human Resources Management – Executing**
        The five basic conflict management techniques are compromise/reconcile, smooth/accommodate, force/direct, withdraw/avoid, and collaborate/problem solve/confront.

12. C   **Section 9.1.2.1 – Human Resources Management – Planning**
        A responsibility assignment matrix (RAM) illustrates the connection between work packages and project team members.

13. B   **Section 4.6.1 – Integration Management – Closing**
        A), C), and D) are all inputs to the Close Project or Phase process.

14. A Section 4.3 – Integration Management – Executing
B), C), and D) are specific project elements to be managed. The question asks for "overall" management.

15. B Section 2.4.2 – Integration Management – Executing
A phase is the collection of logically related project activities that culminate in completing a deliverable.

16. A Section 4.3.3.4 – Integration Management – Executing
Iterations occur as a result of technology decisions, procurement choices, quality definitions, etc. and may affect other knowledge areas. Updating the project management plan is necessary in order to keep in step with the changes occurring on a project.

17. C Section 4.0 – Integration Management – Initiating
A) and D) are some of the activities carried out in a project; B) is a process group, not a knowledge area.

18. A Section 4.1.2.1 – Integration Management – Initiating
B) make-or-buy decisions occur with procurement management *after* a charter has been developed; C) lessons learned may be used in the creation of a charter, but A) is a better answer since we are talking about assessing the inputs needed to develop the charter; D) a risk register captures risk events that may or may not occur on a project and the response plans for them, and they are typically created after the charter.

19. C Section 4.0 & 5.3.3.1 – Integration Management – Initiating
A) are limitations and may be real or perceived; B) are uncertain but hopefully educated guesses; D) are a type of constraint.

20. C Section Overview – Integration Management – Initiating
A) is the definition of integration management; B) defines an application area; D) defines a project management process group.

21. D **Section 4.5 – Integration Management – Monitoring and Controlling**
The Perform Integrated Change Control process also includes the activities associated with managing changes to deliverables, organizational process assets, project documents, and the project management plan.

22. A **Section 4.2.1 – Integration Management – Planning**
B) is a technique for developing the project management plan; C) are different from enterprise environmental factors; D) is an organizational process asset.

23. C **Section 12.4 – Procurement Management – Closing**
A) is a procurement file; B) is a quality audit; D) is a performance measurement.

24. A **Section 12.2 – Procurement Management – Executing**
This is the knowledge area that includes all the processes and activities needed to identify, define, combine, unify, and coordinate project management activities.

25. A **Section 12.1 – Procurement Management – Planning**
B) and C) occur in the Conduct Procurements process; D) occurs in the Control Procurements process.

26. A **Section 12.1 – Procurement Management – Planning**
In a fixed-price-incentive-fee contract, the seller may receive more than the fixed price if certain criteria are met.

27. B **Section 8.2.2.3 – Quality Management – Executing**
Process analysis may include affinity diagrams, process decision program charts, interrelationship digraphs, tree diagrams, prioritization matrices, or network diagrams.

28. C **8.3 – Quality Management – Monitoring and Controlling**
Although A) could be correct, C) is a more specific answer; B) is the definition of attribute sampling; D) is the definition of prevention.

15

29. D   Section 8.1.1.5 – Quality Management – Planning
A) and B) are part of the project management plan; C) is an organizational process asset.

30. B   Section 11.6 – Risk Management – Monitoring and Controlling
Risks will change during the course of a project. As early risks close and the project progresses, other risks will be identified.

31. A   Section 11.2 – Risk Management – Planning
Risk continually changes throughout a project due to changes in situations. Risks must be regularly reviewed and discussed to ensure proactive attention.

32. A   Section 11.1 – Risk Management – Planning
B) takes place during the Identify Risks process; C) takes place during the Perform Quantitative Risk Analysis process; D) takes place during the Perform Qualitative Risk Analysis process.

33. C   Section 11.0 – Risk Management – Planning
A) risk management should address both positive and negative risks; B) issues are risks that have happened; D) catastrophic events are handled at the organization level, not the project level.

34. D   Section 11.4 – Risk Management – Planning
The party should be held outside because the expected monetary value if the party is held outside is $1,600 which is greater than $920 if it is held inside. Of course, you can only choose whether to hold the party inside or outside; you cannot choose whether it rains or not.

35. D   Section 11.3 – Risk Management – Planning
The risk rating helps determine risk urgency.

36. B   Section 5.5.3 – Scope Management – Monitoring and Controlling
The primary focus of the Validate Scope process is the acceptance of work results.

37. B **Section 5.6.2.1 – Scope Management – Monitoring and Controlling**
A) would include formal policies or templates to be used to control scope; C) earned value techniques are used to measure, but they require analysis to determine causes; D) quality metrics are also measurement tools.

38. A **Section 5.4 – Scope Management – Planning**
B) and C) a network diagram will show the schedule activity dependencies and the critical path; D) is the definition of an organizational breakdown structure.

39. B **Section 5.3 – Scope Management – Planning**
A) is an input to the Create WBS process; C) is an input to the Develop Project Charter process; D) expert judgment is a technique for the Define Scope process, but inspection is a technique for the Control Quality process.

40. B **Section 5.2.3.1 – Scope Management – Planning**
A) requirements documentation is a project document, not the project management plan; C) links product requirements and deliverables; D) requirements are an input to the Define Scope process, and the project scope statement is an output of that process.

41. A **Section 5.1 – Scope Management – Planning**
B) The main benefit of the Collect Requirements process is to determine what is required to meet stakeholder needs; C) the main benefit the Define Scope process is to determine which requirements are included in the scope; D) the main benefit of the Create WBS process is that it provides a structured detail of what's included in the project.

42. C **Section 13.3 – Stakeholder Management – Executing**
A) and B) stakeholders must be identified and a plan developed before the team can get to the point of minimizing resistance to a project.

43. A **Section 13.1 – Stakeholder Management – Initiating**
The stakeholder register is the primary output of the Identify Stakeholders Process.

15

44. D **Section 13.1 – Stakeholder Management – Initiating**
Understanding stakeholders' expectations of the project as well as their level of interest in the project will assist the project manager in planning the project appropriately.

45. B **Section 13.1 – Stakeholder Management – Initiating**
A) may help to understand what regulators need, but this would take place in the Plan Stakeholder Management process; C) occurs in the Control Stakeholder Engagement process; D) is part of the Manage Stakeholder Engagement process.

46. A **Section 13.4.1 – Stakeholder Management – Monitoring and Controlling**
Inputs to the Control Stakeholder Engagement process are the project management plan (from the Develop Project Management Plan process), issue log (from the Manage Stakeholder Engagement process), work performance data (from the Direct and Manage Project Work process), and project documents.

47. C **Section 13.2.2.3 – Stakeholder Management – Planning**
A) is a tool used specifically for project team members; B) is an output of Identify Stakeholders; D) this tool is used to link the origin of product requirements to project deliverables.

48. B **Section 6.7.2.1 – Time Management – Monitoring and Controlling**
When reading questions, make sure you focus on what is being asked. This question is specifically about schedule, not cost.

49. A **Section 6.4 – Time Management – Planning**
B) is part of the Define Activities process; C) is part of the Plan Schedule Management process; D) is part of the Develop Schedule process.

50. C **Section 6.6.2.2 – Time Management – Planning**
The critical path is the longest path through the network, and it also identifies the duration of the project. Here, A-D-G-H-I is the critical path.

APPENDIX C

GLOSSARY

This glossary is a supplement to the *PMBOK® Guide*. Some of these terms are not in the *PMBOK® Guide*'s glossary but may be used in test questions.

100% rule: the WBS should represent the total work at the lowest levels and should roll up to the higher levels so that nothing is left out, and no extra work is planned to be performed.

Accuracy: an assessment of correctness in which the closer a result is to a specified value, the more accurate the result.

Acknowledge: indicates receipt of a message by a receiver, but does not indicate that the receiver understood or agreed.

Active listening: the receiver confirms listening by nodding, eye contact, and asking questions for clarification.

Activity attributes: similar to a WBS dictionary because they describe the detailed attributes of each activity. Examples of these attributes are description, predecessor and successor activities, and the person responsible for completing an activity.

Activity contingency reserve: budget for a specific WBS activity within the cost baseline that is allocated for identified risks that are accepted and for which contingent or mitigating responses are developed.

Affiliation power: power that results from whom you know or whom an individual has access to.

Agreements: any documents or communications that define the initial intentions of a project. They can take the form of a contract, memorandum of understanding (MOU), letter of agreement, verbal agreement, email, etc.

Application area: a category of projects that share components that may not be present in other categories of projects. For example, approaches to information technology projects are different from those for residential development projects, so each is a different application area.

15

Attribute sampling: a method of measuring quality that consists of noting the presence (or absence) of some characteristic (the attribute) in each of the units under consideration. After each unit is inspected, a decision is made to accept a lot, reject it, or inspect another unit.

Authority: the right to make decisions necessary for the project or the right to expend resources.

Backward pass: used to determine the late start and late finish dates of activities.

Benchmark: comparing actual or planned project practices to those of comparable projects to identify best practices and generate ideas for improvement. Benchmarks provide a basis for measuring performance.

Bidder conference: the buyer and potential sellers meet prior to the contract award to answer questions and clarify requirements; the intent is for all sellers to have equal access to the same information.

Budget at Completion (BAC): the sum of all budgets established for the work to be performed.

Business value: the entire value of a business; the total sum of all tangible and intangible elements.

Buyer: the performing organization, client, customer, contractor, purchaser, or requester seeking to acquire goods and services from an external entity (the seller). The buyer becomes the customer and key stakeholder.

Capability maturity model integration (CMMI): defines the essential elements of effective processes. It is a model that can be used to set process improvement goals and provide guidance for quality processes.

Change control: the procedures used to identify, document, approve (or reject), and control changes to the project baselines.

Change log: a comprehensive list of changes made during a project.

Change management: the process for managing change in the project. A change management plan should be incorporated into the project management plan.

Chart of accounts: the financial numbering system used to monitor project costs by category. It is usually related to an organization's general ledger.

Code of accounts: the numbering system for providing unique identifiers for all items in the work breakdown structure. It is hierarchical and can go to multiple levels, each lower level containing a more detailed description of a project deliverable. The WBS contains clusters of elements that are child items related to a single parent element; for example, parent item 1.1 contains child items 1.1.1, 1.1.2, and 1.1.3.

Code of conduct: a guide for practitioners in a profession that describes the expectations the practitioners have of themselves and of others.

Colocation: project team members are physically located close to one another in order to improve communication, working relations, and productivity.

Commercial-off-the-shelf (COTS): a product or service that is readily available from many sources; selection of a seller is primarily driven by price.

Constraint: a restriction or limitation that may force a certain course of action or inaction.

Contingency plan: a planned response to a risk event that will be implemented only if the risk event occurs.

Contingency reserve: budget within the cost baseline or performance measurement baseline that is allocated for identified risks that are accepted and for which contingent or mitigating responses are developed.

Contract: the binding agreement between a buyer and seller.

Control account: the management control point at which integration of scope, budget, and schedule takes place and at which performance is measured.

Control limits: the area composed of three standard deviations on either side of the centerline or mean of a normal distribution of data plotted on a control chart, which reflects the expected variation in the data.

Crashing: using alternative strategies for completing project activities (such as using outside resources) for the least additional cost. Crashing should be performed on tasks on the critical path. Crashing the critical path may result in additional or new critical paths.

Crashing costs: costs incurred as additional expenses above the normal estimates to speed up an activity.

Critical path: the path with the longest duration within the project. It is sometimes defined as the path with the least float (usually zero float). The delay of a task on the critical path will delay the completion of the project.

Culture: everything that people have, think and do as members of their society and that is shared by at least one other person

Decision theory: a technique for assisting in reaching decisions under uncertainty and risk. It points to the best possible course, whether or not the forecasts are accurate.

Decode: the term for the receiver translating a message into an idea or meaning.

Decomposition: the process of breaking down a project deliverable into smaller, more manageable components. In the Create WBS process, the results of decomposition are deliverables, whereas in the Define Activities process, project deliverables are further broken down into schedule activities.

Design of experiments: a statistical method for identifying which factors may influence specific variables of a product or process either under development or in production.

Deliverable: Any unique and verifiable product, result, or capability to perform a service that is required to be produced to complete a process, phase, or project.

Direct costs: costs incurred directly by a project.

Effective listening: the receiver attentively watches the sender to observe physical gestures and facial expressions. In addition, the receiver contemplates responses, asks pertinent questions, repeats or summarizes what the sender has sent, and provides feedback.

Encode: the term for the sender translating an idea or meaning into a language for sending.

Enterprise environmental factors: external or internal factors that can influence a project's success. These factors include controllable factors such as the tools used in managing projects within the organization and uncontrollable factors that have to be considered by the project manager such as market conditions or corporate culture.

Estimate to complete: the estimated additional costs to complete activities or the project.

Expert judgment: judgment based on expertise appropriate to the activity. It may be provided by any group or person, either within the organization or external to it.

Expert power: power that results from an individual's knowledge, skills, and experience.

Fallback plan: a response plan that will be implemented if the primary response plan is ineffective.

Fast tracking: overlapping or performing in parallel project activities that would normally be done sequentially. Fast tracking may increase rework and project risk.

Feedback: affirming understanding and providing information.

Finish-to-finish: a logical relationship in which the predecessor must finish before the successor can finish.

Finish-to-start: a logical relationship in which the predecessor must finish before the successor can start. This is the default relationship for most software packages.

Fixed costs: nonrecurring costs that do not change if the number of units is increased.

Float: the amount of time that a scheduled activity can be delayed without delaying the end of the project. It is also called slack or total float. Float is calculated using a forward pass (to determine the early start and early finish dates of activities) and a backward pass (to determine the late start and late finish dates of activities). Float is calculated as the difference between the late finish date and the early finish date. The difference between the late start date and the early start date always produces the same value for float as the preceding computation.

Free float: the amount of time that a schedule activity can be delayed without delaying the early start date of any successor or violating a schedule constraint.

Forward pass: used to determine the early start and early finish dates of activities.

Gantt chart: a bar chart that shows activities against time. Although the traditional early charts did not show task dependencies and relationships, modern charts often show dependencies and precedence relationships. These popular charts are useful for understanding project schedules and for determining the critical path, time requirements, resource assessments, and projected completion dates.

Good practice: a specific activity or application of a skill, tool, or technique that has been proven to contribute positively to the execution of a process.

Grade: a category or rank used to distinguish items that have the same functional use but do not share the same requirements for quality.

Hammock: summary activities used in a high-level project network diagram.

Heuristics: rules of thumb for accomplishing tasks. Heuristics are easy and intuitive ways to deal with uncertain situations; however, they tend to result in probability assessments that are biased.

15

Indirect costs: costs that are part of doing business and are shared among all ongoing projects.

Input: a tangible item internal or external to the project that is required by a process for the process to produce its output.

Inspection: examining or measuring to verify whether an activity, component, product, result, or service conforms to specified requirements.

Issue: a risk event that has occurred.

Issue log: A project document used to document and monitor elements under discussion or in dispute between project stakeholders.

Knowledge area: a collection of processes, inputs, tools, techniques, and outputs associated with a topical area. Knowledge areas are a subset of the overall project management body of knowledge that recognizes "good practices."

Lag: the amount of time a successor's start or finish is delayed from the predecessor's start or finish. In a finish-to-start example, activity A (the predecessor) must finish before activity B (the successor) can start. If a lag of three days is also defined, it means that B will be scheduled to start three days after A is scheduled to finish.

Lead (negative lag): the amount of time a successor's start or finish can occur before the predecessor's start or finish. In a finish-to-start example, activity A (the predecessor) must finish before activity B (the successor) can start. A lead of three days means that B can be scheduled to start three days before A is scheduled to finish.

Leadership: the ability to get an individual or group to work toward achieving an organization's objectives while accomplishing personal and group objectives at the same time.

Lean Six Sigma: a business improvement methodology that strives to eliminate non-value added activities and waste from processes and products.

Legitimate power: formal authority that an individual holds as a result of his or her position.

Letter contract: a written preliminary contract authorizing the seller to begin work immediately; it is often used for small-value contracts.

Letter of intent: this is *not* a contract but simply a letter, without legal binding, that says the buyer intends to hire the seller.

Level of effort: An activity that does not produce definitive end products and is measured by the passage of time.

Logical relationships: there are four logical relationships between a predecessor and a successor: finish-to-start, finish-to-finish, start-to-start, and start-to-finish.

Malcolm Baldrige award: the national quality award given by the U.S. National Institute of Standards and Technology. Established in 1987, the program recognizes quality in business and other sectors. It was inspired by Total Quality Management.

Management reserve: a dollar value, not included in the project budget, that is set aside for unplanned changes to project scope or time that are not currently anticipated.

Milestone: a significant point or event in a project, program, or portfolio.

Milestone chart: a bar chart that only shows the start or finish of major events or key external interfaces (e.g., a phase kickoff meeting or a deliverable); a milestone consumes *no* resource and has *no* duration; these charts are effective for presentations and can be incorporated into a summary Gantt chart.

Multi-criteria decision analysis: this technique utilizes a decision matrix to provide a systematic analytical approach for establishing criteria such as risk levels, uncertainty, and valuation to evaluate and rank many ideas.

Network diagram: a schematic display of project activities showing task relationships and dependencies; the PDM is useful for forcing the total integration of the project schedule, for simulations and "what-if" exercises, for highlighting critical activities and the critical path, and for determining the projected completion date.

Noise: anything that compromises the original meaning of a message.

Nonverbal communication: about 55% of all communication, based on what is commonly called body language.

Objective: something toward which work is to be directed, a strategic position to be attained, a purpose to be achieved, a result to be obtained, a product to be produced, or a service to be performed.

Operation: ongoing work performed by people, constrained by resources, planned, executed, monitored, and controlled. Unlike a project, operations are repetitive; e.g., the work performed to carry out the day-to-day business of an organization is operational work.

Opportunities: risk events or conditions that are favorable to a project.

Opportunity costs: costs of choosing one alternative over another and giving up the potential benefits of the other alternative.

Organizational breakdown structure (OBS): a type of organizational chart, different from a responsibility assignment matrix (RAM), in which work package responsibility is related to the organizational unit responsible for performing that work. It may be viewed as a very detailed use of a RAM with work packages of the work breakdown structure (WBS) and organizational units as its two dimensions.

Organizational process assets: any formal or informal processes, plans, policies, procedures, guidelines, and on-going or historical project information such as lessons learned, measurement data, project files, and estimates versus actuals.

15

Organizational project management maturity model (OPM3®): focuses on an organization's knowledge, assessment, and improvement elements.

Output: a deliverable, result, or service generated by the application of various tools or techniques within a process.

Paralingual communication: optional vocal effects, the tone of voice that may help communicate meaning.

Parking lot: a technique for capturing ideas and recording them for later use.

Penalty (coercive, punishment) power: power that results from an ability to take away something of value to another.

Percent complete: the amount of work completed on an activity or WBS component.

Performance domain: a broad category of duties and responsibilities that define a role. A performance domain expresses the actual actions of the project manager in that particular domain.

Phase: one of a collection of logically related project activities usually resulting in the completion of one or more major deliverables. A project phase is a component of a project life cycle.

Planning package: a component of the WBS that is a subset of the control account to support known uncertainty in project deliverables. Planning packages will include information on a deliverable but without any details associated with schedule activities.

Point of total assumption: in a fixed price contract, the point above which the seller will assume responsibility for all costs; it generally occurs when the contract ceiling price has been exceeded.

Portfolio: a collection of programs, projects, and additional work managed together to facilitate the attainment of strategic business goals.

Power: the ability to influence people in order to achieve needed results.

15

Precision: a measure of exactness based on the interval of measurement. The smaller the interval, the more precise.

Predecessor: the activity that must happen first when defining dependencies between activities in a network.

Prevention: keeping errors out of a process.

Privity: the contractual relationship between the two parties of a contract. If party A contracts with party B, and party B subcontracts to party C, there is no privity between party A and party C.

Process: a collection of related actions performed to achieve a predefined desired outcome. The *PMBOK® Guide* defines a set of 47 project management processes, each with various inputs, tools, techniques, and outputs. Processes can have predecessor or successor processes, so outputs from one process can be inputs to other processes. Each process belongs to one and only one of the five process groups and one and only one of the ten knowledge areas.

Process group: a logical grouping of a number of the 47 project management processes. There are five process groups, and all are required to occur at least once for every project. The process groups are performed in the same sequence each time: initiating, planning, executing, more planning and executing as required, and ending with closing. The monitoring and controlling process group is performed throughout the life of the project. Process groups can be repeated for each phase of the project life cycle. Process groups are not phases. Process groups are independent of the application area or the life cycle utilized by the project.

Process quality: specific to the type of product or service being produced and the customer expectations, the level of process quality will vary. Organizations strive to have efficient and effective processes in support of the product quality expected. For example, the processes associated with building a low-quality, low-cost automobile can be just as efficient as, if not more efficient than, the processes associated with building a high-quality, high-cost automobile.

Product life cycle: the collection of stages that make up the life of a product. These stages are typically introduction, growth, maturity, and retirement.

Product quality: specific to the type of product produced and the customer requirements, product quality measures the extent to which the end product(s) of the project meets the specified requirements. Product quality can be expressed in terms that include, but are not limited to, performance, grade, durability, support of existing processes, defects, and errors.

Program: a group of related projects managed in a coordinated way; e.g., the design and creation of the prototype for a new airplane is a project, while manufacturing 99 more airplanes of the same model is a program.

Progressive elaboration: the iterative process of increasing the level of detail in a project management plan as greater amounts of information and more accurate estimates become available.

Project: work performed by people, constrained by resources, planned, executed, monitored, and controlled. It has definite beginning and end points and creates a unique outcome that may be a product, service, or result.

Project charter: a document issued by the project initiator or sponsor that formally authorizes the existence of a project and provides the project manager with the authority to apply organizational resources to project activities.

Project deliverable: a unique and verifiable product, result, or capability that is an output of the project itself.

Project life cycle: the name given to the collection of various phases that make up a project. These phases make the project easier to control and integrate. The result of each phase is one or more deliverables that are utilized in the next few phases. The work of each phase is accomplished through the iterative application of the initiating, planning, executing, monitoring and controlling, and closing process groups.

Project management: the ability to meet project requirements by using various knowledge, skills, tools, and techniques to accomplish project work. Project work is completed through the iterative application of initiating, planning, executing, monitoring and controlling, and closing process groups. Project management is challenged by competing and changing demands for scope (customer needs, expectations, and requirements), resources (people, time, and cost), risks (known and unknown), and quality (of the project and product).

Project management information system (PMIS): the collection of tools, methodologies, techniques, standards, and resources used to manage a project. These may be formal systems and strategies determined by the organization or informal methods utilized by project managers.

Project management methodology: any structured approach used to guide the project team through the project life cycle. This methodology may utilize forms, templates, and procedures standard to the organization.

Project network schedule calculations: there are three types of project network schedule calculations: a forward pass, a backward pass, and float. A forward pass yields early start and early finish dates, a backward pass yields late start and late finish dates, and these values are used to calculate total float.

Project objective: the purpose toward which a project is initiated.

Project quality: typically defined within the project charter, project quality is usually expressed in terms of meeting stated schedule, cost, and scope objectives. Project quality can also be addressed in terms of meeting business objectives that have been specified in the charter. Solving the business problems for which the project was initiated is a measure of the quality for the project.

Quality: the degree to which a set of inherent characteristics satisfies the stated or implied needs of the customer. To measure quality successfully, it is necessary to turn implied needs into stated needs via project scope management.

15

Quality objective: a statement of desired results to be achieved within a specified time frame.

Quality policy: a statement of principles for what the organization defines as quality.

Referent (charisma) power: power that results from a project manager's personal characteristics.

Requirements traceability matrix: a matrix for recording each requirement and tracking its attributes and changes throughout the project life cycle to provide a structure for changes to product scope. Projects are undertaken to produce a product, service, or result that meets the requirements of the sponsor, customer, and other stakeholders. These requirements are collected and refined through interviews, focus groups, surveys, and other techniques. Requirements may also be changed through the project's configuration management activities.

Residual risk: when implementing a risk response plan, the risk that cannot be eliminated.

Resource calendar: a calendar that documents the time periods in which project team members can work on a project.

Resource leveling: a technique in which start and finish dates are adjusted based on resource constraints with the goal of balancing demand for resources with the available supply.

Resource optimization techniques: techniques that are used to adjust the start and finish dates of activities that adjust planned resource use to be equal to or less than resource availability.

Responsibility assignment matrix (RAM): a structure that relates project roles and responsibilities to the project scope definition.

Reward power: power that results from an ability to give something of value to another.

Risk: an uncertain event or condition that could have a positive or negative impact on a project's objectives.

Risk appetite: the degree of uncertainty an entity is willing to take on in anticipation of a reward.

Risk threshold: the measures, along the level of uncertainty or the level of impact, at which a stakeholder may have a specific interest. Risk will be tolerated under the threshold and not tolerated over the threshold.

Risk tolerance: the degree, amount, or volume of risk that an organization or individual will withstand.

Rolling wave planning: a progressive elaboration technique that addresses uncertainty in detailing all future work for a project. Near-term work is planned to an appropriate level of detail; however, longer term deliverables are identified at a high level and decomposed as the project progresses.

Schedule activity: an element of work performed during the course of a project. It is a smaller unit of work than a work package and the result of decomposition in the Define Activities process of project time management. Schedule activities can be further subdivided into tasks.

Scheduling charts: there are four types of scheduling charts: the Gantt chart, the milestone chart, the network diagram, and the time-scaled network diagram.

Scope baseline: the approved detailed project scope statement along with the WBS and WBS dictionary.

Scope creep: the uncontrolled expansion of a product or project scope without adjustments to time, cost, and resources.

Secondary risk: when implementing a risk response, a new risk that is introduced as a result of the response.

Seller: the bidder, contractor, source, subcontractor, vendor, or supplier who will provide the goods and services to the buyer. The seller generally manages the work as a project, utilizing all processes and knowledge areas of project management.

Single source: selecting a seller without competition. This may be appropriate if there is an emergency or prior business relationship.

15

Six Sigma: an organized process that utilizes quality management for problem resolution and process improvement. It seeks to identify and remove the causes of defects.

Sole source: selecting a seller because it is the only provider of a needed product or service.

Stakeholder: an individual, group, or organization who may affect, be affected by, or perceive itself to be affected by a decision, activity, or outcome of a project.

Stakeholder register: a project document that includes the identification, assessment, and classification of project stakeholders.

Standard: a document that describes rules, guidelines, methods, processes, and practices that can be used repeatedly to enhance the chances of success.

Standard deviation: the measurement of the variability of the quantity measured, such as time or costs, from the average.

Start-to-finish: a logical relationship in which the predecessor must start before the successor can finish; this is the least used and some software packages do not even allow it.

Start-to-start: a logical relationship in which successor can start as soon as the predecessor starts.

Statistical sampling: involves choosing part of a population of interest for inspection.

Statistical terms: the primary statistical terms are the project mean, variance, and standard deviation.

Subproject: a component of a project. Subprojects can be contracted out to an external enterprise or to another functional unit.

Successor: the activity that happens second or subsequent to a previous activity when defining dependencies between activities in a network.

Sunk costs: money already spent; there is no more control over these costs. Since these are expended costs they should not be included when determining alternative courses of action.

Tailor: the act of carefully selecting processes and related inputs and outputs contained within the *PMBOK® Guide* to determine a subset of specific processes that will be included within a project's overall management approach.

Team building: the process of getting a diverse group of individuals to work together effectively. Its purpose is to keep team members focused on the project goals and objectives and to understand their roles in the big picture.

Technique: a defined systematic series of steps applied by one or more individuals using one or more tools to achieve a product or result or to deliver a service.

Threat: a risk event or condition that is unfavorable to a project.

Time-scaled network diagram: a combination of a network diagram and a bar chart that shows project logic, activity durations, and schedule information.

Tolerance: the quantified description of acceptable variation for a quality requirement.

Tool: a tangible item such as a checklist or template used in performing an activity to produce a product or result.

Transmit message: the term for using a communication method to deliver a message.

Triangular distribution or **three-point estimating**: takes the average of three estimated durations: the optimistic value, the most likely value, and the pessimistic value. By using the average of three values rather than a single estimate, a more accurate duration estimate for the activity is obtained.

Variable costs: costs that increase directly with the size or number of units.

Virtual teams: groups of people with shared objectives who fulfill their roles with little or no time spent meeting face to face.

Warranty: assurance that the products are fit for use or the customer receives compensation. Warranties could cover downtime and maintenance costs.

WBS dictionary: houses the details associated with the work packages and control accounts. The level of detail needed will be defined by the project team.

Weighted three-point estimating or **beta/PERT**: the program evaluation and review technique (PERT) uses the three estimated durations of three-point estimating but weighs the most likely estimate by a factor of four. This weighted average places more emphasis on the most likely outcome in calculating the duration of an activity. Therefore, it produces a curve that is skewed to one side when possible durations are plotted against their probability of occurrence.

What-if scenario analysis: the process of evaluating scenarios in order to predict their effect on project objectives.

Work breakdown structure (WBS): a framework for defining project work into smaller, more manageable pieces; it defines the total scope of the project using descending levels of detail.

Work package: the lowest level of a WBS; cost estimates are made at this level.

Work performance data: the raw observations and measurements identified during activities being performed to carry out project work.

Work performance information: the performance data collected from various controlling processes, analyzed in context, and integrated based on relationships across areas.

Work performance reports: the physical or electronic representation of work performance information compiled in project documents and intended to generate decisions, actions, or awareness.

Workarounds: unplanned responses to risks that were previously unidentified or accepted.

APPENDIX D

BIBLIOGRAPHY

This study guide and the *PMBOK® Guide* provide enough material for most experienced project managers to pass the exam. However, if you feel that you need additional materials, here are some books that we have found useful and that we reference in the study guide.

Brake, Terence, Danielle Walker, and Thomas Walker. *Doing Business Internationally: The Guide to Cross-cultural Success.* New York: McGraw-Hill, 1995.

Cleland, David, Karen M. Bursic, Richard Puerzer, and A. Yaroslav Vlasak, eds. *Project Management Casebook.* Newtown Square, PA: Project Management Institute, 1998.

Clemen, Robert T. *Making Hard Decisions: An Introduction to Decision Analysis*, Second Edition. Pacific Grove, CA: Duxbury Press, 1996.

Ferraro, Gary P. *The Cultural Dimension of International Business*, Fourth Edition. Upper Saddle River, NJ: Prentice-Hall, 2002.

Fleming, Quentin W. and Joel M. Koppelman. *Earned Value Project Management*, Second Edition. Newtown Square, PA: Project Management Institute, 1996.

Garner, Bryan A., ed. *Black's Law Dictionary*, Eighth Edition. New York: Thomson West, 2004.

Ireland, Lewis R. *Quality Management for Projects and Programs.* Newtown Square, PA: Project Management Institute, 1991.

Kerzner, Harold. *Project Management: A Systems Approach to Planning, Scheduling, and Controlling*, Eighth Edition. New York: John Wiley & Sons, 2003.

Lewis, James P. *Fundamentals of Project Management.* New York: American Management Association, 1997.

15

----------. *Project Planning, Scheduling and Control.* Chicago: Probus Publishing, 1991.

Meredith, Jack R. and Samuel J. Mantel, Jr. *Project Management: A Managerial Approach*, Fourth Edition. New York: John Wiley & Sons, 2000.

Project Management Institute. *A Guide to the Project Management Body of Knowledge*, Fifth Edition (*PMBOK® Guide*). Newtown Square, PA: Project Management Institute, 2012.

----------. *Code of Ethics and Professional Conduct.*

----------. *PMI Lexicon of Project Management Terms.*

----------. *PMI CAPM Exam Content Outline—2013.*

----------. *Practice Standard for Estimating and Practice Standard for Earned Value Management*, Second Edition.

----------. *Principles of Project Management.* Newtown Square, PA: Project Management Institute, 1997.

----------. *Project Management Experience and Knowledge Self-Assessment Manual.* Newtown Square, PA: Project Management Institute, 2000.

----------. *Project Management Professional (PMP) Examination Specification.* Newtown Square, PA: Project Management Institute, 2005.

Rosen, Robert, Patricia Digh, Marshall Singer, and Carl Phillips. *Global Literacies: Lessons on Business Leadership and National Cultures.* New York: Simon & Schuster, 2000.

Rosenau, Milton D., Jr. *Successful Project Management, A Step-by-Step Approach with Practical Examples*, Third Edition. New York: John Wiley & Sons, 1998.

15

Trompenaars, Fons and Charles Hampden-Turner. *Riding the Waves of Culture: Understanding Diversity in Global Business*, Second Edition. New York: McGraw-Hill, 1998.

Verma, Vijay K. *Human Resource Skills for the Project Manager*. Newtown Square, PA: Project Management Institute, 1996.

----------. *Managing the Project Team*. Newtown Square, PA: Project Management Institute, 1995.

----------. *Organizing Projects for Success*. Newtown Square, PA: Project Management Institute, 1995.

Wideman, R. Max, ed. *A Framework for Project and Program Management Integration*. Newtown Square, PA: Project Management Institute, 1991.

----------. *Project and Program Risk Management: A Guide to Managing Project Risks and Opportunities*. Newtown Square, PA: Project Management Institute, 1992.

Wysocki, Robert K., Robert Beck Jr., and David B. Crane. *Effective Project Management: How to Plan, Manage, and Deliver a Project on Time and Within Budget*. New York: John Wiley & Sons, 2000.

15

PROJECT INSIGHT™ AND METAFUSE, INC.

Project Insight® (www.projectinsight.net) is portfolio and project management software for small- to medium-sized organizations. Project Insight allows project teams to operate more efficiently and productively on projects, tasks, issues, and assets with its cloud based solution. The software is powerful for experienced project managers, yet easy for team members to learn and adopt.

Key Features of Project Insight™ Enterprise Project Management Software

The key features of this software are:
- Project requests
- Project prioritization
- Intelligent scheduling
- Resource management and allocation
- Document management
- Approvals
- Issue tracking
- Workflows
- Budgeting and costing
- Time and expense tracking
- Dashboards and reports
- Portfolio management
- Outlook integration
- Permissions and security
- Customizable
- Web Services APIs and SDK

Project Insight® follows the Project Management Institute's standards and is compliant with the *PMBOK® Guide*.

15

INDEX

16

16

16

O

P